GREEK LYRIC

II

LCL 143

GREEK LYRIC
II

ANACREON, ANACREONTEA
CHORAL LYRIC
FROM OLYMPUS TO ALCMAN

EDITED AND TRANSLATED BY

DAVID A. CAMPBELL

HARVARD UNIVERSITY PRESS
CAMBRIDGE, MASSACHUSETTS
LONDON, ENGLAND

ISBN 0-674-99158-3

Printed in Great Britain by St Edmundsbury Press Ltd,
Bury St Edmunds, Suffolk, on acid-free paper.
Bound by Hunter & Foulis Ltd, Edinburgh, Scotland.

CONTENTS

In memory of
F. J.
and George

πρὸ γόων δὲ μνᾶστις

PREFACE

This volume contains the fragments of Anacreon, the third great composer of solo song, Sappho and Alcaeus having occupied volume I. The *Anacreontea* are added as an appendage, although they were not composed until several centuries after Anacreon; and since little has been written about them in English in recent years I have supplied a comparatively full introduction to them. Volume II continues with the earliest writers of choral poetry, notably Terpander and Alcman; the other choral poets will follow in volumes III and IV.

Again, I am happy to acknowledge my gratitude for Research Grants awarded by the University of Victoria and Leave Fellowships granted by the Social Sciences and Humanities Research Council of Canada, which allowed me to enjoy six months of Study Leave in 1979, 1983 and 1986. I wish to thank my Research Assistants, Dr. Caroline A. Overman, Miss Vicki R. Cameron, Mr. J. Bruce McKinnon and Mr. John J. Koval for their help, the Librarian and staff of the McPherson Library, University of Victoria, for obtaining rare books and periodicals, Mrs.

PREFACE

Philippa Goold, associate editor of the Loeb Classical Library, for the endless patience and good humour with which she corrected proofs and improved the appearance of volumes I and II, and once again Mrs. A. Nancy Nasser for typing the manuscript.

UNIVERSITY OF VICTORIA   DAVID A. CAMPBELL
December 1987

ANACREON
AND THE
ANACREONTEA

INTRODUCTION

Solo song: Anacreon

Anacreon was born in the Ionian city of Teos in Asia Minor. When Harpagus, Cyrus' general, attacked the Greek coastal cities, the population of Teos, Anacreon among them, sailed to Thrace, where they founded Abdera *c.* 540 B.C. Anacreon is next heard of at the court of Polycrates of Samos, whose tyranny is dated to 533–522 (test. 1 n. 2). Fr. 493 suggests that he went there not directly from Abdera but from Athens. After the murder of Polycrates Anacreon was taken to Athens by Hipparchus, son of Peisistratus, who during the tyranny of his brother Hippias (527–510 B.C.) was responsible for cultural affairs. Anacreon may have lived on in Athens after the murder of Hipparchus in 514 B.C., or he may have gone to Thessaly: epigrams written for the Thessalian ruler Echecratidas and his wife Dyseris are attributed to him (frr. 107, 108D.). If he did visit Thessaly, he must have returned to Athens and may have spent much of his later life there: he is said to have sung the praises of Critias, grandfather of the Athenian politician of that name (fr. 495: cf. 500), and to have known and enjoyed the poetry of Aeschylus, who staged his first play between *c.* 499 and 496 B.C. and won his first victory in 484 (see fr. 412).

3

His statue was seen on the Acropolis by Pausanias
(test. 10). He is said to have lived 85 years (test. 8),
and Eusebius says that he 'was well-known' in 536/5
(test. 2): he may have been born *c.* 570 and died *c.* 485.

Most of his poetry was concerned with love and
wine: Maximus of Tyre summed up its content as
'the hair of Smerdies and Cleobulus, the pipes of
Bathyllus and Ionian song' (Anacr. fr. 471), and
according to Cicero it was all erotic (test. 20). The
symposium must have provided the occasion for its
performance: Critias indeed called him 'the excite-
ment of the drinking-party' (Anacr. fr. 500). Samian
politics appear twice: see frr. 348, 353. Critias refer-
red to his choral poetry (Anacr. fr. 500), but apart
from one dubious fragment of his Maiden-songs (501)
it is lost.

References survive to Books 1, 2 and 3 of his
works, but it seems that there were five books in all
(test. 13). His poetry was probably edited first by
Aristophanes of Byzantium *c.* 200 B.C. and 40 or 50
years later by Aristarchus (ib. n. 2). Scholarly work
had begun in the 4th century with Heraclides Pon-
ticus and Chamaeleon (see fr. 372), and Alexan-
drians from Zenodotus, the first librarian, to the 1st
century B.C. Didymus devoted attention to him.

The Anacreontea

The manuscript

The *Anacreontea* are preserved in the 10th century
manuscript [1] which contains the *Palatine Antho-*

---

[1] See Alan Cameron, *G.R.B.S.* 11 (1970) 339 ff. A. Diller in
Serta Turyniana (1974) 520 f. says the scribe J worked
c. 930–950.

logy. This manuscript had an eventful history [2]: it was seen by Salmasius in the library at Heidelberg in 1607, but how or when it came there is uncertain. It was already in two parts,[3] the first volume containing Books 1–13 of the *Anthology*, the second and smaller volume Books 14 and 15, the *Anacreontea* (ff. 675–90) and other material. In 1623 after the sack of Heidelberg it was given to Pope Gregory XV. In 1797 Napoleon took it, recently rebound in its two volumes, from the Vatican to Paris. After 1815 both volumes should have been returned to Heidelberg: the larger volume is now there (Cod. Gr. 23), but the other was overlooked by the Heidelberg librarian and never left Paris. It is in the Bibliothèque Nationale (Cod. Gr. Suppl. 384).

The poems, however, were first edited in Paris in 1554 by Stephanus (Henri Estienne), who had copied the text from 'an old manuscript' he had seen three years earlier in Louvain; whether this was our Palatine manuscript has been disputed,[4] but it is likely that it was,[5] since Stephanus' apograph, which sur-

---

[2] See the prefaces to C. Preisendanz, *Carmina Anacreontea* (which has a photograph of the first page of the *Anacreontea*) and *Anthologia Palatina* (facsimile), Gow-Page, *Hellenistic Epigrams* xxxiii ff.

[3] Preisendanz, pref. to *A.P.* col. viii.

[4] E.g. Rose, pref. to his edition iii ff., Preisendanz, pref. v ff.

[5] West, pref. vii f.

vives in the University of Leyden, and his editions agree so closely with its text.[6]

Content of the poems

The poem which stands first in the collection refers symbolically to the influence of Anacreon: the writer accepts a garland from Anacreon's head and places it on his own; the consequence stated explicitly is that he has been in love ever since; but the poem may be read as an introductory piece in which the poet acknowledges that he writes of love and wine in the manner of Anacreon. Similarly in 60(b), the last of the Palatine collection, we find, 'Imitate Anacreon, the famous singer. Drain your cup to the boys, your lovely cup of words', where the last phrase shows that the writer has poetry in mind as well as erotic conviviality. The author of 7 adopts the persona of Anacreon, but in 15 and 20 the references to him are in the third person. Lines of Anacreon are quoted or alluded to in 47. 8 f. and 52(b) (cf. 60B. 1) and there are many verbal echoes. Bathyllus, the boy whose good looks and pipe-playing were themes of Anacreon's poetry (see test. 11 n. 5, fr. 471), figures also in the *Anacreontea*: his home is still in Samos (17. 45 f.), but he has no further identity, being simply the ideal boy of the poet's fantasies and dreams.

[6] For the influence of the poems on European lyric from the 16th c. onwards see Michael Baumann, *Die Anakreonteen in englischen Übersetzungen* (Heidelberg 1974), James Hutton, *The Greek Anthology in France and in the Latin Writers of the Netherlands to the Year 1800* (Ithaca, N.Y., 1946), L. A. Michelangeli, *Anacreonte e la sua fortuna nei secoli* (Bologna 1922), Herbert Zeman, *Die deutsche anakreontische Dichtung* (Stuttgart 1972).

ANACREONTEA

Poem 5, in which the writer gives instructions to a silversmith for the creation of a cup, lists in fact the subjects which occupy the writers of the *Anacreontea*: spring, the rose, wine, Bacchus, Cyprian Aphrodite, the Loves, the Graces, the vine, handsome boys; if one adds poems inspired by or giving orders for works of art, the list is almost complete. Love is the commonest subject, wine not far behind; and the two are often united, beautiful Lyaeus keeping company with beautiful Cythere (43. 13 f.), Dionysus with the Paphian (20. 6 f., 49. 1 ff.) or the Loves (44. 1 f.). The pieces on works of art (3, 4, 5, 16, 17, 54, 57) form another important group; there are addresses to the cicada (34) and the rose (55) and a piece on gold and the poet's lyre (58). All these subjects are favourites also of the poets of the *Anthology*. In 60(a) the writer toys briefly with a mythological subject, the love of Apollo for Daphne; the picture described in 54 is of Europa and the bull; and the address to the rose (55) ends with a mock-heroic account of the flower's birth. For the most part, however, the poets are happy to abjure epic themes in favour of lighter material (2, 23, 26; symbolically in 4). They will occasionally nod in Homer's direction with an allusion to the *Iliad* (4. 1–11, 14. 12 f., 33. 2 f.), but their echoes of the lyric poets are more frequent.[7]

Metres

The poems are written in hemiambics (catalectic iambic dimeters) or in anaclasts (ionic dimeters with

[7] E.g. Archilochus, 8. 1 ff.; Alcaeus, 60(b). 11 ff.; Ibycus, 25. 1 ff., 44. 6 ff.; Theognis, 29. 5 ff., 32. 9 ff.; even Pindar, 43. 11 f., 60(b). 3 f.; and also the *Bacchae* of Euripides, 41. 5, 43. 5 f.

anaclasis) or, in the case of 19 and 20, in metres
which may have been regarded as legitimate forms of
these. Both rhythms are often called 'anacreontic'.
They are rarely mixed: our text of 48 gives 7
hemiambics followed by 3 anaclasts; in 49 the first 4
lines are probably intended for anaclasts (or ionic
dimeters: 2, 4), the last 6 for hemiambics; both poems
are probably late; see also Anacreon 505(d), where
Baxter inserted τὸν before Ἔρωτα to make the
hemiambic into an anaclast.

(1) The hemiambic or iambic dimeter catalectic, a
seven-syllable line of the pattern ⏖–⏑–|⏑––, is
found in Anacreon 429, 430. In a few late poems
hemiambics are found in company with acatalectic
dimeters ⏖–⏑–|⏖–⏑–, for which see Anacreon 427,
428. In 45 vv. 3–6 fall into couplets of alternating
acatalectics and catalectics; 5 begins with 9 lines of
fumbling hemiambics and continues with a similar
alternation, also fumbling (vv. 10 and 18 are re-
cognisable acatalectics) [8]; 58 introduces acatalectics
in pairs (15 f., 32 f.) and in a group of three (23 ff.); 20
(which has a choriamb for the first iambic metron:
see below) has 2 catalectics (2, 6) among
acatalectics.

Writers introduced variety in two ways [9]:
(a) by substituting a choriamb for the first iambic
metron, –⏑⏑–|⏑––: examples at 4. 16, 17, 19 (i.e. in
the latest version of the poem), 20. 2, 6 (see above),

---

[8] See M. Brioso Sánchez, *Anacreontea: Un ensayo para su
datación* 20 f.
[9] For 47. 7, 9, 11 (⏑–––|⏑––) see next note: they might
perhaps have found justification in the text of Anacreon;
58. 2, 5, 8 (⏖–⏑–|–––) are hard to accept, 49. 6
(⏑–⏑⏑–––) impossible.

36. 15, 39. 3 (perhaps also 5), 47. 6, 12, 51. 1–5 (4 is acatalectic), 54. 8. Hadrian, writing a Latin epitaph on his horse in the first half of the 2nd century A.D., used equal numbers of this line and hemiambics, mostly in alternation (Bücheler ii 2 no. 1522);

(b) by a sort of anaclasis which produced the pherecratean, $\cup$–|–$\cup\cup$–|–: so 5. 19 (cf. 5. 1, 11), 21. 2, 36. 6, 16, 47. 3 (doubtful), 49. 4, 5, 51. 6. Poem 19 is written entirely in the rhythm –––$\cup\cup$––.

(2) Anaclasts, eight-syllable lines of the pattern $\cup\cup$–$\cup$–$\cup$––, are ionic dimeters ($\cup\cup$––|$\cup\cup$––) with anaclasis (reversal: lit. 'bending back') of the 4th and 5th syllables. Pure ionics were admitted by Anacreon in 356(a). 5, (b). 5, 395. 5, 11, and are common in the *Anacreontea*.

The following variations are found [10]:

(a) ––$\cup$–$\cup$–– (resulting in a hemiambic) by contraction of the first two short syllables: see 17. 45, 18. 15, 42. 12, 43. 14, 16, 52(a). 2, 4, 5, 7, and cf. 52(b). 3;

(b) $\cup\cup$–$\cup\cup\cup$ $\cup$–– by resolution of the 5th syllable: see 42. 15, 43. 3, 46. 6;

(c) ––$\cup$ $\cup\cup\cup$–– by a combination of (a) and (b): see 44. 5, and cf. the catalectic ionic tetrameters of Callimachus (fr. 761 Pfeiffer);

(d) –$\cup\cup$ $\cup$–$\cup$–– with substitution of –$\cup\cup$ for $\cup\cup$– at the beginning of the line: see 34. 7, 49. 1, 59. 1;

---

[10] Even 50. 6, 16, 22 ($\cup\cup$–––$\cup$––) and 40. 6 (cf. 40. 8), 52(b). 3 (––––$\cup$––), which one might tend to regard as unacceptable variations, gain support from Anacr. 346 (2). 3. In 41 v. 1 and perhaps vv. 5 and 6 show –$\cup\cup$–$\cup\cup$––. In late poems scansion of lines is uncertain when we cannot tell what system of prosody was acceptable to the poet: stress accent plays an increasingly important role.

(e) $-\cup-\cup-\cup--$, an anaclast with long first syllable: see 38. 16, 40. 4, 50. 26, 27, 60. 9.

Pure ionic dimeters produced the following variation:

(f) $---|\cup\cup--$ by contraction of the first two short syllables: see 44. 2; poem 19 is written entirely in this rhythm: see 1(b) above.

Although the two 'anacreontic' metres have different origins, their aesthetic effect is exactly alike. They are suited for frivolity rather than profundity of thought. Sentences tend to be short: when they are long, as in 56 or 59. 1 ff., the shortness of the sub-units of the sentence keeps the thought clear. Parataxis, as in Anacreon 395, is common: see e.g. poem 25.

Date of the poems

It is astonishing that for three centuries after Stephanus' edition scholars should have been reluctant to abandon the attribution to Anacreon. Language, prosody and the treatment of the subject-matter should have shown beyond doubt that the poems were not composed before the Hellenistic period, most of them perhaps not until the Roman and Byzantine eras. The Alexandrian scholars who quoted from the poetry of Anacreon made no mention of the *Anacreontea*.

Few poems give any clue to the date of their composition: contemporary allusions do not belong to amatory and convivial verse. Edmonds tried to date 14 by the absence of Rome in the catalogue of love-affairs; but a Greek poet using a Greek poet as his model would avoid mention of Rome: the list of places begins (at home?) with Athens, moves to

Corinth,[11] then to the east coast of the Aegean from north to south, to Syria, Egypt and Crete in the eastern Mediterranean, and finally to the furthest west and east. A comic poem need pay no attention to political reality.

In 27 the writer refers to the headgear of the Parthians as their distinguishing feature. Parthian history extends from 247 B.C. to shortly after 200 A.D., and Parthian traders could have been seen in Antioch, the western terminus of their trade-route to the Mediterranean; or the author might have been one of the Greeks who lived in Parthia in the settlements of Alexander and the Seleucids.

The famous poem on the cicada (34) has been closely studied in recent years: Albrecht Dihle (*Harv. Stud.* 71, 1966, 107 ff.) argued from the language, from what he took to be prosodic irregularities, and from the alleged identification in the poem of the Stoic ἀπάθεια and the Platonic ὁμοίωσις θεῷ (an identification 'particularly important in early Christian moral teaching from the time of Clement of Alexandria onwards, especially in monastic literature') for a date between 350 and 580 A.D.; M. Brioso Sánchez (*Emerita* 38, 1970, 311 ff.) rightly rejected much of Dihle's reasoning and argued for a date between 200 and 500 A.D., an age of pseudoscience and pedantry. Textual problems are of first importance: if the ms. reading is kept in vv. 7 (with χ' ὁπόσα), 8, 15 and 17 or in any one of these lines, the date of composition will be later than 400 A.D. (see

[11] See 14 n. 1.

below).[12] The cicada attracted the attention of the epigrammatists from Anyte and Leonidas onwards (*A.P.* 7. 190, 6. 120); note especially Meleager's address (*A.P.* 7. 196).

A valuable piece of chronological evidence is provided by Aulus Gellius, who in his *Attic Nights* (see Sa. test. 53) quotes a version of 4, describing it as 'charming little verses of the aged Anacreon'. Gellius was born *c.* 130 A.D., and his book was perhaps published shortly before 180. We have three versions of the poem, and it is probable that Gellius' is not the oldest: see 4 n. 5 and Bergk, *P.L.G.* iii 298 f.

What seems to be the oldest form of 4 is found together with 8 in the *Palatine Anthology* (i.e. earlier in the same ms. as the *Anacreontea*).[13] They are numbers 48 and 47 of Book XI, and since 23–46 and 49–50 of that book are from the *Garland* of Philip, it is possible[14] that they too came from Philip's collection; if they did, they are most likely to have been composed between *c.* 90 B.C. (the date of Meleager's

---

[12] Hanssen, who did valuable work on the comparative dating of the poems, put 34 in the 2nd c. B.C. Edmonds' second test (B), for which see below, also points to an early date. The relevant figure in his table (p. 12) is 2.57 by my calculation: his figure 2.43 is identical with that for Anacreon himself (p. 7), mine not much different. Giangrande (*Q.U.C.C.* 19, 1975, 195 ff.) regards vv. 7, 8, 15, 17 as isosyllabic. West, obelizing and emending the text, puts 34 in his earliest group.

[13] They are also in the *Planudean Anthology* and in syll. cod. Paris. suppl. 352 = *Anecd. Par.* iv 376s. Cramer.

[14] No more than 'possible', since 23–46 form an alphabetic sequence (in reverse order) to which 47 and 48 do not belong. 43–46 and 49 are all convivial poems (like 47 and 48) by five different authors.

ANACREONTEA

Garland) and *c.* 40 A.D. (Philip's *Garland*). It is signi-
ficant that 8 like 4 appears in a shorter version in
the *Anthology*. It seems likely that these were the
earliest versions: Bergk (p. 299) showed how 4 may
have grown from the 11-line poem of the *Anthology*
to the 16-line poem quoted by Gellius and finally to
the 21-line version of the *Anacreontea* with its strong
suggestions of late date.

Poem 6 is found in the *Planudean Anthology* in the
seventh and last book, the Ἐρωτικά (388 in the
Planudean Appendix), and it is ascribed there to one
Julianus. The Aldine edition added 'ex-prefect of
Egypt', thus identifying him with the 6th century
poet, some 70 of whose epigrams were included in the
Cycle of Agathias. But Julianus is a common name,
and the seven lines carry no indication of late date.
The poem has an anomalous position in Book 7 of
the *Planudean Anthology* (see Gow, *The Greek Antho-
logy* 57 f.): could it at some time have been attach-
ed as a pendant to 16. 387,[15] the last of the series
on stelae in the Hippodrome at Constantinople from
Book 4 of the *Planudean Anthology* (see Gow p. 46
with n. 2)? 387 ends with the word στέφος, the garland
that might be worn by the charioteer Julianus[16]: the
attribution of our poem (στέφος πλέκων . . .) to
Julianus might be the mistake of a lemmatist.

The Christian writers Clement and Hippolytus
quote *c.* 200 A.D. *Anacreontea* which are not in the
Palatine manuscript: see Anacr. 505(d) and 60–62 B.
These were either not known to the anthologist who

---

[15] It now follows it in the *Planudean Appendix*.
[16] For this Julianus see the index to Alan Cameron,
Porphyrius the Charioteer.

compiled our collection of *Anacreontea* [17] or else
were rejected by him.

Study of the vocabulary of the poems has given
some interesting results: Brioso Sánchez [18] lists 11
words which on our present evidence we must call
late: εὐτελίζω (28. 10), ἀναθάλπω (33. 21) (Anacreon is
fond of ἀνα- compounds), and ἐφευρετής (38. 3), not
found before the 1st century A.D.; ψαλίζω (10. 4), κλα-
δίσκος (18. 13), ταινίη = "breastband" (22. 13) and ἄ-
στονος (56. 6), not before the 2nd century; ταρσά (n. pl.)
(10. 3) and παντορέκτης (11. 11), not before the 3rd
century; ληνοβάτης (4. 16) and κισσοστεφής (48. 5), not
before the 4th century, and he adds three others
which may also be late (although, like κισσοστεφής,
they might have been invented at any time by a poet
of modest enterprise): πολύκωμος (42. 14), ἀβροχαίτας
(43. 8) and μεθυδώτας (49. 4). One might add μάργαρον
(22. 14) and the transitive βρύω (46. 2). [19]

Brioso Sánchez's study of the syntax of the
poems [20] led him to the conclusion that they belong

---

[18] *Anacreontea* 13 f.; see also Giangrande (loc. cit.) for
possible vulgarisms.
[19] Brioso Sánchez lists only 3 *hapax legomena*: ἐρωτιδεῖς
(25. 13), ἀναιμόσαρκος (34. 17) and the doubtful ἀχανδής
(58. 35); there are others: ἡμίλεπτος (25. 10), φίλυμνος (34. 16),
ἀνεμό-τροπος or -τροφος (38. 14), δαϊκτής (42. 10), κατάκισσος
(43. 5), λυσίφρων (49. 2), λυσιπαίγμων (50. 10), μελιστής, 'singer'
(60b. 8).
[20] Pp. 14 ff.: he deals with the use of the optative,
prepositions, particles, comparatives and superlatives and
the vocative with ὦ. Some of his conclusions need to be
modified: e.g. the ascendancy of μετά over σύν is due in part
to its convenience as a line-opener in anaclasts (e.g. 37. 6
μετὰ παρθένων ἀθύρων).

in general to the last centuries of the Roman Empire and the early days of the Byzantine era. Their affinities are with the prose of the Septuagint, the New Testament and papyri and with poetry of the 2nd century B.C. onwards.

The most rewarding field of study for the relative chronology of the poems has been the examination of the effect of the stress accent on composition. According to Paul Maas (*Greek Metre*, tr. H. Lloyd-Jones, p. 13), the distinction between vowels in point of quantity ended about 400 A.D.; from then onwards they had absolute equality in time value as in Modern Greek. The first line of poem 40 (ἐπειδὴ βροτὸς ἐτύχθην) is the clearest possible example: it purports to be an anaclast (∪∪–∪–∪––), but the accented syllable has taken the place of the long syllable of quantitative composition.

The influence of accent in the *Anacreontea* has been studied by Hanssen [21] (whose conclusions were used by Crusius in *R.E.*), Edmonds [22] and most recently Brioso Sánchez.[23] They examined the hemiambics and anaclasts of writers ranging from Anacreon and Euripides (*Cycl.* 495 ff.) to Byzantine writers, studying in particular the incidence of accent on the penultimate syllable of the line and fitting the poems of our collection into the chron-

---

[21] *Verhandlungen der 36 Vers. d. Phil. in Karlsruhe*, 1882, p. 284 ff., *Philol.* Suppl. 5. 2, p. 199 ff.

[22] *Anacreontea* 6 ff. Edmonds used three other tests also; of these test (C) produced 'nothing much', test (D) sometimes gave corroborative evidence, test (A) was much more helpful but gave a freakish result for the crucial figure of Synesius.

[23] *Anacreontea: Un ensayo* 41 ff.

ological framework so obtained. Their results do not coincide: Hanssen did not use the method rigorously; and Edmonds used fewer authors, relied also on other tests, and based his calculations on his own text with its large number of original emendations. Brioso Sánchez's figures are the most trustworthy; but he rightly noted the danger inherent in calculations based on short poems, where the statistics may be misleading. His conclusions may be accepted for the longer poems, for the short poems only when his figures are very high or very low: there must be a large area of doubt on either side of his border-line *c.* 400 A.D. Again, the results will obviously depend on the text that is adopted; and finally allowance must be made for writers who may have deliberately copied ancient practice more closely than others.[24]

The results of these three scholars, together with those of Sitzler,[25] which were based on other criteria, are as follows: the poems are listed in numerical order for the sake of easy reference.

(1) Hanssen formed 3 groups:
- (a) (dated to the last centuries B.C. and to 1–138 A.D.): 1, 4, 6–35, 39, 47, 51
- (b) (138–400 A.D.): 36, 42–44, 46, 48, 49, 53, 55–58
- (c) (after 400 A.D.): 2, 3, 5, 37, 38, 40, 41, 45, 50, 52, 54, 59, 60.

(2) Sitzler's classification was straightforward:
- (a) (earliest) 1–20 except for 2, 3, 5
- (b) (rather later) 21–34
- (c) (late) 35–60.

---

[24] See West, *Greek Metre* 169.
[25] 'Zu den Anakreonteen', *Woch. für Klass. Phil.* 30/31 (1913) col. 858 f.

His grouping is similar to that of the latest editor, West (see below).

(3) Edmonds formed four groups, the first three of which were distinguished by subject-matter, by use of Doricisms and by frequency of pure Ionic lines:

(a) earliest in groups i–iii (some perhaps 2nd century B.C.; mostly 50 B.C.–50 A.D.): 3, 4, 6, 11, 15, 16, 23, 24, 27, 35, 55, 56, 57 and perhaps 8, 14, 39, 45, 47, 51, 60(b); of these he singled out as the oldest of all 3, 11, 23, 35

(b) (latest, 350–580 A.D.): 5, 12, 18, 20–22, 26, 31, 37, 40–42, 44, 46, 50, 52(a) and (b), 58, 59.

(4) Brioso Sánchez has two groups:

(a) the earlier (1st century A.D.? 100–400 A.D.): 1, 2, 4 (vv. 1–15, 20), 5, 6, 8 (vv. 1–10), 9–11, 13–17, 19, 20, 23–25, 27, 28, 29 (vv. 5–14), 30, 33–36, 39, 43–45, 47, 49, 51, 52(b), 54–58

(b) the later (400–600 A.D.): 3, 4 (vv. 16–19, 21), 7, 8 (vv. 11–15), 12, 18, 21, 22, 26, 29 (vv. 1–4), 31, 32, 37, 38, 40–42, 46, 48, 50, 52(a), 53, 59.

(5) West divides the poems into three groups on the basis of their prosody (pref. xiii f.):

(a) those which conform to ancient practice or can be made to do so by slight textual emendation: 1–4, 7–36, 39, 42–44, 46, 48, 51, 52(a), 53, 55, 56, 59, 60(a), 60(b)

(b) a degenerate group, in which *a, ι* and *υ* may be wrongly scanned, unaccented *η, ω* and diphthongs at the end of a word may be shortened, and *-ος, -ον* etc. may be lengthened before a vowel: 6, 37, 38, 47, 50, 52(b), 54, 57, 58

(c) the worst group, in which unaccented long vowels are regarded as short, accented short

17

vowels as long: 5, 40, 41, 45, 49.

According to West, the collection was put together from four sources, two containing earlier poems, two later:

(a) 1–20 (except 2, 3 and 5), Hellenistic in spirit, classical in prosody, written in Ionic dialect, and arranged by metre, 1–15 being hemiambic, 16–18 anaclasts, 19–20 unique. Poem 2 was later placed next to 1 as an alternative introductory poem to the collection, 3 and 5 next to 4 because of their subject-matter.

(b) 21–34, mainly about love, but written with less charm than the first group and with no mention of Anacreon or Bathyllus; also in Ionic and arranged by metre, 21–27 hemiambic, 28–34 anaclasts.

(c) 35–53, often convivial in character, showing metrical licence and corrupt prosody (see group (c) above), Doric forms and degenerate language; arrangement is not by metre.

(d) 54–60, sometimes longer and with longer sentences, Doric forms, and a more academic and self-conscious manner.

The compiler of the collection worked on the same lines as Cephalas, compiler of the *Greek Anthology*, and may have belonged like him to the 9th century.

SELECT BIBLIOGRAPHY
(Anacreon, *Anacreontea*)

Bergk, T. *Poetae Lyrici Graeci*, vol. iii [4], Leipzig, 1882

Brioso Sánchez, M. *Anacreontea: Un ensayo para su datación*, Salamanca, 1970; *Anacreónticas, Texto revisado y traducido*, Madrid, 1981

Bowra, C. M. *Greek Lyric Poetry from Alcman to Simonides* [2], Oxford, 1961

Campbell, D. A. *Greek Lyric Poetry: A Selection of Early Greek Lyric, Elegiac and Iambic Poetry*, London, 1967; *The Golden Lyre: The Themes of the Greek Lyric Poets*, London, 1983

Diehl, E. *Anthologia Lyrica Graeca*, vol. i [2], Leipzig, 1949–52

Edmonds, J. M. *Lyra Graeca*, vol. ii [2], London, 1931; *Elegy and Iambus* (vol. ii) *with the Anacreontea*, London, 1931

Fränkel, H. *Early Greek Poetry and Philosophy*, trans. by M. Hadas and J. Willis, Oxford, 1975

Friedländer, P. (with H. B. Hoffleit) *Epigrammata: Greek Inscriptions in Verse from the Beginnings to the Persian Wars*, Berkeley and Los Angeles, 1948

Gentili, B. *Anacreon*, Rome, 1958

Gerber, D. *Euterpe: An Anthology of Early Greek Lyric, Elegiac and Iambic Poetry*, Amsterdam, 1970

Giangrande, G. 'On the text of the Anacreontea', *Q.U.C.C.* 19 (1975) 177–210

BIBLIOGRAPHY

Kirkwood, G. M. *Early Greek Monody*, Ithaca, 1974

Page, D. L. *Poetae Melici Graeci*, Oxford, 1962 (*P.M.G.*); *Lyrica Graeca Selecta*, Oxford, 1968 (*L.G.S.*); *Supplementum Lyricis Graecis*, Oxford, 1974 (*S.L.G.*); *Epigrammata Graeca*, Oxford, 1975; *Further Greek Epigrams*, Cambridge, 1981 (*F.G.E.*)

Preisendanz, C. *Carmina Anacreontea*, Leipzig, 1912

West, M. L. *Iambi et Elegi Graeci ante Alexandrum Cantati*, 2 vols., Oxford, 1971 (*I.E.G.*); *Greek Metre*, Oxford, 1982; *Carmina Anacreontea*, Leipzig, 1984

ANACREON
AND THE
ANACREONTEA

ANACREON

TESTIMONIA VITAE ATQUE ARTIS

1 *Sud.* A 1916 (i 171s. Adler)

'Ανακρέων, Τήϊος, λυρικός, Σκυθίνου υἱός, οἱ δὲ
Εὐμήλου, οἱ δὲ Παρθενίου, οἱ δὲ 'Αριστοκρίτου
ἐδόξασαν. ἔγραψεν ἐλεγεῖα καὶ ἰάμβους, 'Ιάδι πάντα
διαλέκτῳ. γέγονε κατὰ Πολυκράτην τὸν Σάμου
τύραννον 'Ολυμπιάδι νβ΄.[1] οἱ δὲ ἐπὶ Κύρου καὶ[2]
Καμβύσου τάττουσιν αὐτὸν κατὰ τὴν νε[3]
'Ολυμπιάδα. ἐκπεσὼν δὲ Τέῳ διὰ τὴν 'Ιστιαίου

---

[1] ξβ΄ Küster   [2] τοῦ Labarbe   [3] Clinton, Adler: κε΄, ηε΄,
νε΄ codd. ξβ΄ Faber, Rohde

(Eusebius).   [4] 'At the time of Cyrus and Polycrates',
according to Athen. 13. 599c (= Sa. test. 8); cf. Aristox. fr. 12
Wehrli: 'Cambyses was contemporary with the tyranny of
Polycrates.' Since Ol. 55 does not fit Cyrus' son Cambyses
III, some scholars emend to Ol. 62, the date when Cambyses
succeeded Cyrus (e.g. Rohde, *Rh. Mus.* 33, 1878, 190).
Others read 'Cyrus the son of Cambyses (II)': see J.
Labarbe, *Ant. Class.* 31, 1962, 184.

ANACREON

BIOGRAPHY

1 *Suda*

Anacreon: a lyric poet of Teos, the son of Scythinus or, according to other authorities, of Eumelus, Parthenius or Aristocritus.[1] He wrote elegiac and iambic poems, all in the Ionic dialect. He lived in the time of Polycrates, the tyrant of Samos, in Olympiad 52 (572/1–569/8 B.C.).[2] But other authorities put him in Olympiad 55 (560/59–557/6 B.C.) at the time of Cyrus[3] and Cambyses.[4] Because of the revolt of

---

[1] Son of Scythinus or Parthenius, acc. to schol. Pl. *Phdr.* 235c; cf. elegiacs in schol. Pind. i 10 Drachm., J. Labarbe *Ant. Class.* 37, 1968, 461–6. Richer, *Portraits of the Greeks* i 77 records a herm (*I.G.* xiv 1133) inscribed Ἀνακ . . . Σκυ . . . Τηι . . . , prob. 'A., son of Scythinus, of Teos'. For the 5th or 4th c. iambic poet Scythinus of Teos see Edmonds, *Elegy and Iambus* ii 244 ff.   [2] Some scholars emend the date to Ol. 62 (532/1–529/8), the traditional date of Polycrates' acme (cf. test. 2). But there were probably two tyrants of this name, the father ruling *c.* 572–540, the son (the Polycrates of Herodotus) ruling 533–522. A.'s contemporary would be the son. Ol. 52 may have seen both the accession of Polycrates I and the births of A. and P. II (J. P. Barron, *CQ* 14, 1964, 210–29: see also fr. 491).   [3] Cf. Zenobius 5. 80 (see fr. 426); Cyrus began his reign in Ol. 55

ἐπανάστασιν ᾤκησεν Ἄβδηρα ἐν Θράκῃ. βίος δὲ ἦν
αὐτῷ πρὸς ἔρωτας παίδων καὶ γυναικῶν καὶ ᾠδάς. καὶ
συνέγραψε παροίνιά τε μέλη καὶ ἰάμβους καὶ τὰ
καλούμενα Ἀνακρεόντεια.

2 Euseb. *Chron.* Ol. 61. 1 (p. 104 Helm, ii 98s. Schöne)

Anacreon lyricus poeta agnoscitur.

3 Aristox. fr. 12 Wehrli (= *F. H. G.* 2. 279. 23)

φ′ γὰρ καὶ ιδ′ ἔτη ἔγγιστα ἀπὸ τῶν Τρωικῶν
ἱστορεῖται μέχρι Ξενοφάνους τοῦ φυσικοῦ καὶ τῶν
Ἀνακρέοντός τε καὶ Πολυκράτους χρόνων καὶ τῆς
ὑπὸ Ἁρπάγου τοῦ Μήδου Ἰώνων πολιορκίας καὶ
ἀναστάσεως, ἣν Φωκεῖς φυγόντες Μασσαλίαν ᾤκισαν.
πᾶσι γὰρ τούτοις ὁμόχρονος ὁ Πυθαγόρας.

Histiaeus he had to leave Teos and settled in Abdera in Thrace.[5] His life was devoted to the love of boys and women and to song. He composed drinking songs and iambics and the so-called *Anacreontea*.[6]

[5] Cf. *Sud.* T 319, Strab. 14. 1. 30 = fr. 505(a). Histiaeus, tyrant of Miletus involved in the Ionian revolt (see Hdt. 5. 35–6; 6. 1), is probably confused by *Suda* with Harpagus, for whom see test. 3.   [6] Late imitations of A.

CHRONOLOGY [1]

2 Eusebius, *Chronicle*

Olympiad 61.1 (536/5) [2]: Anacreon the lyric poet is well known.

[1] See also test. 8, Sa. test. 8.   [2] So Jerome and Armenian version; a variant reading gives Ol. 62. 2 (531/0 B.C.). The next entry records the accession of Polycrates (II) and his brothers in 533/2. See also A. A. Mosshammer, *The Chronicle of Eusebius* 297–300.

3 Aristoxenus, *Life of Pythagoras*

It is recorded that approximately 514 years elapsed between the Trojan War and the time of Xenophanes the physicist,[1] Anacreon, Polycrates, the blockade and destruction of Ionia by Harpagus the Mede [2] and the migration of the Phocaeans to Marseilles to escape it. For Pythagoras was contemporary with all these.

[1] Flor. 538/7 B.C. (Euseb.); but the traditional date of the fall of Troy (e.g. in Eratosthenes) was 1184 B.C.   [2] *c.* 540 B.C.; cf. Hdt. 1. 162–8, Strab. 6. 1. 1.

4 Ael. *V. H.* 9. 4 (p. 102 Dilts)

Πολυκράτης ὁ Σάμιος ἐν Μούσαις ἦν καὶ
'Ανακρέοντα ἐτίμα τὸν Τήιον καὶ διὰ σπουδῆς ἦγε καὶ
ἔχαιρεν αὐτῷ καὶ τοῖς ἐκείνου μέλεσιν. οὐκ ἐπαινῶ δὲ
αὐτοῦ τὴν τρυφήν.

5 Apul. *Flor.* 15. 51, 54 (p. 20s. Helm)

. . . ante aram Bathylli statua a Polycrate ty-
ranno dicata, qua nihil videor effectius cognovisse
. . . verum haec quidem statua esto cuiuspiam
puberum, qui Polycrati tyranno dilectus Anacreon-
teum amicitiae gratia cantilat.[1]

[1] Helm: quos P.t. dilectos Anacreon Teius a.g.c., Salmasius

6 [Pl.] *Hipparch.* 228bc

καὶ ἐπ' 'Ανακρέοντα τὸν Τήιον πεντηκόντορον
στείλας ἐκόμισεν εἰς τὴν πόλιν, Σιμωνίδην δὲ τὸν

Bull. Corresp. Hell. 66 (1942) 248–54.

ANACREON

4 Aelian, *Historical Miscellanies* [2]

Polycrates of Samos loved the arts, and he honoured and favoured Anacreon of Teos, delighted with both the man and his poetry.[3] But I do not praise his luxury.[4]

[1] For anecdotes about A. see Tzetzes *Chil.* 4. 131. 235 ff., Stob. *Flor.* 93. 78, Max. Tyr. 21. 7.   [2] Continued at fr. 414.   [3] For A. and Polycrates see fr. 483, Paus. 1. 2. 3, Ael. *V. H.* 12. 25; Hdt. 3. 121 says A. was with him when he was murdered in 522 B.C.   [4] The word, used here of Polycrates, is used of A. by Jul. *Mis.* 337a, Athen. 10. 429b (=test. 18), *A. P.* 7. 33. 1; cf. Ar. *Thesm.* 159–63.

5 Apuleius, *Flowers of Rhetoric*

Before the altar [1] is a statue of Bathyllus [2] dedicated by the tyrant Polycrates. I think I have never come across anything more perfect . . . This statue may be taken to represent one of the youths of the court—one who was loved by the tyrant Polycrates and is singing a song of Anacreon for friendship's sake.[3]

[1] Of the temple of Hera in Samos.   [2] See test. 11 n. 5.   [3] Text uncertain: perhaps 'one of the youths who were loved by the tyrant P. and of whom Anacreon of Teos sings for friendship's sake'.

6 (Plato), *Hipparchus*

Hipparchus sent a fifty-oared ship to fetch Anacreon of Teos to Athens,[1] and induced Simonides of

[1] Cf. frr. 412, 495, 500 for A.'s stay in Athens; for the archaeological evidence see S. Papaspyridi-Karouzou,

Κεῖον ἀεὶ περὶ αὐτὸν εἶχεν μεγάλοις μισθοῖς καὶ
δώροις πείθων . . .

7 Schol. Pind. *Isthm.* 2. 1b (iii 213 Drachmann)

ταῦτα δὲ τείνει καὶ εἰς τοὺς περὶ Ἀλκαῖον καὶ
Ἴβυκον καὶ Ἀνακρέοντα καὶ εἴ τινες τῶν πρὸ αὐτοῦ
δοκοῦσι περὶ τὰ παιδικὰ ἠσχολῆσθαι· οὗτοι γὰρ
παλαιότεροι Πινδάρου· Ἀνακρέοντα γοῦν ἐρωτη-
θέντα, φασί, διατί οὐκ εἰς θεοὺς ἀλλ᾽ εἰς παῖδας
γράφεις τοὺς ὕμνους; εἰπεῖν, ὅτι οὗτοι ἡμῶν θεοί εἰσιν.

8 [Luc.] *Macr.* 26 (i 81 Macleod)

Ἀνακρέων δὲ ὁ τῶν μελῶν ποιητὴς ἔζησεν ἔτη
πέντε καὶ ὀγδοήκοντα . . .

9 Val. Max. 9. 12. ext. 8 (p. 462 Kempf)

sicut Anacreonti quoque, quem usitatum humanae
vitae modum supergressum passae uvae suco tenues

Ceos by high pay and presents to be always at his side.[2]

[2] For the whole passage cf. Aristot. *Ath. Pol.* 18, Ael. *V. H.* 8. 2.

7 Scholiast on Pindar, *Isthmians*

This refers to Alcaeus and Ibycus and Anacreon and anyone else before Pindar who may have devoted his attention to his favourite boy: for these writers were older than Pindar. They say that when Anacreon was asked why he did not write hymns to gods but to boys, he replied, 'Because they are my gods.'

DEATH

8 (Lucian), *On Longevity*

Anacreon the lyric poet lived eighty-five years [1] . . .

[1] I.e. until *c.* 485 B.C.; according to schol. Aes. *P.V.* 128 (=Anacr. 412) he lived long enough to enjoy the works of Aeschylus, whose first plays were performed *c.* 499–6 (first victory 484).

9 Valerius Maximus, *Memorable Deeds and Sayings* (on unusual deaths)

The same was true of Anacreon, who surpassed the common span of human life [1] but perished when a single pip obstinately stuck in his withered throat

[1] He fell ill once but recovered: Him. *Or.* 69. 35 (=Anacr. 494).

et exiles virium reliquias foventem unius grani per-
tinacior in aridis faucibus mora [1] absumpsit.

[1] Madvig: codd. umor

10 Paus. 1. 25. 1 (i 55 Rocha-Pereira)

ἔστι δὲ ἐν τῇ Ἀθηναίων ἀκροπόλει καὶ Περικλῆς ὁ
Ξανθίππου καὶ αὐτὸς Ξάνθιππος, ὃς ἐναυμάχησεν ἐπὶ
Μυκάλῃ Μήδοις. ἀλλ᾽ ὁ μὲν Περικλέους ἀνδριὰς
ἑτέρωθι ἀνάκειται, τοῦ δὲ Ξανθίππου πλησίον ἕστηκεν
Ἀνακρέων ὁ Τήϊος, πρῶτος μετὰ Σαπφὼ τὴν
Λεσβίαν τὰ πολλὰ ὧν ἔγραψεν ἐρωτικὰ ποιήσας· καὶ
οἱ τὸ σχῆμά ἐστιν οἷον ᾄδοντος ἂν ἐν μέθῃ γένοιτο
ἀνθρώπου.

11 *Anth. Plan.* 306 = Leonidas xxxi Gow-Page

πρέσβυν Ἀνακρείοντα χύδαν σεσαλαγμένον οἴνῳ
    θάεο † δινωτοῦ στρεπτὸν ὕπερθε λίθου †,
ὡς ὁ γέρων λίχνοισιν ἐπ᾽ ὄμμασιν ὑγρὰ δεδορκὼς
    ἄχρι καὶ ἀστραγάλων ἕλκεται ἀμπεχόναν,

as he sustained his poor remaining strength with
raisin-juice.[2]

[2] Cf. Pliny, *N. H.* 7. 7, Politian, *Nutricia* (*Opera Omnia* I.
543), Petrus Crinitus, *de Honesta Disciplina* 2. 6, *A. P.* 7. 33.

PORTRAITS

10 Pausanias, *Description of Greece*

On the Athenian acropolis there are statues of
Pericles and his father Xanthippus, who fought the
Persians in the naval engagement off Mycale.[1] But
Pericles' statue is on one side, while near Xan-
thippus stands Anacreon of Teos, the first poet after
Sappho of Lesbos to make love his main theme. The
statue represents him as a man singing when he is
drunk.[2]

[1] 479 B.C.; see fr. 493.   [2] The statue in the Carlsberg
Glyptothek in Copenhagen is probably not a copy of the
Acropolis statue. *A.P.* 9. 599 mentions a statue in Teos, W.
Peek, *Gr. Vers-Inschriften* i 1792. 1–3 one in Cyzicus.

11 *Planudean Anthology:* Leonidas of Tarentum, *On Anacreon* [1]

Look at old [2] Anacreon, dishevelled and unsteady
with wine, bent over the inlaid stone(?).[3] See how
the old man gazing amorously with lascivious eyes[4]

[1] Cf. *Anth. Plan.* 307–9, all possibly on the statue men-
tioned by Pausanias (test. 10). Representations of Ana-
creon are catalogued in Richter, *Portraits of the Greeks*
i 75–8.   [2] A. was habitually depicted in art and literature
(esp. the *Anacreontea*) as old: cf. e.g. fr. adesp. 35 = *P. M. G.*
953 (quoted in Sa. test. 8).   [3] Obscure: see Gow–Page
H. E. ii 341.   [4] Cf. test. 12. 3.

διссῶν δ' ἀρβυλίδων τὰν μὲν μίαν οἷα μεθυπλήξ
  ὤλεσεν, ἐν δ' ἑτέρᾳ ῥικνὸν ἄραρε πόδα.
μέλπει δ' ἠὲ Βάθυλλον ἐφίμερον ἠὲ Μεγιστᾶν
  αἰωρῶν παλάμᾳ τὰν δυσέρωτα χέλυν·
ἀλλά, πάτερ Διόνυσε, φύλασσέ μιν, οὐ γὰρ ἔοικεν
  ἐκ Βάκχου πίπτειν Βακχιακὸν θέραπα.

12 *Anth. Pal.* 7. 27 = Antipater of Sidon xv Gow-Page

εἴης ἐν μακάρεσσιν, Ἀνάκρεον, εὖχος Ἰώνων,
  μήτ' ἐρατῶν κώμων ἄνδιχα μήτε λύρης·
ὑγρὰ δὲ δερκομένοισιν ἐν ὄμμασιν οὖλον ἀείδοις
  αἰθύσσων λιπαρῆς ἄνθος ὕπερθε κόμης,
ἠὲ πρὸς Εὐρυπύλην τετραμμένος ἠὲ Μεγιστῆν
  ἢ Κίκονα Θρηκὸς Σμερδίεω πλόκαμον,
ἡδὺ μέθυ βλύζων, ἀμφίβροχος εἵματα Βάκχῳ,
  ἄκρητον θλίβων νέκταρ ἀπὸ στολίδων·
τρισσοῖς γάρ, Μούσαισι Διωνύσῳ καὶ Ἔρωτι,
  πρέσβυ, κατεσπείσθη πᾶς ὁ τεὸς βίοτος.

trails his robe to his ankles. Stricken by wine he has lost one of his two shoes, but keeps a wrinkled foot in the other. He singing of delightful Bathyllus [5] or of Megisteus,[6] holding in his hand the love-lorn lyre. Father Dionysus, guard him, for it is not right for the servant of Bacchus to fall because of Bacchus.

[5] Cf. *Anth. Plan.* 307, *A. P.* 7. 30, 31, test. 5, frr. 402, 471, 503.   [6] Cf. *Anth. Plan.* 307, *A. P.* 7. 25, 27, frr. 352–3, 416.

EPITAPH [1]

12 *Palatine Anthology:* Antipater of Sidon, *On Anacreon*

Anacreon, glory of the Ionians, may you among the dead not be without your beloved revels or your lyre; but gazing amorously with lascivious eyes may you sing clear-voiced, shaking the garland on your perfumed hair, turning towards Eurypyle [2] or Megisteus or the Ciconian [3] locks of Thracian Smerdies,[4] as you spout forth sweet wine, your robe quite drenched with Bacchus, wringing unmixed nectar from its folds; for all your life, old man, was poured out as an offering to these three—the Muses, Dionysus and Eros.

[1] Cf. *A. P.* 7, 23–26, 28–33.   [2] Cf. *A. P.* 7. 31, fr. 372.
[3] The Cicones were a Thracian tribe.   [4] Cf. *A. P.* 7. 25, 29, 31, frr. 346(6), 347, 366, 402, 414, 503.

13 *Anth. Pal.* 9. 239 = Crinagoras vii Gow-Page

βύβλων ἡ γλυκερὴ λυρικῶν ἐν τεύχεϊ τῷδε
πεντὰς ἀμιμήτων ἔργα φέρει χαρίτων
† Ἀνακρείοντος, ἃς ὁ Τήιος ἡδὺς πρέσβυς
ἔγραψεν ἢ παρ᾽ οἶνον ἢ σὺν Ἱμέροις †.
δῶρον δ᾽ εἰς ἱερὴν Ἀντωνίῃ ἤκομεν ἠῶ
κάλλευς καὶ πραπίδων ἔξοχ᾽ ἐνεγκαμένη.

3 ἡδὺς πρέσβυς codd. κύκνος Jacobs   4 ἢ σὺν Ἱμέροις cod. P
corrector: caret P

14 Trich. *de nov. metr.* (p. 369 Consbruch)

τοῦτο τὸ καταληκτικὸν δίμετρον (sc. ἰαμβικὸν) καὶ
ἡμίαμβον παρ᾽ ἡμῖν ὀνομάζεται· ἐπίσημον δέ ἐστι καὶ
τοῖς παλαιοῖς Ἀνακρεόντειον λέγεται, ὡς πολλῷ αὐτῷ
κεχρημένου τοῦ Ἀνακρέοντος.

ANACREON

ANCIENT EDITIONS [1]

13 *Palatine Anthology:* Crinagoras

The delightful quintet [2] of lyric books inside this
case brings works of inimitable charm—Anacreon's,
which the pleasant old man from Teos wrote over the
wine or with the help of the Desires. We come as a
gift for the holy day [3] of Antonia, [4] whose beauty and
wisdom are unexcelled.

[1] See also Alc. test. 11; for ancient commentators see Sa.
test. 22 (Didymus), Sa. test. 39 (Clearchus); others were
Aristophanes of Byzantium (fr. 408), Aristarchus and
Taenarus (fr. 352), Heraclides Ponticus (Plut. *Per.* 27 on
fr. 372), Chamaeleon (fr. 372), Zenodotus (frr. 408, 431); cf.
fr. 461. Aristoxenus alluded to him (Sa. test. 37
n. 2).   [2] Books 1, 2 and 3 of A.'s lyrics are attested. They
were prob. edited by Aristophanes of Byzantium and by
Aristarchus: see Heph. pp. 68, 74 Consbr. (=fr. 348, Alc.
test. 11), Gentili *Anacreon* xxvi ff.   [3] Prob. her birthday.
[4] Prob. Antonia Minor, daughter of Mark Anthony and
Octavia and mother of Germanicus and the emperor
Claudius.

METRES [1]

14 Trichas, *On the Nine Metres*

The iambic dimeter catalectic is also known to us
as the hemiambic. It is important, and the ancients
call it the anacreontic because Anacreon used it
extensively. [2]

[1] For further references see the indexes to *Grammatici
Latini* (Keil) and Hephaestion, *Enchiridion* (Consbruch)
under 'Anacreon' and '*anacreonteum metrum*', B. Gentili,
Anacreon 108–115, Anacr. fr. 499.   [2] E.g. at fr. 429: cf.
'Mar. Vict.' (Aphthonius) (vi 153 Keil).

15 Mall. Theod. *de metr.* (vi 593 Keil) (de ana-
creontico)

quod maxime fit sonorum, si primus pes anapaes-
tus ponatur, post duo iambi, deinde syllaba.

16 Hermog. *Id.* 2. 3 (p. 322 Rabe)

ἔννοιαι τοίνυν εἰσὶν ἀφελείας ἁπλῶς μὲν εἰπεῖν αἱ
καθαραί· . . . ἰδίως δ᾽ ἂν λέγοιντο ἀφελεῖς αἱ τῶν
ἀπλάστων ἠθῶν καὶ ὑπό τι νηπίων, ἵνα μὴ ἀβελτέρων
λέγῃ τις, οἷον τὸ περὶ πραγμάτων διεξιέναι τινῶν καὶ
λέγειν αὐτὰ μηδεμιᾶς ἀνάκης οὔσης μηδὲ ἐπερωτῶντός
ινος, ὡς τὰ πολλὰ ἔχει τῶν Ἀνακρέοντος . . .

17 *Anth. Pal.* 4. 1. 35s. = Meleager i Gow-Page

ἐν δ᾽ ἄρ᾽ Ἀνακρείοντα, τὸ μὲν γλυκὺ κεῖνο μέλισμα
νέκταρος, εἰς δ᾽ ἐλέγους ἄσπορον ἀνθέμιον . . .

ANACREON

15 Mallius Theodorus, *On Metres*

The anacreontic [1] sounds most impressive if it has an anapaest in the first foot, then two iambs plus one syllable. [2]

[1] E.g. at fr. 395; for modern analysis see e.g. D. S. Raven, *Greek Metre* 67.   [2] Cf. schol. B. Heph., Append. Dionys., Append. Rhetor. (pp. 285, 316, 343 Consbr.).

THE VERDICT OF ANTIQUITY [1]

16 Hermogenes, *Kinds of Style* (on simplicity)

In general, thoughts which are pure are thoughts of simplicity . . . More particularly, one would call 'simple' the thoughts of unaffected and to some extent childlike, not to say stupid, natures. For example, it is 'simple' to go over events and recount them when there is no necessity and no-one is asking a question. Most of Anacreon is like this . . .

[1] Cf. also Dion. Hal. on Sa. fr. 1, Sa. testt. 8, 39, 42, 47–49, 52–54, Alc. test. 27, *Anacreont.* 7. 2, 15. 7, 60(b). 7.

17 *Palatine Anthology*: The Garland of Meleager

And he entwined Anacreon, whose sweet lyric song is indeed of nectar, but a bloom which cannot be transplanted into elegiacs. [1]

[1] Meleager had to exclude from his anthology the greater part of A.'s poetry as being lyric, not elegiac.

18 Athen. 10. 429b (ii 433 Kaibel)

ἄτοπος δὲ ὁ Ἀνακρέων ὁ πᾶσαν αὐτοῦ τὴν ποίησιν
ἐξαρτήσας μέθης. τῇ γὰρ μαλακίᾳ καὶ τῇ τρυφῇ
ἐπιδοὺς ἑαυτὸν ἐν τοῖς ποιήμασι διαβέβληται, οὐκ
εἰδότων τῶν πολλῶν ὅτι νήφων ἐν τῷ γράφειν καὶ
ἀγαθὸς ὢν προσποιεῖται μεθύειν οὐκ οὔσης ἀνάγκης.

19 Hor. *Carm.* 4. 9. 9s.

nec, si quid olim lusit Anacreon,
delevit aetas.

'Acro' *ad. loc.* (i 356 Keller)

ideo lusit quia iocis et conviviis digna cantavit.

20 Cic. *Tusc.* 4. 71

nam Anacreontis quidem tota poesis est amatoria.

ANACREON

18 Athenaeus, *Scholars at Dinner*

Anacreon, who made all his poetry depend on the subject of intoxication,[1] is unusual. For he is attacked as having given himself over in his poetry to laxity and luxury, since most people are unaware that he was sober while he composed and that he was an upright man,[2] who merely pretended to be drunk, though there was no necessity for his doing so.

[1] Cf. Ov. *Ars Am.* 3. 329–31, Sext. Emp. *Adv. Gramm.* 1. 298, Porph. on Hor. *A. P.* 85.   [2] Socrates refers to 'the wise A.' (Pl. *Phdr.* 235b); cf. frr. 363, 500.

19 Horace, *Odes*

. . . nor has time destroyed Anacreon's playful poems.[1]

'Acro' on the passage:

. . . 'playful', because he wrote poems suited to merry-making and convivial occasions.

[1] See Sa. test. 53, Alc. test. 27, Luc. *Symp.* 17, *V. H.* 2. 15 for their performance at dinners.

20 Cicero, *Tusculan Disputations*

All of Anacreon's poetry is erotic.[1]

[1] Clem. Al. *Strom.* 1. 78 says A. invented love-poetry. For Cic.'s derogatory tone cf. Philod. *de Mus.* 14. 8–13 (the Stoic Diogenes said A. corrupted the young by his ideas), Plut. *Per.* 2.

ANACREON

346 P. Oxy. 2321

(1) fr. 1

οὐδε . . . [.]σ . φ . . ạ . . [. . .] . . [
φοβερὰς δ᾽ ἔχεις πρὸς ἄλλωι
3 φρένας, ὦ καλλιπρό[σ]ωπε παίδ[ων·

καί σε δοκεῖ μὲν ἐ[ν δό]μοισι[ν
πυκινῶς ἔχουσα [μήτηρ
6 ἀτιτάλλειν· σ[.] . [. . . .] . . . [

τὰς ὑακιν[θίνας ἀρ]ούρας
ἵ]να Κύπρις ἐκ λεπάδνων
9 . . . .]΄[.]α[ς κ]ατέδησεν ἵππους·

. . . . . .]δ᾽ ἐν μέσωι κατῆ⟨ι⟩ξας
. . . . . .]ωι δι᾽ ἄσσα πολλοὶ
12 πολ]ιητέων φρένας ἐπτοέαται.

λεωφ]όρε λεωφόρ᾽ Ἡρο[τ]ίμη,

suppl. Lobel praeter 4 Lloyd-Jones, 5 Gallavotti 9 ἐρο]
ἐσσα[ς Gentili

ANACREON

Frr. 346–7 are papyrus finds; frr. 348–50 are attributed to Book 1, 351 to Book 1 or 2, 352–4 to Book 2, 355–6 to Book 3. The rest cannot be assigned to any book: frr. 357–445 are arranged on metrical principles, 446–60 have consecutive words but are too short for such arrangement, 461–87 are isolated words in alphabetical order, 488–98 contain references to the content of various poems.

Papyrus fragments of Anacreon published in 1986 by M. W. Haslam (Ox. Pap. LIII 3695) reveal a coincidence with fr. 443 and provide tatters of what seems to be mainly erotic verse.

346 Oxyrhynchus papyrus (2nd c. A.D.)

(1) . . . nor . . . but you have a timid heart as well, you lovely-faced boy, and (your mother) thinks that she tends you (at home), keeping a firm hold on you; (but you escaped to?) the fields of hyacinth, where Cyprian Aphrodite tied her (lovely?) horses freed from the yoke; and you darted down in the midst of the (throng?), so that many of the citizens have found their hearts fluttering.

Herotima,[1] public highway, public highway [2] . . .

[1] Probably the beginning of a new poem; if not, we must translate 'you lovely-faced girl' in v. 3 above.   [2] See 446.

GREEK LYRIC

(2) fr. 4

> χα]λεπωι δ᾽ ἐπυκτάλιζο[ν
>]ἀνορέω τε κἀνακύπτω[
>] . ωι πολλὴν ὀφείλω
>]ν χάριν ἐκφυγὼν Ἔρωτα[
> 5]νυσε παντάπασι δεσμ[ῶν
>]. χαλεπῶν δι᾽ Ἀφροδίτη[ν.
>]φέροι μὲν οἶνον ἄγγε[ι
>]φέροι δ᾽ ὕδω[ρ] πάφλ[αζον,
>] . ε καλέοι[. .]ιν[
> 10]χαρις, ἄρτ[. .]ς δ[
>] . [

suppl. Lobel praeter   7 Latte   8 πάφλ[αζον Gentili   1 vel χαλεπῶς   2 νῦν δ᾽] Peek   5 Δεύ[νυσε Gentili   6 τῶ]ν Gentili   10 ἄρτ[ιο]ς Peek

(3) frr. 11+3

> 4]ννυχ[
>] ειδεμ . [
> ἡδύ τε καὶ π[
>
> 7 ἀλλ᾽ ἐρόεντα[
> δῶρα πάρεστ[ι
> Πιερίδων, β[
>
> 10 κα[ὶ] Χάρισιν,[

4 ἐ]ννυχ[Peek   8 suppl. Peek

42

ANACREON

(2) . . . and I was boxing with a tough opponent,[1] (but now) I look up and raise my head again . . . I owe many thanks, (Dionysus?), for having escaped Love's bonds completely, bonds made harsh by Aphrodite. Let[2] wine be brought in a jar, let bubbling water be brought, let . . . be summoned . . . grace, (perfect?) . . .

[1] Presumably Eros: cf. 396.   [2] No need to see the beginning of a new poem here, especially if the supplement 'Dionysus' is correct.

(3) . . . by night . . . sweet and . . . But the lovely gifts of the Pierian Muses[1] are here . . . and (to) the Graces[2] . . .

[1] Cf. Archil. 1. 2.   [2] Poem ends two verses later.

(4) fr. 6

```
                        ] . ος, χαλ . [
                     ] . α χαροπο . [
          ] πάννυχος πετοίμην [
      5   ἰ]χθυοέντων δὲ λιπ[ὼν
          ] χρυσολόφου[[ς]] Παλλάδ[ος
          ] τηλόθεν . [
          ἄ]νθεσιν β[
          ο]ἰκία δ' ὑψ[ηλὰ
     10        ] . οναε[
```

5 suppl. dubit. Gallavotti   6, 8 suppl. Lobel   9 Peek, Barigazzi

(5) fr. 9

```
      1   ]μεριμ[ν-    2 'Αφρο]δίτην
```

(6) fr. 14 (schol.) πρ(ὸς) Σμερδ(ίην)

347 P. Oxy. 2322 fr. 1

```
          καὶ κ[όμη]ς, ἥ τοι κατ' ἀβρὸν
      2   ἐσκία[ζ]εν αὐχένα·

          νῦν δὲ δὴ σὺ μὲν στολοκρός,
          ἡ δ' ἐς αὐχμηρὰς πεσοῦσα
          χεῖρας ἀθρόη μέλαιναν
      6   ἐς κόνιν κατερρύη

          τλημόν[ω]ς τομῆι σιδήρου
          περιπεσο[ῦ]σ'· ἐγὼ δ' ἄσηισι
          τείρομαι· τί γάρ τις ἔρξηι
     10   μηδ' ὑπὲρ Θρήικης τυχών;
```

(4) . . . flashing (sea?) . . . all night long I might fly . . . and leaving the . . . of fishy (waters?) . . . (of) gold-crested Pallas Athene . . . from afar . . . flowers . . . high palace . . .

(5) . . . care . . . Aphrodite . . .

(6) (scholiast) addressed to Smerdies [1]

[1] See test. 12 n.4.

347 Oxyrhynchus papyrus (2nd or early 3rd c. A.D.) fr. 1

. . . and of the hair, which shadowed your soft neck; and now, look! You are bald, and your hair has fallen into coarse hands and tumbled in a heap in the black dust, having encountered miserably the cutting blade of iron; and I am worn away with distress: for what is one to do if he has not succeeded even for the sake of Thrace [1]?

[1] Prob. 'who has failed to save the hair of Thracian Smerdis': see frr. 402, 414, test. 12.

οἰκτρὰ δὴ φρονεῖν ἀκού[ω
τὴν ἀρίγνωτον γυναῖ[κα
πολλάκις δὲ δὴ τόδ' εἰπ[εῖν
14   δαίμον' αἰτιωμέ[ν]ην·

ὠ]ς ἂν εὖ πάθοιμι, μῆτερ,
εἴ] μ' ἀμείλιχον φέρουσα
π]όντον ἐσβάλοις θυίοντα [
18   π]ορφ[υρ]έοισι κύμασι[

].[ ]..[ ]..[

suppl. Lobel   7 τλήμον[ο]ς spatio brevius

347A = Sa. 213C

348 Heph. *Poem.* 4. 8 (p. 68s. Consbruch)

κοινὸν δέ ἐστι κατὰ σχέσιν τὸ δύο ⟦συστήμασιν⟧ ὑποπεπτωκός, καθάπερ τὸ πρῶτον Ἀνακρέοντος ᾆσμα·

γουνοῦμαί σ' ἐλαφηβόλε
ξανθὴ παῖ Διὸς ἀγρίων
δέσποιν' Ἄρτεμι θηρῶν·

I [2] hear that the easily-recognised lady is sad at heart and often speaks these words as she blames her fate: 'It would be a blessing for me, mother, if you carried me and threw me into the relentless sea that rages with its dark waves . . .'

[2] Prob. the beginning of a new (and incomplete) poem: 'the easily-recognised lady' may be a well-known courtesan left nameless by A.

347A = Sa. 213C (first words of poems by Sappho, Alcaeus, Anacreon)

348 Hephaestion, *On Poems*

The type which allows two classifications in strophic correspondence is 'common', e.g. the first song [1] of Anacreon, 'I beseech you . . . beasts' etc.[2]: in the current edition [3] the stanza ('strophe') has eight lines, and the song is monostrophic [4]; but the stanza can be differently divided into a triad plus a pentad with a pherecratean concluding both the three-line and the five-line sections.

I beseech you, deer-shooter, fair-haired child of Zeus, Artemis, queen of wild beasts, who now some-

[1] I.e. the first poem of Book 1.   [2] All eight lines are quoted by the scholiast.   [3] That of Aristarchus: see test. 13 n. 2.   [4] I.e., has a repeated eight-line stanza.

GREEK LYRIC

ἤ κου νῦν ἐπὶ Ληθαίου
5 δίνῃσι θρασυκαρδίων
ἀνδρῶν ἐσκατορᾷς πόλιν
χαίρουσ', οὐ γὰρ ἀνημέρους
ποιμαίνεις πολιήτας.

κατὰ μὲν γὰρ τὴν νῦν ἔκδοσιν ὀκτάκωλός ἐστιν ἡ στροφή, καὶ τὸ
ᾆσμά ἐστι μονοστροφικόν. δύναται δὲ καὶ ἑτέρως διαιρεῖσθαι εἴς τε
τριάδα καὶ πεντάδα ἡ στροφή, ὥστε Φερεκράτειον εἶναι τὸ
τελευταῖον τοῦ συστήματος τοῦ ἐκ τῶν τριῶν κώλων καὶ τῶν πέντε.

cf. Heph. *Ench.* 1. 4, schol. A Heph., schol. B Heph.,
Choerob. (pp. 3, 172, 262, 192 Consbr.), Ioh. Sicel. ap. *Rhet.
Gr.* vi 128 Walz, Apostol. *Cent.* v 59a (ii 351 L.–S.), Anal.
Gramm. ed. Keil 10. 26, Atil. Fortunat. Gramm. vi 298. 2,
300. 1, 10 Keil, schol. B *Il.* 21. 470 (v 234 Erbse), Eust. *Il.*
1247. 9, Ap. Dysc. *Synt.* 1. 92 (ii 77 Uhlig), Ar. Byz. fr. 383B
Slater

4 ἵκου Heph. *Ench.* codd. DI, schol. A Heph., Ioh. Sicel. (ἵκευ
Wilamowitz) ἤκου Heph. codd. dett. recc.

349 *Et. Gen.* (p. 43 Calame)=*Et. Mag.* 713. 7

σίλλοι· ἐπισκώμματα, κατὰ τροπὴν τοῦ τ εἰς σ τίλλοι τινές.
τίλλειν δὲ τὸ σκώπτειν, ὡς λέγει Ἀνακρέων ἐν τῷ πρώτῳ·

οὗτος δηῦτ' Ἰηλυσίους
τίλλει τοὺς κυανάσπιδας.

cf. *Et. Gen.* (p. 30 Calame)=*Et. Mag.* 463. 9 s.v. ἴαλλοι, Orion.
148. 11

1 οὗτος δηῖ τ' ἀλυσίους *Et. Gen.* (σίλλοι) cod. A οὗτος δύ τ'
ἀλυσίους cod. B δεῦτε Ἰηλυσίους *Et. Gen.* (ἴαλλοι) cod. A tantum
Ἰηλυσίους cod. B δηῦτε Bergk   2 τοὺς κυανάσπιδας *Et. Gen.*
(σίλλοι) cod. A τοὺς κυν- cod. B (sim. *Et. Mag.*) χακασπιδάς *Et.
Gen.* (ἴαλλοι) cod. A κασπίδας cod. B (χαλκασπίδας e.g. corr.
Calame)

where by the eddies of the Lethaeus [5] look down on a city [6] of bold-hearted men and rejoice, since the citizens whom you shepherd are not untamed.[7]

[5] Tributary of the Maeander.   [6] Magnesia, near which was the temple of Artemis Leucophryene.   [7] Civilised Greeks under Persian rule; A. may have prayed for help for the Magnesians in the remainder of the poem: see Bowra, *G. L. P.* 274; Page, *Studi . . . L. Castiglioni* 2. 661 ff. thinks the citizens are the Persians.

349 *Etymologicum Genuinum*

σίλλοι: 'gibes', used by some for τίλλοι with a change of τ to σ; τίλλειν is 'to mock': cf. Anacreon Book 1:

Once again this man plucks (i.e. mocks) the blue-shielded men of Ialysus.[1]

[1] An indication that Rhodes was part of the empire of Polycrates of Samos.

GREEK LYRIC

350 Phot. (p. 123 Reitzenstein)

ἀνασύρειν καὶ ἀνασεσυρμένην· εἰώθαμεν χρῆσθαι τῷ ὀνόματι ἐπὶ τῶν φορτικῶν ἠαναισχυντούντων. Ἀνακρέων ἐν ά.

ἐν αἱ cod., corr. Reitzenstein

351 *Et. Mag.* 713. 26

σινάμωροι πολεμίζουσι θυρωρῷ

ἐν δευτέρῳ Ἀνακρέων. μεμορημένοι φησὶ πρὸς τὸ σίνεσθαι.

cf. *Et. Gen.* (p. 43 Calame) σινάμωροι· ἐν β''Ἀνακρέων (cod. A), ἐν α''Α. (cod. B)

θυρωροὶ codd., corr. Bergk

352 Athen. 15. 671d–672a (iii 484s. Kaibel)

καὶ ὁ Κύνουλκος· ἐπεὶ περὶ στεφάνων ζητήσεις ἤδη γεγόνασιν, εἰπὲ ἡμῖν τίς ἐστιν ὁ παρὰ τῷ χαρίεντι Ἀνακρέοντι Ναυκρατίτης στέφανος, ὦ Οὐλπιανέ. φησὶν γὰρ οὕτως ὁ μελιχρὸς ποιητής (fr. 434). καὶ διὰ τί παρὰ τῷ αὐτῷ ποιητῇ λύγῳ τινὲς στεφανοῦνται; φησὶν γὰρ ἐν τῷ δευτέρῳ τῶν μελῶν·

⟨ὁ⟩ Μεγιστῆς δ᾽ ὁ φιλόφρων δέκα δὴ μῆνες ἐπεί τε
στεφανοῦταί τε λύγῳ καὶ τρύγα πίνει μελιηδέα.

ὁ γὰρ τῆς λύγου στέφανος ἄτοπος· πρὸς δεσμοὺς γὰρ καὶ πλέγματα ἡ λύγος ἐπιτήδειος. εἰπὲ οὖν ἡμῖν τι περὶ τούτων ζητήσεως ἀξίων ὄντων . . . · ὁ Δημόκριτος ἔφη· Ἀρίσταρχος ὁ γραμματικώτατος, ἑταῖρε, ἐξηγούμενος τὸ χωρίον ἔφη ὅτι καὶ λύγοις ἐστεφανοῦντο οἱ ἀρχαῖοι. Ταίναρος δὲ ἀγροίκων εἶναι λέγει στεφάνωμα τὴν λύγον.

cf. Athen. 673d–674a, Anacr. 496

1 ὁ add. Gaisford   δ᾽ om. 673d   ἐπειδὴ 673d

ANACREON

350 Photius, *Lexicon*

ἀνασύρειν ('to pull up') and ἀνασεσυρμένην ('with her clothes pulled up'): we normally use the word of vulgar or shameless people. Anacreon in Book 1.[1]

[1] But in which sense?

351 *Etymologicum Magnum*

Mischievously they fight with the doorkeeper.[1]

Anacreon in Book 2.[2] By σινάμωροι ('mischievous') he means 'destined (μεμορημένοι) to do mischief (σίνεσθαι).'

[1] Or 'Mischievous men fight . . .'. Cf. Sa. 110(a).   [2] One ms. has 'Book 1'.

352 Athenaeus, *Scholars at Dinner*

Cynulcus said, 'Since questions about garlands have come up, tell us, Ulpian, what 'the garland of Naucratis' is in the charming Anacreon; for the sweet poet says (fr. 434); and why in the same poet are some people garlanded with willow? In Book 2 of his songs he says:

The kindly Megistes has for ten months now garlanded himself with willow and drunk the honeysweet must.[1]

The garland of willow is absurd, since willow is suitable for ropes and wicker-work. So tell us something about these things, since they deserve investigation . . .' Democritus said, 'The eminent grammarian Aristarchus in his explanation of the passage, my friend, said the ancients used to make garlands even from willow. Taenarus says that country people used willow for garlands . . .'

[1] A. E. Harvey, *C. Q.* n.s. 7 (1957) 222 n. 1 suggests that A. is mocking the garlands and drink of Megistes, for whom see test. 11 n. 6.

353 Schol. Hom. *Od.* 21. 71 (ii 698 Dindorf)

μύθου· νῦν τῆς στάσεως. ὅθεν καὶ ᾿Ανακρέων τοὺς ἐν τῇ Σάμῳ ἁλιεῖς ὄντας στασιαστάς φησι·

> μυθιῆται
> δ᾿ ἀνὰ νῆσον ὦ Μεγιστῆ
> διέπουσιν ἱρὸν ἄστυ,

ἀντὶ τοῦ στασιασταί.

cf. Eust. *Od.* 1901. 44, *Et. Gen.* (p. 37 Calame)=*Et. Mag.* 593. 46 (᾿Α. ἐν τῷ β´ τῶν μελῶν), Apoll. Soph. *Lex. Hom.* 114. 3 (p. 558 de Villoison), Antig. Caryst. *Mir.* 120; voc. μυθιήτης ap. Ap. Dysc. *Conj.* 524 (p. 255 Schneider), alios (v. Page ad loc.)

2 Buttmann: ἀννήσω schol. Hom. ἐν νήσῳ Eust.

354 Ammon. *Diff.* 135 (p. 35 Nickau)

διαβόητος καὶ ἐπιβόητος διαφέρει. διαβόητος μὲν γάρ ἐστιν ὁ ἐπ᾿ ἀρετῇ ἐγνωσμένος, ἐπιβόητος δ᾿ ὁ μοχθηρὰν ἔχων φήμην. ᾿Ανακρέων ἐν δευτέρῳ·

> καί μ᾿ ἐπίβωτον
> κατὰ γείτονας ποήσεις.

cf. *Et. Gud.* 355. 30 de Stef., *Et. Vat.* gr. 1708 (ap. Gentili), Eust. *Od.* 1856. 12

1 ἐπίβωτον Eust. -βόητον cett.

355 *Suda* (iv 507 Adler)

τὰ Ταντάλου τάλαντα τανταλίζεται· διεβεβόητο ὁ Τάνταλος ἐπὶ πλούτῳ, ὡς καὶ εἰς παροιμίαν διαδοθῆναι. οὗτος γὰρ πλούσιος Φρὺξ ἐπὶ ταλάντοις διεβεβόητο, Πλουτοῦς καὶ Διὸς λεγόμενος. κέχρηται δὲ τῇ παροιμίᾳ καὶ ᾿Ανακρέων ἐν τρίτῳ.

cf. Phot. s.v. Ταντάλου τάλαντα (p. 570 Porson), Arsen. =Apostol. *Cent.* 16. 16 (ii 660 L.–S.)

ANACREON

353 Scholiast on *Odyssey*

μῦθος ('word, tale') now means 'rebellion, civil strife'; and so Anacreon says of the rebellious fishermen in Samos

and in the island, Megistes, the talkers hold sway over the sacred city,

using μυθιῆται, 'talkers', instead of στασιασταί, 'rebels'.[1]

[1] According to Antigonus they were led by one Herostratus; for political opposition to Polycrates see Hdt. 3. 44 f.

354 Ammonius, *On Similar but Different Words*

διαβόητος and ἐπιβόητος are different in meaning: the man known for his virtue is διαβόητος, 'famous', the man with a bad reputation is ἐπιβόητος, 'notorious': cf. Anacreon Book 2:

and you will make me notorious among the neighbours.

355 *Suda*

'His talents would tantalise Tantalus'[1]: Tantalus was famous for his wealth and has become proverbial for it. He was a wealthy Phrygian, famous for his talents, reputedly the son of Pluto (Lady Wealth) and Zeus. Anacreon uses the proverb in Book 3.

[1] Lit. 'he equals Tantalus in talents', a talent being a large sum of money. See also P. Oxy. 3695 fr. 3.

GREEK LYRIC

356 Athen. 10. 427ab (ii 428s. Kaibel)

παρὰ δὲ Ἀνακρέοντι εἶς οἴνου πρὸς δύο ὕδατος·

(a)

> ἄγε δὴ φέρ' ἡμὶν ὦ παῖ
> κελέβην, ὅκως ἄμυστιν
> προπίω, τὰ μὲν δέκ' ἐγχέας
> ὕδατος, τὰ πέντε δ' οἴνου
> 5 κυάθους ὡς ἀνυβρίστως
> ἀνὰ δηὗτε βασσαρήσω.

καὶ προελθὼν τὴν ἀκρατοποσίαν Σκυθικὴν καλεῖ πόσιν·

(b)

> ἄγε δηὗτε μηκέτ' οὕτω
> πατάγῳ τε κἀλαλητῷ
> Σκυθικὴν πόσιν παρ' οἴνῳ
> μελετῶμεν, ἀλλὰ καλοῖς
> 5 ὑποπίνοντες ἐν ὕμνοις.

cf. Athen. 11. 475c, Eust. *Od.* 1476. 31, Porphyr. in Hor. *Carm.* 1. 27. 1 (p. 35 Holder) protreptice ode est haec ad hilaritatem, cuius sensus sumptus est ab Anacreonte ex libro tertio

5s. Pauw: ἂν ὑβριστιώσανα Athen.

357 Dio Chrys. *Or.* 2. 62 (i 29 von Arnim)

τούτοις γε μὴν ξυνέπεται μηδὲ εὐχὰς εὔχεσθαι τὸν βασιλέα τοῖς ἄλλοις ὁμοίας μηδὲ αὖ τοὺς θεοὺς καλεῖν οὕτως εὐχόμενον ὥσπερ ὁ Ἰώνων ποιητὴς Ἀνακρέων·

> ὦναξ, ᾧ δαμάλης Ἔρως
> καὶ Νύμφαι κυανώπιδες
> πορφυρῆ τ' Ἀφροδίτη
> συμπαίζουσιν, ἐπιστρέφεαι
> 5 δ' ὑψηλὰς ὀρέων κορυφάς·
> γουνοῦμαί σε, σὺ δ' εὐμενὴς

ANACREON

356 Athenaeus, *Scholars at Dinner*

But in Anacreon the mixture is one part wine to two parts water:

Come, boy, bring me a bowl, so that I may drink without stopping for breath; pour in ten ladles of water and five of wine, that I may once again play the Bacchant with decorum;

and further on he calls the drinking of unmixed wine Scythian drinking:

Come again, let us no longer practise Scythian drinking with clatter and shouting over our wine, but drink moderately amid beautiful songs of praise.[1]

[1] From Book 3 of Anacreon (Porphyrio); the quotations must come from the same poem.

357 Dio Chrysostom, *Orations*

It follows that the king should not offer prayers like those of other men nor call on the gods in prayer after the manner of the Ionian poet Anacreon:

Lord, with whom Love the subduer and the blue-eyed Nymphs and radiant Aphrodite play, as you haunt the lofty mountain peaks, I beseech you: come

ἔλθ' ἡμίν, κεχαρισμένης
δ' εὐχωλῆς ἐπακούειν·
Κλεοβούλῳ δ' ἀγαθὸς γένεο
10 σύμβουλος, τὸν ἐμόν γ' ἔρω-
τ', ὦ Δεόνυσε, δέχεσθαι.

cf. Hdn. i 79 Lentz, Aelian. *N. A.* 4. 2 (i 218 Scholfield),
Hsch. Δ 170 (i 402 Latte), Himer. *Or.* 9. 19 (p. 84 Colonna)

10 γ' Kan. δ' codd.

358 Athen. 13. 599c (iii 321 Kaibel)

Χαμαιλέων δ' ἐν τῷ περὶ Σαπφοῦς καὶ λέγειν τινάς φησιν εἰς
αὐτὴν πεποιῆσθαι ὑπὸ Ἀνακρέοντος τάδε·

σφαίρῃ δηῦτέ με πορφυρῇ
βάλλων χρυσοκόμης Ἔρως
νήνι ποικιλοσαμβάλῳ
συμπαίζειν προκαλεῖται·
5 ἡ δ', ἐστὶν γὰρ ἀπ' εὐκτίτου
Λέσβου, τὴν μὲν ἐμὴν κόμην,
λευκὴ γάρ, καταμέμφεται,
πρὸς δ' ἄλλην τινὰ χάσκει.

cf. *Et. Sorb.* ap. *Et. Mag.* 448. 29

1 Barnes (-έη): πορφυρενι codd.   3 Seidler: ποικίλος
λαμβάνω Athen. ποικίλους (ω super ου script.) ἀμβάλω *Et. Sorb.*
5 Barnes: ἀπευκτικοῦ Athen.

359 'Hdn.' *Fig.* (*Rhet. Gr.* viii 599s. Walz)

ἔστι δὲ τὸ τοιοῦτον σχῆμα καὶ παρά τισι τῶν ποιητῶν . . . παρὰ
μὲν οὖν Ἀρχιλόχῳ (115 West), παρὰ δὲ Ἀνακρέοντι ἐπὶ τριῶν·

Κλεοβούλου μὲν ἔγωγ' ἐρέω,
Κλεοβούλῳ δ' ἐπιμαίνομαι,
Κλεόβουλον δὲ διοσκέω.

3 Bergk: δὲ διοσκνέω, διὸς κνέων alia codd. (v. West *I. E. G.*
i 46)

56

to me with kindly heart, hear my prayer and find it acceptable: give Cleobulus good counsel, Dionysus, that he accept my love.[1]

[1] Considered a complete poem by some; for Cleobulus cf. 359, 360, 402, 471, Max. Tyr. 21. 7.

358 Athenaeus, *Scholars at Dinner* [1]

Chamaeleon in his treatise *On Sappho* actually declares that some say it was to her that the following lines were addressed by Anacreon:

Once again golden-haired Love strikes me with his purple ball and summons me to play with the girl in the fancy sandals; but she—she comes from Lesbos with its fine cities—finds fault with my hair because it is white, and gapes after another—girl.[2]

[1] See Sa. test. 8.   [2] Prob. a complete poem.

359 'Herodian', *On Figures of Speech*

The figure polyptoton (repetition of a word in different cases) can be found in some of the poets: in Archilochus (fr. 115) and in Anacreon, who uses three cases:

I love Cleobulus, I am mad about Cleobulus, I gaze at Cleobulus.

GREEK LYRIC

360 Athen. 13. 564d (iii 244 Kaibel)

καὶ ἡ Σαπφὼ δὲ πρὸς τὸν ὑπερβαλλόντως θαυμαζόμενον τὴν μορφὴν καὶ καλὸν εἶναι νομιζόμενόν φησιν· (fr. 138). ὁ δ' Ἀνακρέων τί φησίν;

> ὦ παῖ παρθένιον βλέπων
> δίζημαί σε, σὺ δ' οὐ κοεῖς,
> οὐκ εἰδὼς ὅτι τῆς ἐμῆς
> ψυχῆς ἡνιοχεύεις.

2 Bergk: οὐκαιεις cod. A οὐκ ἀίεις epitom. οὐ κλύεις Erfurdt

361 Str. 3. 2. 14 (i 232 Kramer)

ὑπολάβοι δ' ἄν τις ἐκ τῆς πολλῆς εὐδαιμονίας καὶ μακραίωνας ὀνομασθῆναι τοὺς ἐνθάδε ἀνθρώπους, καὶ μάλιστα τοὺς ἡγεμόνας, καὶ διὰ τοῦτο Ἀνακρέοντα μὲν οὕτως εἰπεῖν·

> ἐγὼ δ' οὔτ' ἂν Ἀμαλθίης
> βουλοίμην κέρας οὔτ' ἔτεα
> πεντήκοντά τε κἀκατὸν
> Ταρτησσοῦ βασιλεῦσαι,

Ἡρόδοτον δὲ (1. 163, 165) καὶ τὸ ὄνομα τοῦ βασιλέως καταγράψαι καλέσαντα Ἀργανθώνιον.

cf. Plin. N. H. 7. 154, 156 (ii 53s. Mayhoff), ps.-Lucian. Macr. 9s. (i 75 Macleod), schol. Dionys. Perieg. 332 (Geogr. Gr. Min. p. 345 Bernhardy) (Ταρτησσός, ἣν καὶ ὁ Ἀνακρέων φησὶ πανευδαίμονα), Phleg. Trall. Macr. 4 (p. 90 Keller)

1 Casaubon: ἐγώ τ' ἂν οὔτ' codd. ἔγωγ' οὔτ' ἂν Mehlhorn

362 Schol. T Hom. Il. 15. 192 (iv 53 Erbse) = Eust. Il. 1012. 1

Ἀττικοὶ τὸν περὶ χειμερίους τροπὰς μῆνα Ποσειδεῶνα καλοῦσιν. Ἀνακρέων·

ANACREON

360 Athenaeus, *Scholars at Dinner*

And Sappho says to the man who is extravagantly admired for his figure and considered handsome (138). And what does Anacreon say?

Boy with the girlish glance,[1] I seek you, but you do not notice, not knowing that you hold the reins of my soul.

[1] Cleobulus? cf. 402.

361 Strabo, *Geography*

One might well believe that it was from their great prosperity that the men of these parts, especially their rulers, got the name of 'long-livers', and that this was why Anacreon said:

I would not wish for Amalthea's horn [1] nor to be king of Tartessus [2] for a hundred and fifty years,

and why Herodotus (1. 163, 165) even gave the name of the king in question, Arganthonius.[3]

[1] Amalthea was the she-goat who nursed the infant Zeus; her horns flowed one with ambrosia, one with nectar, the prototype of the horn of plenty, *cornu copiae.*   [2] District and city at the mouth of the Baetis (mod. Guadalquivir).   [3] Acc. to Hdt. Arg. ruled Tartessus for 80 of his 120 years.

362 Scholiast on *Iliad*

The people of Attica call the month of the winter solstice Poseideon: cf. Anacreon:

μεὶς μὲν δὴ Ποσιδηίων
ἔστηκεν † νεφέλη δ' ὕδωρ
⟨   ⟩ βαρὺ δ' ἄγριοι
χειμῶνες κατάγουσι. †

2ss. schol. Hom. ut supra; ἔστηκε, νεφέλαι δ' ὕδατι βαρύνονται,
ἄγριοι δὲ χειμῶνες παταγοῦσι Eust. νεφέλας δ' ὕδωρ | βαρύνει, Δία
τ' ἄγριοι | χειμῶνες κατάγουσι Bergk

363 Athen. 15. 687e (iii 520s. Kaibel)

καὶ ὁ σοφὸς δὲ Ἀνακρέων λέγει που·

τί μὲν πέτεαι
συρίγγων κοϊλώτερα
στήθεα χρισάμενος μύρῳ;

τὰ στήθη παρακελευόμενος μυροῦν, ἐν οἷς ἐστιν ἡ καρδία, ὡς καὶ
ταύτης δηλονότι παρηγορουμένης τοῖς εὐώδεσι.

1 Page: τί μὴν Athen.   τί μὲν ⟨οὐ⟩ ci. Page   2 Bergk:
κοιλότερα Athen.

364 Ap. Dysc. *Synt.* 3. 74 (ii 338s. Uhlig)

καὶ δὴ παρείπετο τῷ χρῶ παραγωγὴ ἡ τοῦ χρῆμι, ὡς φημί, ἀφ'
οὗ τρίτον πρόσωπον χρῆσι ὡς φησί, ἐξ οὗ τὸ χρή ἐν ἀποκοπῇ
ἀπετελεῖτο ὁμοίως τῷ παρὰ Ἀνακρέοντι·

σὲ γάρ
φη Ταργήλιος ἐμμελέως
δισκεῖν

cf. Ap. Dysc. *Adv.* 543 (p. 133 Schneider)=*Anecd. Gr.* ii 543
Bekker, schol. T Hom. *Il.* 5. 256 (ii 42 Erbse), Choerob. in
Theod. *Can.* ii 25 Hilgard=*Anecd. Oxon.* iv 411 Cramer (τὸ
δὲ Ταργήλιος ὄνομά ἐστι δαίμονος), Lex. Messan. *De iota
ascripto* ed. Rabe, *Rh. Mus.* 47 (1892) 410

ANACREON

See, the month of Poseideon has come, the clouds (are heavy with?) water, and the wild storms (crash?).[1]

[1] Or 'the wild storms bring the sky-god down' (cf. Hor. *Epod.* 13. 1): text uncertain.

363 Athenaeus, *Scholars at Dinner* [1]

And the wise Anacreon says somewhere:

Why are you all of a flutter, anointing with perfume your breast that is hollower than the pipes of Pan?

He urges the perfuming of the breast, in which the heart lies, clearly because the heart too is soothed by sweet scents.

[1] The passage follows Alc. 362 (second fragment); Athen.'s comment fits the Alc. passage, not the text of Anacr., which is mockery of an old man.

364 Apollonius Dyscolus, *Syntax*

The variant form χρῆμι, like φημί, existed alongside of χρῶ; the third person was χρῆσι, like φησί, and from it the abbreviated form χρή was created, like φη ('says') in Anacreon:

for Targelius [1] says you throw the discus beautifully.

[1] A daemon or lesser deity, in whose honour the Thargelia may originally have been held.

365 *Et. Gen.* (p. 22 Calame) = *Et. Mag.* 259. 28 = Hdn.
ii 330s., 492 Lentz

Δεύνυσος· ὁ Διόνυσος. ᾿Ανακρέων·

> πολλὰ δ᾽ ἐρίβρομον
> Δεόνυσον,

ἀπὸ τοῦ Διόνυσος, τοῦ ῾ι᾽ τραπέντος εἰς ῾ε᾽ Δεόνυσος· οὕτως γὰρ
Σάμιοι προφέρονται. καὶ συναιρέσει Δεύνυσος, ὡς Θεόδοτος
Θεύδοτος.

2 Δεύ- codd.

366 Eust. *Od.* 1542. 47

> ἀλλ᾽ ὦ τρὶς κεκορημένε
> Σμερδίη

παρὰ ᾿Ανακρέοντι· ἤγουν πολλάκις ἐκσεσαρωμένε.

cf. Eust. *Il.* 725. 35, Suet. π. βλασφ. pp. 63, 104 Taillardat,
Hsch. K 3607 (ii 511 Latte)

367 Schol. A Hom. *Il.* 3. 219 (i 399 Erbse)

πρὸς τὸ ἀστεμφές, ὅτι τὸ ἀμετακίνητον. ὁ γὰρ ᾿Ανακρέων·

> σὺ γὰρ ἦς ἔμοι-
> γ᾽ ἀστεμφής

1 εἰς (‘you are’) Bergk

368 *Et. Gen.* (p. 37 Calame)

μύθεαι· δεύτερον πρόσωπον παθητικοῦ ἐνεστῶτος. τοιοῦτόν ἐστι
παρὰ τῷ ᾿Ανακρέοντι·

> Λευκίππην ἔπι δίνεαι,

ἰωνικῶς.

λευκίππη cod. A λευκίππων cod. B corr. Hoffmann ἐπιδίνεαι
codd.

ANACREON

365 *Etymologicum Genuinum*

Deunysus = Dionysus; cf. Anacreon:

> often loud-roaring Deunysus;

the ι of Dionysus has been changed to ε to give Deonysus, the form used by the Samians [1]; contraction results in Deunysus, as in Theudotus for Theodotus.

[1] A. would actually have used this form.

366 Eustathius on *Odyssey* 5. 306 (τρισμάκαρες Δαναοί, 'thrice-happy Greeks')

> Come, thrice-swept Smerdies, . . .

in Anacreon, i.e. often swept out.[1]

[1] 'Foppish'? or with obscene sense?

367 Scholiast on *Iliad* 3. 219 (ἀστεμφές, 'stiff')

The mark (διπλῆ) [1] is against ἀστεμφές, which means 'inflexible'; cf. Anacreon:

> for you were inflexible towards me.

[1] Made by a grammarian in the margin of the text.

368 *Etymologicum Genuinum*

μύθεαι, 'you say': 2nd person present passive: so δίνεαι in Anacreon:

> you are in a spin about Leucippe.

The form is Ionic.

GREEK LYRIC

369 *Et. Gen.* (p. 38 Calame) = *Et. Mag.* 601. 20 = Hdn. (ii 253 Lentz)

νένοται· ἢ ἀπὸ τοῦ νενόηται κατὰ συγκοπὴν τοῦ ‘ η ’ ἢ ἀπὸ τοῦ νένωται κατὰ συστολήν . . . καὶ παρ᾽ Ἀνακρέοντι ἡ μετοχή, οἷον

>   ὁ δ᾽ ὑψηλὰ νενωμένος

370 Schol. Eur. *Hec.* 361 (i 39 Schwarz)

τὴν κάσιν· Ἀνακρέων·

>   οὔτ᾽ ἐμὴν ἀπαλὴν κάσιν·

σεσημείωται δὲ ὅτι τὴν θήλειαν κάσιν εἶπεν, εἰ μὴ ἀποκοπή ἐστι τοῦ κασιγνήτην.

Bergk: οὔτε μὲν cod. M τότε μ᾽ cod. A

371 Chrysipp. π. ἀποφ. 22 (*S. V. F.* ii 57 Arnim)

. . . οὐ Ἀνακρέων οὕτως ἀπεφήνατο·

>   οὐ δηῦτ᾽ † ἔμπεδός † εἰμι
>   οὐδ᾽ ἀστοῖσι προσηνής.

1 οὐδ᾽ εὐπέμπελός Bergk   εἰμ᾽ ⟨ἔγωγ᾽⟩? Page

372 Athen. 12. 533ef (iii 177 Kaibel)

Χαμαιλέων δ᾽ ὁ Ποντικὸς ἐν τῷ περὶ Ἀνακρέοντος προθεὶς τὸ

>   ξανθῇ δ᾽ Εὐρυπύλῃ μέλει
>   ὁ περιφόρητος Ἀρτέμων,

τὴν προσηγορίαν ταύτην λαβεῖν τὸν Ἀρτέμωνα διὰ τὸ τρυφερῶς βιοῦντα περιφέρεσθαι ἐπὶ κλίνης.

cf. schol. Ar. *Ach.* 850 (p. 23 Dübner), Plut. *Per.* 27 (i 2. 32 Ziegler), Zenob. ap. Miller *Mélanges* 356, Plin. *N. H.* 34. 56 (v 182 Mayhoff), Hsch. Π 1831 (iii 318 Schmidt)

ANACREON

369 *Etymologicum Genuinum*

νένοται, 'he is minded': the form is derived either from νενόηται with the η dropped or from νένωται with the vowel shortened . . . Anacreon has the participle:

> but he, being high-minded, . . .

370 Scholiast on Euripides, *Hecuba* (τὴν . . . κάσιν, 'the sister')

Cf. Anacreon:

> nor my tender sister.

It is marked as exceptional because he uses κάσις as a feminine noun, unless of course it is a shortened form of κασιγνήτη.

371 Chrysippus, *Negatives*

. . . then Anacreon did not [1] express himself as follows:

> This time I am not (obstinate?) [2] nor easy-going with my fellow-citizens.

[1] Part of a Stoic exercise in logic.   [2] Text uncertain.

372 Athenaeus, *Scholars at Dinner*

Chamaeleon of Pontus in his treatise *On Anacreon* quotes these lines:

> Fair-haired Eurypyle is in love with that litter-rider Artemon,

and explains that Artemon got this name because he lived luxuriously and was carried about in a litter.[1]

[1] Continued at 388. For Eurypyle see test. 12 n.2.

GREEK LYRIC

373 Heph. *Ench.* 10. 4 (p. 33s. Consbruch)

τὸ δὲ τὴν δευτέραν ἰαμβικὴν ἔχον καλεῖται Πριάπειον, οἷον·

ἠρίστησα μὲν ἰτρίου λεπτοῦ μικρὸν ἀποκλάς,
οἴνου δ' ἐξέπιον κάδον· νῦν δ' ἁβρῶς ἐρόεσσαν
ψάλλω πηκτίδα τῇ φίλῃ κωμάζων †παιδὶ ἁβρῆι†.

cf. Athen. 11. 472e (1–2 κάδον, Ἀνακρέοντος), 14. 646d (1–2 κάδον, Ἀνακρέων), Poll. 10. 70 (ii 209 Bethe), Apoll. Soph. *Lex. Hom.* (p. 846 de Villoison), Eust. *Od.* 1654. 17, Apostol. *Cent.* 6. 86c (ii 450 L.–S.)

3 παιδὶ ἁβρῆι Heph. codd. ΑΙ ποδὶ ἁβρῇ cod. Η   nomen proprium fort. latet: Πολιάρχῃ Wilamowitz

374 Athen. 14. 634c (iii 399 Kaibel)

πολλάκις καὶ αὐτὸς ἐν ἐννοίᾳ γίνομαι, μουσικῆς ὢν ἐραστής, περὶ τῆς μαγάδιδος καλουμένης, πότερον αὐλῶν εἶδος ἢ κιθάρας ἐστίν. ὁ μὲν γὰρ ἥδιστος Ἀνακρέων λέγει που·

ψάλλω δ' εἴκοσι
   † χορδαῖσι μάγαδιν † ἔχων,
ὦ Λεύκασπι, σὺ δ' ἡβᾷς.

cf. 14. 634f, 635cd (=Posidon. 292, i 254s. Edelstein-Kidd), Poll. 4. 61 (i 219 Bethe)

1s. εἴκοσι ⟨Λυδὸν⟩ | χορδῇσιν μαγάδην ἔχων Bergk

375 Athen. 4. 177a–182c (i 397 Kaibel)

οἴδαμεν δὲ καὶ τοὺς ἡμιόπους καλουμένους, περὶ ὧν φησιν Ἀνακρέων·

τίς ἐρασμίην
τρέψας θυμὸν ἐς ἥβην τερένων ἡμιόπων ὑπ' αὐλῶν
ὀρχεῖται;

εἰσὶ δ' οἱ αὐλοὶ οὗτοι ἐλάσσονες τῶν τελείων ... εἰσὶν δ' οἱ αὐτοὶ τοῖς παιδικοῖς καλουμένοις, οἷς οὐκ οὖσιν ἐναγωνίοις πρὸς τὰς εὐωχίας χρῶνται. διὸ καὶ τέρενας αὐτοὺς κέκληκεν ὁ Ἀνακρέων.

2 Mehlhorn: ἐσέβην Athen.   Casaubon: τέρεν ὡς ἡμίοπον Athen.

ANACREON

373 Hephaestion, *Handbook on Metres*

The antispastic tetrameter catalectic which has an iambic in the second metron is called priapean, e.g.[1]

I dined by breaking off a small piece of thin honeycake, but I drained a jar of wine. Now I tenderly strike my lovely lyre in a serenade to my dear girl.[2]

[1] Attributed to Anacreon by Athenaeus.   [2] Text of last words uncertain: perhaps a proper name, e.g. 'my dear Poliarche'.

374 Athenaeus, *Scholars at Dinner*

I myself, being a music-lover, have often wondered whether the instrument called the magadis is a sort of pipes or a type of lyre; for the sweet Anacreon says somewhere:

Holding the magadis I strike its twenty strings,[1] while you, Leucaspis, enjoy the fun of youth.

[1] Text uncertain. Athen. goes on to quote authors who seem to speak of the magadis as a pipe.

375 Athenaeus, *Scholars at Dinner*

We know also of pipes called half-size, about which Anacreon says:

Who has turned his thoughts to lovely youth and dances to the tender half-size pipes [1]?

These pipes are smaller than the complete ones . . . They are the same as the so-called 'child-pipes', which are not suitable for public festivals but are used at parties. This is why Anacreon calls them 'tender'.

[1] Pipes with three holes instead of six.

GREEK LYRIC

376 Heph. *Poem*. 7. 2 (p. 71 Consbruch)

εἰσὶ δὲ ἐν τοῖς ποιήμασι καὶ οἱ ἀρρενικῶς οὕτω καλούμενοι ἐπῳδοί, ὅταν μεγάλῳ στίχῳ περιττόν τι ἐπιφέρηται, οἷον· (Archil. frr. 172. 1s., 182)... ὅταν δὲ ἔμπαλιν ἡ τάξις ᾖ, προῳδὸς καλεῖται, ὡς παρὰ Ἀνακρέοντι·

> ἀρθεὶς δηὖτ' ἀπὸ Λευκάδος
> πέτρης ἐς πολιὸν κῦμα κολυμβῶ μεθύων ἔρωτι.

cf. Philostrat. *Imag*. 1. 15 (ii 317 Kayser), Apostol. *Cent*. 3. 90c (ii 308 L.–S.)

377 Schol. T Hom. *Il*. 24. 278 (v 571 Erbse)

Μυσοὶ πλησίον ὄντες Ἐνετῶν· ὅθεν ἡμιόνων γένος· ἢ ὡς καὶ παρὰ Μυσοῖς διαφόρων ὄντων. Ἀνακρέων·

> ἱπποθόρων δὲ Μυσοὶ
> εὗρον μεῖξιν ὄνων

πρὸς ἵππους, ἐξ ὧν ἡμίονοι.

1 Bergk: -θορον cod.   δὲ Bekker καὶ cod.   2 Bergk: εὑρεῖν cod.

378 Schol. Ar. *Av*. 1372 (p. 249 White)

ἀναπέτομαι δή· παρὰ τὰ Ἀνακρέοντος·

> ἀναπέτομαι δὴ πρὸς Ὄλυμπον πτερύγεσσι κούφῃς
> διὰ τὸν Ἔρωτ'· οὐ γὰρ ἐμοὶ ⟨— ∪⟩ θέλει συνηβᾶν.

διὸ καὶ τὸ χ ἔχουσι οἱ δύο στίχοι.

cf. Heph. *Ench*. 9. 3 (p. 30 Consbr.), epitom. Heph. 5 (p. 360 Consbr.)

2 ⟨παῖς ἐ⟩θέλει Porson

68

ANACREON

376 Hephaestion, *On Poems*

In poems there are also the so-called epodes—the noun is masculine—when an addition is made to a long line, e.g. Archilochus, 172. 1 f., 182; but when the order is reversed [1] it is called a pro-ode, as in Anacreon:

See, once again I climb up and dive from the Leucadian cliff [2] into the grey waves, drunk with love.

[1] I.e. the shorter line comes first.   [2] See Sa. test. 23.

377 Scholiast on Homer, *Iliad* 24. 278 ('mules which the Mysians once gave Priam')

'Mysians' because they were neighbours of the Enetians, from whom came the breed of mules,[1] or because Mysian mules were particularly fine. Cf. Anacreon:

and the Mysians discovered the breeding of mare-mounting asses

with horses, whence come mules.

[1] Cf. *Il.* 2. 852.

378 Scholiast on Aristophanes, *Birds* ('See, I fly up')

This comes from Anacreon's lines:

See, I fly up on light wings to Olympus in search of Love; for (the boy) does not wish to enjoy the fun of youth with me.[1]

That is why the two lines have the χ.[2]

[1] Cf. 445, Sa. 163.   [2] Marginal mark used by Aristarchus to indicate something noteworthy.

GREEK LYRIC

379 Lucian. *Herc.* 8 (i 22 Macleod)

ὥστε ἰσχὺς μὲν καὶ τάχος καὶ κάλλος καὶ ὅσα σώματος ἀγαθὰ
χαιρέτω, καὶ ὁ Ἔρως ὁ σός, ὦ Τήιε ποιητά, ἐσιδών με,

(a)   ὑποπόλιον γένειον χρυσοφαέννων,

εἰ βούλεται,

(b)   πτερύγων † ἢ ἀετοῖς † παραπετέσθω,

καὶ ὁ Ἱπποκλείδης οὐ φροντιεῖ.

ita Bergk: Ἔρως, ὅς μ' ἐσιδὼν γένειον | ὑποπόλιον χρυσοφαέννων
πτερύγων ἀήταις | παραπέτεται

380 Himer. *Or.* 47. 1 (p. 189s. Colonna)

χαῖρε φίλον φῶς χαρίεντι μειδιῶν προσώπῳ·

μέλος γάρ τι λαβὼν ἐκ τῆς λύρας εἰς τὴν σὴν ἐπιδημίαν προσοίσο-
μαι, ἡδέως μὲν ἂν πείσας καὶ αὐτοὺς τοὺς αὐτοὺς λόγους λύραν μοι
γενέσθαι καὶ ποίησιν, ἵνα τι κατὰ σοῦ νεανιεύσωμαι, ὁποῖον
Σιμωνίδης ἢ Πίνδαρος κατὰ Διονύσου καὶ Ἀπόλλωνος. ἐπεὶ δὲ
ἀγέρωχοί τε ὄντες καὶ ὑψαύχενες ἄφετοί τε καὶ ἔξω μέτρων
ἀθύρουσιν, ὀλίγα παρακαλέσας τὴν ποίησιν, δοῦναί μοί τι μέλος
Τήιον (ταύτην γὰρ φιλῶ τὴν Μοῦσαν) ἐκ τῶν ἀποθέτων τῶν
Ἀνακρέοντος τοῦτόν σοι φέρων τὸν ὕμνον ἔρχομαι καί τι καὶ αὐτὸς
προσθεὶς τῷ ᾄσματι· ὦ φάος Ἑλλήνων καὶ τῶν ὅσοι Παλλάδος
ἱερὸν δάπεδον Μουσάων τ' ἄλση νεμόμεθα.

¹ The opening words of a speech addressed in Athens to the
proconsul Basilius.

381 Atil. Fort. *Ars* 28 (vi 301 Keil) (de metris Horatii)

apud Anacreontem

(a)   εἶμι λαβὼν † εἰσάρας †,

Sappho (fr. 153); secundum colon Anacreon sic:

(a) ἐς Ἥρης Bergk

ANACREON

379 Lucian, *Heracles*

So goodbye, strength and swiftness and beauty and all physical excellence; let your Love, poet of Teos, glance at

my greying beard

and then, if he so wishes,

fly past me on wings of shining gold.

Hippoclides won't mind.[1]

[1] See Hdt. 6. 126 ff.; exact text of Anacr. uncertain.

380 Himerius, *Orations* [1]

Hail, dear light, with a smile on your lovely face—

for I shall take a song from the lyre and bring it in honour of your visit. I should gladly have persuaded the words themselves to be my lyre and poetry, so that I might sing of you with youthful abandon, as did Simonides and Pindar of Dionysus and Apollo; but the words are proud and stiff-necked, ranging without restraint and frisking beyond the confines of their rhythms; and so I made a small request of Poetry to give me a song of Teos—that is the Muse I love—from the stores of Anacreon; and I come with this hymn of praise for you, having myself made an addition to the song: 'Oh light of the Greeks and of all of us who dwell in the holy plain of Pallas and the groves of the Muses.'

381 Atilius Fortunatianus (on the metre of Horace, *Odes* 1. 8)

The metre of the first line is in Anacreon,

(a)   I shall take it and go (to Hera's temple?)

and in Sappho (fr. 153). The metre of the second is in Anacreon, as follows:

(b) ἀσπίδα ῥίψας ποταμοῦ καλλιρόου παρ' ὄχθας,

Sappho sic (fr. 128).

(b) Bergk: ἀσπίδα ριψ' ἐς ποταμὸν ιλλιροου (κα super ιλ script.) τροχοὰς cod. A ασπιδα ριψες ποταμον ιλλιροου τροχοας cod. B

---

382 Heph. *Ench.* 9. 2 (p. 30 Consbruch)

τρίμετρα (sc. χοριαμβικὰ καταληκτικά) δὲ οἷον τὸ Ἀνακρέοντος·

δακρυόεσσάν τ' ἐφίλησεν αἰχμήν

cf. epitom. Heph. 5 (p. 360 Consbr.), schol. Hermog. *Id.* 1. 5 (vii 988 Walz *Rhet. Gr.*)

---

383 Athen. 11. 475f (iii 46 Kaibel)

Ἀνακρέων·

οἰνοχόει δ' ἀμφίπολος μελιχρὸν
οἶνον τρικύαθον κελέβην ἔχουσα.

2 ἐς κελέβην τ. χέουσα West

---

384 Schol. Pind. *Isthm.* 2. 13 (iii 215 Drachmann)

τοιοῦτον δέ τι καὶ Ἀνακρέων εἴρηκε, καὶ μή ποτε ἡ ἀπότασίς ἐστιν ἐς τὰ ὑπ' ἐκείνου εἰρημένα· φησὶ γάρ·

οὐδ' ἀργυρῆ κω τότ' ἔλαμπε Πειθώ.

cf. Tzetz. *Chil.* 8. 828s. (p. 315 Kiessling)

ἀργυρέα, -ρέους codd. Bergk: κ̄ κότε cod. B. πώποτε cod. D Barnes: πυθώ codd.

(b)

throwing down his (my?) shield by the banks of the fair-flowing river,

and in Sappho (fr. 128).

382 Hephaestion, *Handbook on Metres*

Choriambic trimeters catalectic as in Anacreon:

and fell in love with the tearful spear.

383 Athenaeus, *Scholars at Dinner* (on κελέβη, 'bowl')

Anacreon has:

and the serving-girl, holding the three-ladle bowl,[1] poured the honey-sweet wine.

[1] Cf. 356, 409 for the terms; metre and text of v. 2 uncertain.

384 Scholiast on Pindar, *Isthmian* 2 ('for in those days the Muse was not yet greedy for gain nor a hireling, nor were sweet soft songs offered for sale by honey-voiced Terpsichore with their faces silvered over')

Anacreon says something similar, and perhaps it is to his words that Pindar is referring:

and in those days Persuasion did not yet shine all silver.

GREEK LYRIC

385 Heph. *Ench*. 9. 3 (p. 30 Consbruch)

πολὺ δ᾽ ἐστὶ καὶ τὸ πρὸς τῇ κατάκλειδι τὴν δευτέραν συζυγίαν
ἰαμβικὴν ἔχον, οἷόν ἐστι παρὰ μὲν Ἀνακρέοντι·

ἐκ ποταμοῦ ᾽πανέρχομαι πάντα φέρουσα λαμπρά.

cf. Apostol. *Cent*. 6. 88c (ii 389 L.–S.)

λαμπρά Heph. καλά Apostol.

386 Heph. *Ench*. 15. 22 (p. 55 Consbruch)

ὥσθ᾽ ὅλον αὐτὸ (sc. τὸ Κρατίνειον) χοριαμβικὸν ἐπίμικτον
γενέσθαι, ὅμοιον Ἀνακρεοντείῳ τῷδε·

Σίμαλον εἶδον ἐν χορῷ πηκτίδ᾽ ἔχοντα καλήν.

387 Heph. *Ench*. 15. 20 (p. 54 Consbruch)

Ἀνακρέων δὲ οὐκ ἰαμβικῷ ἀλλὰ χοριαμβικῷ ἐπιμίκτῳ πρὸς τὰς
ἰαμβικὰς ἐπήγαγε τὸ ἰθυφαλλικόν·

τὸν μυροποιὸν ἠρόμην Στράττιν εἰ κομήσει.

cf. Poll. 7. 177 (ii 100 Bethe) (μυροποιός· οὕτω δὲ Ἀνακρέων)

μυρο- Poll. λυρο- Heph.

388 Athen. 12. 533f (iii 177 Kaibel)

καὶ γὰρ Ἀνακρέων αὐτὸν (sc. τὸν Ἀρτέμωνα) ἐκ πενίας εἰς
τρυφὴν ὁρμῆσαί φησιν ἐν τούτοις·

πρὶν μὲν ἔχων βερβέριον, καλύμματ᾽ ἐσφηκωμένα,
καὶ ξυλίνους ἀστραγάλους ἐν ὠσὶ καὶ ψιλὸν περὶ
3 πλευρῇσι ⟨δέρμ᾽ ᾖει⟩ βοός,
νήπλυτον εἴλυμα κακῆς ἀσπίδος, ἀρτοπώλισιν
καθελοπόρνοισιν ὁμιλέων ὁ πονηρὸς Ἀρτέμων,
6 κίβδηλον εὑρίσκων βίον,

74

ANACREON

385 Hephaestion, *Handbook on Metres*

A common form of choriambic tetrameter catalectic has the second metron iambic as well as the close; cf. Anacreon:

I come up from the river bringing (the washing) all bright.[1]

[1] Presumably the beginning of a poem; the speaker is a woman.

386 Hephaestion, *Handbook on Metres*

And so the whole verse (the cratinean) becomes a mixed choriambic like Anacreon's

I saw Simalus in the chorus holding his lovely lyre.

387 Hephaestion, *Handbook on Metres*

Anacreon added the ithyphallic ($-\cup-\cup--$) not to an iambic length but to a choriambic with iambic admixture ($-\cup\cup-|\cup-\cup-$):

I asked Strattis the perfumer [1] whether he would let his hair grow long.

[1] 'The lyre-maker' in Hephaestion's text, 'the perfumer' in Pollux.

388 Athenaeus, *Scholars at Dinner* [1]

Indeed Anacreon says in the following lines that Artemon shot from poverty to luxury:

He used to go about in an old cap,[2] a wasped hood, with wooden dice in his ears and around his ribs a hairless oxhide, the unwashed wrapping of a wretched shield—that scoundrel Artemon, consorting with bread-women and ready whores, devising a

[1] The passage follows 372. [2] A unique noun, meaning uncertain.

75

πολλὰ μὲν ἐν δουρὶ τιθεὶς αὐχένα, πολλὰ δ᾽ ἐν τροχῷ,
πολλὰ δὲ νῶτον σκυτίνῃ μάστιγι θωμιχθείς, κόμην
9 πώγωνά τ᾽ ἐκτετιλμένος·
νῦν δ᾽ ἐπιβαίνει σατινέων χρύσεα φορέων καθέρματα
† παῖς Κύκης † καὶ σκιαδίσκην ἐλεφαντίνην φορεῖ
12 γυναιξὶν αὕτως ⟨ἐμφερής⟩.

3 suppl. Bergk 4 Schoemann: νεόπλουτον cod. A
νεόπλυτον cod. E 11 παῖς ὁ K. Hermann 12 suppl.
Schoemann

389 Athen. 10. 433ef (ii 443 Kaibel)

τὸ δίψος γὰρ πᾶσιν ἰσχυρὰν ἐπιθυμίαν ἐμποιεῖ τῆς περιττῆς
ἀπολαύσεως· . . . Ἀνακρέων·

φίλη γάρ εἰς ξείνοισιν· ἔασον δέ με διψέοντα πιεῖν.

Page: εισξεινεις cod.

390 Athen. 1. 21a (i 45s. Kaibel)

ἔταττον γὰρ τὸ ὀρχεῖσθαι ἐπὶ τοῦ κινεῖσθαι καὶ ἐρεθίζεσθαι.
Ἀνακρέων·

καλλίκομοι κοῦραι Διὸς ὠρχήσαντ᾽ ἐλαφρῶς.

cf. Eust. *Od.* 1942. 4

391 Schol. Pind. *Ol.* 8. 42c (i 248 Drachmann)

ἐπὶ στέφανον τεῦξαι· μεταφορικῶς τὸ τεῖχος. στέφανος γὰρ
ὥσπερ τῶν πόλεων τὰ τείχη. καὶ Ἀνακρέων·

νῦν δ᾽ ἀπὸ μὲν στέφανος πόλεως ὄλωλεν.

Bergk: πόλ. στέφ. codd.

fraudulent living; often he had his neck in the stocks, often on the wheel; often his back was flogged with a leather whip and his hair and beard plucked out. But nowadays the son of Cyce rides in a carriage [3] wearing gold earrings, and he carries an ivory parasol exactly like the ladies.

[3] A woman's vehicle.

389 Athenaeus, *Scholars at Dinner*

For thirst causes in everyone a powerful desire for excessive satisfaction; . . . cf. Anacreon:

You are a friendly girl to strangers, so let me drink: I'm thirsty.

390 Athenaeus, *Scholars at Dinner*

For they used the word 'dance' to express movement and excitement [1]; cf. Anacreon:

The fair-haired daughters of Zeus danced lightly.

[1] The quotation from Ion which follows illustrates the second (metaphorical) use: 'his heart danced'.

391 Scholiast on Pindar, *Olympian* 8 ('to make a crown')

'Crown' is used metaphorically for 'wall', since the walls of a city are, as it were, its crown: cf. Anacreon:

But now the crown of the city [1] is destroyed.

[1] Possibly Teos (see testt. 1, 3).

77

392 *Et. Gen.* (p. 29 Calame) = *Et. Mag.* 429. 50 = Zonar. 990 = Hdn. *Orthogr.* (ii 517 Lentz)

ἡμετέρειος· κτητικόν ἐστι· σημαίνει δὲ τὸν τοῦ ἡμετέρου. ἀπὸ τοῦ ἡμέτερος, ἡμετέρειος· ἐχρήσατο δὲ τῇ λέξει ᾿Ανακρέων·

> οὔτε γὰρ ἡμετέρειον οὔτε καλόν

393 Heph. *Ench.* 15. 10 (p. 51 Consbruch)

κέχρηται δὲ καὶ ᾿Ανακρέων (sc. τῷ ἐγκωμιολογικῷ) ἐν πλείοσιν ᾄσμασιν·

> ὀρσόλοπος μὲν ῎Αρης φιλεῖ μεναίχμην

394 Heph. *Ench.* 7. 2 (p. 21 Consbruch)

ὕστερον δὲ καὶ ᾿Ανακρέων τούτῳ τῷ μέτρῳ (sc. τῷ δακτυλικῷ τετραμέτρῳ εἰς δισύλλαβον καταληκτικῷ) καὶ ὅλα ᾄσματα συνέθηκεν·

(a)   ἡδυμελὲς χαρίεσσα χελιδοῖ

καὶ

(b)   μνᾶται δηῦτε φαλακρὸς ῎Αλεξις.

cf. Mar. Plot. Sacerd. (vi 514 Keil)

395 Stob. 4. 51. 12 (v 1068 Hense) (περὶ θανάτου καὶ ὡς εἴη ἄφυκτος)

᾿Ανακρέοντος·

> πολιοὶ μὲν ἡμὶν ἤδη
> κρόταφοι κάρη τε λευκόν,
> χαρίεσσα δ᾿ οὐκέτ᾿ ἤβη
> πάρα, γηραλέοι δ᾿ ὀδόντες,
> 5 γλυκεροῦ δ᾿ οὐκέτι πολλὸς
> βιότου χρόνος λέλειπται·

ANACREON

392 *Etymologicum Genuinum*

ἡμετέρειος is a possessive adjective meaning 'belonging to what is ours', derived from ἡμέτερος. Anacreon used the word:

> neither from our land nor beautiful

393 Hephaestion, *Handbook on Metres* [1]

Anacreon used the encomiologic metre in many songs:

> Warlike Ares loves a staunch fighter.

[1] See Alc. 383.

394 Hephaestion, *Handbook on Metres*

Later [1] Anacreon composed whole poems in this metre (the dactylic tetrameter catalectic with disyllabic close):

(a)
> Sweet-singing, graceful swallow

and

(b)
> Once again bald Alexis goes wooing.

[1] Heph. has quoted Archil. 195.

395 Stobaeus, *Anthology* (on death and its inevitability)

From Anacreon:

My temples are already grey and my head is white; graceful youth is no more with me, my teeth are old, and no long span of sweet life remains now. And so I

δια ταῦτ' ἀνασταλύζω
θαμὰ Τάρταρον δεδοικώς·
Ἀίδεω γὰρ ἐστι δεινὸς
10 μυχός, ἀργαλῆ δ' ἐς αὐτὸν
κάτοδος· καὶ γὰρ ἑτοῖμον
καταβάντι μὴ ἀναβῆναι.

2 τε Bergk δὲ codd.   11 κεῖ γὰρ West

396 Athen 11. 782a (iii 18 Kaibel)

ἔθος δ' ἦν πρότερον ἐν τῷ ποτηρίῳ ὕδωρ ἐμβάλλεσθαι, μεθ' ὃ τὸν
οἶνον. . . . Ἀνακρέων·

φέρ' ὕδωρ, φέρ' οἶνον, ὦ παῖ, φέρε ⟨δ'⟩ ἀνθεμόεντας
ἡμὶν
στεφάνους· ἔνεικον, ὡς δὴ πρὸς Ἔρωτα πυκταλίζω.

cf. Demetr. *Eloc.* 5 (p. 4 Raderm.) (μεθύοντος γὰρ ὁ ῥυθμὸς
ἀτεχνῶς γέροντος), anon. metr. (P. Oxy. 220 col. vii 3–6
=Heph. p. 404 Consbr.), *Et. Gen.* (p. 26 Calame)=*Et. Mag.*
345. 32, Orion. 62. 30, Eust. *Il.* 1322. 53, lap. inscr. ed.
G. Vuillemot (*Mém. de la Soc. éduenne* 51, 1966, 31ss.)

1 δ' suppl. Casaubon   2 ὡς δὴ Orion ὡς ἤδη Et. Gen. ὡς μὴ
Athen. Eust. lapis ὡς ἂν Dobree

397 Athen. 15. 674cd (iii 490 Kaibel)

ἐκάλουν δὲ καὶ οἷς περιεδέοντο τὸν τράχηλον στεφάνους ὑποθυμί-
δας· . . . Ἀνακρέων·

πλεκτὰς
δ' ὑποθυμίδας περὶ στήθεσι λωτίνας ἔθεντο.

cf. Athen. 15. 678d

Dindorf: ὑποθυμιάδας (bis) Athen.

often weep in fear of Tartarus: for the recess of Hades is grim, and the road down to it grievous; and it is certain that he who goes down does not come up again.

396 Athenaeus, *Scholars at Dinner*

It was the custom to pour into the cup first water and then the wine . . . ; cf. Anacreon:

Bring water, boy, bring wine, bring me garlands of flowers: fetch them, so that I may box against Love.[1]

Demetrius, *On Style*

The rhythm is exactly that of an old man drunk.

[1] The poem has been found with a portrait of Anacreon on a 2nd c. A.D. mosaic at Autun: see also 429 and M. and A. Blanchard, *R. E. A.* 75 (1973) 268 ff.

397 Athenaeus, *Scholars at Dinner*

They called the garlands which they fastened around their necks ὑποθυμίδες [1]; . . . cf. Anacreon:

and they placed over their breasts woven garlands of lotus.

[1] Athen. quotes also Alc. 362, Sa. 94. 15 f.

398 Schol. A Hom. *Il.* 23. 88 (v 382 Erbse) (ἀμφ' ἀστραγάλοισι χολωθείς)

αἱ πλείους τῶν κατὰ ἄνδρα ἀμφ' ἀστραγάλησιν ἐρίσσας (Bekker: ἐρύσας cod.), καὶ ἔστιν Ἰωνικώτερον·

> ἀστραγάλαι δ' Ἔρωτός εἰσιν
> μανίαι τε καὶ κυδοιμοί,

Ἀνακρέων.

399 Schol. Eur. *Hec.* 934 (i 74 Schwartz)

καὶ δωριάζειν τὸ γυμνουμένας φαίνεσθαι τὰς γυναῖκας. Ἀνακρέων·

> ἐκδῦσα κιθῶνα δωριάζειν

cf. Eust. *Il.* 975. 38

Fick: χιτῶνα codd.

400 Heph. *Ench.* 12. 5 (p. 39 Consbruch)

τὸ δὲ ⟨δίμετρον τὸ⟩ ἀκατάληκτον (sc. τὸ ἰωνικὸν ἀπ' ἐλάσσονος) κατὰ τὸν ἀνακλώμενον χαρακτῆρα πολὺ παρὰ τῷ Ἀνακρέοντί ἐστι·

> παρὰ δηῦτε Πυθόμανδρον
> κατέδυν Ἔρωτα φεύγων.

ANACREON

398 Scholiast on *Iliad* ('in anger over the dice')

Most of the 'individual' texts have 'in a quarrel over the dice' with the feminine form ἀστραγάλη, which is more Ionic; cf. Anacreon:

The dice of Love are madness and uproar.

399 Scholiast on Euripides, *Hecuba*

The expression 'to play the Dorian' is used of women showing themselves naked; cf. Anacreon:

to take off her (your) chiton and play the Dorian.

400 Hephaestion, *Handbook on Metres*

The ionic *a minore* dimeter acatalectic with anaclasis [1] is frequent in Anacreon:

Once again I went down to Pythomander's [2] to escape Love.

[1] With 4th and 5th syllables interchanged.   [2] Meaning obscure; perhaps 'I sought refuge with P.'

GREEK LYRIC

401 Str. 14. 2. 27 (iii 140 Kramer)

τοῦ δὲ περὶ τὰ στρατιωτικὰ ζήλου τά τε ὄχανα ποιοῦνται τεκμή-
ρια καὶ τὰ ἐπίσημα καὶ τοὺς λόφους· ἅπαντα γὰρ λέγεται Καρικά.
Ἀνακρέων μέν γέ φησιν·

> διὰ δηῦτε Καρικουργέος
> ὀχάνου χεῖρα † τιθέμενοι †

cf. Eust. *Il.* 367. 23, 707. 61, schol. A Hom. *Il.* 8. 193 (i 278
Di.), *Et. Gen.* (p. 31 Calame)=*Et. Gud.* 297. 43=*Et. Mag.*
489. 36

2 ὀχάνου Str., Eust. 367 -οιο schol. Hom., Ett., Eust. 707
τιθέμενοι, τιθέναι, τιθέμεναι codd. τέθειμαι Edmonds

402 Max. Tyr. 18.9 (p. 232s. Hobein)

ἡ δὲ τοῦ Τηίου σοφιστοῦ τέχνη τοῦ αὐτοῦ ἤθους καὶ τρόπου. καὶ
γὰρ πάντων ἐρᾷ τῶν καλῶν καὶ ἐπαινεῖ πάντας. μεστὰ δὲ αὐτοῦ τὰ
ᾄσματα τῆς Σμέρδιος κόμης καὶ τῶν Κλεοβούλου ὀφθαλμῶν καὶ
τῆς Βαθύλλου ὥρας. ἀλλὰ καὶ τούτοις τὴν σωφροσύνην ὁρᾷς·

(a)

> ἔραμαι ⟨δέ⟩ τοι συνηβᾶν,

φησίν,

> χαρίεν γὰρ † ἔχεις ἦθος. †

καὶ αὖθις

(b)

> καλὸν εἶναι τῷ Ἔρωτι τὰ δίκαιά φησιν.

ἤδη δέ που καὶ τὴν τέχνην ἀπεκαλύψατο·

(c)

> ἐμὲ γὰρ † λόγων † εὕνεκα παῖδες ἂν φιλέοιεν·
> χαρίεντα μὲν γὰρ ᾄδω, χαρίεντα δ᾽ οἶδα λέξαι.

(a) 1 δέ suppl. Bergk   2 ἔσχες ἦθος Barnes ἦθος ἴσχεις
Hiller   (c) 1 λόγων ⟨ἐμῶν⟩, ⟨νέοι⟩ λόγων ci. Bergk λόγων
⟨μελέων τ᾽⟩ Blass   2 Valckenaer: διδῶ codd.

84

ANACREON

401 Strabo, *Geography*

As evidence for the Carians' enthusiasm for soldiering shield-holds, shield-emblems and crests are adduced, since they are all called Carian. Anacreon says:

Once again (I have put my?) hand through the Carian-made shield-strap.[1]

[1] Continued at Alc. 388. Is Anacreon fighting against Love?

402 Maximus of Tyre, *Orations*

The art of the craftsman of Teos is of the same kind and character[1]: he is in love with all who are beautiful and praises them all. His poems are full of the hair of Smerdis and the eyes of Cleobulus and the youthful beauty of Bathyllus. But even in these verses you may see his moderation: he says:

(a)

and I long to enjoy the fun of youth with you, for you have graceful ways;

and again he says that

(b)

just deeds are beautiful in Love's view;

and he has surely revealed his art when he says

(c)

for children might love me for my words: for I sing graceful songs and I know how to speak graceful words.

[1] Cf. Sa. test. 20.

GREEK LYRIC

403 Hsch. E 5936 (ii 195 Latte)

ἕρμα· ἔρεισμα ⟦ἢ ἔργμα⟧ ἢ τὸν πετρώδη καὶ ἐπικυματιζόμενον ὥστε μὴ βλέπειν τόπον τῆς θαλάσσης. καὶ Ἀνακρέων·

> ἀσήμων
> ὑπὲρ ἑρμάτων φορέομαι.

cf. Alc. 306 (i) col. i, Harp. s.v. ἕρμα (i 134 Dind.), Phot. s.v. ἑρμάν (15. 1 Pors.), *Sud.* E 3026 (ἑρμᾶν), Zonar. 860 (ἑρμᾶν)

404 Phot. (p. 111 Reitzenstein)

μεταβάλλουσι δ᾽ οἱ Ἴωνες τὸ τελευταῖον 'α' . . . Ἀνακρέων·

> νεότης τε κὐγιείη

405 Schol. Hes. *Theog.* 767 (v. M. L. West, *Philol.* 110, 1966, 154)

. . . χθόνιον δὲ καὶ τὸν στυγνόν, ὡς Ἀνακρέων·

> χθόνιον δ᾽ ἐμαυτὸν ἦγον.

ἤγων, ἦγον, ἦρεν codd.

406 Apoll. Soph. *Lex. Hom.* s.v. θέσθαι (p. 87 Bekker)

. . . καὶ γὰρ ὁ θησαυρὸς θεσμὸς λέγεται, καθάπερ καὶ Ἀνακρέων λέγει·

> ἀπὸ δ᾽ ἐξείλετο θεσμὸν μέγαν.

cf. *Et. Gen.* (p. 30 Calame)=*Et. Mag.* 448. 16

407 Schol. Pind. *Ol.* 7. 5a (i 200 Drachmann)

προπίνειν ἐστὶ κυρίως τὸ ἅμα τῷ κράματι τὸ ἀγγεῖον χαρίζεσθαι. Ἀνακρέων·

> ἀλλὰ πρόπινε
> ῥαδινοὺς ὦ φίλε μηρούς,

ἀντὶ τοῦ χαρίζου.

ANACREON

403 Hesychius, *Lexicon*

ἕρμα: a support; or a rocky place in the sea, hidden from view by the waves; cf. Anacreon:

> I am carried over hidden reefs.[1]

[1] Prob. metaphorically of a stormy love affair; cf. Alc. 306 (i) col. i.

404 Photius, *Lexicon*

The Ionians change the final α (to η) . . . ; cf. Anacreon:

> youth and health

405 Scholiast on Hesiod, *Theogony* (θεοῦ χθονίου, 'the god of the lower world')

χθόνιος, 'of the lower world', may mean 'sullen', as in Anacreon:

> I behaved sullenly.

406 Apollonius, *Homeric Lexicon*

For θησαυρός, 'treasure', is also called θεσμός, as in Anacreon:

> and carried away a great treasure.

407 Scholiast on Pindar

Properly speaking προπίνειν, 'to pledge', means to make a gift of the cup along with the mixture of wine; cf. Anacreon:

> Come, pledge me, dear boy, your slender thighs,

where πρόπινε, 'pledge', is used instead of χαρίζου, 'grant'.

408 Aelian. *N. A.* 7. 39 (ii 152ss. Scholfield)

ὅσοι λέγουσι θῆλυν ἔλαφον κέρατα οὐ φύειν, οὐκ αἰδοῦνται τοὺς
τοῦ ἐναντίου μάρτυρας· . . . ᾿Ανακρέων ἐπὶ θηλείας φησίν·

> ἀγανῶς οἷά τε νεβρὸν νεοθηλέα
> γαλαθηνὸν ὅς τ᾽ ἐν ὕλῃ κεροέσσης
> ἀπολειφθεὶς ἀπὸ μητρὸς ἐπτοήθη.

πρὸς δὲ τοὺς μοιχῶντας τὸ λεχθὲν καὶ μέντοι καὶ φάσκοντας δεῖν
ἐροέσσης γράφειν ἀντιλέγει κατὰ κράτος ᾿Αριστοφάνης ὁ Βυζάντιος
(fr. 378 Slater).

cf. Athen. 9. 396d, schol. Pind. *Ol.* 3. 52 (i 120 Dr.), Eust. *Il.*
711. 34, Poll. 5. 76 (i 282 Bethe)

409 Athen. 10. 430d (ii 436s. Kaibel)

ὁ δ᾽ ᾿Ανακρέων ἔτι ζωρότερον (sc. κιρνάναι κελεύει τὸν οἶνον) ἐν
οἷς φησι·

> καθαρῇ δ᾽ ἐν κελέβῃ πέντε ⟨τε⟩ καὶ τρεῖς ἀνα-
> χείσθω.

τε suppl. Dindorf   ἀναχείσθων ci. Bergk

410 Athen. 15. 674c (iii 490 Kaibel)

ἐστεφανοῦντο δὲ καὶ τὸ μέτωπον, ὡς ὁ καλὸς ᾿Ανακρέων ἔφη·

> ἐπὶ δ᾽ ὀφρύσιν σελίνων στεφανίσκους
> θέμενοι θάλειαν ἑορτὴν ἀγάγωμεν
> Διονύσῳ

cf. Eust. *Od.* 1908. 55, schol. Pind. *Ol.* 3. 19 (i 110 Dr.)

ANACREON

408 Aelian, *On the Nature of Animals*

Those who say the female deer has no horns do not respect the witnesses to the contrary: . . . Anacreon says of a female deer:

Gently,[1] like a new-born sucking fawn, who is frightened, left in the woods away from his horned mother.

Those who corrupt the text,[2] actually saying that the correct reading is ἐροέσσης, 'lovely mother', are vigorously attacked by Aristophanes of Byzantium.

[1] Perhaps 'I draw near you gently, as though you were a . . . fawn'.   [2] E.g. Zenodotus, acc. to the scholiast on Pindar *Ol.* 3. 52; but see G. M. Bolling, *T.A.P.A.* 71, 1940, 40 ff.

409 Athenaeus, *Scholars at Dinner*

Anacreon orders a still stronger mixture[1] in these words:

and let the mixture be poured in a clean bowl, five (of wine) and three (of water).

[1] The passage follows Alc. 346.

410 Athenaeus, *Scholars at Dinner*

They also garlanded their brows, as handsome Anacreon said:

and let us place garlands of celery on our brows and celebrate a rich festival for Dionysus.

GREEK LYRIC

411 Heph. *Ench.* 12. 4 (p. 39 Consbruch)

τῶν δὲ τριμέτρων (sc. ἰωνικῶν τῶν ἀπ᾽ ἐλάσσονος) τὸ μὲν
ἀκατάληκτον παρὰ τῇ Σαπφοῖ (fr. 134), παρὰ δὲ ᾽Ανακρέοντι

(a)   ἀπό μοι θανεῖν γένοιτ᾽· οὐ γὰρ ἂν ἄλλη
        λύσις ἐκ πόνων γένοιτ᾽ οὐδάμα τῶνδε,

τὸ δὲ καταληκτικὸν ⟨ἑτέρως ἐσχημάτισται⟩·

(b)   Διονύσου σαῦλαι Βασσαρίδες

cf. Arsen. = Apostol. *Cent.* 3. 60b (ii 301 L.–S.)

412 Schol. M. Aes. *P. V.* 128 (p. 15 Dindorf)

ὁ ῥυθμὸς ᾽Ανακρεόντειός ἐστι κεκλασμένος πρὸς τὸ θρηνητικόν.
ἐπεδήμησε γὰρ τῇ ᾽Αττικῇ Κριτίου ἐρῶν καὶ ἠρέσθη λίαν τοῖς
μέλεσι τοῦ τραγικοῦ. ἐχρῶντο δὲ αὐτοῖς οὐκ ἐν παντὶ τόπῳ ἀλλ᾽ ἐν
τοῖς θρηνητικοῖς . . . ἐστι δὲ ταῦτα ὅμοια τῷ·

        οὐ δηὖτέ μ᾽ ἐάσεις μεθύοντ᾽ οἴκαδ᾽ ἀπελθεῖν;

Page: οὐδ᾽ αὖ μ᾽ ἐάσεις cod.   interrogat. sign. add. Bergk

413 Heph. *Ench.* 12. 4 (p. 39 Consbruch)

καὶ τῷ βραχυκαταλήκτῳ δὲ (sc. τῷ ἀπ᾽ ἐλάσσονος ἰωνικῷ
τετραμέτρῳ) ᾽Ανακρέων ὅλα ᾆσματα συνέθηκεν·

        μεγάλῳ δηὖτέ μ᾽ Ἔρως ἔκοψεν ὥστε χαλκεὺς
        πελέκει, χειμερίῃ δ᾽ ἔλουσεν ἐν χαράδρῃ.

90

ANACREON

411 Hephaestion, *Handbook on Metres*

Among ionic *a minore* trimeters examples of the acatalectic are Sappho's (fr. 134) and Anacreon's:

(a)

May death be mine, for there could be no other release from these troubles [1];

but the catalectic line is formed differently [2]:

(b)

The hip-swaying Bassarids [3] of Dionysus

[1] Prob. the troubles of love.　　[2] With ∪∪−− contracted to −−− in the second foot.　　[3] Female worshippers of D.

412 Scholiast on Aeschylus, *Prometheus Bound*

The anacreontic rhythm is a broken rhythm [1] suited to lament. Anacreon lived in Attica when he was in love with Critias, and he took great delight in the songs of the tragedian (Aeschylus).[2] They did not use the rhythms indiscriminately but only in passages of lament . . . The passage is similar in rhythm to

Once again, won't you let me go home, now that I am drunk?

[1] I.e. the ionics undergo anaclasis.　　[2] See test. 8 n.1 and fr. 495.

413 Hephaestion, *Handbook on Metres*

Anacreon wrote whole songs in the ionic *a minore* tetrameter brachycatalectic:

Once again Love has struck me like a smith with a great hammer and dipped me in the wintry torrent.[1]

[1] To temper the metal.

GREEK LYRIC

414 Stob. 4. 21. 24 (iv 491 Hense) (κατὰ κάλλους)

Φαβωρίνου· . . . πρὸς ταῦτα γελοῖος ἂν φανείη ὁ Ἀνακρέων καὶ μικρολόγος τῷ παιδὶ μεμφόμενος ὅτι τῆς κόμης ἀπεκείρατο, λέγων ταῦτα·

> ἀπέκειρας δ᾽ ἁπαλῆς κόμης ἄμωμον ἄνθος·

ἀλλ᾽ ὦ Ἀνάκρεον μικρὸν ἐπίμεινον καὶ ὄψει πάντα ἀποκεκαρμένα.

Athen. 12. 540e (iii 191 Kaibel)

ἄξιον θαυμάζειν τὸν τύραννον (sc. Πολυκράτη) ὅτι οὐδαμόθεν ἀναγέγραπται γυναῖκας ἢ παῖδας μεταπεμψάμενος, καίτοι περὶ τὰς τῶν ἀρρένων ὁμιλίας ἐπτοημένος, ὡς καὶ ἀντερᾶν Ἀνακρέοντι τῷ ποιητῇ, ὅτε καὶ δι᾽ ὀργὴν ἀπέκειρε τὸν ἐρώμενον.

Aelian. V. H. 9. 4 (p. 102 Dilts)

Ἀνακρέων ἐπήνεσε Σμερδίην θερμότερον τὰ παιδικὰ Πολυκράτους, εἶτα ἤσθη τὸ μειράκιον τῷ ἐπαίνῳ . . . ἐζηλοτύπησε δὲ Πολυκράτης ὅτι τὸν Σμερδίην ἐτίμησε, καὶ ἑώρα τὸν ποιητὴν ὑπὸ τοῦ παιδὸς ἀντιφιλούμενον, καὶ ἀπέκειρε τὸν παῖδα ὁ Πολυκράτης, ἐκεῖνον μὲν αἰσχύνων, οἰόμενος δὲ λυπεῖν τὸν Ἀνακρέοντα. ὁ δὲ οὐ προσεποιήσατο αἰτιᾶσθαι τὸν Πολυκράτη σωφρόνως καὶ ἐγκρατῶς, μετήγαγε δὲ τὸ ἔγκλημα ἐπὶ τὸ μειράκιον, ἐν οἷς ἐπεκάλει τόλμαν αὐτῷ καὶ ἀμαθίαν ὁπλισαμένῳ κατὰ τῶν ἑαυτοῦ τριχῶν. τὸ δὲ ᾆσμα τὸ ἐπὶ τῷ πάθει τῆς κόμης Ἀνακρέων ᾀσάτω· ἐμοῦ γὰρ αὐτὸς ἄμεινον ᾄσεται.

ANACREON

414 Stobaeus, *Anthology* (against beauty)

Favorinus [1]: . . . and so Anacreon would seem to be ridiculous and petty in blaming the boy [2] for cutting off his hair when he says:

You have cut off the perfect flower of your soft hair.

Anacreon, wait a moment and you will see everything cut off.

[1] 2nd c. A.D. rhetorician.   [2] Smerdies: see test. 12 n. 4.

Athenaeus, *Scholars at Dinner*

It is remarkable that the tyrant Polycrates is nowhere recorded as having summoned either women or boys to his court, although he was passionately devoted to the company of males, to the extent of being a rival of the poet Anacreon at the time when in anger he cut off the hair of his beloved boy.

Aelian, *Historical Miscellanies* [1]

Anacreon praised Smerdies, the favourite of Polycrates, too warmly, and the youth enjoyed the praise . . . ; but Polycrates was jealous that Anacreon had honoured Smerdies, and seeing that the youth returned the poet's love he cut off the boy's hair to disgrace him and cause Anacreon grief. But Anacreon, showing good sense and self-control, did not presume to blame Polycrates but rather turned his reproach on the boy in the words which upbraided his rashness and folly in taking arms against his own hair. Let Anacreon sing the song on what happened to the hair: he will sing it better than I.

[1] Continued from test. 4.

GREEK LYRIC

415 Athen. 10. 427d (ii 429s. Kaibel)

ἦν ἀπ' ἀρχῆς τὸ μὲν σπένδειν ἀποδεδομένον τοῖς θεοῖς, ὁ δὲ κότταβος τοῖς ἐρωμένοις. ἐχρῶντο γὰρ ἐπιμελῶς τῷ κοτταβίζειν ὄντος τοῦ παιγνίου Σικελικοῦ, καθάπερ καὶ Ἀνακρέων ὁ Τήιος πεποίηκε·

> Σικελὸν κότταβον ἀγκύλῃ †δαΐζων†

cf. Hsch. A 575 (i 23 Latte)

cens. Ien.: Σικελικὸν Athen.   λατάζων ci. Wilamowitz

416 *Et. Mag.* 2. 47

παρὰ τὸ ἀβακὴς οὖν γίνεται ἀβακῶ, ὥσπερ εὐσεβὴς εὐσεβῶ. γίνεται δὲ καὶ ἀβακίζω· φησὶν Ἀνακρέων·

> ἐγὼ δὲ μισέω
> πάντας ὅσοι χθονίους ἔχουσι ῥυσμοὺς
> καὶ χαλεπούς· μεμάθηκά σ', ὦ Μεγιστῆ,
> τῶν ἀβακιζομένων,

ἀντὶ τοῦ τῶν ἡσυχίων καὶ μὴ θορυβωδῶν.

cf. *Anecd. Par.* iv 84 Cramer = Zonar. s.v. ἀβάκησαν
2 ὅσοι Bergk οἱ, οἵ codd.   ῥυθμοὺς, ῥυμοὺς codd.   3 μεμαθήκασιν ὡς μεγίστη codd., corr. Hemsterhuys, Bergk

417 Heraclit. *Alleg. Hom.* 5 (p. 5s. Buffière)

καὶ μὴν ὁ Τήιος Ἀνακρέων ἑταιρικὸν φρόνημα καὶ σοβαρᾶς γυναικὸς ὑπερηφανίαν ὀνειδίζων τὸν ἐν αὐτῇ σκιρτῶντα νοῦν ὡς ἵππον ἠλληγόρησεν οὕτω λέγων·

> πῶλε Θρηικίη, τί δή με
>   λοξὸν ὄμμασι βλέπουσα
> 2 νηλέως φεύγεις, δοκεῖς δέ
>   μ' οὐδὲν εἰδέναι σοφόν;
> ἴσθι τοι, καλῶς μὲν ἄν τοι
>   τὸν χαλινὸν ἐμβάλοιμι,

94

ANACREON

415 Athenaeus, *Scholars at Dinner*

In the beginning the libation was given to the gods as their due, the cottabus [1] to the beloved: they assiduously practised the cottabus, a Sicilian game, as the poem of Anacreon of Teos shows:

(throwing the drops of?) the Sicilian cottabus with curved arm.

[1] See Alc. 322.

416 *Etymologicum Magnum* [1]

From ἀβακής, 'quiet', comes ἀβακῶ, 'I am quiet', just as εὐσεβῶ, 'I am reverent', comes from εὐσεβής, 'reverent'. There is also the form ἀβακίζω, 'I am quiet'; cf. Anacreon:

But I hate all who have sullen and difficult ways. I have learned that you, Megistes, are one of the quiet ones.

He uses ἀβακιζομένων, 'quiet', in the sense of 'peaceful, causing no disturbance'.[2]

[1] The passage follows Sa. 120.   [2] This may be wrong: 'quiet' probably = 'sullen' (lit. 'underground') and 'difficult' (Page, *Wien. Stud.* 79, 1966, 30 ff.); cf. 352 n. 1.

417 Heraclitus, *Homeric Allegories*

Moreover [1] Anacreon of Teos, abusing the meretricious spirit and arrogance of a haughty woman, used the 'allegory' of a horse to describe her frisky disposition:

Thracian filly, why do you look at me from the corner of your eye and flee stubbornly from me, supposing that I have no skill? Let me tell you, I

[1] The passage follows Alc. 6.

4 ἡνίας δ' ἔχων στρέφοιμί
σ' ἀμφὶ τέρματα δρόμου·
νῦν δὲ λειμῶνάς τε βόσκεαι
κοῦφά τε σκιρτῶσα παίζεις,
6 δεξιὸν γὰρ ἱπποπείρην
οὐκ ἔχεις ἐπεμβάτην.

cf. Himer. *Or*. 9. 19 (p. 84 Colonna), cod. Vat. gr. 12 fol. 99ʳ
(v. *Herm*. 96, 1968, 238)

4 Bergk: στρέφοιμ' ἀμφὶ codd.

418 Heph. *Ench*. 6. 4 (p. 19 Consbruch)

καὶ τῶν ἀκαταλήκτων δὲ (sc. τῶν τροχαϊκῶν) τὸ τετράμετρόν
ἐστιν ἔνδοξον, οἷον τουτὶ τὸ Ἀνακρέοντος·

κλῦθί μεο γέροντος, εὐέθειρα χρυσόπεπλε κούρα.

cf. schol. B Heph. (p. 271 Consbr. bis)

419 *Anth. Pal*. 13. 4

Ἀνακρέοντος· τετράμετρον·

ἀλκίμως σ' ὦ 'ριστοκλείδη πρῶτον οἰκτίρω φίλων·
ὤλεσας δ' ἥβην ἀμύνων πατρίδος δουληΐην.

420 Iulian. *Misopogon* 366b (i 473 Hertlein)

ἤδη γάρ, ὡς καὶ ὑμεῖς αὐτοὶ συνορᾶτε, πλησίον ἐσμὲν ἐθελόντων
θεῶν

εὖτέ μοι λευκαὶ μελαίνησ' ἀναμεμείξονται τρίχες,

ὁ Τήιος ἔφη ποιητής.

could neatly put the bridle on you and with the reins in my hand wheel you round the turnpost of the race-course; instead, you graze in the meadows and frisk and frolic lightly, since you have no skilled horseman to ride you.

418 Hephaestion, *Handbook of Metres*

Among the trochaic acatalectic lines the tetrameter is noteworthy, e.g. Anacreon's:

Hear an old man's prayer, you maiden [1] of the lovely hair and golden robe.

[1] Probably a goddess.

419 *Palatine Anthology*

Tetrameters of Anacreon:

Foremost among my brave friends, Aristoclides, I pity you: you lost your youth, keeping slavery from your country.

420 Julian, *The Beard-hater*

For now, as you can see for yourselves, I am near the time,[1] if the gods so will,

when white hairs shall mingle with my black,

as the poet of Teos said.

[1] Julian was 30.

GREEK LYRIC

421 *Epim. Hom.* (*Anecd. Oxon.* i 288 Cramer) = Hdn. π. παθ. fr. 149 (ii 225 Lentz)

καὶ Ἀνακρέων·

αἱ δέ μεο φρένες
ἐκκεκωφέαται.

cf. *Et. Gen.* (p. 25 Calame), *Et. Mag.* 322. 22

422 *Et. Mag.* 714. 38 (s.v. σῖτος)

ἔστι γὰρ καὶ σίω διὰ τοῦ ʼιʼ, ᾧ χρῆται Ἀνακρέων, οἷον·

Θρηκίην σίοντα χαίτην.

cf. Ioh. Charac. π. ὀρθογρ. (Egenolff, *Philol.* 59, 1900, 618ss.)

ὁρικὴν Char.

423 (=S313) Hdn. *de barb. et soloec.* (ap. Ammon. ed. Valckenaer p. 193) + *Anecd. Gr.* ii 177 de Villoison + cod. Mutin. (ed. Bühler, *Mus. Crit.* 4, 1969, 9ss.)

σολοίκους δὲ ἔλεγον οἱ παλαιοὶ τοὺς βαρβάρους· ὁ γὰρ Ἀνακρέων φησί·

(a)   κοίμισον δέ, Ζεῦ, σόλοικον φθόγγον,

(b)   μή πως βάρβαρα βάξῃς

cf. Eust. *Il.* 368. 2

δέ codd. AB Valck.: carent rell.   Ζεῦ codd. Marc. 489, 512: carent rell.

424 Ammon. *Diff.* 120 (p. 31 Nickau)

γῆμαι τοῦ γήμασθαι διαφέρει, ὅτι γαμεῖ μὲν ὁ ἀνήρ, γαμεῖται δὲ ἡ γυνή . . . καὶ Ἀνακρέων (sc. τὴν διαφορὰν τετήρηκεν αὐτῶν) διασύρων τινὰ ἐπὶ θηλύτητι·

ANACREON

421 *Homeric Parsings* (on the form μεμετρέαται, 'have been measured')

Cf. Anacreon:

> and my wits have been numbed.

422 *Etymologicum Magnum*

For σείω, 'shake', also has the form σίω, which Anacreon uses, e.g.

> shaking his (your) Thracian locks [1]

[1] With ref. to Smerdis? Cf. 402, 414, test. 12.

423 Herodian, *On Non-Greek Words and Solecisms*

The ancients called barbarous speakers 'solecians'; Anacreon says:

(a)

> and silence the solecian speech, Zeus,

(b)

> lest you speak the language of barbarians.

424 Ammonius, *On Similar but Different Words*

The active voice γῆμαι, 'to marry', differs from the middle voice γήμασθαι, 'to get married', in that the man 'marries', the woman 'gets married' . . . ; Anacreon observes the distinction when he ridicules someone for his effeminacy:

GREEK LYRIC

καὶ θάλαμος ἐν †ᾧ† κεῖνος οὐκ ἔγημεν ἀλλ'
ἐγήματο.

cf. *Impr.* 3 (v. Ammon. *Diff.* ed. Nickau p. 140), *Anecd. Gr.* ii
375 Bachmann, *Et. Gud.* 310. 19 de Stef., Eust. *Od.* 1678. 59

ἐν ᾧ codd. ἔνθα Hoffmann οὗ West

425 Plut. *de commun. notit.* 20, 1068b (vi. 2. 82 Pohlenz-
Westman)

διψῶντες οὖν ὕδατος οὐκ ἔχουσι χρείαν οὐδ' ἄρτου πεινῶντες·

ξείνοισίν ἐστε μειλίχοισ' ἐοικότες
στέγης τε μοῦνον καὶ πυρὸς κεχρημένοις.

Heph. *Ench.* 5. 2 (p. 16 Consbruch)

ἔστι δὲ ἐπίσημα ἐν αὐτῷ (sc. τῷ ἰαμβικῷ) ἀκατάληκτα μὲν
δίμετρα, οἷον τὰ Ἀνακρεόντεια ὅλα ᾄσματα γέγραπται (fr. 428),
τρίμετρα δέ· ἔστε ξ. μ. ἐοικότες.

ἐ. ξέν- codd., transposuit Barnes (ξείν- Gentili)

426 Zenob. *Cent.* 5. 80 (i 152 Leutsch-Schneidewin)

φασὶ τοὺς Κᾶρας πολεμουμένους ὑπὸ Δαρείου τοῦ Πέρσου κατά
τινα παλαιὰν μαντείαν εἰρημένην αὐτοῖς τοὺς ἀλκιμωτάτους προσ-
θέσθαι συμμάχους ἐλθεῖν εἰς Βραγχίδας καὶ τὸν ἐκεῖ θεὸν ἐρωτῆσαι
εἰ Μιλησίους πρόσθοιντο συμμάχους· τὸν δὲ ἀποκρίνασθαι·

πάλαι ποτ' ἦσαν ἄλκιμοι Μιλήσιοι.

οὗτος δὲ ὁ στίχος εἴρηται τὸ πρότερον παρὰ Ἀνακρέοντι, ὃς ἤκμασε
μάλιστα κατὰ Κῦρον τὸν Πέρσην.

cf. schol. Ar. *Plut.* 1002 (ἰσχυροί ποτ' ἦσαν οἱ Μ., ὡς καὶ
Ἀνακρέων φησί), schol. *Vesp.* 1060ss. (Timocreonti Rhodio
adscribit), Athen. 12. 523f (iii 155s. Kaibel), Hsch. H 878 (ii
297 Latte), Phot. s. vv. ἦσάν ποτ' ἦσαν, Diodor. 10. 25. 2 (ii 213
Vogel), al.

and the chamber in which he did not marry but got married.

425 Plutarch, *On Common Notions: Against the Stoics*

So when they are thirsty they have no need of water, when they are hungry no need of bread:

You are like gentle guests, needing only shelter and fire.

Hephaestion, *Handbook on Metres*

Noteworthy forms of the iambic are dimeters acatalectic, such as those in which whole poems of Anacreon are written,[1] and trimeters: 'You are like gentle guests.'

[1] See 428.

426 Zenobius, *Proverbs*

They say that the Carians,[1] when at war with Darius of Persia, in obedience to an old oracle bidding them take the bravest men as allies, went to Branchidae and asked the god there if they should take the Milesians as allies; and the god replied:

Once long ago the Milesians were brave.

But the line is found before this in Anacreon, who flourished about the time of Cyrus the Persian.

[1] Acc. to the scholiast on Aristophanes it was to Polycrates of Samos that the oracle was given.

427 Athen. 10. 446f–447a (ii 471 Kaibel)

καὶ γένηται ἡ παρ' Ἀνακρέοντι καλουμένη ἐπίστιος. φησὶ γὰρ ὁ μελοποιός·

> μηδ' ὥστε κῦμα πόντιον
> λάλαζε, τῇ πολυκρότῃ
> σὺν Γαστροδώρῃ καταχύδην
> πίνουσα τὴν ἐπίστιον.

τοῦτο δ' ἡμεῖς ἀνίσωμά φαμεν.

428 Heph. *Ench.* 5. 2 (p. 16 Consbruch)

ἐστὶ δὲ ἐπίσημα ἐν αὐτῷ ἀκατάληκτα μὲν δίμετρα οἷον τὰ Ἀνακρεόντεια ὅλα ᾆσματα γέγραπται·

> ἐρέω τε δηὖτε κοὐκ ἐρέω
> καὶ μαίνομαι κοὐ μαίνομαι.

cf. schol. B Heph. (p. 267 Consbr.), Apostol. *Cent.* 7. 88b (ii 419 L–S), schol. Ar. *Plut.* 253 (p. 338 Dübner)

429 Heph. *Ench.* 5. 3 (p. 16 Consbruch)

καταληκτικὸν δὲ δίμετρον (sc. ἰαμβικὸν) τὸ καλούμενον Ἀνακρεόντειον οἷον·

> ὁ μὲν θέλων μάχεσθαι,
> πάρεστι γάρ, μαχέσθω.

cf. lap. inscr. (v. fr. 396), ubi post μαχέσθω haec fortasse: ἐ[μοὶ δὲ δὸς] προ[πίνειν|με]λιχρ[ὸν οἶνον,] ὦ [παῖ] (M. et A. Blanchard), Anacreont. 47. 8s., schol. Ar. *Plut.* (p. 342 Dübner), schol. B Heph. (p. 267 Consbr.), anon. P. Oxy. 220 col. x (Heph. p. 406 Consbr.), Mar. Plot. Sacerd. (vi 520 Keil)

ANACREON

427 Athenaeus, *Scholars at Dinner*

And let us have what Anacreon calls the hearth-cup; for that lyric poet says:

> and do not babble like the wave of the sea, swilling down the hearth-cup with the wily[1] Gastrodora.[2]

We call it the cup of equal shares.

[1] Or 'noisy'.　　[2] Presumably a comic version of a woman's name, e.g. Metrodora.

428 Hephaestion, *Handbook on Metres* [1]

Noteworthy forms of the iambic are dimeters acatalectic, such as those in which whole poems of Anacreon are written, e.g.

> Once again I love and I do not love, I am mad and I am not mad.

[1] Cf. 425.

429 Hephaestion, *Handbook on Metres*

The iambic dimeter catalectic is the so-called anacreontean, e.g.

> He who wants to fight—let him fight, for he may.[1]

[1] The lines are on the Autun mosaic (see 396 n.1): the fragmentary sequel has been conjecturally restored as 'but give me honey-sweet wine to drink a toast, boy.'

GREEK LYRIC

430 Ptol. *De voc. diff.* (Heylbut *Herm.* 22, 1887, 409) = Ammon. *Diff.* 298 (p. 78 Nickau)

λεία· . . . διὰ δὲ τοῦ 'ι' γραφόμενον ἐπίρρημά ἐστιν ἐπιτάσεως δηλωτικόν, ⟨ἐάν τε ἐκτείνηται⟩ ἐάν τε συστέλληται ὡς παρὰ Ἀνακρέοντι·

> λίην δὲ δὴ λιάζεις

431 Zonar. 1512 (s.v. πανδοκεῖον)

τὸν δὲ μοχλὸν ἐν τῷ 'χ' καὶ Ἀττικοὶ καὶ Δωριεῖς καὶ Ἴωνες πλὴν Ἀνακρέοντος. οὗτος δὲ μόνος σχεδὸν τὸ 'κ', Ζηνόδοτος δὲ ⟨μοχλόν⟩.

> κοὖ μοκλὸν ἐν θύρῃσι διξῆσιν βαλών
> ἥσυχος κατεύδει.

cf. Phryn. p. 308 Lobeck, p. 362 Rutherford

1 Bergk: καὶ οὐ, οὔρῃσι δίζῃσι Zonar.

432 *Et. Gen.* (p. 34 Calame) = *Et. Mag.* 523. 4 = Hdn. (i 251, i 446, ii 901 Lentz)

τὸ δὲ κνύζα, ὡς λέγει Ἡρωδιανός, εἰ μὲν ἐπὶ τοῦ φυτοῦ, συγκοπή ἐστιν . . . , εἰ δὲ ἐπὶ τοῦ παρεφθαρμένου καὶ ἐρρυσωμένου, οὐ συγκοπή ἐστιν ἀλλ' ἀπὸ τοῦ κνύω, ἀφ' οὗ κνύος ἡ φθορά . . . · γίνεται κνύζα, ὡς παρ' Ἀνακρέοντι ἐν ἰάμβῳ, οἷον·

> κνυζή τις ἤδη καὶ πέπειρα γίνομαι
> σὴν διὰ μαργοσύνην.

cf. Eust. *Od.* 1746. 13, *Et. Gud.* 330. 59

κνυζῇ, κνύζει, κνύζα, κνίζη codd.   γίνομαι *Et. Gen.*, Eust., γενομένη *Et. Mag.*

ANACREON

430 Ptolemaeus, *Differences in Words*

λεία, 'plunder': . . . when it is written with ι for ει it is an adverb denoting intensity, whether the ι is long or short as in Anacreon:

> but you go too far.

431 Zonaras, *Lexicon* (on the spelling of πανδοκεῖον)

The form μοχλός, 'bolt', with a χ is found in Attic, Doric and Ionic except for Anacreon, who is almost alone in writing it with a κ, though Zenodotus (would read μοχλός):

> and though he does not draw a bolt on his double door he sleeps peacefully.

432 *Etymologicum Genuinum*

As Herodian says, κνύζα, if it means the plant 'fleabane', is an abbreviation (of κόνυζα), but if it means 'spoiled', 'wrinkled', it is not an abbreviation but comes from κνύω, 'scratch', from which comes κνύος, 'itch' . . . ; it becomes κνύζα, as in an iambus (i.e. a satirical poem) of Anacreon:

> Already I[1] am becoming a wrinkled[2] old thing, over-ripe fruit, thanks to your lust.[3]

[1] The speaker is feminine.   [2] Or 'itchy': meaning uncertain.   [3] See C. Brown, *C.Q.* 34 (1984) 37 ff.

433 Athen. 11. 498a–c (iii 98 Kaibel)

'Ησίοδος δ' ἐν τῷ δευτέρῳ Μελαμποδίας σὺν τῷ 'π' σκύπφον λέγει (frr. 271, 272 M.-W.)· . . . ὁμοίως εἴρηκε καὶ 'Ανακρέων·

> ἐγὼ δ' ἔχων σκύπφον 'Ερξίωνι
> τῷ λευκολόφῳ μεστὸν ἐξέπινον.

ἀντὶ τοῦ προέπινον.

cf. Eust. *Il*. 900. 16

434 Athen. 15. 671de (iii 484 Kaibel)

ἐπεὶ περὶ στεφάνων ζητήσεις ἤδη γεγόνασιν, εἰπὲ ἡμῖν τίς ἐστιν ὁ παρὰ τῷ χαρίεντι 'Ανακρέοντι Ναυκρατίτης στέφανος, ὦ Οὐλπιανέ· φησὶν γὰρ οὕτως ὁ μελιχρὸς ποιητής·

> στεφάνους δ' ἀνὴρ τρεῖς ἕκαστος εἶχεν,
> τοὺς μὲν ῥοδίνους, τὸν δὲ Ναυκρατίτην.

cf. Poll. 6. 107 (ii 31 Bethe) Ναυκρατίτῃ στεφάνῳ (σάμψυχος οὗτος ἦν), Hsch. N 123 (ii 698 Latte) (ὁ βύβλινος ἢ ὁ ἐκ φιλύρας ἢ ὁ σαμψύχινος)

435 Athen. 1. 12a (i 26 Kaibel)

παρ' ὅλην δὲ τὴν συνουσίαν παρέκειντο αἱ τράπεζαι πλήρεις, ὡς παρὰ πολλοῖς τῶν βαρβάρων ἔτι καὶ νῦν ἔθος ἐστί,

> κατηρεφέες παντοίων ἀγαθῶν

κατὰ 'Ανακρέοντα.

436 Athen. 6. 229b (ii 15 Kaibel)

χωρὶς δὲ τοῦ 'τ' στοιχείου Ἴωνες ἤγανον λέγουσιν, ὡς 'Ανακρέων·

> χειρά τ' ἐν ἠγάνῳ βαλεῖν.

cf. Eust. *Od*. 1862. 12, *Il*. 244. 46, 701. 18

ANACREON

433 Athenaeus, *Scholars at Dinner*

Hesiod in Book 2 of the *Melampodia* uses σκύπφος, 'cup', with a π . . . ; Anacreon has it too:

and I held a full cup and drained it to white-crested Erxion,

using ἐξέπινον, 'drained it', instead of προέπινον, 'drank it to the health of'.

434 Athenaeus, *Scholars at Dinner* [1]

Since questions about garlands have come up, tell us, Ulpian, what 'the garland of Naucratis' [2] is in the charming Anacreon; for that sweet poet says:

and each man had three garlands, two of roses and the other a garland of Naucratis.

[1] See 352.   [2] Variously explained as a garland of marjoram, papyrus, lime or (Athen. 675f ff.) myrtle.

435 Athenaeus, *Scholars at Dinner*

The tables remained full for the entire feast,[1] as is still the custom today among many foreign races,

covered with all manner of good things,

as Anacreon puts it.

[1] In *Od.* 1. 138 ff.

436 Athenaeus, *Scholars at Dinner*

The Ionians say ἤγανον, 'frying-pan', without the initial τ, as in Anacreon:

to put (his) hand in the frying-pan.

437 *Et. Gen.* (p. 34 Calame)=*Et. Gud.* 333. 22=*Et. Mag.*
524. 50=*Et. Sym.*=*Et. Vat. gr.* 1708

κόκκυξ· ὄρνεον ἐαρινὸν παραπλήσιον ἱέρακι· ἢ ὄρνεον δειλότατον,
ὡς Ἀνακρέων φησίν·

$$\text{ἐγὼ δ' ἀπ' αὐτῆς † φεύγω † ὥστε κόκκυξ.}$$

φάγω *Et. Sym.* ἔφυγον? Page

438 *Et. Gen.* (p. 29 Calame)=*Et. Mag.* 433. 44

ἠπεροπευτής· . . . ἢ παρὰ τὸ ἔπω, τὸ λέγω, γίνεται ὀπεύς . . .
καὶ . . . μετὰ τοῦ 'α' τοῦ σημαίνοντος τὸ κακὸν καὶ τοῦ 'περ'
περιττοῦ συνδέσμου, ἀπεροπεύς, ὁ τῷ λόγῳ κακῶς χρώμενος καὶ
ἀπατῶν, οἷον (*Od.* 11. 364)· καὶ ἀπεροπός, ὡς παρ' Ἀνακρέοντι,
οἷον·

$$\text{βούλεται † ἀπεροπὸς † ἡμὶν εἶναι,}$$

καὶ θηλυκῶς ἀπεροπή.

ἀπεροπεύς τις ἡμὶν? Page

439 Hsch. Γ 1013 (i 395 Latte)

γυναῖκες εἰλίποδες· διὰ τὴν δέσιν τῶν σκελῶν καὶ πλοκὴν τὴν
κατὰ τὴν συνουσίαν. καὶ Ἀνακρέων·

$$\text{πλέξαντες μηροῖσι † πέρι μηρούς}$$

cf. *Sud.* M 1470 (iii 429 Adler) Εὔπολις εἰλίποδας (sc. τὰς πόρνας
φησίν), Eust. *Od.* 1394. 40, 1921. 66

πλέξαντες . . . | μηροῖσιν Hoffmann

440 Prisc. *De metr. Ter.* (iii 427 Keil)

Anacreon teste Heliodoro

$$\text{† ὁρᾶν ἀεὶ † λίην πολλοῖσι γὰρ μέλεις.}$$

hic iambus quartum spondeum habet.

ANACREON

437 *Etymologicum Gudianum*

Cuckoo: a spring bird the size of a falcon; a very cowardly bird, as Anacreon says:

> and I (fled?) from her like a cuckoo.

438 *Etymologicum Genuinum* (on the derivation of ἠπεροπευτής, 'deceiver')

. . . or ὀπεύς comes from ἔπω, 'I say' . . . and with the prefix ἀ- denoting evil and the redundant link περ we have ἀπεροπεύς, one who makes evil use of language and cheats, as in *Od.* 11. 364, and ἀπεροπός as in Anacreon, e.g.

> he wants to deceive us [1];

the feminine form is ἀπεροπή.

[1] Presumably the speaker is a woman.

439 Hesychius, *Lexicon*

'leg-rolling women' [1]: because they wind their legs together or intertwine them during intercourse; cf. Anacreon:

> twining thighs around thighs.

[1] Attributed to the comic poet Eupolis. Homer uses the adjective of oxen 'with rolling gait'.

440 Priscian, *On the Metres of Terence*

According to Heliodorus Anacreon has:

> . . . too much [1]; for many men are in love with you.

This iambic line has a spondee in the fourth foot.

[1] Text corrupt.

441 Schol. T Hom. *Il.* 17. 542 (iv 405 Erbse) = *Anecd. Par.* iii 287 Cramer

κατὰ ταῦρον ἐδηδώς· ἡ διακοπὴ τῆς λέξεως τὸν εἰς πολλὰ διεσπασμένον παρέστησε ταῦρον, οὐ τοῦ μέτρου ἀπαιτοῦντος. παρῆν γὰρ φάναι ταῦρον κατεδηδώς. καὶ Ἀνακρέων·

(a)   διὰ δὲ δειρὴν ἔκοψε μέσην

(b)   κὰδ δὲ λῶπος ἐσχίσθη

cf. Eust. *Il.* 1001. 39

442 Schol. T Hom. *Il.* 19. 21s. (iv 576 Erbse)

οἷ᾽ ἐπιεικὲς ἔργα· ἐν ἑαυτῷ τὸ πρᾶγμα τὴν ὑπερβολὴν ἔχον ὑπεροχὴν οὐκ ἐπιδέχεται μείζονα. καὶ Ἀνακρέων·

κωμάζει † δὲ ὡς ἂν δεῖ † Διόνυσος,

αὐτὸν αὑτῷ συγκρίνας.

δεῖ: δὴ ci. Schneidewin

443 Schol. Soph. *Ant.* 134 (p. 224 Papageorgiu)

ὅτι δὲ τανταλωθεὶς σημαίνει τὸ διασεισθεὶς μαρτυρεῖ καὶ Ἀνακρέων·

† μελαμφύλλῳ δάφνᾳ χλωρᾷ τ᾽ ἐλαίᾳ τανταλίζει †

⟨ἐν⟩ μελ. Bergk

444 Plut. *Amator.* 4 (iv 341 Hubert)

οὕτως εἷς Ἔρως ⟦ὁ⟧ γνήσιος ὁ παιδικός ἐστιν, οὐ

πόθῳ στίλβων,

ὡς ἔφη τὸν παρθένιον Ἀνακρέων, οὐδὲ μύρων ἀνάπλεως καὶ

γεγανωμένος.

ἀλλὰ λιτὸν αὐτὸν ὄψει . . .

ANACREON

441 Scholiast on *Iliad* ('having devoured a bull')

The tmesis (i.e. the separation of the prefix κατά from the verb ἐδηδώς) represented the rending of the bull into many pieces; it was not demanded by the metre, for he could have said ταῦρον κατεδηδώς; cf. Anacreon:

(a)

> and (he) cut through the middle of the neck,

(b)

> and the robe was torn right down.

442 Scholiast on *Iliad* ('armour such as the handiwork of gods should be')

The subject already involves hyperbole and does not allow greater exaggeration; cf. Anacreon:

> and he revels like Dionysus,

where the poet compares Dionysus with himself.

443 Scholiast on Sophocles, *Antigone*

τανταλωθείς, 'swung', means 'violently shaken', as Anacreon testifies:

> shakes . . . (among?) [1] the dark-leaved laurel and green olive.

[1] Text uncertain. See P. Oxy. 3695 fr. 3.

444 Plutarch, *Dialogue on Love*

There is, then, one genuine Love, the love of boys: he is not

> glistening with desire,

as Anacreon says of the love of girls, nor drenched with perfumes and

> gleaming;

when you see him, he will be unadorned . . .

GREEK LYRIC

445 Himer. *Or.* 48. 4 (p. 197s. Colonna)

νῦν ἔδει μοι Τηίων μελῶν, νῦν ἔδει μοι τῆς Ἀνακρέοντος λύρας,
ἥν, ὅταν ὑπὸ παιδικῶν ἐκεῖνος ὑπεροφθῇ ποτε, καὶ κατ' αὐτῶν
Ἐρώτων οἶδεν ἐργάσασθαι· εἶπον ἂν πρὸς αὐτοὺς τὰ ἐκείνου
ῥήματα·

> ὑβρισταὶ καὶ ἀτάσθαλοι καὶ οὐκ εἰδότες
> ἐφ' οὓς τὰ βέλη κυκλώσεσθε.

τάχα δ' ἂν καὶ ἠπείλησα τὴν ἀπειλὴν ἣν Ἀνακρέων ἀπειλεῖ τοῖς
Ἔρωσιν· ἐκεῖνος γάρ ποτε ἐρασθεὶς ἐφήβου καλοῦ, ἐπειδήπερ ἑώρα
τὸν ἔφηβον ὀλίγον αὐτοῦ φροντίζοντα, λύραν ἁρμόσας ἠπείλει τοῖς
Ἔρωσιν, εἰ μὴ αὐτῷ τιτρώσκοιεν αὐτίκα τὸν ἔφηβον, μηκέτι μέλος
εὔφημον εἰς αὐτοὺς ἀνακρούσασθαι.

446 *Sud.* M 1470 (iii 429 Alder)

μυσάχνη· ἡ πόρνη παρὰ Ἀρχιλόχῳ (fr. 209 West) ...
Ἀνακρέων δὲ

> πανδοσίαν

καὶ

> λεωφόρον

(v. 346. 1. 13) καὶ

> μανιόκηπον.

Eust. *Il.* 1329. 95 καὶ μὴν ὁ Ἀνακρέων τὴν τοιαύτην οὐ πάνυ
σφοδρῶς ἀλλὰ περιεσκεμμένως πανδοσίαν ὠνείδισε καὶ λεωφόρον
καὶ

> πολύυμνον,

al. (e Suet. π. βλασφ. pp. 51, 94 Taillardat)

112

ANACREON

445 Himerius, *Orations*

Now I should have had songs of Teos and the lyre of Anacreon which he, whenever scorned by a beloved boy, knows how to use against the Loves themselves. I would have addressed them in his words:

You are violent and wicked, and you do not know against whom you will hurl your weapons.

Perhaps too I would have uttered the threat made against the Loves by Anacreon: he once loved a handsome youth, and when he saw that the youth paid little attention to him he tuned his lyre and threatened that if the Loves did not at once wound the youth, he would never again strike up a song in their praise.[1]

[1] Cf. 378.

446 *Suda*

μυσάχνη, 'dirty': used of a whore by Archilochus ... Anacreon has

generous giver,

and

public highway

(cf. 346) and

sex-mad.

Eustathius on *Iliad*

Moreover Anacreon with more caution than violence reproached this sort of woman as 'generous giver', 'public highway', and

much-sung.

GREEK LYRIC

447 *Et. Gen.* (p. 42 Calame) = *Et. Mag.* 703. 27 = *Et. Vat. gr.*
1708 = *Et. Gud.* 492. 18 = Zonar. 1608 = Hdn. (ii 577 Lentz)

ὅτι δὲ ῥαγεὶς ἔλεγον τοὺς βαφεῖς καὶ ῥέγος τὸ βάμμα σαφὲς
᾽Ανακρέων ποιεῖ·

ἁλιπόρφυρον ῥέγος·

καὶ παρὰ ᾽Ιβύκῳ (fr. 316).

448 Hsch. A 7926 (i 268 Latte)

ἄστυ Νυμφέων

τὴν Σάμον ᾽Ανακρέων, ἐπεὶ ὕστερον εὔυδρος ἐγένετο.

cf. Athen. 15. 672b

449 Pl. *Theages* 125de

ΣΩ. ταῦτ᾽ ἐστὶν ἅπερ ἔφη ᾽Ανακρέων τὴν Καλλικρίτην ἐπίστασ-
θαι· ἢ οὐκ οἶσθα τὸ ᾆσμα;

ΘΕ. ἔγωγε.

ΣΩ. τί οὖν; τοιαύτης τινὸς καὶ σὺ συνουσίας ἐπιθυμεῖς ἀνδρὸς
ὅστις τυγχάνει ὁμότεχνος ὢν Καλλικρίτῃ τῇ Κυάνης καὶ

ἐπίσταται τυραννικά,

ὥσπερ ἐκείνην ἔφη ὁ ποιητής, ἵνα καὶ σὺ ἡμῖν τύραννος γένῃ καὶ τῇ
πόλει;

450 Serv. in Verg. *Aen.* 1. 749 (i 209 Thilo-Hagen)
bibebat amorem adlusit ad convivium. sic Anacreon:

ἔρωτα πίνων

114

ANACREON

447 *Etymologicum Genuinum*

They called dyers ῥαγεῖς and dye ῥέγος; Anacreon makes this clear:

> sea-purple dye;

so in Ibycus 316.

448 Hesychius, *Lexicon*

> city of the Nymphs:

Anacreon's description of Samos: it later [1] got a fine water-supply.

[1] The famous aqueduct may have been complete when A. was at Samos: see Barron, *C. Q.* 14, 1964, 214 with n.3. Athenaeus says the Samian temple of Hera was founded by the Leleges and Nymphs.

449 Plato, *Theages*

Socrates. This is what Anacreon said Callicrite understood; or do you not know the poem?

Theages. I know it.

Socrates. Well, do you want to keep that sort of company? To associate with a man who is a fellow-craftsman of Callicrite, daughter of Cyane, and

> understands tyranny,

as the poet said she did, so that you may become tyrant over us and the city?

450 Servius on Virgil, *Aeneid* ('she drank love')

An allusion to the drinking-party; so in Anacreon:

> drinking love [1]

[1] Cf. *Anacreont.* 6. 5.

451 Prisc. *Inst. Gramm.* vii 7 (ii 289 Keil) (de vocat. cas. primae declin.)

. . . cum graecorum quoque poetae similiter inveniantur protulisse vocativos in supra dicta terminatione. Ἀνακρέων·

ἤλιε καλλιλαμπέτη

posuit pro καλλιλαμπέτα.

cf. *Et. Mag.* 670. 19, *Anecd. Oxon.* iii 389, 390 Cramer, Choerob. in Theod. (i 164 Hilgard)

452 *Et. Gen.* (p. 34s. Calame) = *Et. Gud.* 339. 22 = *Et. Mag.* 530. 17

κορώνη· . . . παρὰ τὸ καῦρον, ὅπερ σημαίνει τὸ κακόν. Ἀνακρέων

κόρωνα βαίνων

φησί.

453 Procl. in Hes. *Op.* 371 (iii 197 Gaisford *Poet. min. Gr.*, 124s. Pertusi)

κωτίλλουσα δὲ σημαίνει ἡδέα λέγουσα. καὶ γὰρ τὴν χελιδόνα κωτίλλειν λέγουσιν, ὡς ἔστι παρὰ Ἀνακρέοντι·

κωτίλη χελιδών

cf. Tzetz. ad loc. (p. 236 Gaisford)

454 Poll. 6. 23 (ii 6 Bethe)

οἰνηρὸς θεράπων

παρὰ Ἀνακρέοντι.

455 Poll. 6. 22 (ii 6 Bethe)

καὶ οἰνοπότης, καὶ

οἰνοπότις γυνή,

ὡς Ἀνακρέων εἶπεν.

ANACREON

451 Priscian, *Grammar* (on the vocative case)

. . . since Greek poets are found to lengthen vocatives in the same way with the above-mentioned termination; cf. Anacreon:

Fair-shining sun;

he uses καλλιλαμπέτη instead of καλλιλαμπέτα.

452 *Etymologicum Genuinum*

κορώνη, 'crow': . . . from καῦρος, 'bad'. Anacreon says:

stepping with arched neck.[1]

[1] I.e. haughtily?

453 Proclus on Hesiod, *Works and Days*

κωτίλλουσα, 'chattering', means 'talking sweetly'; they say the swallow also 'chatters', as in Anacreon:

the chattering swallow.

454 Pollux, *Vocabulary*

wine-waiter

in Anacreon.

455 Pollux, *Vocabulary*

'Wine-drinker', and in the feminine

wine-drinking woman,

as in Anacreon.

456 Schol. Ap. Rhod. 3. 106 (p. 220 Wendel)

'Ανακρέων δὲ ἐπὶ τάχους ἔταξε τὸ ῥαδινόν·

ῥαδινοὺς πώλους

457 Choerob. in Theodos. (ii 80 Hilgard) = *Anecd. Oxon.* iv
185, 415 Cramer = *Anecd. Gr.* iii 1287 Bekker

σημειούμεθα παρὰ τῷ ποιητῇ τό· τά μοι ῥερυπωμένα κεῖται (*Od.*
6. 59) . . . καὶ τὸ

ῥεραπισμένῳ νώτῳ

παρὰ τῷ 'Ανακρέοντι, ὅτι ταῦτα διὰ τοῦ 'ρ' ἀνεδιπλασιάσθησαν.

cf. *Anecd. Par.* iv 226 Cramer, Hdn. ii 789 Lentz, schol.
Hom. *Od.* 6. 59 (i 299 Dindorf)

fort. -μένῳ | νώτῳ Page vel ῥ. ⟨δὲ⟩: v. Gentili

458 Clem. Alex. *Paid.* 3. 11. 69 (i 274 Stählin)

αἱ δὲ γυναικεῖοι κινήσεις καὶ θρύψεις καὶ χλιδαὶ κολουστέαι
παντελῶς· τὸ γὰρ ἁβροδίαιτον τῆς περὶ τὸν περίπατον κινήσεως καὶ
τὸ

σαῦλα βαίνειν,

ὥς φησιν 'Ανακρέων, κομιδῇ ἑταιρικά.

459 Schol. Ap. Rhod. 3. 120 (p. 221 Wendel)

μάργος "Ερως· κατὰ μετωνυμίαν, ὁ μαργαίνειν ποιῶν, ὡς . . . καὶ
'Ανακρέων·

τακερὸς δ' "Ερως·

118

ANACREON

456 Scholiast on Apollonius of Rhodes

Anacreon used ῥαδινός, 'slender', to denote speed [1]:

slender colts.

[1] An improbable statement.

457 Choeroboscus, *On the Canons of Theodosius*

We note in Homer the expression (*Od.* 6. 59) . . . and in Anacreon

flogged back,

since in these forms the reduplication has the letter ρ (i.e. ῥερ- instead of ἐρρ-).

458 Clement of Alexandria, *The Schoolmaster*

Womanish movements and pampered and luxurious habits are to be cut out completely; for effeminacy of movement in walking and

going along with hips swaying,

as Anacreon [1] puts it, are thoroughly meretricious.

[1] Cf. Semon. 18.

459 Scholiast on Apollonius of Rhodes

'mad Love': by metonymy, Love who makes men mad; . . . so in Anacreon:

and melting Love.

460 Serv. in Verg. *Aen.* 11. 550 (ii 544 Thilo-Hagen)

caroque oneri timet: Anacreon

$$\phi\acute{o}\rho\tau o\nu\ \text{"}E\rho\omega\tau o\varsigma,$$

id est onus amoris.

461 Orion (3. 11 Sturz)

$$\dot{a}\beta\rho\acute{o}\varsigma\cdot$$

ὁ κούφως βαίνων, κατὰ στέρησιν τοῦ βάρους. οὕτως ἐν ὑπομνή-
ματι Ἀνακρέοντος εὗρον.

462 Poll. 7. 172 (ii 99 Bethe)

$$\chi\acute{\eta}\lambda\iota\nu o\nu$$

δὲ

$$\ddot{a}\gamma\gamma o\varsigma\ \ddot{\epsilon}\chi o\nu\ \pi\upsilon\theta\mu\acute{\epsilon}\nu a\varsigma\ \dagger\ \dot{a}\gamma\gamma\epsilon o\sigma\epsilon\lambda\acute{\iota}\nu\omega\nu\ \dagger$$

ὅταν εἴπῃ Ἀνακρέων, τὸ ἐκ σχοινίων πλέγμα δηλοῖ.
cf. Hsch. K 2417 (ii 468 Latte)

463 Str. 14. 1. 3 (iii 93 Kramer)

Τέω δὲ Ἀθάμας μὲν πρότερον (sc. κτίζει), διόπερ

$$\text{Ἀθαμαντίδα}$$

καλεῖ αὐτὴν Ἀνακρέων.
cf. Steph. Byz. s.v. Τέως (i 619 Meineke)=Hdn. (i 104 Lentz)

464 Hsch. A 1866 (i 67 Latte)

$$A\dot{\iota}\theta o\pi\acute{\iota}\eta\varsigma\ \pi a\hat{\iota}\delta a\cdot$$

τὸν Διόνυσον. Ἀνακρέων. ἄλλοι τὸν οἶνον, ἄλλοι τὴν Ἄρτεμιν.
Bergk: Αιθιοπεις cod.

ANACREON

460 Servius on Virgil, *Aeneid*

'and fears for his dear burden': cf. Anacreon:

> Love's burden.

461 Orion, *Lexicon*

> graceful,

treading lightly, weightlessly.[1] So I have found it in a commentary on Anacreon.

[1] A fanciful derivation from ἀ- and βάρος is being offered.

462 Pollux, *Vocabulary*

When Anacreon says

> a plaited basket containing celery-stalks,

he means one of plaited reeds.

463 Strabo, *Geography*

Teos was founded first by Athamas, and that is why Anacreon calls it

> Athamantis

(daughter of Athamas).

464 Hesychius, *Lexicon*

> child of Aethopia:

i.e. Dionysus, according to Anacreon. Others use the expression for wine,[1] others for Artemis.[2]

[1] Cf. Homer's αἴθοπα οἶνον, 'sparkling wine'.   [2] See 'Sa.' 157D.

465 *Et. Gen.* (p. 34 Calame) = *Et. Mag.* 514. 27

κινάκης· ἀκινάκης παρὰ Σοφοκλεῖ (fr. 1061 Pearson). τὸ μὲν
ἀνακρεόντειον ἐὰν χωρὶς τοῦ ‘ι’ γράφεται, γέγονεν ἔκθλιψις τοῦ ‘ι’
καὶ κρᾶσις τοῦ ‘ω’ καὶ ‘α’·

τὠκινάκῃ,

ὥσπερ ὦ "Απολλον ὤπολλον· ἐὰν δὲ ἔχῃ τὸ ‘ι’, δηλονότι ἀφαιρέσει
τοῦ ‘α’, οἷον ἀστεροπή στεροπή . . .

τῶ κινάκης *Et. Gen.*

466 Phot. *Lex.* (p. 69 Reitzenstein) = *Anecd. Gr.* i 373 Bekker

ἀκταινῶσαι·

ἀντὶ τοῦ ὑψῶσαι καὶ ἐξᾶραι καὶ μετεωρίσαι. πεποίηται δὲ οὕτως·
ἐστὶ δένδρον ὃ καλεῖται ἀκτή, ἀφ’ οὗ τὰ ἀκόντια τέμνεται. οὕτως
'Ανακρέων.

467 Hsch. A. 3659 (i 128 Latte)

ἀμιθά⟨ς⟩·

ἔδεσμα ποιόν, καὶ ἄρτυμα, ὡς 'Ανακρέων.

cf. A 3690 ἀμαμιθάδες

468 Eust. *Od.* 1538. 50 (e Suet. π. βλασφ. pp. 56, 100 Taillardat)

ἀνήλατος,

φασί, παρὰ 'Ανακρέοντι ὁ ἀπειθής· ἀπὸ ὑποζυγίων.

122

ANACREON

465 *Etymologicum Genuinum*

κινάκης is used by Sophocles for ἀκινάκης, 'scimitar'. The form in Anacreon is written without the ι (i.e. without the iota subscript): the ι has been elided and the letters ωα have undergone crasis to give τὠκινάκῃ (for τῷ ἀκινάκῃ),

> with his scimitar,

as ὦ Ἄπολλον becomes ὤπολλον. If it is written with the ι (i.e. τῷ κινάκῃ), then clearly the initial α has been dropped, as in ἀστεροπή, στεροπή etc.

466 Photius, *Lexicon*

ἀκταινῶσαι

> to raise,

'to lift, to elevate'. The word is derived [1] from ἀκτῆ, 'elder', a tree from which javelins (ἀκόντια) are cut; so Anacreon.

[1] Very doubtfully.

467 Hesychius, *Lexicon*

ἀμιθάς:

> mince-meat,

a type of food or condiment, as in Anacreon.

468 Eustathius on *Odyssey*

> undrivable,

they say, means 'disobedient' in Anacreon, a usage derived from mule-driving.

GREEK LYRIC

469 *Et. Sorb.* (ap. *Et. Mag.* 159. 50 adn. Gaisford)

ἀστράβη·

. . . εἰς ᾽Ανακρέοντα εἴρηται καὶ ἀστραφὴ καὶ ἐπὶ ὀχήματος ἐφ᾽ οὗ
ἀσφαλῶς κάθηνται.

470 Hsch. A 8360 (i 282 Latte)

αὐτάγητοι·

ἀγάμεναι ἑαυτὰς καὶ θαυμαστικῶς ἔχουσαι ἑαυτῶν. ῎Ιων ᾽Αλκμήνῃ
(fr. 8 Nauck²). ἔνιοι δὲ αὐθάδεις. καὶ ᾽Ανακρέων οὕτω κέχρηται.

471 Max. Tyr. 37. 5 (p. 432 Hobein)

οὕτω καὶ ᾽Ανακρέων Σαμίοις Πολυκράτην ἡμέρωσεν κεράσας τῇ
τυραννίδι ἔρωτα, Σμερδίου καὶ Κλεοβούλου κόμην καὶ αὐλοὺς
Βαθύλλου καὶ ᾠδὴν ᾽Ιωνικήν.

Hor. *Epod.* 14. 9ss.

> non aliter Samio dicunt arsisse Bathyllo
>   Anacreonta Teium
> qui persaepe cava testudine flevit amorem
>   non elaboratum ad pedem.

Et. Gen. s.v. ᾽Αρίστυλλος (p. 16 Calame) = Hdn. (ii 205 Lentz)
= *Et. Mag.* 142. 56

καὶ παρὰ τὸ Βαθυκλῆς Βάθυλλος, ὁ ἐρώμενος ᾽Ανακρέοντος.

cf. *Et. Gen.* s.v. Βάθυλλος (p. 19 Calame) ὄνομα κύριον . . .
γέγονε δὲ ὑποκοριστικῶς)

124

ANACREON

469 *Etymologicum Sorbonicum*

ἀστράβη,

saddle:

Anacreon used the form ἀστραφή to mean a carriage on which one sits securely.[1]

[1] Text and interpretation uncertain: see Gentili ad loc. (fr. 146).

470 Hesychius, *Lexicon*

αὐτάγητοι: 'self-admiring women, marvelling at themselves': so Ion in his *Alcmena* (fr. 8); but in some writers it means

stubborn:

Anacreon uses it in this sense.

471 Maximus of Tyre, *Orations*

In this way also Anacreon softened the tyranny of Polycrates over the Samians by mingling it with love—the hair of Smerdies and Cleobulus, the pipes of Bathyllus [1] and Ionian song.

Horace, *Epodes*

Not otherwise, they say, did Anacreon of Teos burn for Samian Bathyllus: often with hollow lyre he sang his sad song of love in no elaborate metre.

Etymologicum Genuinum

From the form Bathycles comes Bathyllus, the name [2] of Anacreon's beloved boy.

[1] Other references to Bathyllus at test. 11 n.5.   [2] A lover's pet-name (*Et. Gen.* s.v.).

472 Athen. 4. 182f (i 398 Kaibel)

τὸν γὰρ βάρωμον καὶ βάρβιτον, ὧν Σαπφὼ (fr. 176) καὶ ᾿Ανακρέων μνημονεύουσι, καὶ τὴν μάγαδιν καὶ τὰ τρίγωνα καὶ τὰς σαμβύκας ἀρχαῖα εἶναι.

4. 175de (i 394 Kaibel)

Νεάνθης ὁ Κυζικηνὸς ἐν α´῾Ωρων εὕρημα λέγει . . . ᾿Ανακρέοντος τὸ βάρβιτον.

473 Eust. Il. 932. 1 (e Suet. π. βλασφ.: v. G. Brugnoli, *Atti Accad. Linc.* 1954, p. 18)

καὶ ὅτι τοὺς οὕτως ἴζοντας ἐπ᾿ ἀμφοτέρους πόδας καὶ

γονυκρότους

τηνικαῦτα δριμέως ἐστὶ προσειπεῖν, καθὰ καὶ οἱ παλαιοὶ δηλοῦσιν, ἐν οἷς φασὶν ὅτι γονύκροτοι οἱ βλαισοί. ᾿Ανακρέων δὲ κέχρηται καὶ ἐπὶ δειλῶν.

474 Poll. 3. 50 (i 170 Bethe)

᾿Ανακρέων δὲ

δίτοκον

τὴν δὶς τεκοῦσαν.

475 *Et. Gen.* (p. 27 Calame) = *Et. Mag.* 385. 9s. = Hdn. (ii 169 Lentz)

ἐσυνῆκεν· ᾿Αλκαῖος (fr. 408)· καὶ ᾿Ανακρέων·

ἐξυνῆκεν,

πλεονασμῷ· οὐκ ἔστι δὲ πλεονασμὸς ἀλλ᾿ ᾿Αττικὴ κλίσις.

Et. Gen. cod. A ἐξυνῆκες

126

ANACREON

472 Athenaeus, *Scholars at Dinner*

For, says Euphorion, the barōmus and the barbitus, which Sappho and Anacreon mention, as well as the magadis, the trigōnon and the sambūca, are all ancient instruments.[1]

Athenaeus, *Scholars at Dinner*

Neanthes of Cyzicus in Book 1 of his *Annals* says that the barbiton was the invention of Anacreon.

[1] See Sa. 176.

473 Eustathius on *Iliad* 13. 281 ('sits on both feet')

Note also that people who sit like this on both feet can be called sarcastically

knock-kneed,

as the ancient writers prove when they call crooked-legged people knock-kneed; but Anacreon uses the term of cowards as well.

474 Pollux, *Vocabulary*

Anacreon uses

twice-bearing

of a woman who has given birth twice.

475 *Etymologicum Genuinum*

Alcaeus has ἐσύνηκεν (fr. 408) and Anacreon ἐξυνῆκεν,

he understood,

with the pleonastic augment; but it is the Attic form, not an example of pleonasm.

GREEK LYRIC

476 Poll. 3. 98 (i 186 Bethe)

μετοχαὶ δὲ τέρπων, ἀλλὰ καὶ ἔτερψεν· τὸ γὰρ ἦδων Ἰωνικόν, καὶ τὸ

$$ἦσε$$

σπάνιον μὲν παρ' ἡμῖν, Ἀνακρέων δ' αὐτὸ εἴρηκεν, Ἴων καὶ ποιητὴς ἀνήρ.

477 Schol. Ar. *Ach.* 1133a (p. 141 Wilson)

διὰ τὸ θερμαίνειν οὖν τὸ στῆθος

$$θωρήσσειν$$

λέγουσι τὸ μεθύειν καὶ ⟨ἀκρο⟩θώρακας τοὺς ἀκρομεθύσους ἐκάλουν. κέχρηται δὲ τῇ λέξει καὶ Ἀνακρέων. ἐστὶ δὲ Ἀττική.

cf. *Sud.* Θ 441 (ii 724 Adler), Zonar. 1068s.

478 Schol. AT Hom. *Il.* 18. 26 (iv 441 Erbse)

μεγαλωστί· Ἀνακρέων·

$$ἰρωστί,$$

Φερεκράτης (fr. 239) ταχεωστί.

cf. Ap. Dysc. *Adv.* 572 (i 162 Schneider) = *Anecd. Gr.* ii 572 Bekker

ἠρωιστί schol. AT ἰερωστί Ap. Dysc.

479 Poll. 5. 96 (i 288 Bethe)

$$κάλυκας$$

παρ' Ὁμήρου (*Il.* 18. 401) τε καὶ Ἀνακρέοντος.

480 Poll. 2. 103 (i 116 Bethe)

Ἀνακρέων δὲ καὶ

$$καταπτύστην$$

εἴρηκεν.

128

ANACREON

476 Pollux, *Vocabulary*

Participles [1] are τέρπων, 'pleasing'; note also ἔτερψεν, 'pleased': the form ἥδων, 'pleasing', is Ionic, and the aorist ἧσε,

> pleased,

is rare with us, though Anacreon, an Ionian and a poet, uses it.

[1] Meaning 'pleasing': other examples follow.

477 Scholiast on Aristophanes, *Acharnians*

So since being drunk heats the breast they call it

> putting on the corslet;

and they used to call the slightly drunk 'top-corsleted'. Anacreon uses the expression, and it is Attic.

478 Scholiast on *Iliad* (on the adverb μεγαλωστί, 'greatly')

cf. Anacreon,

> sacredly,

and Pherecrates, 'swiftly'.

479 Pollux, *Vocabulary* (on ornaments for the female head)

> flower-buds

in Homer and Anacreon.

480 Pollux, *Vocabulary*

Anacreon also uses the separate feminine form of κατάπτυστος,

> abominable (woman).

481 Schol. M Aes. *Pers.* 42 (p. 22 Dähnhardt)

ἁβροδιαίτων . . . Λυδῶν· . . . ἁβροδίαιτοι δὲ οὗτοι, ὅθεν καὶ τὸ παρ' Ἀνακρέοντι

λυδοπαθεῖς τινες

ἀντὶ τοῦ ἡδυπαθεῖς.

cf. Athen. 15. 690bc (iii 526 Kaibel), Eust. *Il.* 1144. 14

482 Schol. Ap. Rhod. 2. 123–129e (p. 135 Wendel)

πόλλ' ἐπιπαμφαλό⟨ωντες⟩· . . .

παμφαλᾶν

γὰρ τὸ μετὰ πτοιήσεως ἐπιβλέπειν. κέχρηται δὲ τῇ λέξει καὶ Ἱππῶναξ (fr. 164) καὶ Ἀνακρέων.

483 Himer. *Or.* 28. 2 (p. 128 Colonna)

ᾖδε δὲ Ἀνακρέων τὴν Πολυκράτους τύχην Σαμίων τῇ θεῷ πεμπόντων (Elter: πέμπουσαν cod.) ἱερά.

Str. 14. 1. 16 (iii 101 Kramer)

τούτῳ συνεβίωσεν Ἀνακρέων ὁ μελοποιός· καὶ δὴ καὶ πᾶσα ἡ ποίησις πλήρης ἐστὶ τῆς περὶ αὐτοῦ μνήμης.

484 *Et. Gen.* s.v. σαλάμβας (p. 43 Calame) = *Et. Mag.* 707. 45

σαλαΐζειν

Ἀνακρέων ἐπὶ τοῦ θρηνεῖν.

cf. Orion. 148. 5 (σηλάζειν)

481 Scholiast on Aeschylus, *Persae* ('soft-living Lydians')

The Lydians do live softly, whence the expression in Anacreon,

> people living in Lydian style,

i.e. in luxurious style.

482 Scholiast on Apollonius of Rhodes ('gazing often')

παμφαλᾶν means

> to gaze with excitement.

It is used by Hipponax and Anacreon.

483 Himerius, *Orations*

And Anacreon sang of the fortune of Polycrates [1] when the Samians were sending offerings to the goddess (Hera).

Strabo, *Geography*

The lyric poet Anacreon lived at the court of Polycrates; indeed his poetry is full of references to him.

[1] For Polycrates see also frr. 471, 491, testt. 4, 5.

484 *Etymologicum Genuinum*

Anacreon uses σαλαΐζειν in the sense of

> to lament.

485 Schol. T Hom. *Il.* 13. 227 (iii 443 Erbse)

νωνύμνους· τινὲς ἀθρηνήτους.

ὕμνον

γὰρ καὶ Ἀνακρέων τὸν θρῆνόν φησιν.

cf. Eust. *Il.* 928. 63

486 Hdn. π. μον. λέξ. α´ 11. 26 (ii 918 Lentz)

Φίλλος·

παρ' Ἀνακρέοντι τὸ ὄνομα.

487 Hdn. π. μον. λέξ. α´ 14. 22 (ii 921 Lentz: cf. i 239, ii 257)

ὁ μέντοι Ἀνακρέων καὶ

χαριτόεις

εἶπεν ἀποδοὺς τὸ ἐντελὲς τῇ λέξει.

488 Greg. Cor. in Hermog. *Meth.* (*Rhet. Gr.* vii 1236 Walz)

αἰσχρῶς μὲν κολακεύει τὴν ἀκοὴν ἐκεῖνα ὅσα εἰσὶν ἐρωτικά, οἷον τὰ Ἀνακρέοντος, τὰ Σαπφοῦς (fr. 156), οἷον γάλακτος λευκοτέρα, ὕδατος ἁπαλωτέρα, πηκτίδων ἐμμελεστέρα, ἵππου γαυροτέρα, ῥόδων ἁβροτέρα, ἱματίου ἑανοῦ μαλακωτέρα, χρυσοῦ τιμιωτέρα.

489 Himer. *Or.* 17. 2 (p. 105 Colonna)

Σαπφὼ καὶ Ἀνακρέων ὁ Τήιος ὥσπερ τι προοίμιον τῶν μελῶν τὴν Κύπριν ἀναβοῶντες οὐ παύονται.

ANACREON

485 Scholiast on *Iliad* (νωνύμνους, 'nameless')

Some use it in the sense of 'unlamented': Anacreon uses ὕμνος,

hymn,[1]

to mean a lament.

[1] But νώνυμνος is derived from ὄνυμα, 'name'.

486 Herodian, *On Anomalous Words*

Phillus:

the name occurs in Anacreon.

487 Herodian, *On Anomalous Words*

Anacreon, however, also gave χαρίεις its full form, χαριτόεις,

graceful.

488 Gregory of Corinth on Hermogenes [1]

The ear is basely flattered by erotic phrases such as those of Anacreon and Sappho; for example, 'whiter than milk', 'more gentle than water', 'more tuneful than lyres', 'haughtier than a mare', 'more delicate than roses', 'softer than a fine robe', 'more precious than gold'.

[1] See Sa. 156: it is uncertain whether any of the examples is from Anacreon.

489 Himerius, *Orations*

Sappho [1] and Anacreon of Teos never cease invoking Cyprian Aphrodite as a prelude to their songs.

[1] See Sa. test. 47.

490 Himer. *Or.* 27. 27 (p. 126 Colonna)

κοσμεῖ μὲν γὰρ Ἀνακρέων τὴν Τηίων πόλιν τοῖς μέλεσι,
κἀκεῖθεν ἄγει τοὺς Ἔρωτας.

491 Himer. *Or.* 29. 22 (p. 132 Colonna)

ἦν Πολυκράτης ἔφηβος, ὁ δὲ Πολυκράτης οὗτος οὐ βασιλεὺς
Σάμου μόνον ἀλλὰ καὶ τῆς Ἑλληνικῆς ἁπάσης θαλάσσης ‘ἀφ’ ἧς
γαῖα ὁρίζεται’. ὁ δ⟨ὲ⟩ ⟦ἤγουν τῆς Ῥόδου secl. Labarbe⟧
Πολυκράτης ἦρα μουσικῆς καὶ μελῶν, καὶ τὸν πατέρα ἔπειθε
συμπρᾶξαι αὐτῷ πρὸς τὸν τῆς μουσικῆς ἔρωτα. ὁ δὲ Ἀνακρέοντα
τὸν μελοποιὸν μεταπεμψάμενος δίδωσι τῷ παιδὶ τούτον τῆς
ἐπιθυμίας διδάσκαλον, ὑφ’ ᾧ τὴν βασιλικὴν ἀρετὴν ὁ παῖς διὰ τῆς
λύρας πονῶν τὴν Ὁμηρικὴν ἔμελλε πληρώσειν εὐχὴν τῷ πατρί,
πολυκρατὴς ⟨καὶ⟩ (add. West) πάντων (Πολυκράτει πάντα R)
κρείσσων ἐσόμενος.

492 Himer. *Or.* 38. 13 (p. 155 Colonna)

ἐπειδὴ καὶ ἡμᾶς, ὦ παῖδες, ὥσπερ τις θεὸς ὅδε ὁ ἀνὴρ φαίνει
οἵους ποιηταὶ πολλάκις εἰς ἀνθρώπων εἴδη μορφάς τε ποικίλας
ἀμείβοντες πόλεις τε εἰς μέσας καὶ δήμους ἄγουσιν, ἀνθρώπων
ὕβριν τε καὶ εὐνομίην ἐφέποντας (Hom. *Od.* 17. 487), οἵαν
Ὅμηρος μὲν Ἀθηνᾶν, Διόνυσον δὲ Ἀνακρέων Εὐριπίδης τ’
ἔδειξαν ...

493 Himer. *Or.* 39. 10 (p. 159s. Colonna)

ἔχαιρε μὲν Ἀνακρέων εἰς Πολυκράτους στελλόμενος τὸν μέγαν
Ξάνθιππον προσφθέγξασθαι, ἡδὺ δ’ ἦν καὶ Πινδάρῳ προσειπεῖν πρὸ
τοῦ Διὸς τὸν Ἱέρωνα.

494 Himer. *Or.* 69. 35 (p. 244 Colonna)

ἥρμοσε μὲν καὶ Ἀνακρέων μετὰ τὴν νόσον τὴν λύραν καὶ τοὺς
φίλους Ἔρωτας αὖθις διὰ μέλους ἠσπάζετο ...

ANACREON

490 Himerius, *Orations*

For Anacreon adorns the city of Teos in his songs,[1] and he brings the Loves from there.

[1] Cf. 463.

491 Himerius, *Orations* [1]

When Polycrates was a youth – he was king, this Polycrates, not only of Samos but of the whole Greek sea 'by which the earth is bounded'[2]—he loved the arts, especially song, and persuaded his father to help him foster his love of the arts; so his father sent for Anacreon, the lyric poet, and gave him to his son to tutor him in his beloved music, and under his supervision the boy worked with his lyre to attain kingly excellence and looked like fulfilling the Homeric prayer[3] for his father by being 'very powerful'[4] and better than anyone else.

[1] See test. 1 n. 2, Ibycus, test. 1.   [2] Perhaps a quotation from Anacreon.   [3] *Il.* 6. 476 ff.   [4] With a play on his name, *poly-krates*.

492 Himerius, *Orations*

And since, my children, this man, as if he were a god, makes us appear like those whom poets often change into mortal shape and various forms and bring into the midst of cities and peoples to deal with the lawlessness and just behaviour of men, as Athena is shown in Homer and Dionysus in Anacreon and Euripides . . .

493 Himerius, *Orations*

Anacreon, when he was being taken to the court of Polycrates, was glad to address the great Xanthippus,[1] and Pindar took pleasure in saluting Hiero before Zeus.

[1] See test. 10, Bowra, *G. L. P.* 301 f.

494 Himerius, *Orations*

Anacreon tuned his lyre after his illness and greeted his dear Loves again in song.

GREEK LYRIC

495 Pl. *Charm.* 157e

ἥ τε γὰρ πατρῴα ὑμῖν οἰκία, ἡ Κριτίου τοῦ Δρωπίδου, καὶ ὑπὸ
'Ανακρέοντος καὶ ὑπὸ Σόλωνος καὶ ὑπ' ἄλλων πολλῶν ποιητῶν
ἐγκεκωμιασμένη παραδέδοται ἡμῖν ὡς διαφέρουσα κάλλει τε καὶ
ἀρετῇ καὶ τῇ ἄλλῃ λεγομένῃ εὐδαιμονίᾳ.

496 Poll. 6. 107 (ii 31 Bethe)

'Ανακρέων δὲ καὶ μύρτοις στεφανοῦσθαί φησι καὶ κοριάννοις καὶ
λύγῳ καὶ Ναυκρατίτῃ στεφάνῳ . . . καὶ ἀνήτῳ.

497 Zenob. *Cent.* 5. 20 (i 123s. Leutsch-Schneidewin)

μέγα φρονεῖ μᾶλλον ἢ Πηλεὺς ἐπὶ τῇ μαχαίρᾳ. μέμνηται ταύτης
'Ανακρέων καὶ Πίνδαρος ἐν Νεμεονίκαις (iv. 58). φασὶ δὲ αὐτὴν
ὑπὸ Ἡφαίστου γενομένην δῶρον Πηλεῖ σωφροσύνης ἕνεκα παρὰ
θεῶν δοθῆναι, ᾗ χρώμενος πάντα κατώρθου καὶ ἐν ταῖς μάχαις καὶ
ἐν ταῖς θήραις.

cf. Zenob. Athoum 2. 79 Miller (*Mélanges* p. 366), Ar. *Nub.*
1063, schol. ad loc. (p. 124 Dübner), Arsen. p. 351 Walz,
Eust. *Il.* 1101. 63

498 Schol. Ap. Rhod. 1. 788–89b (p. 69 Wendel)

καλῆς διὰ παστάδος· . . . καλῆς δὲ ἤτοι ὅτι βασίλεια τὰ οἰκήματα
ἢ ὅτι ἐρωτικά. τοιαῦτα γὰρ τὰ τῶν ἐρώντων, ὡς καὶ 'Ανακρέων ἐπὶ
ἐρωμένης φησίν· ⟨   ⟩.

ANACREON

495 Plato, *Charmides*

Socrates (to Charmides and Critias). Your father's house, the house of Critias, son of Dropides, has been celebrated by Anacreon [1] and Solon [2] and many other poets, so that it is famed in tradition as being pre-eminent in beauty, in virtue and in all else that is called happiness.

[1] Cf. 412, 500.   [2] Frr. 22, 22a.

496 Pollux, *Vocabulary*

Anacreon says he garlands himself with myrtle and coriander and willow and with the garland of Naucratis . . . and with anise.[1]

[1] See 352, 434, Sa. 191, Alc. 436.

497 Zenobius, *Proverbs*

'He is more proud than Peleus of his sword.' This proverb is mentioned by Anacreon and by Pindar in his *Nemeans*. They say that the sword was made by Hephaestus and was a gift to Peleus from the gods in reward for his virtue; when he used it he was always successful both in battle and in the chase.

498 Scholiast on Apollonius of Rhodes ('through a beautiful porch')

. . . 'beautiful' either because the building was royal or because of its love interest; for that is how lovers speak: so Anacreon says of the woman he loves, . . .[1]

[1] The quotation is lost.

GREEK LYRIC

MISCELLANEA

499 (a) Caes. Bass. (vi 261 Keil)

quae omnia genera hendecasyllabi Catullus et Sappho et Anacreonta et alios auctores secutus non tamquam vitiosa vitavit sed tamquam legitima inseruit.

(b) 'Mar. Vict.' (Aphthonius) (vi 109 Keil)

asclepiadeum . . . prima adempta syllaba anacreontion dabit, sic: saevis trepidant carbasa flatibus.

(c) 'Mar. Vict.' (Aphthonius) (vi 88 Keil)

trimetrum catalecticum anacreontium, ita: amor te meus o pulchra puella.

500 Athen. 13. 600de (iii 323s. Kaibel)

(Ἔρωτα) ὃν ὁ σοφὸς ὑμνῶν αἰεί ποτε Ἀνακρέων πᾶσίν ἐστιν διὰ
στόματος. λέγει οὖν περὶ αὐτοῦ καὶ ὁ κράτιστος Κριτίας τάδε·

> τὸν δὲ γυναικείων μελέων πλέξαντά ποτ᾽ ᾠδὰς
> ἡδὺν Ἀνακρείοντα Τέως εἰς Ἑλλάδ᾽ ἀνῆγεν,
> συμποσίων ἐρέθισμα, γυναικῶν ἠπερόπευμα,
> αὐλῶν ἀντίπαλον, φιλοβάρβιτον, ἡδύν, ἄλυπον.
> οὔποτέ σου φιλότης γηράσεται οὐδὲ θανεῖται,
> ἔστ᾽ ἂν ὕδωρ οἴνῳ συμμειγνύμενον κυλίκεσσι
> παῖς διαπομπεύῃ προπόσεις ἐπιδέξια νωμῶν,
> παννυχίδας θ᾽ ἱερὰς θήλεις χοροὶ ἀμφιέπωσιν,
> πλάστιγξ θ᾽ ἡ χαλκοῦ θυγάτηρ ἐπ᾽ ἄκραισι καθίζῃ
> κοττάβου ὑψηλαῖς κορυφαῖς Βρομίου ψακάδεσσιν.

138

ANACREON

499 (*on the metres of Anacreon*)

(a) Caesius Bassus, *On Metres*

Catullus, following Sappho, Anacreon and other authors, did not avoid all these types [1] of (phalaecian) hendeca-syllabic as being faulty: he included them as legitimate.

[1] Lines beginning with trochee or iamb instead of spondee.

(b) 'Marius Victorinus' (Aphthonius) *Grammar*

If the first syllable is removed from the (lesser) asclepiad, an anacreontic will result with the form $--\cup\cup--\cup\cup-\cup-$.

(c) the same

. . . an antispastic trimeter catalectic gives an anacreontic [1] of the form $\cup--\cup\cup--\cup\cup--$.

[1] For other units labelled anacreontic see Servius, *Cent. Metr.* (iv 458 ff. Keil) and passages listed by Page, *P.M.G.* 499 (fin.), together with testt. 14, 15.

500 Athenaeus, *Scholars at Dinner*

And wise Anacreon, who is on everyone's lips, is always singing the praises of Love; and so the excellent Critias [1] says this of him: 'Sweet Anacreon, who once wove the songs for women's melodies,[2] was brought to Greece by Teos, the excitement of the drinking-party, the deceiver of women, the rival of the pipes, lover of the lyre, sweet healer of pain: never shall love of you grow old or die, so long as the boy carries round the water mixed with wine for the cups, dispensing the toasts from left to right; so long as female choirs [2] perform the night-long rites; so long as the scale-pan, daughter of bronze, sits on the high summit of the cottabus [3] to receive the drops of the Bromian.' [4]

[1] 5th c. politician and poet.   [2] None of A.'s maiden-songs survives, but see 501.   [3] See 415.   [4] Dionysus, god of wine.

GREEK LYRIC

cf. Lucian. *Ver. Hist.* 2. 15 οἱ μὲν οὖν χοροὶ ἐκ παίδων εἰσὶν καὶ παρθένων, ἐξάρχουσι δὲ καὶ συνᾴδουσιν Εὔνομός τε ὁ Λοκρὸς καὶ Ἀρίων ὁ Λέσβιος καὶ Ἀνακρέων καὶ Στησίχορος, *Anth. Pal.* 7. 24. 6 (Ἀνακρέων) παννύχιος κρούων τὸν φιλόπαιδα χέλυν, 7. 29. 2 (Ἀνακρέοντος) ἡ γλυκερὴ νυκτιλάλος κιθάρη, 7. 31. 2 (Ἀνάκρεον) κώμου καὶ πάσης κοίρανε παννυχίδος.

501 Schol. *Il.* 21. 162s. (P. Oxy. 221 vii 5–12: vol. ii 62s.)(v 91 Erbse)

5   ϙαι . α[.]ανακ[
ἐν Παρθενείοις·

        πα[ῖς δ'] Ἀστερ[οπαίου γε-

γένημαι, ὅς πο[.] θιαν [. .]ας ἀμ (φοτέραι-
σι χερσὶ ῥῖπτεν καὶ [. .]αμ[
ὁ δὲ χαλκέοις θρασυ[

        ν
10 πεη⟦ν⟧ χὠμοπτολι[
μάχαι θαυμαινετ . . [
λεων ἱέντα ῥόμ[βον

suppl. Grenfell-Hunt   5 καὶ [π]ὰ[ρ'] Ἀνακ[ρέοντι suppl. Platt

502(a) = Alc. test. 27, (b) = Sa. test. 47

140

ANACREON

Lucian, *A True Story*

Their choruses (sc. on the Island of the Blessed) are of boys and girls, and Eunomus of Locri, Arion of Lesbos, Anacreon and Stesichorus lead them and sing with them.

Palatine Anthology

'Simonides', *On Anacreon*: . . . striking all night long his boy-loving lyre.

Antipater of Sidon, *On Anacreon*: your sweet lyre that talked all night long.

Dioscorides, *On Anacreon*: lord of the revel and every night-long rite.

501 Scholiast on *Iliad* ('the hero Asteropaeus attacked him with spears in both hands, since he was ambidextrous')

. . . (so in Anacreon?) [1] in his Maiden-songs:

and I am the son of Asteropaeus, who threw . . . with both hands and . . .; but he (with) bronze (weapons), bold man . . . and from the same city . . . battle . . . was admired . . . throwing whirling (javelins) . . .

[1] Dialect and subject-matter make the supplement uncertain.

502 (a) = Alc. test. 27, (b) = Sa. test. 47

GREEK LYRIC

503 Pap. ed. Schubart, *Ber. Sächs. Akad. d. Wiss. Leipzig* (1950) n. 38, pp. 72ss.

F col. ii 59ss.

> . . . ἐν]θυμούμενο[ν μὲν] Σωκράτους ὅσ[ους ἐ]ραστὰς ἔλαβ[εν ἐν] γήραι, ἔνθυμ [ούμε]νον δὲ αὐτοῦ κ[αὶ] Ἀνακρέοντος ὡ[ς χα]ρίεις ἡμεῖν κα[ὶ νῦν] δοκεῖ αὐτοῖς ὁ [βίος] καὶ † πολιαῖς † · γῆρ[ας] ἄμουσον μὲν [ὁμο]λογουμένως [αἰσ]χρόν, μουσικὸ[ν δ]ὲ Ἄπολλον ὡς χαρίεν. ἀλλὰ τὴν Σμερ[δί]ου καὶ Βαθύλλου κλ[. . .]ν (fin. col.)

'πολιοῖς exspectasses' Page

504 = eleg. 3

505 (INCERTI AUCTORIS)

(a) Str. 14. 1. 30 (iii 110 Kramer)

> καὶ ἡ Τέως δὲ ἐπὶ χερρονήσῳ ἵδρυται λιμένα ἔχουσα. ἐνθένδ' ἐστὶν Ἀνακρέων ὁ μελοποιός, ἐφ' οὗ Τήιοι τὴν πόλιν ἐκλιπόντες εἰς Ἄβδηρα ἀπῴκησαν Θρᾳκίαν πόλιν οὐ φέροντες τὴν τῶν Περσῶν ὕβριν, ἀφ' οὗ καὶ τοῦτ' εἴρηται·

> > Ἄβδηρα καλὴ Τηίων ἀποικίη.

Anacr. ded. Crusius

(b) Str. 14. 1. 17 (iii 101 Kramer)

> Συλοσῶν δ' ἀπελείφθη μὲν ἰδιώτης ὑπὸ τοῦ ἀδελφοῦ, Δαρείῳ δὲ . . . χαρισάμενος ἐσθῆτα, ἧς ἐπεθύμησεν ἐκεῖνος φοροῦντα ἰδών, οὔπω δ' ἐβασίλευε τότε, βασιλεύσαντος ἀντέλαβε δῶρον τὴν τυραννίδα. πικρῶς δ' ἦρξεν, ὥστε καὶ ἐλειπάνδρησεν ἡ πόλις· κἀκεῖθεν ἐκπεσεῖν συνέβη τὴν παροιμίαν·

> > ἔκητι Συλοσῶντος εὐρυχωρίη.

Anacr. ded. Crusius

(c) = inc. auct. 1 (Lobel-Page, Voigt): v. vol. i, p. 438

142

ANACREON

503 Papyrus of 1st-2nd c. A.D.

. . . bearing in mind how many lovers Socrates had in his old age and how delightful the life of Socrates or Anacreon still seems to us, even (when they were grey-haired?). Old age without the arts is admittedly foul, but old age with the arts—Apollo,[1] how delightful it is! But . . . of Smerdies and Bathyllus . . .

[1] Schubart thought the words of Anacreon might be represented from here onwards.

504 = elegiac fr. 3

505 Fragments of uncertain authorship ascribed by some to Anacreon

(a) Strabo, *Geography*

Teos is situated on a peninsula, and it has a harbour. It is the birthplace of Anacreon, the lyric poet, in whose day the Teians abandoned their city and moved to Abdera in Thrace, since they would not tolerate the insolence of the Persians; whence these words:

Abdera, fair colony of the Teians.

(b) Strabo, *Geography* (on Samos)

Syloson was left a private citizen by his brother (Polycrates); but he presented Darius with a robe which he coveted when he saw him wearing it, and so Darius, when he eventually became king, gave Syloson the tyranny in return. His rule was so harsh that Samos became short of men. This was the origin of the saying,

thanks to Syloson there is plenty of room.

(c) = 'Sappho or Alcaeus' fr. 1

(d) Clem. Al. *Strom.* 6. 14. 7 (ii 434 Stählin)

'Ανακρέοντος γὰρ ποιήσαντος·

Ἔρωτα γὰρ τὸν ἁβρὸν
μέλομαι βρύοντα μίτραις
πολυανθέμοις ἀείδειν·
ὅδε καὶ θεῶν δυναστής,
ὅδε καὶ βροτοὺς δαμάζει,

Εὐριπίδης γράφει (fr. 431. 1)· Ἔρως γὰρ ἄνδρας οὐ μόνους
ἐπέρχεται.

Fulgent. *Mit.* 1. 20 (p. 31 Helm)

Iuppiter enim, ut Anacreon antiquissimus auctor
scripsit, dum adversus Titanas, id est Titani filios qui frater
Saturni fuerat, bellum adsumeret et sacrificium caelo
fecisset, in victoriae auspicium aquilae sibi adesse
prosperum vidit volatum. pro quo tam felici omine,
praesertim quia et victoria consecuta est, in signis bellicis
sibi aquilam auream fecit tutelaeque suae virtuti dedicavit,
unde et apud Romanos huiuscemodi signa tracta sunt.

'Acro' in Hor. *Carm.* 4. 9. 9 (i 356 Keller)

Anacreon autem saturam scripsit, amicus Lisandri.

(e) Schol. Scorial. Arat. *Phaen.* Σ III 3 (v. *R. É. G.* 73, 1960,
273s., *Helikon* 1, 1961, 493ss.)

Οἰνοπίωνι· ὁ Διονύσου καὶ Ἀριάδνης παῖς ἐν Χίῳ τῇ νήσῳ ᾤκει,
ταύτης βασιλεύων, ὡς Ἀνακρέων φησίν·

ὅτι μὴ Οἰνοπίων.

ANACREON

(d) Clement of Alexandria, *Miscellanies*

For when Anacreon [1] had written,

For I am eager to sing of tender Love, his head garlanded with luxuriant flowers: he is the ruler over gods, he is the subduer of mortals,

Euripides wrote, 'For Love assails not men alone.'

[1] The lines almost certainly belong to the *Anacreontea*.

Fulgentius, *Mythologies*

According to Anacreon,[1] a most ancient author, when Zeus was beginning warfare against the Titans, i.e. the sons of Titan, brother of Cronus, and had sacrificed to Heaven, he saw an eagle fly nearby as a favourable omen for victory. In return for this happy omen, and particularly because it was indeed followed by victory, he put a golden eagle on his war standards and dedicated it as a protection for his valour; from these are derived the Roman standards of this type.

[1] Probably a later Anacreon: see *R.E.* Suppl. 1 p. 76 (Anakreon 1a).

'Acro' on Horace, *Odes* [1]

Moreover Anacreon wrote satire [2]; he was the friend of Lysander.

[1] The passage follows test. 19.   [2] E.g. 388; the text of the following words is doubtful: some emend 'friend' to 'enemy'.

(e) Scholiast on Aratus, *Phaenomena* 640

Oenopion: son of Dionysus and Ariadne; lived on the island of Chios and ruled over it, as Anacreon [1] says:

except Oenopion.

[1] Probably the later Anacreon, cited by Fulgentius in (d) above, an Alexandrian writer, author of another *Phaenomena*.

GREEK LYRIC

(f) = S317 *S.L.G.*   crateris inscriptio, ed. E. Vermeule, *Antike Kunst, Heft* 1. 8 (1965) 34ss.

ὤπολλον, σέ γε καὶ μάκαι[ραν

505A = S 314 *S. L. G.*   Theod. π. κλίσ. τῶν εἰς -ων βαρυτόνων (ed. A. Hilgard, *Excerpta ex libris Herodiani*, Leipzig 1887, p. 21)

τεράμων τεράμωνος· σεσημείωται δὲ ἡ χρῆσις παρὰ Πλάτωνι ἐν Σοφιστῇ (cf. 221a καλάμοις) τῷ διαλόγῳ· ὁ γὰρ Ἀνακρέων ὡς μετοχικὸν

τεράμοντος

ἔκλινεν. σημαίνει δὲ τὸν κάλαμον.

ELEGI

eleg. 1 Heph. *Ench.* 1. 6 (p. 5 Consbruch)

καὶ παρ' Ἀνακρέοντι ἐν Ἐλεγείαις·

οὐδέ τί τοι πρὸς θυμόν, ὅμως γε μένω σ' ἀδοιάστως

Bergk: μὲν ὡς codd.

eleg. 2 Athen. 11. 463a (iii 8 Kaibel)

καὶ ὁ χαρίεις δ' Ἀνακρέων φησίν·

οὐ φιλέω ὃς κρητῆρι παρὰ πλέῳ οἰνοποτάζων
  νείκεα καὶ πόλεμον δακρυόεντα λέγει,
ἀλλ' ὅστις Μουσέων τε καὶ ἀγλαὰ δῶρ' Ἀφροδίτης
  συμμίσγων ἐρατῆς μνήσκεται εὐφροσύνης.

1 φιλέω ὃς epit. φιλεος cod. A

146

ANACREON

(f) Inscription on a calyx krater (*c.* 513–508 B.C.)[1]

Apollo, (I beseech) you and blessed (Artemis)

[1] The words proceed from the mouth of one Ecphantides, the host at a symposium: the vase-painter is Euphronius.

505A Theodosius, *On the Declension of barytone words* [1] *in* -ων

τεράμων, genitive τεράμωνος: this usage of Plato in his dialogue *The Sophist* [2] is noted as remarkable, since Anacreon declined the noun like a participle, genitive τεράμοντος. It means

reed.

[1] I.e. words with the acute accent on the penultimate syllable.   [2] I.e. τεράμωσι, but the word has been ousted in our mss. by the common word καλάμοις.

ELEGIAC FRAGMENTS

eleg. 1 Hephaestion, *Handbook on Metres* (on the internal correption in ἀδοιάστως)

. . . and in Anacreon's *Elegiacs*:

nor is it at all to your liking; and yet I await you unhesitatingly

eleg. 2 Athenaeus, *Scholars at Dinner*

And the delightful Anacreon says:

I do not like the man who while drinking his wine beside the full mixing-bowl talks of strife and tearful war: I like him who by mingling the splendid gifts of the Muses and Aphrodite remembers the loveliness of the feast.

eleg. 3 = *P.M.G.* 504   Schol. Hom. *Od.* 8. 294 (i 382s Dindorf)

μετὰ Σίντιας ἀγριοφώνους· . . . καὶ Ἀνακρέων δὲ ὡς πολεμικῶν μέμνηται·

τί μοι (φησί) τῶν ἀγκυλοτόξων
† φιλοκιμέρων καὶ Σκυθέων † μέλει;

2 φιλοκιμέως cod. Q ὦ φίλε Κιμμερίων Schneidewin

eleg. 4 Athen. 11. 460c (iii 2 Kaibel)

ὁ δὲ Ἀνακρέων ἔφη·
οἰνοπότης δὲ πεποίημαι.

eleg. 5 'Longinus' *de subl.* 31. 1 (p. 37 Russell)

. . .θρε]πτικώτατον καὶ γόνιμον, τὸ δ' Ἀνακρέοντος οὐκέτι·
Θρηϊκίης ⟨πώλου⟩ ἐπιστρέφομαι.

πώλου suppl. Bergk

eleg. 5A *Anth. Pal.* 10. 70. 7s. (Macedonius)

τὴν γὰρ Ἀνακρείοντος ἐνὶ πραπίδεσσι φυλάσσω
παρφασίην ὅτι δεῖ φροντίδα μὴ κατέχειν.

eleg. 3 Scholiast on *Odyssey* ('to the wild-speaking Sintians'[1])

. . . Anacreon too mentions them as being warlike:

What do I care, my friend, for the Cimmerians with their curving bows and the Sintians [2]?

[1] Early inhabitants of Lemnos.   [2] Text corrupt.

eleg. 4 Athenaeus, *Scholars at Dinner*

And Anacreon says:

and I have become a wine-drinker.[1]

[1] Cf. 455.

eleg. 5 'Longinus', *On Sublimity* (on colloquial expressions)

. . . most [1] productive and fruitful, but not Anacreon's:

I turn my thoughts to the Thracian (filly?).

[1] The words follow a lacuna: text of 'Longinus' and Anacreon uncertain; see 417. 1 for the filly.

eleg. 5A *Palatine Anthology*: Macedonius the Consul

. . . for I keep in mind the advice of Anacreon,[1] that

we should not keep hold of worry.

[1] Probably not the exact words of A.; the ref. may well be to the *Anacreontea*: cf. 38. 16, 40. 5.

GREEK LYRIC

EPIGRAMMATA

100D. = i *F.G.E.*   *Anth. Pal.* 7. 226 (Plan.)

Ἀνακρέοντος Τηΐου· εἰς Ἀγάθωνα στρατιώτην ἐν Ἀβδήροις·

Ἀβδήρων προθανόντα τὸν αἰνοβίην Ἀγάθωνα
    πᾶσ' ἐπὶ πυρκαϊῆς ἥδ' ἐβόησε πόλις·
οὔ τινα γὰρ τοιόνδε νέων ὁ φιλαίματος Ἄρης
    ἠνάρισε στυγερῆς ἐν στροφάλιγγι μάχης.

cf. *Sud.* II 2437 (v. 1), AI 227 (vv. 1–2), H 369 (vv. 3–4) (iv 207, ii 173, 572 Adler)

101D. = ii *F.G.E.*   *Anth. Pal.* 7. 160 (Plan.)

Ἀνακρέοντος· εἰς Τιμόκριτον ἀριστέα·

κάρτερος ἐν πολέμοις Τιμόκριτος, οὗ τόδε σᾶμα·
    Ἄρης δ' οὐκ ἀγαθῶν φείδεται ἀλλὰ κακῶν.

ANACREON

EPIGRAMS

Meleager included in his Garland epigrams attributed to Anacreon (test. 17), and eighteen carry his name in the Palatine Anthology. Some may be authentic, e.g. 100, 107, 108, but certainty is impossible: the author's name was not added to epitaphs or dedications before the end of the 5th c. B.C., and there is seldom any corroborative evidence about the authorship. Some are demonstrably later than Anacreon, e.g. 114, 115, 'Simon. 156D.' and probably 105; the manner of 102 and the content of 113 point to Hellenistic authorship.

100D. *Palatine Anthology*

Anacreon of Teos: on the soldier Agathon at Abdera

The mighty Agathon who died for Abdera was mourned at the pyre by this whole city; for in the whirl of hateful battle blood-loving Ares never slew any youth such as he was.[1]

[1] Perhaps an elegiac lament rather than a true epitaph.

101D. *Palatine Anthology*

Anacreon: on the heroism of Timocritus

Timocritus, whose tomb [1] this is, was strong in the wars: Ares spares not the brave but the cowards.

[1] The Doric form σᾶμα makes attribution to Anacreon uncertain: see also Friedländer-Hoffleit, *Epigrammata* 69.

102D. = iii *F.G.E.   Anth. Pal.* 7. 263 (Plan.)

'Ανακρέοντος Τηΐου· εἰς Κλεηνορίδην ναυαγήσαντα·

καὶ σέ, Κλεηνορίδη, πόθος ὤλεσε πατρίδος αἴης
   θαρσήσαντα νότου λαίλαπι χειμερίη·
ὥρη γάρ σε πέδησεν ἀνέγγυος, ὑγρὰ δὲ τὴν σὴν
   κύματ' ἀφ' ἱμερτὴν ἔκλυσεν ἡλικίην.

103D. = ix *F.G.E.   Anth. Pal.* 6. 138

  τοῦ αὐτοῦ (sc. 'Ανακρέοντος)· ὁμοίως (i.e., ut 110D., ἀνάθημα τῷ 'Απόλλωνι: perperam?)

πρὶν μὲν Καλλιτέλης ἱδρύσατο, τόνδε δ' ἐκείνου
   ἔγγονοι ἐστήσανθ', οἷς χάριν ἀντιδίδου.

cf. *I. G.* I² 834 (1 πριμ —hιδρυσατ[, 2 ἔ]γ[γ]ονοι ἐστησαν[   )
1 μ' ἱδρ- *Anth.*   2 ἔκγονοι ἐστάσανθ' *Anth.*

104D. = vi *F.G.E.   Anth. Pal.* 6. 135

  τοῦ αὐτοῦ (sc. 'Ανακρέοντος)· ἀνάθημα τῷ Διὶ παρὰ Φειδόλα·

οὗτος Φειδόλα ἵππος ἀπ' εὐρυχόροιο Κορίνθου
   ἄγκειται Κρονίδᾳ, μνᾶμα ποδῶν ἀρετᾶς.

ANACREON

102D. *Palatine Anthology*

Anacreon of Teos: on Cleënorides, who was shipwrecked

You too, Cleënorides, were destroyed by your desire for your fatherland, when you put your trust in the wintry blast of the south wind; for the weather, with which no covenant is possible, shackled you, and the wet waves washed away your lovely youth.[1]

[1] Like 100D., perhaps elegiac lament rather than epitaph.

103D. *Palatine Anthology*

Anacreon [1]

Calliteles was the first to put your figure [2] here; this one was set up by his descendants [3]: show gratitude to them.

[1] Ascription doubtful: see C. A. Trypanis, *C. Q.* 45 (1951) **33.**
[2] The lines were inscribed on an Athenian herm, perhaps *c.* 450 B.C. (Pfohl), too late for Anacreon.   [3] Or 'his grandchildren'.

104D. *Palatine Anthology*

Anacreon [1]: a dedication to Zeus by Pheidolas

This horse of Pheidolas from spacious Corinth is dedicated to the son of Cronus to commemorate the excellence of his feet.[2]

[1] Note Doric forms, appropriate for a Corinthian patron.
[2] Pheidolas' sons won the horse-race at Olympia in 508 B.C.: see Paus. 6.13.9 and Page, *F.G.E.* 401f.

105D. = iv *F.G.E.*   *Anth. Pal.* 6. 346

'Ανακρέοντος·

Τελλίᾳ ἱμερόεντα βίον πόρε, Μαιάδος υἱέ,
   ἀντ' ἐρατῶν δώρων τῶνδε χάριν θέμενος·
δὸς δέ μιν εὐθυδίκων Εὐωνυμέων ἐνὶ δήμῳ
   ναίειν αἰῶνος μοῖραν ἔχοντ' ἀγαθήν.

¹ Reiske: τελαίαι ἡμερ- cod. P

106D. = xiv *F.G.E.*   *Anth. Pal.* 6. 143

   τοῦ αὐτοῦ (sc. 'Ανακρέοντος)· ἀνάθημα τῷ Ἑρμῇ παρὰ Τιμώνακτος·

εὔχεο Τιμώνακτι θεῶν κήρυκα γενέσθαι
   ἤπιον, ὅς μ' ἐρατοῖς ἀγλαΐην προθύροις
Ἑρμῇ τε κρείοντι καθέσσατο· τὸν δ' ἐθέλοντα
   ἀστῶν καὶ ξείνων γυμνασίῳ δέχομαι.

3 Valckenaer: κρειόεντι cod. P

107D. = xiii *F.G.E.*   *Anth. Pal.* 6. 142

   τοῦ αὐτοῦ (sc. 'Ανακρέοντος)· ἀνάθημα τῷ Διονύσῳ·

σάν τε χάριν, Διόνυσε, καὶ ἀγλαὸν ἄστεϊ κόσμον
   Θεσσαλίας μ' ἀνέθηκ' ἀρχὸς Ἐχεκρατίδας.

ANACREON

105D. *Palatine Anthology*

Anacreon [1]

Give Tellias a life to be desired, son of Maia,[2] in gratitude for these lovely gifts; and grant that he dwell among the fair-judging people of Euonymon [3] enjoying good fortune all his days.

[1] Probably a 4th c. poem: a Tellias of Euonymon is known from an inscription dated *c.* 325.   [2] Hermes: Tellias may have offered his gifts at a herm.   [3] A deme of Attica.

106D. *Palatine Anthology*

Anacreon [1]: a dedication to Hermes by Timonax

Pray that the herald of the gods [2] be kind to Timonax, who set me up to adorn the lovely porch and glorify the lord Hermes; I welcome all comers to the gymnasium, citizen or stranger.

[1] Probably of late date (Trypanis *loc. cit.*).   [2] Hermes: the herm addresses the passer-by.

107D. *Palatine Anthology*

Anacreon [1]: a dedication to Dionysus

In gratitude to you, Dionysus, and as a splendid adornment to the city [2] I was set up by Echecratidas, lord of Thessaly.

[1] Note Doric forms. Echecratidas lived in the first half of the 5th c.   [2] Pharsalus or Athens?

155

GREEK LYRIC

108D. = vii *F.G.E.*   *Anth. Pal.* 6. 136

τοῦ αὐτοῦ (sc. Ἀνακρέοντος)· ἀνάθημα·

Πρηξιδίκη μὲν ἔρεξεν, ἐβούλευσεν δὲ Δύσηρις,
εἷμα τόδε· ξυνὴ δ' ἀμφοτέρων σοφίη.

cf. *Sud.* EI 141 (ii 528 Adler) ἐν ἐπιγράμμασι (vv. 1–2)

109D. = xi *F.G.E.*   *Anth. Pal.* 6. 140

τοῦ αὐτοῦ (sc. Ἀνακρέοντος)· ἀνάθημα παρὰ Μελάνθου τῇ
Σεμέλῃ (perperam)·

παιδὶ φιλοστεφάνῳ Σεμέλας ἀνέθηκε Μέλανθος
μνᾶμα χοροῦ νίκας, υἱὸς Ἀρηιφίλου.

1 Barnes: -στεφάνου cod. P   μ' ἀνέθηκε Hecker

110D. = viii *F.G.E.*   *Anth. Pal.* 6. 137

τοῦ αὐτοῦ (sc. Ἀνακρέοντος)· ἀνάθημα τῷ Ἀπόλλωνι παρὰ
Ναυκράτους·

πρόφρων, Ἀργυρότοξε, δίδου χάριν Αἰσχύλου υἱῷ
Ναυκράτει, εὐχωλὰς τάσδ' ὑποδεξάμενος.

111D. = xii *F.G.E.*   *Anth. Pal.* 6. 141

τοῦ αὐτοῦ (sc. Ἀνακρέοντος)· ἀνάθημα τῇ Ἀθηνᾷ·

ῥυσαμένα Πύθωνα δυσαχέος ἐκ πολέμοιο
ἀσπὶς Ἀθηναίης ἐν τεμένει κρέμαται.

cf. *Sud.* Δ 1634 (ii 149 Adler) ἐν ἐπιγράμμασι (vv. 1–2)
2 κρέμαμαι Bergk

156

ANACREON

108D. *Palatine Anthology*

Anacreon: a dedication

This robe was made by Praxidice and designed by Dyseris [1]: its art is common to both.

[1] Wife of Echecratidas (see 107D.)

109D. *Palatine Anthology*

Anacreon: a dedication by Melanthus to Semele [1]

Melanthus, son of Areïphilus, dedicated me to the garland-loving son of Semele to commemorate the victory of his chorus.[2]

[1] In fact to Dionysus; note Doric forms.   [2] Perhaps in a dithyrambic contest at a festival of Dionysus.

110D. *Palatine Anthology*

Anacreon: a dedication to Apollo by Naucrates

Accept these votive offerings, lord of the silver bow, and show kindly gratitude to Naucrates, son of Aeschylus.

111D. *Palatine Anthology*

Anacreon: a dedication to Athena

The shield which rescued Python from the foul din of war hangs in the precinct of Athena.[1]

[1] Cf. Alc. 428(a). Note Doric forms.

112D. = x *F.G.E.   Anth. Pal.* 6. 139

τοῦ αὐτοῦ (sc. 'Ανακρέοντος)· ἀνάθημα παρὰ Πραξαγόρα·

Πραξαγόρας τάδε δῶρα θεοῖς ἀνέθηκε, Λυκαίου
   υἱός, ἐποίησεν δ' ἔργον 'Αναξαγόρας.

113D. = v *F.G.E.   Anth. Pal.* 6. 134 (Plan.)

   'Ανακρέοντος· ἀνάθημα·

ἡ τὸν θύρσον ἔχουσ' Ἑλικωνιὰς ἥ τε παρ' αὐτὴν
   Ξανθίππη Γλαύκη τ' εἰς χορὸν ἐρχόμεναι
ἐξ ὄρεος χωρεῦσι, Διωνύσῳ δὲ φέρουσι
   κισσὸν καὶ σταφυλήν, πίονα καὶ χίμαρον.

1 ἡ δὲ Plan.   2 Γ. δ' ἡ σχεδὸν ἐρχομένη Plan.

114D. = xvii *F.G.E.   Anth. Pal.* 9. 715 (Plan.)

   'Ανακρέοντος·

βουκόλε, τὰν ἀγέλαν πόρρω νέμε, μὴ τὸ Μύρωνος
   βοίδιον ὡς ἔμπνουν βουσὶ συνεξελάσῃς.

ANACREON

112D. *Palatine Anthology*

Anacreon: a dedication by Praxagoras

Praxagoras, son of Lycaeus, dedicated these gifts to the gods. Anaxagoras [1] was the craftsman.

[1] Perhaps Anaxagoras of Aegina, who made the bronze statue of Zeus offered at Olympia after Plataea (479 B.C.) (Paus. 5. 23. 3).

113D. *Palatine Anthology*

Anacreon: a dedication [1]

She with the thyrsus is Heliconias, next to her is Xanthippe, then Glauce; they are coming from the mountain to join the chorus, bearing ivy and grapes and a plump kid for Dionysus.

[1] Rather, a description of a painting.

114D. *Palatine Anthology*

Anacreon [1]

Herdsman, graze your herd far from here, lest thinking Myron's heifer to be alive you drive it off with your cattle.

[1] The sculptor Myron worked *c.* 480–455 B.C.; on poems inspired by his bronze *Cow* see Gow–Page, *H. E.* ii 63 f.; the present piece and the next are Hellenistic or later.

GREEK LYRIC

115D. = xviii *F.G.E.*   *Anth. Pal.* 9. 716 (Plan.)

τοῦ αὐτοῦ (sc. Ἀνακρέοντος)·

βοίδιον οὐ χοάνοις τετυπωμένον, ἀλλ᾽ ὑπὸ γήρως
χαλκωθὲν σφετέρῃ ψεύσατο χειρὶ Μύρων.

Simon. 101D. = xv *F.G.E.*   *Anth. Pal.* 6. 144

τοῦ αὐτοῦ (post lacunam: sc. Ἀνακρέοντος?)

Στροίβου παῖ, τόδ᾽ ἄγαλμα, Λεώκρατες, εὖτ᾽ ἀνέθηκας
Ἑρμῇ, καλλικόμους οὐκ ἔλαθες Χάριτας.

etiam post *Anth. Pal.* 6. 213 (τοῦ αὐτοῦ, sc. Σιμωνίδου) cf. lap.
inscr. ed. Wilhelm *Jahresh. d. Oest. Arch. Inst. Wien* 2
(1899) 221: 1 Σ]τροι[βο]π[α]ιτο[δαγαλ]μα: λεο[, 2 ἑρμει-
καλλικομωσουκελαθεσ[: in utroque loco alterum exhibet
distichon *Anth. Pal.* cod. P:

> οὐδ᾽ Ἀκαδήμειαν πολυγαθέα, τῆς ἐν ἀγοστῷ
> σὴν εὐεργεσίην τῷ προσιόντι λέγω.

cf. *Sud.* A 315 (i **33** Adler) ἐν ἐπιγράμμασι (vv. 2b–4), *Anecd.
Par.* iv 87 Cramer (v. 4)

Simon. 156D. = xvi *F.G.E.*   *Anth. Pal.* 6. 145

τοῦ αὐτοῦ (post eandem lacunam: sc. Ἀνακρέοντος?)·
ἀνάθημα Σοφοκλέους ποιητοῦ τῶν τραγῳδιῶν·

βωμοὺς τούσδε θεοῖς Σοφοκλῆς ἱδρύσατο πρῶτος,
ὃς πλεῖστον Μούσης εἷλε κλέος τραγικῆς.

ANACREON

115D. *Palatine Anthology*

Anacreon [1]

This heifer, which was never struck in the mould but turned into bronze on account of its old age, Myron pretended to be the work of his own hand.

[1] See 114D. n.1.

Simonides 101D. *Palatine Anthology*

Anacreon? [1]:

Leocrates, son of Stroebus, when you dedicated this statue to Hermes you did not escape the notice of the fair-tressed Graces. [2]

[1] There is a lacuna in the ms. before these lines, so that it is uncertain whether the words 'By the same author' refer to Anacreon; the lines occur also after 6. 213, where they are ascribed to Simonides. They have been found in an inscription dated 500–450 B.C. Leocrates was an Athenian general in 479 and in 459.   [2] The *Anthology* in both places has a second couplet, which was not on the stone: 'nor of the delightful Academy, in a corner of which I proclaim to all visitors your kind service.'

Simonides 156D. *Palatine Anthology*

Anacreon? [1]: a dedication by the tragic poet Sophocles

Sophocles was the first to set up these altars to the gods: it was he who won the greatest glory from the Muse of Tragedy.

[1] This poem is ascribed to 'the same author' as the previous one; it is clearly later than Anacreon.

ANACREONTEA

1

'Ανακρέων ἰδών με
ὁ Τήιος μελῳδὸς
ὄναρ λέγων προσεῖπεν,
κἀγὼ δραμὼν πρὸς αὐτὸν
5 περιπλάκην φιλήσας.
γέρων μὲν ἦν, καλὸς δέ,
καλὸς δὲ καὶ φίλευνος·
τὸ χεῖλος ὦζεν οἴνου,
τρέμοντα δ' αὐτὸν ἤδη
10 Ἔρως ἐχειραγώγει.
ὁ δ' ἐξελὼν καρήνου
ἐμοὶ στέφος δίδωσι·
τὸ δ' ὦζ' 'Ανακρέοντος.
ἐγὼ δ' ὁ μωρὸς ἄρας
15 ἐδησάμην μετώπῳ·
καὶ δῆθεν ἄχρι καὶ νῦν
ἔρωτος οὐ πέπαυμαι.

titulus: 'Ανακρέοντος Τηίου συμποσιακὰ ἡμιάμβια καὶ ἀνακρεόντια καὶ τρίμετρα   3 Stephanus: προεῖπεν cod.

THE ANACREONTEA [1]

1

Anacreon, the singer from Teos, saw me and spoke to me in a dream; and I ran to him and kissed him and embraced him. He was an old man but handsome, handsome and amorous; his lips smelled of wine, and since he was now shaky Love was leading him by the hand. He took the garland from his head and gave it to me, and it smelled of Anacreon. Fool that I was, I held it up and fastened it on my brow— and to this very day I have not ceased to be in love.

[1] The title in the ms. is 'Convivial poems of Anacreon of Teos in hemiambics, anacreontea and trimeters': 'anacreontea' is used for 'anaclasts' (Ionic dimeters with anaclasis) as in P. Oxy. 220 col. vii (p. 404 Consbruch) and later writers (see pp. 285, 316 f., 343, 394 f. Consbruch); by 'trimeters' may be meant the 'cucullii', pairs of ionic trimeters used by Byzantine writers to separate anacreontic strophes, but there are none in the ms. (see West's Preface, p. v).

2

δότε μοι λύρην Ὁμήρου
φονίης ἄνευθε χορδῆς,
φέρε μοι κύπελλα θεσμῶν,
φέρε μοι νόμους κεράσσας,
5 μεθύων ὅπως χορεύσω,
ὑπὸ σώφρονος δὲ λύσσης
μετὰ βαρβίτων ἀείδων
τὸ παροίνιον βοήσω.
δότε μοι λύρην Ὁμήρου
10 φονίης ἄνευθε χορδῆς.

titulus: τοῦ αὐτοῦ βασιλι⟨κόν⟩   4 West: κεράσσω cod.   9s.
om. Stephanus, alii

3

ἄγε, ζωγράφων ἄριστε,
λυρικῆς ἄκουε Μούσης·
5 γράφε τὰς πόλεις τὸ πρῶτον
6 ἱλαράς τε καὶ γελώσας,
3 φιλοπαίγμονάς τε Βάκχας
4 †ἑτεροπνόους ἐναύλους·†
ὁ δὲ κηρὸς ἂν δύναιτο,
γράφε καὶ νόμους φιλούντων.

vv. 3s. post v. 6 transp. Scaliger, post v. 8 West; lac. post 2, 4
indic. Bergk   3 Barnes: -παίγμονες δὲ Βάκχαι cod.
4 in marg. cod. ἑτεροπόρους: ἑτεροπνόοις ἐν αὐλοῖς Faber
7 δύνηται Barnes (cf. 16. 8)

4

τὸν ἄργυρον τορεύων
Ἥφαιστέ μοι ποίησον
πανοπλίαν μὲν οὐχί·
τί γὰρ μάχαισι κἀμοί;

2

Give [1] me Homer's lyre, but without the murderous string [2]; bring me cups of ordinances, bring them after mixing in laws, so that when I am drunk I may dance and in a sane madness [3] sing to the lyres and shout the drinking-song.

Give me Homer's lyre, but without the murderous string.

[1] Called 'a royal song' by the lemmatist: prob. a song for the symposiarch, who superintended the mixing of wine and water at a party (cf. *LSJ* s.v. βασιλεύς V).   [2] Cf. Anacr. eleg. 2.   [3] Cf. Anacr. 356.

3

Come, finest of painters, listen to the lyric Muse: paint first the cities, happy and laughing, and the playful Bacchants (with their double pipes?) [1]; and if the wax [2] is able, paint too the customs of lovers.

[1] Lines 3–4 are here placed after 5–6, but the corruption may be deeper.   [2] On which encaustic painting was done.

4

Work your silver, Hephaestus, and make me not a suit of armour [1]—what have I to do with battles?—

[1] As for Achilles, *Il.* 18.

5 ποτήριον δὲ κοῖλον
ὅσον δύνῃ βαθύνας.
ποίει δέ μοι κατ' αὐτοῦ
μήτ' ἄστρα μήτ' Ἅμαξαν,
μὴ στυγνὸν Ὠρίωνα.
10 τί Πλειάδων μέλει μοι,
τί γὰρ καλοῦ Βοώτου;
ποίησον ἀμπέλους μοι
καὶ βότρυας κατ' αὐτῶν
καὶ μαινάδας τρυγώσας,
15 ποίει δὲ ληνὸν οἴνου,
ληνοβάτας πατοῦντας,
τοὺς σατύρους γελῶντας
καὶ χρυσοῦς τοὺς Ἔρωτας
καὶ Κυθέρην γελῶσαν
20 ὁμοῦ καλῷ Λυαίῳ,
Ἔρωτα κἀφροδίτην.

cf. *Anth. Pal.* 11. 48 (Plan.) (Ἀνακρέοντος), *Anecd. Par.* iv
376s. Cramer, Aul. Gel. 19. 9. 6

titulus: τοῦ αὐτοῦ εἰς ποτήριον ἀργυροῦν   1 τορεύσας *Anth.*
(Plan.), *Par.*, Gell.   3 om. *Anth., Par.*   4 om. *Anth.*
(Plan.), *Par.*   6 βάθυνον *Anth.* (Plan.), *Par.*, Gell.
9 om. Gell.   10, 11 om. *Anth.* (Plan.), *Par.*   pro 12–21 ἀλλ'
ἀμπέλους χλοώσας/καὶ βότρυας γελῶντας/σὺν τῷ καλῷ Λυαίῳ
Anth. (Plan.), *Par.*   post 13 καὶ χρυσέους πατοῦντας/ ὁμοῦ
καλῷ Λυαίῳ/Ἔρωτα καὶ Βάθυλλον Gell.

5

καλλιτέχνα, τόρευσον
ἔαρος κύπελλον ἤδη·
τὰ πρῶτ' ἡμῖν τὰ τερπνὰ
ῥόδα φέρουσιν Ὧραι·
5 ἀργύρεον δ' ἁπλώσας
ποτὸν ποίει μοι τερπνόν.

but rather a hollow cup, as deep as you can. Put no
stars on it for me, no Wain,[2] no gloomy Orion: what
do I care about the Pleiads or the fair Ploughman?
Put vines on for me with bunches of grapes on them
and Bacchants picking them; put a wine-press and
men treading it, the satyrs laughing, Loves all in
gold, Cythere[3] laughing together with handsome
Lyaeus,[4] Love and Aphrodite.[5]

[2] Cf. *Il.* 18. 485 ff.   [3] Aphrodite.   [4] Dionysus, 'the
Loosener'.   [5] The version in the *Palatine Anthology*,
probably the oldest, ends '. . . no gloomy Orion, but
sprouting vines and laughing bunches of grapes, together
with handsome Lyaeus'; Gellius' version ends '. . . with
bunches of grapes on them and, all in gold, treading them
together with handsome Lyaeus, Love and Bathyllus.' The
version in the *Anacreontea* is a clumsy, late expansion:
'Aphrodite' repeats 'Cythere', 'Love' follows 'Loves', 16, 17,
19 have an unexpected choriambic opening (or false
quantities), 18 has a false quantity, ληνοβάτης, 'treader' (16),
is a late word.

5

Fine craftsman, make a springtime cup at once:
the Seasons are bringing us the first delightful roses;
beat the silver thin and make my drink delightful.

τῶν τελετῶν παραινῶ
μὴ ξένον μοι τορεύσῃς,
μὴ φευκτὸν ἱστόρημα·
10 μᾶλλον ποίει Διὸς γόνον,
Βάκχον Εὔιον ἡμῖν.
μύστις νάματος ἢ Κύπρις
ὑμεναίους κροτοῦσα·
χάρασσ' Ἔρωτας ἀνόπλους
15 καὶ Χάριτας γελώσας·
ὑπ' ἄμπελον εὐπέταλον
εὐβότρυον κομῶσαν
σύναπτε κούρους εὐπρεπεῖς,
ἂν μὴ Φοῖβος ἀθύρῃ.

titulus: ἄλλο εἰς τὸ αὐτὸ ποτήριον τοῦ αὐτοῦ Ἀνακρέοντος
4 Bergk: φέρουσαν ὥρην cod.   12 De la Fosse: ἢ cod.
13 Pauw, Stephanus: ὑμεναίοις κροτῶσα cod.   19 ἀθύρει,
supra η, cod.

6

στέφος πλέκων ποτ' εὗρον
ἐν τοῖς ῥόδοις Ἔρωτα,
καὶ τῶν πτερῶν κατασχὼν
ἐβάπτισ' εἰς τὸν οἶνον,
5 λαβὼν δ' ἔπινον αὐτόν·
καὶ νῦν ἔσω μελῶν μου
πτεροῖσι γαργαλίζει.

cf. Anth. Plan. lib. vii fin. (= Anth. Gr. 16. 388) (Ἰουλιανοῦ)
titulus: τοῦ αὐτοῦ εἰς Ἔρωτα   5 Barnes: ἔπιον codd.

7

λέγουσιν αἱ γυναῖκες·
'Ἀνάκρεον, γέρων εἶ·

ANACREONTEA

As for festive rites, I request that you engrave no loathsome foreign tale: rather put there for us the child of Zeus, Bacchus, Evius.[1] To initiate us in the drinking let there be the Cyprian,[2] clapping the rhythm of the wedding-songs; carve Loves unarmed and laughing Graces; under a spreading leafy vine covered with bunches of grapes add handsome youths, unless Phoebus is playing there.[3]

[1] Cult titles of Dionysus.   [2] Aphrodite.   [3] Prosody crude: a late poem.

6 [1]

Once when I was weaving a garland I found Love among the roses. I held him by his wings and plunged him in my wine, then I took it and drank him down [2]; and now inside my body he tickles me with his wings.

[1] Ascribed in *Planudean Anthology* to Julianus; in the Aldine edition he is identified with a 6th c. prefect of Egypt, but there is no indication of late date in the poem.   [2] Cf. Anacr. 450.

7

The ladies say, 'Anacreon, you are old. Take a

λαβὼν ἔσοπτρον ἄθρει
κόμας μὲν οὐκέτ' οὔσας,
5 ψιλὸν δέ σευ μέτωπον.'
ἐγὼ δὲ τὰς κόμας μέν,
εἴτ' εἰσὶν εἴτ' ἀπῆλθον,
οὐκ οἶδα· τοῦτο δ' οἶδα,
ὡς τῷ γέροντι μᾶλλον
10 πρέπει τὸ τερπνὰ παίζειν,
ὅσῳ πέλας τὰ Μοίρης.

titulus: ἄλλο εἰς ἑαυτόν   8 Stephanus: τὸ δὲ ex τόδε corr. cod.

8

οὔ μοι μέλει τὰ Γύγεω,
τοῦ Σάρδεων ἄνακτος·
οὐδ' εἷλέ πώ με ζῆλος,
οὐδὲ φθονῶ τυράννοις.
5 ἐμοὶ μέλει μύροισιν
καταβρέχειν ὑπήνην,
ἐμοὶ μέλει ῥόδοισιν
καταστέφειν κάρηνα·
τὸ σήμερον μέλει μοι,
10 τὸ δ' αὔριον τίς οἶδεν;
ὡς οὖν ἔτ' εὔδι' ἔστιν,
καὶ πῖνε καὶ κύβευε
καὶ σπένδε τῷ Λυαίῳ,
μὴ νοῦσος, ἤν τις ἔλθῃ,
15 λέγῃ, 'σὲ μὴ δεῖ πίνειν.'

cf. *Anth. Pal.* 11. 47 (Plan.) (Ἀνακρέοντος), *Anecd. Par.* iv 376 Cramer, cod. Par. 1630

titulus: εἰς τὸ ἀφθόνως ζῆν   3 οὔθ' αἱρέει με χρυσός *Anth.* (Plan.), *Par.*   4 οὐκ αἰνέω τυράννους *Anth.*   11–15 om. *Anth.* (Plan.), *Par.*, Par. 1630   15 σε μηδὲ πίνειν Stephanus

mirror and look: your hair is no longer there, and your brow is bare.' But I do not know whether my hair is still there or has gone; I do know that the closer Fate is, the more fitting it is for the old man to enjoy his fun and games.

8

I do not care about the wealth of Gyges, lord of Sardis: I have never envied him, and I have no grudge against tyrants.[1] I care about drenching my beard with perfumes, I care about garlanding my head with roses; I care about today: who knows tomorrow[2]? So while skies are still cloudless drink, play dice and pour libation to Lyaeus,[3] lest some disease come and say, 'You must not drink.'

[1] Vv. 1–4 are based on Archil. 19. 1–3.   [2] The version in the *Palatine Anthology* ends here.   [3] See 4 n.4.

9

ἄφες με, τοὺς θεούς σοι,
πιεῖν, πιεῖν ἀμυστί·
θέλω, θέλω μανῆναι.
ἐμαίνετ' Ἀλκμαίων τε
5 χὠ λευκόπους Ὀρέστης
τὰς μητέρας κτανόντες·
ἐγὼ δὲ μηδένα κτάς,
πιὼν δ' ἐρυθρὸν οἶνον
θέλω, θέλω μανῆναι.
10 ἐμαίνετ' Ἡρακλῆς πρὶν
δεινὴν κλονῶν φαρέτρην
καὶ τόξον Ἰφίτειον.
ἐμαίνετο πρὶν Αἴας
μετ' ἀσπίδος κραδαίνων
15 τὴν Ἕκτορος μάχαιραν·
ἐγὼ δ' ἔχων κύπελλον
καὶ στέμμα τοῦτο χαίτης,
οὐ τόξον, οὐ μάχαιραν,
θέλω, θέλω μανῆναι.

titulus: εἰς ἑαυτὸν μεμεθυσμένον   16 Stephanus: ἔχω cod.
17 Stephanus: χαῖτες cod.

10

τί σοι θέλεις ποιήσω,
τί σοι, λάλη χελιδόν;
τὰ ταρσά σευ τὰ κοῦφα
θέλεις λαβὼν ψαλίξω;
5 ἢ μᾶλλον ἔνδοθέν σευ
τὴν γλῶσσαν, ὡς ὁ Τηρεὺς
ἐκεῖνος, ἐκθερίξω;
τί μευ καλῶν ὀνείρων

9

Allow me, in heaven's name, to drink, to drink without stopping for breath: I want to be mad, I want to be mad. Alcmaeon and white-footed Orestes went mad when they had killed their mothers [1]: I have killed no-one, but after drinking the red wine I want to be mad, I want to be mad. Heracles went mad once, brandishing his terrible quiver and the bow of Iphitus [2]; Ajax went mad once, waving Hector's sword with his shield [3]: I have my cup and this garland on my hair, no bow and no sword, and I want to be mad, I want to be mad.

[1] Alcmaeon, son of Amphiaraus and Eriphyle, killed his traitorous mother on his father's instructions; Orestes killed Clytemnestra to avenge his father Agamemnon; 'white-footed' perhaps because barefoot in his madness. [2] Heracles killed Iphitus and took his bow, later using it to kill his wife Megara and their children.   [3] Ajax's shield was famous (*Il.* 7. 219); after fighting against him Hector gave him his sword (*Il.* 7. 303). Ajax went mad when the armour of Achilles was awarded to Odysseus.

10

What shall I do with you, what shall I do with you, chattering swallow? Shall I take your nimble wings and clip them with my scissors or cut out your tongue like Tereus [1]? Why did you snatch away

[1] Tereus cut off the tongue of his sister-in-law Philomela so that she could not tell that he had raped her; she was later turned into a swallow.

ὑπορθρίαισι φωναῖς
10 ἀφήρπασας Βάθυλλον;

titulus: τοῦ αὐτοῦ εἰς χελιδόνα   2 Stephanus: λάλευ cod.

11

Ἔρωτα κήρινόν τις
νεηνίης ἐπώλει·
ἐγὼ δέ οἱ παραστὰς
'πόσου θέλεις' ἔφην 'σοὶ
5 τὸ τευχθέν ἐκπρίωμαι;'
ὁ δ' εἶπε δωριάζων
'λάβ' αὐτόν, ὁππόσου λῆς.
ὅπως ⟨δ'⟩ ἂν ἐκμάθῃς πᾶν,
οὐκ εἰμὶ κηροτέχνας,
10 ἀλλ' οὐ θέλω συνοικεῖν
Ἔρωτι παντορέκτᾳ.'
'δὸς οὖν, δὸς αὐτὸν ἡμῖν
δραχμῆς, καλὸν σύνευνον.'
Ἔρως, σὺ δ' εὐθέως με
15 πύρωσον· εἰ δὲ μή, σὺ
κατὰ φλογὸς τακήσῃ.

titulus: τοῦ αὐτοῦ εἰς Ἔρωτα κήρινον   5 τυχθέν in marg.
cod.   8 suppl. Faber   νιν, πᾶν supra, cod.   9 Barnes:
-νης cod.   11 παντορέκτη ex -α corr. cod.

12

οἱ μὲν καλὴν Κυβήβην
τὸν ἡμίθηλυν Ἄττιν
ἐν οὔρεσιν βοῶντα
λέγουσιν ἐκμανῆναι.
5 οἱ δὲ Κλάρου παρ' ὄχθαις

Bathyllus from my lovely dreams with your early morning songs?

11

A youth was selling a wax Love. I stopped by his side and said, 'How much do you want for your handiwork?' He replied in Doric, 'Take him at your price. To tell you the whole story, I am no wax-modeller: it's just that I have no wish to live with Love, the villain.' 'Then give me him, give me him for a drachma: he'll make a fine bedfellow.' Love, set me on fire at once: if you don't, you will melt in flames.

12

Some say half-woman Attis went mad shouting for lovely Cybebe in the mountains.[1] Some drink the

[1] A devotee of Cybebe or Cybele, the Great Mother, Attis castrated himself in the mountains of Phrygia.

δαφνηφόροιο Φοίβου
λάλον πιόντες ὕδωρ
μεμηνότες βοῶσιν.
ἐγὼ δὲ τοῦ Λυαίου
10 καὶ τοῦ μύρου κορεσθεὶς
καὶ τῆς ἐμῆς ἑταίρης
θέλω, θέλω μανῆναι.

titulus: εἰς Ἄττιν τοῦ αὐτοῦ

13

θέλω, θέλω φιλῆσαι.
ἔπειθ' Ἔρως φιλεῖν με·
ἐγὼ δ' ἔχων νόημα
ἄβουλον οὐκ ἐπείσθην.
5 ὁ δ' εὐθὺ τόξον ἄρας
καὶ χρυσέην φαρέτρην
μάχῃ με προὐκαλεῖτο.
κἀγὼ λαβὼν ἐπ' ὤμων
θώρηχ', ὅπως Ἀχιλλεύς,
10 καὶ δοῦρα καὶ βοείην
ἐμαρνάμην Ἔρωτι.
ἔβαλλ', ἐγὼ δ' ἔφευγον.
ὡς δ' οὐκέτ' εἶχ' ὀιστούς,
ἤσχαλλεν, εἶτ' ἑαυτὸν
15 ἀφῆκεν εἰς βέλεμνον·
μέσος δὲ καρδίης μευ
ἔδυνε καί μ' ἔλυσεν·
μάτην δ' ἔχω βοείην·
τί γὰρ βάλωμεν ἔξω,
20 μάχης ἔσω μ' ἐχούσης;

titulus: τοῦ αὐτοῦ εἰς Ἔρωτα   1 secl. West   6 Stephanus: -σίην cod.   16 Stephanus: κραδίης cod.   18 'post vers. excidit aliquid velut καὶ δοῦρα καὶ θώρηκα' Crusius   19 Stephanus: βάλομεν cod.

babbling water of bay-bearing Phoebus by the slopes of Claros [2] and go mad and shout. I want to have my fill of Lyaeus [3] and perfume and my girl and to go mad, I want to go mad.

[2] Oracle of Apollo near Colophon in Asia Minor: its well provided the priest with inspiration.   [3] See 4 n.4.

13

I want to love, I want to love. [1] Love urged me to love, but I was a fool and was not persuaded. So he immediately took up his bow and golden quiver and challenged me to a fight. I hung my corslet from my shoulders, like Achilles, and took my spears and ox-hide shield and began fighting with Love. He shot and I ran; when he had no arrows left, he was distressed; then he hurled himself for a javelin, pierced the middle of my heart and loosened my limbs. My shield (and spears and corslet) [2] are useless: why hurl weapons from me when the fight is within me?

[1] West deletes the line.   [2] Crusius' supplement.

14

εἰ φύλλα πάντα δένδρων
ἐπίστασαι κατειπεῖν,
εἰ κύματ' οἶδας εὑρεῖν
τὰ τῆς ὅλης θαλάσσης,
5 σὲ τῶν ἐμῶν ἐρώτων
μόνον ποῶ λογιστήν.
πρῶτον μὲν ἐξ Ἀθηνῶν
ἔρωτας εἴκοσιν θὲς
καὶ πεντεκαίδεκ' ἄλλους.
10 ἔπειτα δ' ἐκ Κορίνθου
θὲς ὁρμαθοὺς ἐρώτων·
Ἀχαΐης γάρ ἐστιν,
ὅπου καλαὶ γυναῖκες.
τίθει δὲ Λεσβίους μοι
15 καὶ μέχρι τῶν Ἰώνων
καὶ Καρίης Ῥόδου τε
δισχιλίους ἔρωτας·
τί φής; ἐκηριώθης;
οὔπω Σύρους ἔλεξα,
20 οὔπω πόθους Κανώβου,
οὐ τῆς ἄπαντ' ἐχούσης
Κρήτης, ὅπου πόλεσσιν
Ἔρως ἐποργιάζει.
τί σοι θέλεις ἀριθμῶ
25 καὶ τοὺς Γαδείρων ἐκτός,
τῶν Βακτρίων τε κινδῶν
ψυχῆς ἐμῆς ἔρωτας;

titulus: τοῦ αὐτοῦ εἰς ἔρωτας   3s. Davisius: κυματῶδες . . .
τὸ cod.   16 Stephanus: Καρίην Ῥόδον τε cod.   18 Bergk:
ἀεὶ κηρωθείς cod.   ἄγει καρωθείς West   22 in marg. Ῥώμης
cod.   24 Scaliger: ἀριθμεῖν cod.   26 τοὺς Brunck

14

If you can count all the leaves of the trees or find
the total of the waves in the whole sea, then I
appoint you sole computer of my loves. First enter
twenty loves from Athens, plus fifteen; next, whole
series of loves from Corinth: it is in Achaea, where
women are beautiful.[1] Enter my loves from Lesbos
and all the way to Ionia, Caria and Rhodes, two
thousand. What's that? You're dazed [2]? I haven't yet
mentioned Syria or the passions of Canobus [3] or of
Crete, which has everything, where Love holds his
revels in the cities. Why should I number my heart's
loves beyond Cadiz or those in Bactria and India?

[1] Corinth was in the Achaean Confederacy from 243 B.C.
till its destruction in 146 B.C.; refounded in 44 B.C., it
became capital of the province of Achaea; cf. *Iliad* 3. 75, 258
'Achaea of the beautiful women'.   [2] Text and translation
doubtful.   [3] Or Canopus, town in Egypt near Alex-
andria.

15

ἐρασμίη πέλεια,
πόθεν, πόθεν πέτασαι;
πόθεν μύρων τοσούτων
ἐπ' ἠέρος θέουσα
5 πνέεις τε καὶ ψεκάζεις;
τίς εἶ, τί σοι μέλει δέ;
''Ανακρέων μ' ἔπεμψε
πρὸς παῖδα, πρὸς Βάθυλλον,
τὸν ἄρτι τῶν ἀπάντων
10 κρατοῦντα καὶ τύραννον.
πέπρακέ μ' ἡ Κυθήρη
λαβοῦσα μικρὸν ὕμνον·
ἐγὼ δ' 'Ανακρέοντι
διακονῶ τοσαῦτα.
15 καὶ νῦν οἴας ἐκείνου
ἐπιστολὰς κομίζω·
καί φησιν εὐθέως με
ἐλευθέρην ποιήσειν.
ἐγὼ δέ, κἢν ἀφῇ με,
20 δούλη μενῶ παρ' αὐτῷ.
τί γάρ με δεῖ πέτασθαι
ὄρη τε καὶ κατ' ἀγροὺς
καὶ δένδρεσιν καθίζειν
φαγοῦσαν ἄγριόν τι;
25 τὰ νῦν ἔδω μὲν ἄρτον
ἀφαρπάσασα χειρῶν
'Ανακρέοντος αὐτοῦ.
πιεῖν δέ μοι δίδωσι
τὸν οἶνον, ὃν προπίνει,
30 πιοῦσα δ' ἀγχορεύω
καὶ δεσπότην κρέκοντα
πτεροῖσι συγκαλύπτω·
κοιμωμένου δ' ἐπ' αὐτῷ

15

Lovely pigeon, where, where have you flown from? As you race on the air you smell of perfumes, you rain perfumes: where did they all come from? Who are you and what is your business?

'Anacreon sent me to a boy, to Bathyllus, now lord and master of all. Cythere [1] sold me in return for a little song; and it is for Anacreon that I perform tasks like this. And what letters I am carrying from him now! And he says he will give me my freedom immediately; but if he does release me, I shall stay with him as his slave. Why should I fly over mountains and fields and sit on trees after eating some wild food? As things are, I eat bread which I snatch from Anacreon's own hands, and for drink he gives me the wine which he drinks to his loves; after drinking I begin to dance, and while my master plays his lyre I shade him with my wings. When he goes to

[1] See 4 n.3.

τῷ βαρβίτῳ καθεύδω.
35 ἔχεις ἅπαντ'· ἄπελθε·
λαλιστέραν μ' ἔθηκας,
ἄνθρωπε, καὶ κορώνης.'

titulus: τοῦ αὐτοῦ εἰς περιστέραν   5 Stephanus: πνίεις cod.
6 Brunck: τίς ἔστι σοι cod.   10 τυράννων West   11 Faber:
με cod.   15 ὁρᾷς Stephanus   30 Hanssen: δ' ἂν χορεύσω
cod.   31 Wahl: ἀνακρέοντ(α) cod.   32 Pauw: σὺν καλύψω
cod., συσκιασω supra.   33 Bergk: -μένη cod.

16

ἄγε, ζωγράφων ἄριστε,
γράφε, ζωγράφων ἄριστε,
' Ροδίης κοίρανε τέχνης,
ἀπεοῦσαν, ὡς ἂν εἴπω,
5 γράφε τὴν ἐμὴν ἑταίρην.
γράφε μοι τρίχας τὸ πρῶτον
ἁπαλάς τε καὶ μελαίνας·
ὁ δὲ κηρὸς ἂν δύνηται,
γράφε καὶ μύρου πνεούσας.
10 γράφε δ' ἐξ ὅλης παρειῆς
ὑπὸ πορφυραῖσι χαίταις
ἐλεφάντινον μέτωπον.
τὸ μεσόφρυον δὲ μή μοι
διάκοπτε μήτε μίσγε,
15 ἐχέτω δ', ὅπως ἐκείνη,
τὸ λεληθότως σύνοφρυ,
βλεφάρων ἴτυν κελαινήν.
τὸ δὲ βλέμμα νῦν ἀληθῶς
ἀπὸ τοῦ πυρὸς ποίησον,
20 ἅμα γλαυκόν, ὡς Ἀθήνης,
ἅμα δ' ὑγρόν, ὡς Κυθήρης.
γράφε ῥῖνα καὶ παρειὰς
ῥόδα τῷ γάλακτι μίξας·

bed, I sleep on the lyre itself. There, you know it all. Go away: you have made me more talkative than a crow, fellow.'

16

Come, best of painters! Paint, best of painters, master of the Rhodian art [1]! Paint my absent girl according to my instructions. First paint her soft black hair; and if the wax [2] is able, make it smell of perfume. Paint her whole cheek and then her ivory brow beneath her dark hair. Do not part her eyebrows nor run them together, but let her keep, as in real life, the black rims of her eyes meeting imperceptibly. Now make her eyes as they are, from fire, both flashing, like Athena's, and moist, like Cythere's.[3] Paint her nose and her cheeks, mingling

---

[1] Painting.   [2] See 3 n.2.   [3] See 4 n.3.

γράφε χεῖλος, οἷα Πειθοῦς,
25 προκαλούμενον φίλημα.
τρυφεροῦ δ' ἔσω γενείου
περὶ λυγδίνῳ τραχήλῳ
Χάριτες πέτοιντο πᾶσαι.
στόλισον τὸ λοιπὸν αὐτὴν
30 ὑποπορφύροισι πέπλοις,
διαφαινέτω δὲ σαρκῶν
ὀλίγον, τὸ σῶμ' ἐλέγχον.
ἀπέχει· βλέπω γὰρ αὐτήν·
τάχα, κηρέ, καὶ λαλήσεις.

titulus: τοῦ αὐτοῦ εἰς κόρην   2 del. Bergk   3 Steph.: ῥοδέης
cod.   16 Steph.: -οφρυν cod.   22 Steph.: ῥῖνας cod.

17   γράφε μοι Βάθυλλον οὕτω,
          τὸν ἑταῖρον, ὡς διδάσκω·
          λιπαρὰς κόμας ποίησον,
          τὰ μὲν ἔνδοθεν μελαίνας,
5   τὰ δ' ἐς ἄκρον ἡλιώσας·
          ἕλικας δ' ἐλευθέρους μοι
          πλοκάμων ἄτακτα συνθεὶς
          ἄφες, ὡς θέλωσι, κεῖσθαι.
          ἁπαλὸν δὲ καὶ δροσῶδες
10   στεφέτω μέτωπον ὀφρὺς
          κυανωτέρη δρακόντων.
          μέλαν ὄμμα γοργὸν ἔστω
          κεκερασμένον γαλήνῃ,
          τὸ μὲν ἐξ Ἄρεος ἕλκον,
15   τὸ δὲ τῆς καλῆς Κυθήρης,
          ἵνα τις τὸ μὲν φοβῆται,
          τὸ δ' ἀπ' ἐλπίδος κρεμᾶται.
          ῥοδέην δ' ὁποῖα μῆλον

roses and cream. Paint her lips like Persuasion's, provoking kisses. Under her soft chin let all the Graces fly around her marble-white neck. Dress the rest of her in robes of light purple, but let her skin show through a little to prove the quality of her body. Enough—I can see her! Soon, wax, you will be talking too.

17

Paint my beloved Bathyllus according to my prescription: make his hair shine, dark beneath but with the ends lightened by the sun; add curling locks falling freely in disorder and let them lie where they wish. Let his soft dewy forehead be garlanded with eyebrows darker than snakes. Let his black eyes be a mixture of ferocity and serenity, taking their ferocity from Ares, their serenity from beautiful Cythere,[1] so that he may inspire terror and also hopeful suspense. Make his downy cheek as rosy as an apple,

[1] See 4 n.3.

χνοίην ποίει παρειήν·
20 ἐρύθημα δ' ὡς ἂν Αἰδοῦς,
δύνασ' εἰ βαλεῖν, ποίησον.
τὸ δὲ χεῖλος οὐκέτ' οἶδα
τίνι μοι τρόπῳ ποιήσεις
ἀπαλὸν γέμον τε πειθοῦς·
25 τὸ δὲ πᾶν ὁ κηρὸς αὐτὸς
ἐχέτω λαλῶν σιωπῇ.
μετὰ δὲ πρόσωπον ἔστω
τὸν Ἀδώνιδος παρελθὼν
ἐλεφάντινος τράχηλος.
30 μεταμάζιον δὲ ποίει
διδύμας τε χεῖρας Ἑρμοῦ,
Πολυδεύκεος δὲ μηρούς,
Διονυσίην δὲ νηδύν·
ἀπαλῶν δ' ὕπερθε μηρῶν,
35 μαλερὸν τὸ πῦρ ἐχόντων,
ἀφελῆ ποίησον αἰδῶ
Παφίην θέλουσαν ἤδη.
φθονερὴν ἔχεις δὲ τέχνην,
ὅτι μὴ τὰ νῶτα δεῖξαι
40 δύνασαι· τὰ δ' ἦν ἀμείνω.
τί με δεῖ πόδας διδάσκειν;
λάβε μισθόν, ὅσσον εἴπῃς.
τὸν Ἀπόλλωνα δὲ τοῦτον
καθελὼν ποίει Βάθυλλον·
45 ἢν δ' ἐς Σάμον ποτ' ἔλθῃς,
γράφε Φοῖβον ἐκ Βαθύλλου.

titulus: εἰς νεώτερον Βάθυλλον   4, 5 Stephanus: τὰς μὲν . . .
τὰς δὲ cod.   18 Bergk: ῥοδινὴν, supra ἐ, cod.   21 Rose:
δύνασαι cod.   24 Stephanus: τὸ cod.   28 Salmasius: τὸ
δ' Ἀ. παρῆλθ cod.   35 μαλερὸν 'sunt qui hic legant'
Stephanus: μηρῶν cod.   39 Stephanus: ὅτι μοι cod.

and, if possible, add a blush like that of Modesty. I do not yet know how you are to make his lip soft and full of persuasion: but let the wax [2] itself have everything, talking silently. After his face make an ivory neck finer than that of Adonis. Give him the chest and two hands of Hermes, the thighs of Polydeuces, the belly of Dionysus [3]; above his soft thighs, thighs with raging fire in them, put a simple member that already desires the Paphian. [4] But your art is grudging: you cannot show his back; that would have been better. Why should I describe the feet? Take your fee, as much as you ask. Take [5] down this Apollo and create Bathyllus; and if ever you come to Samos, paint Phoebus from Bathyllus.

[2] See 3 n.2.　　[3] Adonis the type of youthful beauty; Hermes the ideal young athlete of the sculptors; Polydeuces (or Pollux) the boxer; Dionysus the youthful god of later Greek art.　　[4] Aphrodite, who rose from the sea near Paphos in Cyprus.　　[5] The last four lines introduce metrical variations and may be a later addition: 'this Apollo' is presumably a picture which is to be replaced by the painting of Bathyllus.

18

δότε μοι, δότ᾽, ὦ γυναῖκες,
Βρομίου πιεῖν ἀμυστί·
ἀπὸ καύματος γὰρ ἤδη
προδοθεὶς ἀναστενάζω.
5 δότε δ᾽ ἀνθέων ἐκείνου
στεφάνους, δόθ᾽, ὡς πυκάζω
τὰ μέτωπά μου 'πίκαυτα·
τὸ δὲ καῦμα τῶν Ἐρώτων,
κραδίῃ, τίνι σκεπάζω;
10 παρὰ τὴν σκιὴν Βαθύλλου
καθίσω· καλὸν τὸ δένδρον,
ἀπαλὰς δ᾽ ἔσεισε χαίτας
μαλακωτάτῳ κλαδίσκῳ·
παρὰ δ᾽ αὐτὸν †ἐρεθίζει†
15 πηγὴ ῥέουσα πειθοῦς.
τίς ἂν οὖν ὁρῶν παρέλθοι
καταγώγιον τοιοῦτο;

titulus: (1) ἄλλο τοῦ αὐτοῦ ἐρωτικόν (2) τοῦ αὐτοῦ ἐρωτικὸν
ᾠδάριον   1 Stephanus: δότε γ. cod.   4 προδοθεὶς ex
πυρωθεὶς corr. cod.   πυρεθεὶς Edmonds   6 Bergk: σ. δ᾽
οἴους π. cod.   7 Edmonds: 'πικαίει cod.   post 9 novum
carmen indicat librarius se ipsum corrigens, add. tit. ἄλλο
εἰς τὸν αὐτόν (sc. Βάθυλλον: cf. 17 tit.!): perperam
11 Salmasius: κάθισο cod.   14 αὐτὸ ψιθυρίζει Bergk

19

αἱ Μοῦσαι τὸν Ἔρωτα
δήσασαι στεφάνοισι
τῷ Κάλλει παρέδωκαν·
καὶ νῦν ἡ Κυθέρεια
5 ζητεῖ λύτρα φέρουσα
λύσασθαι τὸν Ἔρωτα.

18

Ladies, give me, give me some Bromian [1] to drink without stopping for breath, for I am already betrayed [2] by the heat and am groaning. Give me garlands of his flowers; give me them so that I may wreath my burned brow. But, my heart, with what shall I ward off the heat of the Loves? I [3] shall sit in the shade of Bathyllus: that is a fine tree, and it shakes its soft tresses on the tenderest of branches; and nearby (whispers?) a spring that flows with persuasion. Who could see such a resting-place and pass it by?

[1] Wine: the Bromian is Dionysus.   [2] Perhaps 'fevered'.
[3] The scribe of our ms. corrected himself to indicate the beginning of a new poem here; many editors have mistakenly followed suit; for Bathyllus' hair and mouth ('full of persuasion') see 17. 3 ff., 22 ff.

19

The Muses tied Love with garlands and handed him over to Beauty. And now Cythereia [1] brings a ransom and seeks to have him released. But if he *is*

[1] Cf. 4 n.3: Aphrodite, mother of Love.

κἂν λύσῃ δέ τις αὐτόν,
οὐκ ἔξεισι, μενεῖ δέ·
δουλεύειν δεδίδακται.

titulus: ἄλλο εἰς Ἔρωτα, τοῦ αὐτοῦ   8 Stephanus: μένει cod.

20

ἡδυμελὴς Ἀνακρέων,
ἡδυμελὴς δὲ Σαπφώ·
Πινδαρικὸν δέ μοι μέλος
συγκεράσας τις ἐγχέοι.
5 τὰ τρία ταῦτά μοι δοκεῖ
καὶ Διόνυσος ἐλθὼν
καὶ Παφίη λιπαρόχροος
καὐτὸς Ἔρως ἂν ἐκπιεῖν.

titulus: ἄλλο   3 Bergk: τόδε cod. δέ τι Hermann
6 Hermann: εἰσελθὼν cod.   8 Hermann: κὰν ἐπίειν cod.

21

ἡ γῆ μέλαινα πίνει,
πίνει δένδρεα δ᾽ αὐτήν.
πίνει θάλασσ᾽ ἀναύρους,
ὁ δ᾽ ἥλιος θάλασσαν,
5 τὸν δ᾽ ἥλιον σελήνη·
τί μοι μάχεσθ᾽, ἑταῖροι,
καὐτῷ θέλοντι πίνειν;

titulus: ἄλλο   2 δὲ δένδρε᾽ αὐτήν Stephanus   δὲ δένδρε᾽ αὖ
γῆν Bergk   3 Heskin (cf. 31. 4): θάλασσα δ᾽ αὔρας cod.

released, he will not leave but will stay: he has learned to be her slave.

20

Anacreon is a sweet singer, Sappho a sweet singer; let them be mixed with a song of Pindar [1] and poured in my cup. I think that if Dionysus came and the Paphian [2] with her gleaming skin and Love himself, they would drink down this trio.

[1] With ref. to Pindar's encomia (e.g. fr. 123 on Theoxenus, 124a for Thrasybulus).　[2] See 17 n.4.

21

The black earth drinks, the trees drink it. The sea drinks the torrents, the sun the sea, the moon the sun. Why fight with me, my friends, if I too want to drink?

22

ἡ Ταντάλου ποτ᾽ ἔστη
λίθος Φρυγῶν ἐν ὄχθαις,
καὶ παῖς ποτ᾽ ὄρνις ἔπτη
Πανδίονος χελιδών.
5 ἐγὼ δ᾽ ἔσοπτρον εἴην,
ὅπως ἀεὶ βλέπῃς με·
ἐγὼ χιτὼν γενοίμην,
ὅπως ἀεὶ φορῇς με.
ὕδωρ θέλω γενέσθαι,
10 ὅπως σε χρῶτα λούσω·
μύρον, γύναι, γενοίμην,
ὅπως ἐγώ σ᾽ ἀλείψω.
καὶ ταινίη δὲ μασθῷ
καὶ μάργαρον τραχήλῳ
15 καὶ σάνδαλον γενοίμην·
μόνον ποσὶν πάτει με.

titulus: ἄλλο εἰς κόρην   10 Stephanus: σεῦ cod.
12 Brunck: ἀλείφω cod.

23

θέλω λέγειν Ἀτρείδας,
θέλω δὲ Κάδμον ᾄδειν,
ἁ βάρβιτος δὲ χορδαῖς
Ἔρωτα μοῦνον ἠχεῖ.
5 ἤμειψα νεῦρα πρώην
καὶ τὴν λύρην ἅπασαν·
κἀγὼ μὲν ᾖδον ἄθλους
Ἡρακλέους· λύρη δὲ
Ἔρωτας ἀντεφώνει.

22

Once Tantalus' daughter [1] became a stone stand-ing among the Phrygian hills; once Pandion's daugh-ter [2] became a bird and flew, a swallow. If only I could be a mirror, so that you would always look at me; a robe, so that you would always wear me; water, that I might wash your skin; perfume, lady, that I might anoint you; a band for your breast, a pearl for your neck, a sandal—only you must trample me underfoot!

[1] Niobe.   [2] Philomela: see 10 n.1.

23

I wish to tell of the sons of Atreus, [1] I wish to sing of Cadmus; but my lyre-strings sing only of Love. The other day I changed the strings, indeed the whole lyre, and began singing of the labours of Heracles: but in answer the lyre sang of the Loves.

[1] Agamemnon and Menelaus; like Cadmus, heroes of epic.

10 χαίροιτε λοιπὸν ἡμῖν,
   ἥρωες· ἡ λύρη γὰρ
   μόνους Ἔρωτας ᾄδει.

titulus: εἰς κιθάραν τοῦ αὐτοῦ   3 ὁ β. Mehlhorn (cf. 15.
34)   11 Stephanus: ἔρωτες cod.

24

Φύσις κέρατα ταύροις,
ὁπλὰς δ᾽ ἔδωκεν ἵπποις,
ποδωκίην λαγωοῖς,
λέουσι χάσμ᾽ ὀδόντων,
5 τοῖς ἰχθύσιν τὸ νηκτόν,
τοῖς ὀρνέοις πέτασθαι,
τοῖς ἀνδράσιν φρόνημα,
γυναιξὶν οὐκ ἔτ᾽ εἶχεν.
τί οὖν; δίδωσι κάλλος
10 ἀντ᾽ ἀσπίδων ἁπασῶν,
ἀντ᾽ ἐγχέων ἁπάντων·
νικᾷ δὲ καὶ σίδηρον
καὶ πῦρ καλή τις οὖσα.

titulus: ἄλλο ἐρωτικόν

25

σὺ μέν, φίλη χελιδόν,
ἐτησίη μολοῦσα
θέρει πλέκεις καλιήν·
χειμῶνι δ᾽ εἰς ἄφαντος
5 ἢ Νεῖλον ἢ ᾽πὶ Μέμφιν.
Ἔρως δ᾽ ἀεὶ πλέκει μευ
ἐν καρδίῃ καλιήν·
Πόθος δ᾽ ὁ μὲν πτεροῦται,
ὁ δ᾽ ᾠόν ἐστιν ἀκμήν,
10 ὁ δ᾽ ἡμίλεπτος ἤδη·

So farewell, heroes [2]: my lyre sings only of the Loves.

[2] Or, keeping ms. reading, 'So welcome, Loves'.

24

Nature gave bulls horns, horses hooves, hares speed, lions a wide mouth full of teeth, fish power to swim, birds flight, men wisdom, women—she had nothing left. And so? She gives them beauty, strong as any shield, strong as any sword. A beautiful woman overcomes even steel or fire.

25

Dear swallow, you come every year and weave your nest in summer, but in winter you disappear, off to the Nile or Memphis; whereas Love is always weaving his nest in my heart: one Desire is getting his wings, another is still an egg, another is half-

βοὴ δὲ γίνετ᾽ αἰεὶ
κεχηνότων νεοττῶν·
Ἐρωτιδεῖς δὲ μικροὺς
οἱ μείζονες τρέφουσιν·
15 οἱ δὲ τραφέντες εὐθὺς
πάλιν κύουσιν ἄλλους.
τί μῆχος οὖν γένηται;
οὐ γὰρ σθένω τοσούτους
Ἔρωτας ἐκβοῆσαι.

titulus: τοῦ αὐτοῦ εἰς χελιδόνα   10 Stephanus: ἡμῖν ληπτὸς
cod.   11 Stephanus: ἀεὶ cod.   19 ἐκσοβῆσαι Pauw

26

σὺ μὲν λέγεις τὰ Θήβης,
ὁ δ᾽ αὖ Φρυγῶν αὐτάς,
ἐγὼ δ᾽ ἐμὰς ἁλώσεις.
οὐχ ἵππος ὤλεσέν με,
5 οὐ πεζός, οὐχὶ νῆες,
στρατὸς δὲ καινὸς ἄλλος
ἀπ᾽ ὀμμάτων με βάλλων.

titulus: ἄλλο ἐρωτικὸν ᾠδάριον

27

ἐν ἰσχίοις μὲν ἵπποι
πυρὸς χάραγμ᾽ ἔχουσιν,
καὶ Παρθίους τις ἄνδρας
ἐγνώρισεν τιάραις.
5 ἐγὼ δὲ τοὺς ἐρῶντας
ἰδὼν ἐπίσταμ᾽ εὐθύς·
ἔχουσι γάρ τι λεπτὸν
ψυχῆς ἔσω χάραγμα.

cum 26 in cod. coniunctum, seiunxit Stephanus

196

hatched already; and there is a continuous shouting from the wide-mouthed chicks; little baby Loves are fed by bigger ones, and when they are fully grown they immediately beget others in their turn. What remedy can there be? I have not the strength to shout down [1] all these Loves.

[1] Perhaps 'to chase them out by shouting'.

26

You tell the story of Thebes, another tells of the war-cries of the Phrygians,[1] I tell how I myself was captured. It was no horse [2] that destroyed me, no infantry, no fleet, but another strange kind of army, striking me with its eyes.

[1] I.e. the Trojans.   [2] As at Troy; or perhaps 'cavalry'.

27

Horses carry the mark of the fire [1] on their haunches; Parthians are recognized by their tiaras. I know lovers as soon as I see them: they carry a fine mark branded on their souls.

[1] I.e. of the branding iron.

28

ὁ ἀνὴρ ὁ τῆς Κυθήρης
παρὰ Λημνίαις καμίνοις
τὰ βέλη τὰ τῶν Ἐρώτων
ἐπόει λαβὼν σίδηρον·
5 ἀκίδας δ' ἔβαπτε Κύπρις
μέλι τὸ γλυκὺ λαβοῦσα·
ὁ δ' Ἔρως χολὴν ἔμισγε.
ὁ δ' Ἄρης ποτ' ἐξ αὐτῆς
στιβαρὸν δόρυ κραδαίνων
10 βέλος ηὐτέλιζ' Ἔρωτος·
ὁ δ' Ἔρως 'τόδ' ἐστίν' εἶπεν
'βαρύ· πειράσας νοήσεις.'
ἔλαβεν βέλεμνον Ἄρης·
ὑπεμειδίασε Κύπρις.
15 ὁ δ' Ἄρης ἀναστενάξας
'βαρύ' φησίν· 'ἆρον αὐτό.'
ὁ δ' Ἔρως 'ἔχ' αὐτό' φησίν.

titulus: ἄλλο τοῦ αὐτοῦ εἰς βέλος

29

χαλεπὸν τὸ μὴ φιλῆσαι,
χαλεπὸν δὲ καὶ φιλῆσαι,
χαλεπώτερον δὲ πάντων
ἀποτυγχάνειν φιλοῦντα.
5 γένος οὐδὲν εἰς Ἔρωτα·
σοφίη, τρόπος πατεῖται·
μόνον ἄργυρον βλέπουσιν.
ἀπόλοιτο πρῶτος αὐτὸς
ὁ τὸν ἄργυρον φιλήσας.
10 διὰ τοῦτον οὐκ ἀδελφός,
διὰ τοῦτον οὐ τοκῆες·
πόλεμοι, φόνοι δι' αὐτόν.

ANACREONTEA

28

Cythere's husband [1] was making the Loves'
weapons of iron in the forge of Lemnos; the Cy-
prian [2] was dipping the points in her sweet honey,
and Love was adding gall. One day Ares came in
from the battlefield brandishing his strong spear and
began to make fun of Love's weapon. Love said, 'This
one is heavy: try it and you will see.' Ares took the
javelin,[3] while the Cyprian smiled quietly; and with
a groan he said, 'It *is* heavy: take it back.' 'Keep it,'
said Love.[4]

[1] Hephaestus: Cythere = Aphrodite.   [2] Aphrodite.   [3] The
point is not clearly made: one would have expected Ares to
be wounded by Love's weapon.   [4] For the love of Ares
and Aphrodite see *Od*. 8. 266 ff.

29

It is hard not to fall in love, it is hard to fall in
love; but hardest of all is to fail in love. Lineage [1] is
nothing to Love, wisdom and character are trampled
underfoot. Money is the only thing they see. Damn
the man who first loved money! Thanks to it we lose
brothers and parents; thanks to it there are wars and

[1] Mehlhorn, with justification, thought that a new poem
begins here; lines 1–4 all have accent on the penultimate
syllable, an indication of late date.

τὸ δὲ χεῖρον· ὀλλύμεσθα
διὰ τοῦτον οἱ φιλοῦντες.

cum 28 in cod. coniunctum, seiunxit Stephanus

30

ἐδόκουν ὄναρ τροχάζειν
πτέρυγας φέρων ἐπ᾽ ὤμων·
ὁ δ᾽ Ἔρως ἔχων μόλιβδον
περὶ τοῖς καλοῖς ποδίσκοις
5 ἐδίωκε καὶ κίχανεν.
τί θέλει δ᾽ ὄναρ τόδ᾽ εἶναι;
δοκέω δ᾽ ἔγωγε πολλοῖς
ἐν ἔρωσί με πλακέντα
διολισθάνειν μὲν ἄλλους,
10 ἑνὶ τῷδε συνδεθῆναι.

titulus: τοῦ αὐτοῦ ὄναρ   6 Zeune: τὸ δ᾽ ὄναρ εἶναι cod.
9 Stephanus: ἄλλοις cod.   10 ἑνί τῳ δὲ Pauw

31

ὑακινθίνῃ με ῥάβδῳ
χαλεπῶς Ἔρως ῥαπίζων
ἐκέλευε συντροχάζειν.
διὰ δ᾽ ὀξέων μ᾽ ἀναύρων
5 ξυλόχων τε καὶ φαράγγων
τροχάοντα τεῖρεν ἱδρώς·
κραδίη δὲ ῥινὸς ἄχρις
ἀνέβαινε, κἂν ἀπέσβην.
ὁ δ᾽ Ἔρως †μέτωπα σείων†
10 ἁπαλοῖς πτεροῖσιν εἶπεν·
‘ σὺ γὰρ οὐ δύνῃ φιλῆσαι;’

titulus: ἄλλο ἐρωτικόν   2 Stephanus: χαλεπὸς cod.   Brunck:
βαδίζων cod.   6 Salmasius: πεῖρεν cod.

murders; and, worst of all, thanks to it we lovers are destroyed.

30

In a dream I seemed to be running, with wings on my shoulders, and Love, with shoes of lead on his pretty feet, was pursuing me and catching me up. What is the meaning of this dream? I think it means that though I have been entangled in many loves and have wriggled free from all the others, I am caught fast in this one.

31

Love, beating me cruelly with a rod tied round with hyacinths,[1] ordered me to run by his side; and as I ran through fierce torrents and thickets and gullies the sweat distressed me, my heart climbed to my nose and I might have perished; but Love fanned [2] my brow with his tender wings and said, 'Can't you love, then?'

[1] Lit. 'with hyacinth rod'; cf. Aphrodite's hyacinth fields at Anacr. 346 fr. 1.   [2] Text and translation doubtful.

32

ἐπὶ μυρσίναις τερείναις
ἐπὶ λωτίναις τε ποίαις
στορέσας θέλω προπίνειν.
ὁ δ᾽ Ἔρως χιτῶνα δήσας
5 ὑπὲρ αὐχένος παπύρῳ
μέθυ μοι διακονείτω·
τροχὸς ἅρματος γὰρ οἷα
βίοτος τρέχει κυλισθείς,
ὀλίγη δὲ κεισόμεσθα
10 κόνις ὀστέων λυθέντων.
τί σε δεῖ λίθον μυρίζειν;
τί δὲ γῇ χέειν μάταια;
ἐμὲ μᾶλλον, ὡς ἔτι ζῶ,
μύρισον, ῥόδοις δὲ κρᾶτα
15 πύκασον, κάλει δ᾽ ἑταίρην·
πρίν, Ἔρως, ἐκεῖ μ᾽ ἀπελθεῖν
ὑπὸ νερτέρων χορείας,
σκεδάσαι θέλω μερίμνας.

titulus: ἄλλο ἐρωτικὸν τοῦ αὐτοῦ   6 Stephanus: διακονεῖτο
cod.   7 Stephanus: γὰρ ἅρματος cod.   12 Stephanus:
καίειν cod.

33

μεσονυκτίοις ποτ᾽ ὥραις,
στρέφετ᾽ ἡνίκ᾽ Ἄρκτος ἤδη
κατὰ χεῖρα τὴν Βοώτου,
μερόπων δὲ φῦλα πάντα
5 κέαται κόπῳ δαμέντα,
τότ᾽ Ἔρως ἐπισταθείς μευ
θυρέων ἔκοπτ᾽ ὀχῆας.
‘τίς’ ἔφην ‘θύρας ἀράσσει
κατά μευ σχίσας ὀνείρους;’

32

I want to make a couch of soft myrtles and lotus plants and drink to my friends; let Love tie his tunic at his neck with papyrus cord and serve me with wine: for life rolls swiftly on like a chariot-wheel, and we shall lie, a handful of dust, when our bones have been loosened.[1] Why perfume a stone? Why pour wine uselessly for soil? No, perfume me while I am still alive, garland my head with roses, summon my girl: before I depart, Love, to join the dances of the dead, I want to scatter my cares.[2]

[1] Variation on Homer's 'his limbs were loosened (in death)'. [2] Strongly influenced by Theognis, e.g. 568, 878, 883.

33

Once in the middle of the night, at the hour when the Bear[1] is already turning by the Ploughman's hand[2] and all the tribes of mortals lie overcome by exhaustion, Love stood at my bolted door and began knocking. 'Who's banging my door?' I said: 'You've

[1] The Great Bear: the Wain, Plough or Dipper. [2] In the constellation Bootes: cf. *Il.* 18. 487 ff., *Od.* 5. 272 ff.

10 ὁ δ' Ἔρως ' ἄνοιγε ' φησίν·
  ' βρέφος εἰμί, μὴ φόβησαι·
  βρέχομαι δὲ κἀσέληνον
  κατὰ νύκτα πεπλάνημαι.'
  ἐλέησα ταῦτ' ἀκούσας,

15 ἀνὰ δ' εὐθὺ λύχνον ἅψας
  ἀνέῳξα καὶ βρέφος μὲν
  ἐσορῶ φέροντα τόξον
  πτέρυγάς τε καὶ φαρέτρην·
  παρὰ δ' ἱστίην καθίξας

20 παλάμαισι χεῖρας αὐτοῦ
  ἀνέθαλπον, ἐκ δὲ χαίτης
  ἀπέθλιβον ὑγρὸν ὕδωρ.
  ὁ δ', ἐπεὶ κρύος μεθῆκε,
  ' φέρε ' φησί ' πειράσωμεν

25 τόδε τόξον, εἴ τι μοι νῦν
  βλάβεται βραχεῖσα νευρή.'
  τανύει δὲ καί με τύπτει
  μέσον ἧπαρ, ὥσπερ οἶστρος.
  ἀνὰ δ' ἄλλεται καχάζων·

30 ' ξένε ' δ' εἶπε ' συγχάρηθι·
  κέρας ἀβλαβὲς μὲν ἡμῖν,
  σὺ δὲ καρδίαν πονήσεις.'

titulus: ἄλλο   2 Bergk: στρεφέτην ὅτ' cod.   9 Stephanus:
σχίζεις cod.   19 καθίσσας Barnes   20 Stephanus: παλάμας
τε cod.   25 Stephanus: ἔστι cod.   31 Bergk: μὲν ἐμοὶ cod.
μένει μοι Michelangeli

34   μακαρίζομέν σε, τέττιξ,
         ὅτε δενδρέων ἐπ' ἄκρων
         ὀλίγην δρόσον πεπωκὼς
         βασιλεὺς ὅπως ἀείδεις.
       5 σὰ γάρ ἐστι κεῖνα πάντα,

shattered my dreams.' Love said, 'Open up! I'm a baby: don't be afraid. I am getting wet, and I have been wandering about in the moonless night.' When I heard this I felt sorry for him and immediately lit a lamp and opened the door and saw a baby with bow, wings and quiver. I made him sit by the hearth, warmed his hands in my palms and squeezed the water from his hair. When the cold had relaxed its grip, he said, 'Come, let's try this bow to see if the string has been at all damaged by the rain.' He drew it and hit me right in the heart,[3] like a stinging gadfly; and he leaped up chuckling and said, 'Stranger, rejoice with me: my bow is undamaged; but your heart will be sore.'

[3] Lit. 'in the middle of the liver'.

34

We count you blessed, cicada, when on the tree-tops, having drunk a little dew, you sing like a king: you own everything that you see in the fields, every-

ὁπόσα βλέπεις ἐν ἀγροῖς
χὠπόσα φέρουσιν ὗλαι.
σὺ δὲ †φιλία† γεωργῶν,
ἀπὸ μηδενός τι βλάπτων·
10 σὺ δὲ τίμιος βροτοῖσιν
θέρεος γλυκὺς προφήτης·
φιλέουσι μέν σε Μοῦσαι,
φιλέει δὲ Φοῖβος αὐτός,
λιγυρὴν δ' ἔδωκεν οἴμην·
15 τὸ δὲ γῆρας οὔ σε τείρει,
σοφέ, γηγενής, φίλυμνε·
ἀπαθής, ἀναιμόσαρκε,
σχεδὸν εἶ θεοῖς ὅμοιος.

titulus: ἄλλο· εἰς τέττιγα ᾠδάριον   5 Stephanus: καινὰ
cod.   7 χὠρόσα Barnes: κορόσα cod.   8 φείδεαι West
15 Stephanus: γέρας εὖσε τηρεῖ cod.   16 Stephanus: γηγενῆ
φίλυπνε cod.   17 Stephanus: ἀπαθὲς cod.

35

Ἔρως ποτ' ἐν ῥόδοισι
κοιμωμένην μέλιτταν
οὐκ εἶδεν, ἀλλ' ἐτρώθη·
τὸν δάκτυλον παταχθεὶς
5 τᾶς χειρὸς ὠλόλυξε.
δραμὼν δὲ καὶ πετασθεὶς
πρὸς τὴν καλὴν Κυθήρην
'ὄλωλα, μῆτερ,' εἶπεν,
'ὄλωλα κἀποθνήσκω·
10 ὄφις μ' ἔτυψε μικρὸς
πτερωτός, ὃν καλοῦσιν
μέλιτταν οἱ γεωργοί.'
ἁ δ' εἶπεν· 'εἰ τὸ κέντρον
πονεῖ τὸ τᾶς μελίττας,

thing that the woods produce. You (spare?) farmers, robbing none of them. You are honoured by mortals as the sweet prophet of summer. The Muses love you and Phoebus himself loves you and has given you a clear song. Age does not distress you, wise one, earth-born,[1] song-lover! You who do not suffer, you whose flesh is bloodless, you are almost like the gods.

[1] The Athenians in the early days wore gold cicada-clasps in their hair, probably to mark their claim to be autochthonous (see Thuc. 1. 2. 5, 1. 6. 3). Ar. *Hist. Anim.* 5. 30 (556b) notes that the cicada larva develops in the ground, so that the insect is literally 'earth-born'.

35

Love once failed to notice a bee that was sleeping among the roses, and he was wounded: he was struck in the finger, and he howled. He ran and flew to beautiful Cythere[1] and said, 'I have been killed, mother, killed. I am dying. I was struck by the small winged snake that farmers call "the bee".' She re-

[1] Aphrodite.

15 πόσον δοκεῖς πονοῦσιν,
   Ἔρως, ὅσους σὺ βάλλεις;'

titulus: ἄλλο εἰς Ἔρωτα   5 Stephanus: τὰς χεῖρας cod.
14 πονεῖς Pauw

36

    ὁ Πλοῦτος εἴ γε χρυσοῦ
    τὸ ζῆν παρεῖχε θνητοῖς,
    ἐκαρτέρουν φυλάττων,
    ἵν', ἂν Θάνατος ἐπέλθῃ,
5   λάβῃ τι καὶ παρέλθῃ.
    εἰ δ' οὖν μὴ τὸ πρίασθαι
    τὸ ζῆν ἔνεστι θνητοῖς,
    τί καὶ μάτην στενάζω;
    τί καὶ γόους προπέμπω;
10 θανεῖν γὰρ εἰ πέπρωται,
    τί χρυσὸς ὠφελεῖ με;
    ἐμοὶ γένοιτο πίνειν,
    πιόντι δ' οἶνον ἡδὺν
    ἐμοῖς φίλοις συνεῖναι,
15 ἐν δ' ἀπαλαῖσι κοίταις
    τελεῖν τὰν Ἀφροδίταν.

titulus: εἰς φιλάργυρον   4 Wakker: ἵν' ασθενεῖν ἐπέλη cod.
8 στεγάζω West

37

    διὰ νυκτὸς ἐγκαθεύδων
    ἁλιπορφύροις τάπησι
    γεγανυμένος Λυαίῳ,
    ἐδόκουν ἄκροισι ταρσῶν
5   δρόμον ὠκὺν ἐκτανύειν
    μετὰ παρθένων ἀθύρων,
    ἐπεκερτόμουν δὲ παῖδες
    ἁπαλώτεροι Λυαίου

plied, 'If the bee-sting is painful, what pain, Love, do you suppose all your victims suffer?' [2]

[2] Cf. 'Theocritus' 19.

36

If Wealth offered life to mortals for gold, then I would persevere in hoarding it, so that if Death came he could take some and pass on. But since mortals cannot buy life, why should I groan in vain, why weep and wail? If I am fated to die, what use is gold? Let me drink, then, and when I have drunk the sweet wine join my friends or on a soft bed perform Aphrodite's rites.

37

While I was sleeping at night under sea-purple blankets, happy under the influence of Lyaeus,[1] I seemed to be running at full speed on the tips of my toes, having fun with some girls; and boys more tender than Lyaeus [2] were teasing me with biting

[1] Dionysus, wine.   [2] Cf. 17 n. 3.

δακέθυμά μοι λέγοντες
10 διὰ τὰς καλὰς ἐκείνας.
ἐθέλοντα δ᾽ ἐκφιλῆσαι
φύγον ἐξ ὕπνου με πάντες·
μεμονωμένος δ᾽ ὁ τλήμων
πάλιν ἤθελον καθεύδειν.

titulus: τοῦ αὐτοῦ ὄναρ   1 Stephanus: διανυκτῶν cod.
11s. Stephanus: ἐθέλοντι . . . μοι cod.   11 Richards: δὲ
φιλῆσαι cod.

38

ἱλαροὶ πίωμεν οἶνον,
ἀναμέλψομεν δὲ Βάκχον,
τὸν ἐφευρετὰν χορείας,
τὸν ὅλας ποθοῦντα μολπάς,
5 τὸν ὁμότροπον Ἐρώτων,
τὸν ἐρώμενον Κυθήρης,
δι᾽ ὃν ἡ Μέθη λοχεύθη,
δι᾽ ὃν ἡ Χάρις ἐτέχθη,
δι᾽ ὃν ἀμπαύεται Λύπα,
10 δι᾽ ὃν εὐνάζετ᾽ Ἀνία.
τὸ μὲν οὖν πῶμα κερασθὲν
ἁπαλοὶ φέρουσι παῖδες,
τὸ δ᾽ ἄχος πέφευγε μιχθὲν
ἀνεμοτρόφῳ θυέλλῃ·
15 τὸ μὲν οὖν πῶμα λάβωμεν,
τὰς δὲ φροντίδας μεθῶμεν·
τί γάρ ἐστί σοι ⟨τὸ⟩ κέρδος
ὀδυνωμένῳ μερίμναις;
πόθεν οἴδαμεν τὸ μέλλον;
20 ὁ βίος βροτοῖς ἄδηλος·
μεθύων θέλω χορεύειν,
μεμυρισμένος τε παίζειν . . .
μετὰ καὶ καλῶν γυναικῶν.

210

words on account of the pretty girls. But when I wanted to kiss them, they all fled from my dream; and I, poor wretch, was left alone and wanted to be asleep again.

38

Let us be merry and drink wine and sing of Bacchus, the inventor of the choral dance, the lover of all songs, leading the same life as the Loves, the darling of Cythere [1]; thanks to him Drunkenness was brought forth, the Grace was born, Pain takes a rest and Trouble goes to sleep. So the drink is mixed and tender boys are bringing it, and grief has fled, mingling with the wind-fed storm: let us take our drink, then, and let our worries go: what is the good of hurting yourself with cares? How can we know the future? Man's life is unclear. I want to be drunk and dance, to perfume myself and have fun (with the handsome youths and) [2] with beautiful women too.

[1] Aphrodite. [2] A line to this effect seems to have been lost.

μελέτω δὲ τοῖς θέλουσι
25 ὅσον ἐστὶν ἐν μερίμναις.
ἱλαροὶ πίωμεν οἶνον,
ἀναμέλψομεν δὲ Βάκχον.

titulus: ἄλλο τοῦ αὐτοῦ εἰς συμπόσιον   1 Stephanus: λιαρὸν
πίομεν cod. (cf. v. 26)   14 -τρόφῳ ex -τρόπῳ corr. cod.
-στρόφῳ Faber   15 Barnes: πόμα cod.   16 τὰ δὲ
φροντίδος Hermann   17 τὸ add. Anna, Fabri filia
18 Portus: ὀδυρώμενος cod.   22 West: δὲ cod.   post
22 fort. deest versus, e.g. μετὰ τῶν καλῶν ἐφήβων Barnes

39

  φιλῶ γέροντα τερπνόν,
  φιλῶ νέον χορευτάν·
  ἂν δ' ὁ γέρων χορεύῃ,
  τρίχας γέρων μέν ἐστιν,
 5 τὰς δὲ φρένας νεάζει.

titulus: ἄλλο εἰς ἑαυτὸν ἢ εἰς ἑταῖρον πρεσβύτην   2 -τάν ex -τήν
corr. cod.

40

  ἐπειδὴ βροτὸς ἐτεύχθην
  βιότου τρίβον ὁδεύειν,
  χρόνον ἔγνων ὃν παρῆλθον,
  ὃν δ' ἔχω δραμεῖν οὐκ οἶδα.
 5 † μέθετέ με, φροντίδες· †
  μηδέν μοι χὔμιν ἔστω.
  πρὶν ἐμὲ φθάσῃ τὸ τέλος,
  παίξω, γελάσω, χορεύσω
  μετὰ τοῦ καλοῦ Λυαίου.

titulus: ἄλλο εἰς ἑαυτόν   1 ex ἐτύχθην corr. cod. (cf. 11. 5)
3 Stephanus: ἔγνον cod.   6 West: καὶ ὑμῖν cod.

212

Those who wish can bother with worries.

Let us be merry and drink wine and sing of Bacchus.

39

I love a pleasant old man, I love a young dancer: and if the old man dances, then he is old as far as his hair is concerned, but young at heart.

40

Since [1] I was created a mortal to journey on the path of life, I can tell the years that I have gone past, but do not know the years I have to run. Let me go, worries: let there be no dealings between you and me. Before death catches up with me, I shall play, I shall laugh and I shall dance with lovely Lyaeus.[2]

[1] The influence of the accent suggests a date not earlier than *c.* 400 A.D. for this poem.   [2] Dionysus.

213

GREEK LYRIC

41

ἦ καλόν ἐστι βαδίζειν,
ὅπου λειμῶνες κομῶσιν,
ὅπου λεπτὸς ἡδυτάτην
ἀναπνεῖ Ζέφυρος αὔρην,
5 κλῆμά τε βάκχιον ἰδεῖν,
χὐπὸ τὰ πέταλα δῦναι,
ἁπαλὴν παῖδα κατέχων
Κύπριν ὅλην πνέουσαν.

titulus: τοῦ αὐτοῦ εἰς τὸ ἔαρ ἤτοι καλοκαίριον   1 West: τί
cod.   3 Barnes: λεπτὴν cod.   5 Mehlhorn: τὸ cod.
Stephanus: εἰδεῖν cod.

42

ποθέω μὲν Διονύσου
φιλοπαίγμονος χορείας,
φιλέω δ᾽, ὅταν ἐφήβου
μετὰ συμπότου λυρίζω·
5 στεφανίσκους δ᾽ ὑακίνθων
κροτάφοισιν ἀμφιπλέξας
μετὰ παρθένων ἀθύρειν
φιλέω μάλιστα πάντων.
φθόνον οὐκ οἶδ᾽ ἐμὸν ἦτορ,
10 φθόνον οὐκ οἶδα δαϊκτήν.
φιλολοιδόροιο γλώττης
φεύγω βέλεμνα κοῦφα·
στυγέω μάχας παροίνους.

214

ANACREONTEA

41

It is a fine thing to walk where the meadows are grassy, where light Zephyr blows the sweetest breeze, to see the branches of Bacchus [1] and to creep under their leaves, embracing a tender girl whose whole body has the fragrance of the Cyprian. [2]

[1] Vines.   [2] Aphrodite. Another late poem.

42

I long for the dances of fun-loving Dionysus, and I love it when I play the lyre with a youth as my drinking companion; but most of all I love to put garlands of hyacinth round my brow and play with girls. My heart knows no envy, I know no heart-rending envy. [1] I avoid the lightweight javelins of the abusive tongue. I hate fights over the wine. At merry

[1] Text uncertain; perhaps 'My heart knows no envy' should be omitted (so Bergk).

πολυκώμους κατὰ δαῖτας
15 νεοθηλέσιν ἅμα κούραις
ὑπὸ βαρβίτῳ χορεύων
βίον ἥσυχον φέροιμι.

titulus: τοῦ αὐτοῦ ἐρωτικὸν ᾠδάριον　　　9 vel 10 fort.
delendus 10 Pauw (cf. Barnes): δαϊκτόν cod.　11 Stephanus:
-λοιδόροισι cod.　　12 Stephanus: ἔφευγε cod.　　15 Bothe:
-θηλαῖσιν cod.　　17 Pauw: φέρωμεν cod. φεροίμην Bergk

43

στεφάνους μὲν κροτάφοισι
ῥοδίνους συναρμόσαντες
μεθύωμεν ἀβρὰ γελῶντες.
ὑπὸ βαρβίτῳ δὲ κούρα
5 κατακίσσοισι βρύοντας
πλοκάμοις φέρουσα θύρσους
χλιδανόσφυρος χορεύῃ.
ἀβροχαίτας δ' ἅμα κοῦρος
στομάτων ἀδὺ πνεόντων
10 κατὰ πηκτίδων ἀθύρῃ
προχέων λίγειαν ὀμφάν.
ὁ δ' Ἔρως ὁ χρυσοχαίτας
μετὰ τοῦ καλοῦ Λυαίου
καὶ τῆς καλῆς Κυθήρης
15 τὸν ἐπήρατον γεραιοῖς
κῶμον μέτεισι χαίρων.

titulus: ἄλλο ἐρωτικὸν ᾠδάριον　　　3 Barnes: μεθύομεν cod.
5 Stanley: βρέμοντας cod.　　7 χορεύῃ ex -ει corr. cod.
8 Stephanus: -χαῖται . . . κοῦροι cod.　　10 Rose: ἀθύρειν
cod.　　14 Stephanus: κυθεριας ex -ειας corr. cod.
16 Stephanus: μεθίῃσι cod.

216

parties with youthful girls, dancing to the lyre, may I take life easy.

43

Let us fasten garlands of roses on our brows and get drunk, laughing gently. Let a gorgeous-ankled girl dance to the lyre carrying the thyrsus [1] with its rich ivy tresses. With her let a boy, soft-haired and with sweet-smelling mouth, play the lyre, pouring forth a clear song. And golden-haired Love with beautiful Lyaeus and beautiful Cythere [2] will join happily in the revel that old men find delightful.

[1] The wand of Bacchants, a fennel rod with a bunch of ivy leaves fastened to the end.   [2] Dionysus and Aphrodite.

44

τὸ ῥόδον τὸ τῶν Ἐρώτων
μίξωμεν Διονύσῳ·
τὸ ῥόδον τὸ καλλίφυλλον
κροτάφοισιν ἁρμόσαντες
5 πίνωμεν ἁβρὰ γελῶντες.
ῥόδον, ὦ φέριστον ἄνθος,
ῥόδον εἴαρος μέλημα,
ῥόδα καὶ θεοῖσι τερπνά,
ῥόδον, ᾧ παῖς ὁ Κυθήρης
10 στέφεται καλοὺς ἰούλους
Χαρίτεσσι συγχορεύων·
στεφάνου με, καὶ λυρίζων
παρὰ σοῖς, Διόνυσε, σηκοῖς
μετὰ κούρης βαθυκόλπου
15 ῥοδίνοισι στεφανίσκοις
πεπυκασμένος χορεύσω.

titulus: ἄλλο ὁμοίως ᾠδάριον· εἰς τὸ ῥόδον   8 del. West
9 Hermann: ὁ παῖς cod.   10 Pauw: καλοῖς ἰούλοις cod.
12 Sitzler: στέψον οὖν cod. στέψον με Bothe   Pauw:
λυρίζω ex λυρίσω corr. cod.

45

ὅταν πίνω τὸν οἶνον,
εὔδουσιν αἱ μέριμναι.
τί μοι πόνων, τί μοι γόων,
τί μοι μέλει μεριμνῶν;
5 θανεῖν με δεῖ, κἂν μὴ θέλω·
τί τὸν βίον πλανῶμαι;
πίωμεν οὖν τὸν οἶνον
τὸν τοῦ καλοῦ Λυαίου·
σὺν τῷ δὲ πίνειν ἡμᾶς
10 εὔδουσιν αἱ μέριμναι.

titulus: τοῦ αὐτοῦ εἰς οἶνον ᾠδάριον   1 πίω Barnes
6 Barnes: τί δὲ τὸν cod.

ANACREONTEA

44

Let us mix the Loves' rose with Dionysus [1]: let us fasten on our brows the rose with its lovely petals and drink, laughing gently. Rose, finest of flowers, rose, darling of spring, rose, delight of the gods also, rose with which Cythere's son [2] garlands his lovely curls [3] when he dances with the Graces, garland me, and in your precinct, Dionysus, I shall play the lyre and, wreathed with my rose garlands, dance with a deep-bosomed [4] girl.

[1] Explained in the following words.   [2] Love, son of Aphrodite.   [3] Lit. the 'down' of his cheeks.   [4] Epic and Pindaric epithet.

45

When I drink wine, my worries go to sleep. What do I care about troubles, about sorrows, about worries? I must die, even if I do not wish to: why puzzle over life? Let's drink the wine of fair Lyaeus [1]; for when we drink, our worries go to sleep. [2]

[1] Dionysus, 'the Loosener'.   [2] Unclassical prosody indicates a late poem.

46

ἴδε πῶς ἔαρος φανέντος
Χάριτες ῥόδα βρύουσιν·
ἴδε πῶς κῦμα θαλάσσης
ἀπαλύνεται γαλήνῃ·
5 ἴδε πῶς νῆσσα κολυμβᾷ·
ἴδε πῶς γέρανος ὁδεύει.
ζαφελῶς δ᾽ ἔλαμψε Τιτάν,
νεφελῶν σκιαὶ δονοῦνται,
τὰ βροτῶν δ᾽ ἔλαμψεν ἔργα,
10 ⟦καρποῖσι γαῖα προκύπτει⟧
καρπὸς ἐλαίας προκύπτει·
βρομίου τρέφεται νᾶμα
κατὰ φύλλον, κατὰ κλῶνα·
θαλέθων ἤνθησε καρπός.

titulus: εἰς τὸ ἔαρ   2 Stephanus: β. ῥ. cod.   7 Bergk:
ἀφελῶς cod.   10 del. Faber   12 tent. West: στρέφεται
cod.   13 Stephanus: κλόνον cod.   D'Orville: καθελων cod.

47

ἐγὼ γέρων μέν εἰμι,
νέων πλέον δὲ πίνω·
κἂν δεήσῃ με χορεύειν,
Σειληνὸν ἐν μέσοισι
5 μιμούμενος χορεύσω
σκῆπτρον ἔχων τὸν ἀσκόν·
ὁ νάρθηξ δ᾽ οὐδέν ἐστιν.
ὁ μὲν θέλων μάχεσθαι
παρέστω καὶ μαχέσθω.
10 ἐμοὶ κύπελλον, ὦ παῖ,
μελίχρουν οἶνον ἡδὺν
ἐγκεράσας φόρησον.

ANACREONTEA

46

See how the Graces swell the rosebuds now that spring has appeared; see how the waves of the sea become gentle in the calm weather; see how the duck dives and the crane makes its journey. Titan [1] shines strongly, the shadows of the clouds are driven on, the fields of mortals shine,[2] the olive-fruit peeps forth, the juice of Bromius [3] fills out by leaf and by branch; the crop flourishes and blossoms.

[1] The Sun-God.   [2] Text of the following lines very uncertain, metre insecure.   [3] Dionysus.

47

I am an old man, but I drink more than the youngsters; and if I have to dance, I shall imitate Silenus and dance in the middle of the ring, with my wine-flask as my support since my fennel-stick is useless. If anyone wants a fight, let him come over here and fight.[1] Mix the sweet honied wine and bring me the cup, boy.

[1] A reminiscence of Anacr. 429, where the lines almost certainly formed the beginning of a poem; the lines are poorly integrated here: perhaps the meaning was intended to be 'If anyone wants to dispute my claim, let him try to outdrink me'. West proposes a system of three five-line stanzas: 1–2, lacuna, 6–7; 8–12; 13–14, 3–5.

221

ἐγὼ γέρων μέν εἰμι,
⟨νέων πλέον δὲ πίνω⟩.

titulus: εἰς ἑαυτόν   4–5 post 13 cod., transp. Lachmann
11 μελιχρὸν Stephanus   14 add. Bergk

48

ὅταν ὁ Βάκχος ἔλθῃ,
εὕδουσιν αἱ μέριμναι,
δοκῶ δ' ἔχειν τὰ Κροίσου.
θέλω καλῶς ἀείδειν,
5 κισσοστεφὴς δὲ κεῖμαι,
πατῶ δ' ἅπαντα θυμῷ.
ὅπλιζ', ἐγὼ δὲ πίνω.
φέρε μοι κύπελλον, ὦ παῖ·
μεθύοντα γάρ με κεῖσθαι
10 πολὺ κρεῖσσον ἢ θανόντα.

titulus: ἄλλο εἰς φιλοπότην· τοῦ αὐτοῦ   1 Stroth: εἰσέλθη cod.
ὅτ' εἰς με Βάκχος ἔλθῃ Barnes   ante v. 7 unum alterumve
versum intercidisse cens. Bergk, velut μέλιχρουν οἶνον ἡδὺν
(47. 11)/ὅπλιζ'

49

τοῦ Διὸς ὁ παῖς ὁ Βάκχος,
ὁ λυσίφρων ὁ Λυαῖος,
ὅταν εἰς φρένας τὰς ἐμὰς
εἰσέλθῃ μεθυδώτας,
5 διδάσκει με χορεύειν.
ἔχω δέ τι καὶ τερπνὸν
ὁ τᾶς μέθας ἐραστάς·
μετὰ κρότων, μετ' ᾠδᾶς
τέρπει με κἀφροδίτα·
10 πάλιν θέλω χορεύειν.

titulus: τοῦ αὐτοῦ εἰς Διόνυσον ἤγουν οἶνον   2 ante Λ. ὁ del.
Barnes   3 εἰς del. Edmonds ἀμάς Rose   10 Heinsius:
καὶ πάλιν cod.

222

I am an old man, but I drink more than the youngsters.

48

When Bacchus comes, my worries go to sleep, and I imagine that I have the wealth of Croesus; I want to sing beautifully; I lie garlanded with ivy and in my heart I disdain the world.[1] Prepare the wine and let me drink it.[2] Bring[3] me a cup, boy, for it is far better that I should lie drunk than lie dead.

[1] Lit. 'I trample everything underfoot'. [2] Text uncertain; a verse may be missing before v. 7. [3] The metre changes here: perhaps the last three lines belong elsewhere.

49

When Zeus' child Bacchus, the Loosener who frees men from their cares, the wine-giver, enters my heart, he teaches me how to dance; and I, the lover of wine, enjoy another pleasure too: along with the dance-beat and song Aphrodite gives me pleasure: I want to dance again.[1]

[1] Metrical irregularities point to a late date.

ὅτ' ἐγὼ πίω τὸν οἶνον,
τότε μὴν ἦτορ ἰανθὲν
. . . .
λιγαίνειν ἄρχεται Μούσας.

5 ὅτ' ἐγὼ πίω τὸν οἶνον,
ἀπορίπτονται μέριμναι
πολυφρόντιδές τε βουλαὶ
ἐς ἁλικτύπους ἀήτας.

9 ὅτ' ἐγὼ πίω τὸν οἶνον,
λυσιπαίγμων τότε Βάκχος
πολυανθέσιν μ' ἐν αὔραις
δονέει μέθη γανώσας.

13 ὅτ' ἐγὼ πίω τὸν οἶνον,
στεφάνους ἄνθεσι πλέξας,
ἐπιθείς τε τῷ καρήνῳ
βιότου μέλπω γαλήνην.

17 ὅτ' ἐγὼ πίω τὸν οἶνον,
μύρῳ εὐώδεϊ τέγξας
δέμας, ἀγκάλαις δὲ κούρην
κατέχων Κύπριν ἀείδω.

21 ὅτ' ἐγὼ πίω τὸν οἶνον,
ὑπὸ κυρτοῖς δὴ κυπέλλοις
τὸν ἐμὸν νόον ἁπλώσας
θιάσῳ τέρπομαι κούρων.

50

When I drink wine, my heart grows warm and . . . begins [1] to sing in clear tones of the Muses.

When I drink wine, my worries and anxious deliberations are thrown to the winds that pound the sea.

When I drink wine, Bacchus who makes men relax with jollity [2] buffets me with fragrant breezes,[3] cheering me with wine.

When I drink wine, I weave garlands with flowers, put them on my head and sing of life's calm weather.

When I drink wine, I wet my body with fragrant perfume and with a girl in my arms I sing of the Cyprian.[4]

When I drink wine, I open up my thoughts under the influence of the rounded cups, and I enjoy the revelling band of boys.

[1] Text uncertain: a line is probably missing. [2] Text uncertain: perhaps 'Bacchus the lyre-player'. [3] Text uncertain. [4] Aphrodite.

25 ὅτ' ἐγὼ πίω τὸν οἶνον,
   τοῦτό μοι μόνον τὸ κέρδος,
   τοῦτ' ἐγὼ λαβὼν ἀποίσω·
   τὸ θανεῖν γὰρ μετὰ πάντων.

titulus: εἰς συμπόσιον τοῦ αὐτοῦ   2 Rose: μὲν cod.   3 versum deesse stat. Hermann   3s. ⟨μέλος⟩ ἅ. λ., ⟨ἀναβάλλεται δὲ⟩ Μούσας West   6 Steph.: ἀπὸ ῥίπτανται cod.   10 λυσιπήμων Pierson   Stephanus: λ. ὅτε μοι B. cod.   11 Stephanus: π. ἐν cod. ὥραις Salmasius   15 τε Mattaire: δὲ cod.   19 Stephanus: ἀγκάλας cod.   22 Rose: δὲ cod.   κυρτοῖσι Brunck   26 τόδε Steph.   Barnes: μόνωι cod.   27 τόδ' Stephanus   28 δεῖ inter γὰρ et μετὰ add. cod.

51

   μή με φύγῃς ὁρῶσα
   τὰν πολιὰν ἔθειραν·
   μηδ', ὅτι σοὶ πάρεστιν
   ἄνθος ἀκμαῖον, τἀμὰ
5 φίλτρα, ⟨φίλα⟩, διώξῃς·
   ὅρα, κἂν στεφάνοισιν
   ὅπως πρέπει τὰ λευκὰ
   ῥόδοις κρίνα πλακέντα.

titulus: εἰς κόρην, τοῦ αὐτοῦ   4 Stephanus: τὰς ἐμὰς cod.   5 Crusius: δῶρα τὰ φίλτρα cod.   τὰς ἐμᾶς | ὥρας φίλτρα δ. West   Stephanus: διώξεις cod.

52(a)

   τί με τοὺς νόμους διδάσκεις
   καὶ ῥητόρων ἀνάγκας;
   τί δέ μοι λόγων τοσούτων
   τῶν μηδὲν ὠφελούντων;
5 μᾶλλον δίδασκε πίνειν
   ἁπαλὸν πῶμα Λυαίου,

When I drink wine, that is all the gain I ask: I shall accept it and take it away; for I must die along with everyone else.[5]

[5] The many metrical faults indicate a late date.

51

Don't look at my grey hair and run! Don't chase away my love,[1] my loved one, simply because you are in the full bloom of youth! Look how well the white lilies woven in garlands go with the roses.

[1] Text uncertain: perhaps 'don't reject my gifts'.

52(a)

Why do you teach me the rules and laws of the rhetoricians? What good to me are all these useless speeches? Teach me rather how to drink the gentle

227

μᾶλλον δίδασκε παίζειν
μετὰ χρυσῆς Ἀφροδίτης.

titulus: τοῦ αὐτοῦ εἰς τὸ ἀνετῶς ζῆν   6 Barnes: πόμα cod.

(b)

πολιαὶ στέφουσι κάραν·
δὸς ὕδωρ, βάλ᾽ οἶνον, ὦ παῖ·
τὴν ψυχήν μου κάρωσον.
βραχὺ μὴ ζῶντα καλύπτεις.
5 ὁ θανὼν οὐκ ἐπιθυμεῖ.

(b) segreg. Crusius   1 κ. σ. Barnes   2 Stephanus:
βαλὼν cod.

53

ὅτ᾽ ἐγὼ ᾽ς νέων ὅμιλον
ἐσορῶ, πάρεστιν ἥβα.
τότε δή, τότ᾽ ἐς χορείην
ὁ γέρων ἐγὼ πτεροῦμαι,
5 παραμαίνομαι, κυβηβῶ.
παράδος· θέλω στέφεσθαι.
πολιὸν δ᾽ ἑκὰς τὸ γῆρας·
νέος ἐν νέοις χορεύσω,
Διονυσίης δέ μοί τις
10 φερέτω ῥοὰν ὀπώρης,
ἵν᾽ ἴδῃ γέροντος ἀλκὴν
δεδαηκότος μὲν εἰπεῖν,
δεδαηκότος δὲ πίνειν,
χαριέντως τε μανῆναι.

titulus: ἄλλο εἰς ἑαυτὸν ὁμοίως   1 West: σὲ (ε del.) νέοις
ὁμίλουν cod.   νέων ὅμιλον iam Stephanus   2 Stephanus:
ἐσορων cod.   3 Stephanus: δὲ cod.   5 Salmasius:
παραμενωμε ex περιμεινόν με corr. cod.   West: κυβήβα
cod.   6 ῥόδα δός Stephanus   7 Bothe: π. δὲ γ. ἐ.
cod.   9 Stephanus: διονυσίοις cod.   10 Baxter: ῥόον (ex
ῥοιὰν corr.) ἀπ᾽ ὀ. cod.   14 Baxter: δὲ cod.

228

draught of Lyaeus,[1] how to play with golden Aphrodite.

[1] Dionysus.

(b)

Grey hairs garland my head. Give me water and add wine, boy! Stupefy my heart! Soon I shall not be alive and you will bury me; and the dead man has no desires.[1]

[1] Crusius detached (b) from (a). (b) has two metrical faults, (a) has none; (a) has paroxytone accent on the last word of every line, an indication of late date, (b) may also be late.

53

When I look at the company of young men, youth returns; at such times in spite of my age I take wing for the dance, I am quite mad, I am frantic. I want to wear a garland: hand me one! Grey old age is far away: I shall dance, a youth among the youths; let someone fetch me Dionysus' liquid harvest, so that he can see the strength of an old man who has learned to speak, has learned to drink, has learned to go mad gracefully.[1]

[1] Cf. Anacr. 402(c). 2.

54

ὁ ταῦρος οὗτος, ὦ παῖ,
δοκεῖ τις εἶναί μοι Ζεύς·
φέρει γὰρ ἀμφὶ νώτοις
Σιδωνίαν γυναῖκα·
5 περᾷ δὲ πόντον εὐρύν,
τέμνει δὲ κῦμα χηλαῖς.
οὐκ ἂν δὲ ταῦρος ἄλλος
ἐξ ἀγέλης λιασθεὶς
ἔπλευσε τὴν θάλασσαν,
10 εἰ μὴ μόνος ἐκεῖνος.

titulus: εἰς τὴν Εὐρώπην   5 Stephanus: παρὰ δὴ (ex δὲ corr.)
cod.   7 Stephanus: οὐκὰν οὖν cod.   8 Bergk: ἐλασθεὶς
cod.

55

στεφανηφόρου μετ᾽ ἦρος
μέλομαι ῥόδον τέρεινον
συνέταιρον ὀξὺ μέλπειν.
τόδε γὰρ θεῶν ἄημα,
5 τόδε καὶ βροτοῖσι χάρμα,
Χάρισίν τ᾽ ἄγαλμ᾽ ἐν ὥραις,
πολυανθέων Ἐρώτων
ἀφροδίσιόν τ᾽ ἄθυρμα·
τόδε καὶ μέλημα μύθοις
10 χαρίεν φυτόν τε Μουσῶν·
γλυκὺ καὶ ποιοῦντι πεῖραν
ἐν ἀκανθίναις ἀταρποῖς,
γλυκὺ δ᾽ αὖ λαβόντι, θάλπειν
μαλακαῖσι χερσί, κοῦφον
15 προσάγοντ᾽ Ἔρωτος ἄνθος.
17 θαλίαις τί κἂν τραπέζαις
Διονυσίαις τ᾽ ἑορταῖς

ANACREONTEA

54

This bull, boy, looks like Zeus to me: he is carrying a Sidonian woman [1] on his back; he is crossing the wide ocean, and he cuts through the waves with his hooves. No other bull would have left the herd and sailed the sea: he alone.

[1] Europa, daughter of Phoenix, 'the Phoenician' (*Il.* 14. 321): the poet is interpreting a picture.

55

Along with spring, the bringer of garlands, I am eager to sing with clear voice of spring's companion,[1] the soft rose. It is the breath of the gods and the joy of mortals, the glory of the Graces in springtime, the delight of the Loves with their rich garlands and of Aphrodite; it is a subject for poetry and the graceful plant of the Muses; it is sweet to find when one is picking one's way along thorny paths, sweet to take and warm in soft hands, to press to one's body, the light flower of Love.[1] At feasts, banquets and festivals of Dionysus what should we

[1] Text and translation uncertain.

δίχα τοῦ ῥόδου γένοιτ' ἄν;
20 ῥοδοδάκτυλος μὲν Ἠώς,
ῥοδοπήχεες δὲ Νύμφαι,
ῥοδόχρους δὲ κἀφροδίτα
παρὰ τῶν σοφῶν καλεῖται.
16 ἀσόφῳ τόδ' αὐτὸ τερπνόν·
τόδε καὶ νοσοῦσιν ἀρκεῖ,
25 τόδε καὶ νεκροῖς ἀμύνει,
τόδε καὶ χρόνον βιᾶται·
χαρίεν ῥόδων δὲ γῆρας
νεότητος ἔσχεν ὀδμήν.
φέρε δὴ φύσιν λέγωμεν·
30 χαροπῆς ὅτ' ἐκ θαλάττης
δεδροσωμένην Κυθήρην
ἐλόχευε πόντος ἀφρῷ
πολεμόκλονόν τ' Ἀθήνην
κορυφῆς ἔδειξεν ὁ Ζεύς,
35 φοβερὰν θέαν Ὀλύμπῳ,
τότε καὶ ῥόδων ἀγητὸν
νέον ἔρνος ἤνθισε χθών,
πολυδαίδαλον λόχευμα·
μακάρων θεῶν δ' ὅμοιον
40 ῥόδον ὡς γένοιτο, νέκταρ
ἐπιτέγξας ἀνέθηλεν
ἀγέρωχον ἐξ ἀκάνθης
φυτὸν ἄμβροτον Λυαῖος.

titulus: εἰς ῥόδον   1 Stephanus: -φόρον cod.   2 Salmasius:
τερινὸν cod.   3 Hermann: σὺνεταιρεῖ αὔξει cod.   ἐραταῖς
κάλυξι μ. tent. West   5 Bothe: βροτῶν cod.   11 πονοῦντ'
ἀγείρειν West   13 Baxter: -τα cod.   14 West: κούφαις
cod.   v.16 post 23 transp. Preisendanz   16 Bothe:
ὦσσοφῶ cod.   Steph.: αυτω cod.   ἀπορῶ τόδ' αὖ, τί τ.
West   17 Rose: τε καὶ cod.   36 Stephanus: ῥόδον cod.
43 Rose: λυαίου ex λυαίωι corr. cod.

232

do without the rose? Rosy-fingered Dawn, rosy-armed Nymphs, rosy-hued Aphrodite—so the poets call them; and the rose gives pleasure also to the unpoetic.[1] It helps the sick, it protects the dead,[2] it defies time: for the rose in its graceful old age keeps the fragrance of its youth. Come, let us tell of its birth: when from the grey waters the sea gave birth to Cythere,[3] all bedewed with foam, and from his head Zeus displayed Athena who loves the battle-din, a fearful sight for Olympus, then earth made wonderful new shoots of roses blossom, her creation of skilled artistry; and that the rose might resemble the blessed gods, Lyaeus[4] sprinkled it with nectar and made it flourish proudly on the thorn, an immortal plant.

[1] Text and translation uncertain.   [2] In wreaths placed on corpses: cf. also *Il.* 23. 185 f.   [3] Aphrodite.   [4] Dionysus.

56

ὁ τὸν ἐν πόνοις ἀτειρῆ,
νέον ἐν πόθοις ἀταρβῆ,
καλὸν ἐν πότοις χορευτὴν
τελέων θεὸς κατῆλθε,
5 ἁπαλὸν βροτοῖσι φίλτρον,
πότον ἄστονον κομίζων,
γόνον ἀμπέλου, τὸν οἶνον,
ἐπὶ κλημάτων ὀπώραις
πεπεδημένον φυλάττων,
10 ἵν᾽, ὅταν τέμωσι βότρυν,
ἄνοσοι μένωσι πάντες,
ἄνοσοι δέμας θεητόν,
ἄνοσοι γλυκύν τε θυμὸν
ἐς ἔτους φανέντος ἄλλου.

titulus: ἄλλο εἰς Διόννσον   6 Stephanus: πόθον cod.
8s. Bergk: π. ὀ./ἐ. κ. φ. cod.   Fabri filia: φυλάττειν cod.
10 Stephanus: τέμνωσι cod.

57

ἆρα τίς τόρευσε πόντον;
ἆρα τίς μανεῖσα τέχνα
ἀνέχευε κῦμα δίσκῳ;
ἐπὶ νῶτα τῆς θαλάττης
5 ἆρα τίς ὕπερθε λευκὰν
ἁπαλὰν χάραξε Κύπριν
νόον ἐς θεοὺς ἀερθείς,
μακάρων φύσιος ἀρχάν;
ὁ δέ νιν ἔδειξε γυμνάν,
10 ὅσα μὴ θέμις δ᾽ ὁρᾶσθαι
μόνα κύμασιν καλύπτει.
ἀλαλημένη δ᾽ ἐπ᾽ αὐτὰ

56

The god who gives the troubled man endurance, the young man courage in love, the dancer beauty in drunkenness, has come down to earth, bringing wine to mortals, a gentle love-charm, a potion to banish grief, the child of the vine. He keeps it shackled in the fruit of the vine-branches so that when men cut the grape-bunches they may all stay healthy— healthy in handsome body, healthy in pleasant mind—till the next year appears.

57

What metalworker created the sea? What inspired art poured waves on a salver? Who with his mind soaring heaven-high took the first step towards immortality [1] by carving on the sea's back soft white Cypris [2]? He showed her naked, covering with the waves only what ought not to be seen. Roaming over

[1] Translation uncertain: perhaps 'carved Cypris, the origin of the race of the immortals'.   [2] Aphrodite.

βρύον ὥς, ὕπερθε λευκᾶς
ἀπαλόχροον γαλήνας
15 δέμας εἰς πλόον φέρουσα,
ῥόθιον παρ' οἶμον ἕλκει.
ῥοδέων δ' ὕπερθε μαζῶν
ἀπαλῆς ἔνερθε δειρῆς
μέγα κῦμα χρῶτα τέμνει.
20 μέσον αὔλακος δὲ Κύπρις
κρίνον ὣς ἴοις ἑλιχθὲν
διαφαίνεται γαλήνας.
ὑπὲρ ἀργύρου δ' ὀχοῦνται
ἐπὶ δελφῖσι χορευταῖς
25 † δολερὸν νόον μερόπων †
Ἔρος Ἵμερος γελῶν τε,
χορὸς ἰχθύων τε κυρτὸς
ἐπὶ κυμάτων κυβιστῶν
† Παφίης τε σῶμα † παίζει,
30 ἵνα νήχεται γελῶσα.

titulus: εἰς δίσκον ἔχοντα Ἀφροδίτην   7 Barnes: νόος cod.
10 Stephanus: χόσα cod.   12 Stephanus: -μένος cod.
13 Bergk: λευκὰν cod.   14 Wahl: -χρόους cod.   16 Sitzler:
πάροιθεν cod.   19 Sitzler: πρῶτα cod.   23 Edmonds: ἀργύρῳ
cod.   Stephanus: ὀρχοῦνται cod.   26 West: γελῶντες cod.
29 Π. ἐς ὄμμα Longepierre Παφίῃ κῶμος ὀπαδεῖ Edmonds

58

ὁ δραπέτας ὁ Χρυσὸς
ὅταν με φεύγῃ κραιπνοῖς
διηνέμοις τε ταρσοῖς
(ἀεὶ δ', ἀεί με φεύγει),
5 οὔ μιν διώκω· τίς γὰρ
μισῶν θέλει τι θηρᾶν;
ἐγὼ δ' ἄφαρ λιασθεὶς

236

the waves like sea-lettuce, moving her soft-skinned body in her voyage over the white calm sea, she pulls the breakers along her path. Above her rosy breasts and below her soft neck a great wave divides her skin. In the midst of the furrow, like a lily wound among violets, Cypris shines out from the calm sea. Over the silver on dancing dolphins ride guileful Love and laughing Desire, and the chorus of bow-backed fish plunging in the waves sports with the Paphian [3] where she swims laughing.[4]

---

[3] Aphrodite.   [4] Text of last sentence uncertain.

58

When Gold, the runaway, flees from me on nimble wind-swift feet—and he is always fleeing, always—I do not pursue him: who wants to chase what he hates? As soon as I am parted from Gold, the run-

τῷ δραπέτᾳ τῷ Χρυσῷ,
ἐμῶν φρενῶν μὲν αὔραις
10 φέρειν ἔδωκα λύπας,
λύρην δ' ἑλὼν ἀείδω
ἐρωτικὰς ἀοιδάς.
πάλιν δ' ὅταν με θυμὸς
ὑπερφρονεῖν διδάξῃ,
15 ἄφνω προσεῖπ' ὁ δραπέτας
φέρων μέθαν μοι φροντίδων,
ἑλών μιν ὡς μεθήμων
λύρης γένωμαι λαροῦ.
ἄπιστ', ἄπιστε Χρυσέ,
20 μάταν δόλοις με θέλγεις·
χρυσοῦ πλέον ⟨τὰ⟩ νεῦρα
πόθους κέκευθεν ἀδεῖς.
σὺ γὰρ δόλων, σύ τοι φθόνων
ἔρωτ' ἔθηκας ἀνδράσιν·
25 λύρη δ' ἄλυπα παστάδων
φιλαμάτων τε κεδνῶν
πόθων κύπελλα κιρνᾷ.
ὅταν θέλῃς δέ, φεύγεις,
λύρης δ' ἐμῆς ἀοιδὰν
30 οὐκ ἂν λίποιμι τυτθόν.
ξείνοισι δ' ἀντὶ Μουσῶν
δολίοις ἀπίστοις ἀνδάνεις.
ἐμοὶ δὲ τῷ λυροκτύπῃ
Μοῦσα φρεσὶν πάροικος·
35 ἀχὰν τεὰν ὀρίνοις,
αἴγλαν τεὰν λαμπρύνοις.

titulus: εἰς χρυσὸν τοῦ αὐτοῦ· ἄλλο   1 Barnes: μ' ὁ cod.
5 Stephanus: οὐ μην cod.   6 Stephanus: το cod.   8 fort.
delendus   16 Anna Fabri: δοι cod.   18 Pauw: λαρον cod.
20 Bergk: μετ' αν cod.   21 Bergk: π. χρυησου ν. cod.

238

away, I give my mind's cares to the winds to carry
off, and I take my lyre and sing love-songs. But just
when my heart teaches me to despise him, suddenly
the runaway speaks to me again, bringing me drunk-
en ideas to make me take him and neglect my sweet
lyre. Faithless, faithless Gold! In vain do you cast a
spell on me with your tricks: the lyre-strings, more
than gold, hold sweet desires. You give men a love of
trickeries and jealousies, but the lyre mixes cups of
desires that bring no harm to bridal chambers and
chaste kisses. When you want to, you run away; but I
would not leave my lyre's song for a moment. You
give pleasure to tricky, faithless strangers instead of
the Muses; but I, the lyre-player, have the Muse
making her home in my heart. You may raise your
lament, you may polish up your glitter [1]!

[1] Text and translation of last sentence insecure.

---

22 West: κεκλυθ αδεις cod.   23–36 in cod. post 60.36
leguntur, transp. Barnes   23 Bergk: δόλωι, φθόνωι cod.
25 D'Orville: λύρην cod.   27 Bergk: κρίνη εχ κρίνει
corr. cod.   31 Preisendanz (ἀντὶ Ραυω): -σιν σὲ δ'
ἀγχιμουσῶν cod.   34 Crusius: μούσαις φρεσὶν ἀποίκους
cod.   35 Preisendanz: ἀχανδέας cod.   36 Preisendanz:
bis in cod.: (i) αἴ. τε λαμπρίοις χαν (ii) αἴ. τελάμπρύνοις

τὸν μελανόχρωτα βότρυν
ταλάροις φέροντες ἄνδρες
μετὰ παρθένων ἐπ' ὤμων,
. . . .
κατὰ ληνοῦ δὲ βαλόντες
5 μόνον ἄρσενες πατοῦσιν
σταφυλήν, λύοντες οἶνον,
μέγα τὸν θεὸν κροτοῦντες
ἐπιληνίοισιν ὕμνοις,
ἐρατὸν πίθοις ὁρῶντες
10 νέον ἐνζέοντα Βάκχον.
ὃν ὅταν πίνῃ γεραιός,
τρομεροῖς ποσὶν χορεύει
πολιὰς τρίχας τινάσσων.
ὁ δὲ παρθένον λοχήσας
15 ἐρατὸς νέος . . . .
. . . . ἐλυσθεὶς
ἀπαλὸν δέμας χυθεῖσαν
σκιερῶν ὕπαιθα φύλλων
βεβαρημένην ἐς ὕπνον.
20 ὁ δ' Ἔρως ἄωρα θέλγων
. . . .
προδότιν γάμων γενέσθαι.
ὁ δὲ μὴ λόγοισι πείθων
τότε μὴ θέλουσαν ἄγχει·
25 μετὰ γὰρ νέων ὁ Βάκχος
μεθύων ἄτακτα παίζει.

titulus: εἰς οἶνον   3 lacunam stat. West   4 West: ληνὸν
cod.   10 Zeune: ἐς ζέοντα cod.   15s. lacunam stat.
Bergk   18 Bergk: ὕπερθε cod.   21 lacunam stat.
Bergk: ⟨παράγει κόρην προδήλων⟩ West   22 Stephanus:
προδότην cod.

Men and girls too carrying the black-skinned bunches of grapes in baskets on their shoulders . . .; and throwing them into the vat they trample the clusters—the men only—releasing the wine, loudly applauding the god [1] in their vintage-songs when they see the lovely young wine [2] bubbling in the jars. When an old man drinks it, he dances on his shaky legs, tossing his grey hair; while a lovely youth, having waylaid a girl, crouching (embraces) her soft body stretched out under the shady leaves, heavy with sleep; and Love with ill-timed magic (urges the girl) to betray her (coming) marriage; and the man who fails to talk the girl round still goes on to squeeze her despite her protest; for Bacchus is drunk and plays disorderly games with the young people.

[1] Dionysus.   [2] Lit. 'Bacchus'.

60(a)

ἀνὰ βάρβιτον δονήσω·
ἄεθλος μὲν οὐ πρόκειται,
μελέτη δ' ἔπεστι παντὶ
σοφίης λαχόντ' ἄωτον.
5 ἐλεφαντίνῳ δὲ πλήκτρῳ
λιγυρὸν μέλος κροαίνων
Φρυγίῳ ῥυθμῷ βοήσω,
ἄτε τις κύκνος Καΰστρου
ποικίλον πτεροῖσι μέλπων
10 ἀνέμου σύναυλος ἠχῇ.
σὺ δέ, Μοῦσα, συγχόρευε·
ἱερὸν γάρ ἐστι Φοίβου
κιθάρη, δάφνη τρίπους τε.
λαλέω δ' ἔρωτα Φοίβου,
15 ἀνεμώλιον τὸν οἶστρον·
σαόφρων γάρ ἐστι κούρα·
τὰ μὲν ἐκπέφευγε κέντρα,
φύσεως δ' ἄμειψε μορφήν,
φυτὸν εὐθαλὲς δ' ἐπήχθη·
20 ὁ δὲ Φοῖβος ᾖε, Φοῖβος,
κρατέειν κόρην νομίζων,
χλοερὸν δρέπων δὲ φύλλον
ἐδόκει τελεῖν Κυθήρην.

titulus: εἰς ᾿Απόλλωνα   3 Stephanus: ἐπέστω πάντη cod.
4 Stephanus: λαχων cod.   9 πολιοῖς Stephanus   14 Ste-
phanus: λαλέων cod.   16 Stephanus: ἐστ' ἀκούσας cod., εὖτ'
ἀκούσῃς in marg.   17 Hiller: τὸν μὲν cod. Stephanus: -γα
cod.   18 Stephanus: -ψα cod.   19 Bergk: ἐπηχεῖ cod.
20 Portus: ἠὲ cod.

242

ANACREONTEA

60(a)

I shall make the lyre-strings vibrate. This is no prize-competition: but everyone who has attained the finest skill in poetry must practise his art. Striking a clear melody with my ivory plectrum I shall shout in Phrygian rhythm [1] like a swan of the Cayster [2] singing with its wings a complex song in unison with the wind's cry. Muse, dance with me: for the lyre like the bay [3] and the tripod is sacred to Phoebus. My theme is the love of Phoebus, that unfulfilled frenzy—for the girl remains chaste: she escaped the sting of his passion and changed her bodily form to take root as a flourishing plant; and Phoebus came, Phoebus, believing that he was master of the girl; but he plucked the green leaves, thinking that he was performing the rites of Cythere. [4]

[1] The poem is in Ionic dimeters with anaclasis, the rhythm associated with the Phrygian Cybebe (see 12 n. 1): cf. Catullus 63.   [2] Cf. *Il.* 2. 460 ff., Pratinas 708. 5: the Cayster is a river on the W. coast of Asia Minor. [3] Greek 'daphne': Daphne, the girl pursued by Apollo, was turned into a baytree.   [4] Aphrodite. There may be considerable corruption in the text: West argues for lacunas at several points after v. 11 ('Muse, dance with me') and proposes other alterations; he does not separate 60(a) and 60(b).

GREEK LYRIC

(b)

ἄγε, θυμέ, πῇ μέμηνας
μανίην μανεὶς ἀρίστην;
τὸ βέλος, φέρε, κράτυνον,
σκοπὸν ὡς βαλὼν ἀπέλθῃς.
5 τὸ δὲ τόξον 'Αφροδίτης
ἄφες, ᾧ θεοὺς ἐνίκα.
τὸν 'Ανακρέοντα μιμοῦ,
τὸν ἀοίδιμον μελιστήν.
φιάλην πρόπινε παισίν,
10 φιάλην λόγων ἐραννήν·
ἀπὸ νέκταρος ποτοῖο
παραμύθιον λαβόντες
φλογερὸν φύγωμεν ἄστρον.

(b) ab (a) separavit Bergk   6 Portus: ὡς cod.   13 Mehl-
horn: φυγόντες cod. in fine (i.e. post 58. 36) legitur τέλος τῶν
'Ανακρέοντος συμποσιακῶν

60B. = fr. 2 West   Hippol. *Haer.* p. 107 Miller

τοῦτο, φησίν, ἐστὶ τὸ ποτήριον τὸ κόνδυ, ἐν ᾧ βασιλεὺς πίνων
οἰωνίζεται. τοῦτο, φησί, κεκρυμμένον εὑρέθη ἐν τοῖς καλοῖς τοῦ
Βενιαμὶν σπέρμασι. λέγουσι δ' αὐτὸ καὶ Ἕλληνες, φησίν, οὕτως
μαινομένῳ στόματι·

φέρ' ὕδωρ, φέρ' οἶνον, ὦ παῖ·
μέθυσόν με καὶ κάρωσον·
τὸ ποτήριον λέγει μου
ποδαπόν με δεῖ γενέσθαι.

τοῦτο, φησίν, ἥρκει μόνον νοηθὲν ἀνθρώποις, τὸ τοῦ 'Ανακρέοντος
ποτήριον ἀλάλως λαλοῦν μυστήριον ἄρρητον, ἄλαλον γάρ, φησί, τὸ
'Ανακρέοντος ποτήριον, ὅπερ αὐτῷ φησιν 'Ανακρέων λαλεῖ ἀλάλῳ
φθέγματι ποδαπὸν αὐτὸν δεῖ γενέσθαι . . .

244

ANACREONTEA

(b)

Come, my heart, why are you mad with the best madness of all [1]? Come, throw your weapon [2] strongly, that you may hit the target and depart; give up the bow of Aphrodite with which she overcame the gods. Imitate Anacreon, the famous singer. Drain your cup to the boys, your lovely cup of words. Let us take comfort from a draught of nectar and avoid the flaming dogstar.[3]

[1] Poetic inspiration; see Pl. *Phdr.* 265b.   [2] Pindaric metaphor for poetic composition: *Ol.* 13. 93 ff., 2. 83 ff.
[3] Cf. Alc. 347. It is not certain that the poem ends here. The ms. concludes with the words 'the end of the convivial poems of Anacreon'.

The following pieces come from sources other than the Palatine ms.; see also Anacr. 505(d).

60B. Hippolytus, *Refutation of all the Heresies*

This, he says, is the cup (κόνδυ) from which the king drinks and which he uses for divination. This is the cup that was found hidden among the fine grain of Benjamin.[1] And the Greeks, he says, mention it also in these wild words:

Bring water, bring wine, boy: make me drunk and stupefy me [2]: my cup tells me what must become of me.

This, he says, would be sufficient for men if only it were understood, this cup of Anacreon which without speaking tells of a secret mystery: Anacreon's cup, he says, is unspeaking, the cup which Anacreon says tells him with unspeaking voice what must become of him . . .

[1] See *Genesis* 44. 1–5.   [2] Cf. *Anacreont.* 52(b). 3.

61B. = fr. 4 West   Schol. Cod. Gud. Eur. *Hec.* 1141

ὡς τό·

τί με φεύγεις τὸν γέροντα;

62B. = fr. 3 West   Greg. Cor. p. 396 Schaefer

τοῖς παρατατικοῖς καὶ τοῖς ἐνεστῶσιν ὁμοίως καὶ ταῖς μετοχαῖς τῶν περισπωμένων καὶ ἁπλῶς εἰπεῖν πάσαις ἐγκλίσεσιν ἐντελῶς κέχρηνται, ὡς ἐν τοῖς Ἀνακρεοντείοις, οἷον·

δοκέει κλύειν γὰρ ἥδε,
λαλέειν τις εἰ θελήσῃ.

ANACREONTEA

61B. Scholiast on Euripides, *Hecuba*

Why do you run from me, the old man?

62B. Gregory of Corinth (on the Ionic dialect)

They use the uncontracted forms of the imperfects, presents and participles of circumflexed verbs, indeed of nearly all the parts of the verb, e.g. in the *Anacreontea*:

for she seems to hear if one wishes to speak.

COMPARATIVE NUMERATION
ANACREON

(The numeration is that which appears in the margin
of Page, *P.M.G.*)

Loeb/Page	Bergk[4]	Diehl	Gentili
346	—	—	60–70
347	—	—	71–73
348	1	1	1
349	13B	15	2
350	—	—	18
351	52	36	27
352	41	21	19
353	16	25	21
354	60	23	20
355	127	—	34
356	63	43	33
357	2	2	14
358	14	5	13
359	3	3	5
360	4	4	15
361	8	8	4
362	6	6	7
363	9	11	17
364	40	14	119
365	11	2 Adn.	16
366	5	9	3
367	7	10	12
368	12B	13	6
369	10	23 Adn.	10
370	12A	12	11

Loeb/Page	Bergk[4]	Diehl	Gentili
371	15	19	9
372	21	16	8
373	17	69	93
374	18	70	96
375	20	18	95
376	19	17	94
377	35	20	117
378	24	52	83
379	25	53	84
380	124	51A	91
381	34 + 28	51	116 + 85
382	31	57	109
383	32	58	110
384	33	59	106
385	23	73	86
386	22	72	88
387	30	71	89
388	21	54	82
389	57	55	108
390	69	63	92
391	72	67	100
392	71	66	101
393	70	74	97
394	67–68	61–62	112–113
395	43	44	36
396	62	27	38
397	39	33	118
398	46	34	111
399	59	35	115
400	61	26	35
401	91	81	47
402A	44	29	23
402B	120	—	120
402C	45	32	22
403	38	31	114
404	—	29A	40
405	64	30	42
406	58	24	39

COMPARATIVE NUMERATION

Loeb/Page	Bergk[4]	Diehl	Gentili
407	66	40	43
408	51	39	28
409	42	22	24
410	54	37	30
411	50 + 55	42 + 48	29 + 32
412	56	49	107
413	47	45	25
414	48	46	26
415	53	41	31
416	74	65	99
417	75	88	78
418	76	91	74
419	114	90	75
420	77	89	77
421	81	94	79
422	49	47	81
423	79	93	122
424	86	87	54
425	84	85	52
426	85	86	53
427	90	80	48
428	89	79	46
429	92	82	49
430	—	83	50
431	88	78	45
432	87	77	44
433	82	75	103
434	83	76	104
435	121	—	121
436	26	50	90
437	29	60	105
438	73	68	98
439	164	—	124
440	93	84	51
441	80	95	80
442	131	—	123
443	78	92	76
444	13A	—	125
445	129	—	127

ANACREON

Loeb/Page	Bergk[4]	Diehl	Gentili
446	156–9	—	163–5
447	138	—	129
448	16 v. 3	—	130
449	118	—	132
450	163	—	131
451	27	50A	87
452	151	—	133
453	154	—	134
454	161	—	135
455	162	—	136
456	165	—	137
457	166	—	41
458	168	—	138
459	169	—	139
460	170	—	140
461	134	—	141
462	37	38	102
463	117	—	142
464	135	—	128
465	136	—	167
466	137	—	143
467	139	—	144
468	140	—	145
469	141	—	146
470	142	—	147
471	—	—	148
472	143	—	149
473	144	—	150
474	145	—	151
475	146	—	152
476	148	—	153
477	147	—	154
478	149	—	155
479	150	—	156
480	152	—	157
481	155	—	158
482	160	—	162
483	—	—	—
484	167	—	166
485	171	—	168

COMPARATIVE NUMERATION

Loeb/Page	Bergk[4]	Diehl	Gentili
486	172	—	169
487	44 Adn.	—	170
488	122	—	173
489	—	—	175
490	—	—	176
491	—	—	—
492	125	—	174
493	126	—	178
494	—	—	—
495	—	—	180
496	123	—	159–61
497	128	—	172
498	119	—	171
499	—	—	—
500	—	—	—
501	—	—	190
502	—	—	—
503	—	—	—
504	—	—	—

ANACREON: ELEGIAC FRAGMENTS

(The numeration is that of West, *I.E.G.*)

West	Bergk	Diehl	Gentili
1	95	97	55
2	94	96	56
3	130	—	126
4	97	99	57
5	96	98	58
(5A)*	98	—	59

*see West *I.E.G.* p. 31

ANACREON

West numbers the iambic fragments of Anacreon as follows:

Loeb/Page	West
419	iamb. 2
420	iamb. 3
421	iamb. 4
424	iamb. 7
425	iamb. 1
431	iamb. 6
432	iamb. 5

ANACREON: EPIGRAMS

(The numeration is that of Diehl)

Diehl	Bergk	Gentili	Page, *F.G.E.*
100	100	191	i
101	101	192	ii
102	113	193	iii
103	104	194	ix
104	102	195	vi
105	112	196	iv
106	111	197	xiv
107	103	198	xiii
108	109	199	vii
109	106	200	xi
110	110	201	viii
111	107	202	xii
112	105	203	x
113	108	204	v
114	115	205	xvii
115	116	206	xviii
Simon. 101	Simon. 150	—	xv
Simon. 156	Simon. 181	—	xvi

COMPARATIVE NUMERATION

(Read: 1 Diehl = 348 Loeb/Page, 2 Bergk =
357 Loeb/Page, etc.)

Bergk⁴	Diehl	Gentili → Loeb/Page		Bergk⁴	Diehl	Gentili → Loeb/Page
1	348	348	348	30	387	405	410
2	357	357	349	31	382	403	411B
3	359	359	366	32	383	402C	415
4	360	360	361	33	384	397	356
5	366	358	359	34	381A	398	355
6	362	362	368	35	377	399	400
7	367	Adesp. 978	362	36	505C	351	395
				37	462	410	505D
8	361	361	372	38	403	462	396
9	363	366	371	39	397	408	406
10	369	367	369	40	364	407	404
11	365	363	370	41	352	415	457
12(A)	370	370	367	42	409	411A	405
12(B)	368	—	—	43	395	356	407
13(A)	444	368	358	44	402A	395	432
13(B)	349	—	—	45	402C	413	431
14	358	364	357	46	398	414	428
15	371	349	360	47	413	422	401
16	353+ 448	372	365	48	414	411B	427
				49	422	412	429
17	373	376	363	50	411A	436	430
18	374	375	350	50(A)	—	451	—
19	376	371	352	51	408	381	440
20	375	377	354	51(A)	—	380	—
21	372+ 388	352	353	52	351	378	425
				53	415	379	426
22	386	409	402C	54	410	388	424
23	385	354	402A	55	411B	389	el. 1
24	378	406	409	56	412	505C	el. 2
25	379	353	413	57	389	382	el. 4
26	436	400	414	58	406	383	el. 5
27	451	396	351	59	399	384	el. 5A
28	381B	505D	408	60	354	437	346
29	437	402A	411A	61	400	394	346
29(A)	—	404	—	62	396	394	346

ANACREON

Bergk[4]	Diehl	Gentili Loeb/Page		Bergk[4]	Diehl	Gentili Loeb/Page
63	356	390	346	88	431	417	386
64	405	Adesp. 957	346	89	428	420	387
				90	427	419	436
65	505D	416	346	91	401	418	380
66	407	392	346	92	429	443	390
67	394	391	346	93	440	423	373
68	394	438	346	94	—	421	376
69	390	373	346	95	—	441	375
70	393	374	346	96	—	—	374
71	392	387	347	97	—	—	393
72	391	386	347	98	—	—	438
72(B)	Adesp. 957	—	—	99	—	—	416
				100	—	—	391
73	438	385	347	101	—	—	392
74	416	393	418	102	—	—	462
75	417	433	419	103	—	—	433
76	418	434	443	104	—	—	434
77	420	432	420	105	—	—	437
78	443	431	417	106	—	—	384
79	423	428	421	107	—	—	412
80	441	427	441	108	—	—	389
81	421	401	422	109	—	—	382
82	433	429	388	110	—	—	383
83	434	430	378	111	—	—	398
84	425	440	379	112	—	—	394
85	426	425	381B	113	—	—	394
86	424	426	385	114	419	—	403
87	432	424	451	115	—	—	399
				116	—	—	381A

COMPARATIVE NUMERATION

Bergk[4]	Gentili		Bergk[4]	Gentili
→ Loeb/Page			→ Loeb/Page	
117	463	377	146	475	469
118	449	397	147	477	470
119	498	364	148	476	471
120	402B	402B	149	478	472
121	435	435	150	479	473
122	488	423	151	452	474
123	496	442	152	480	475
124	380	439	153	373Adn.	476
125	492	444	154	453	477
126	493	el. 3	155	481	478
127	355	445	156	446	479
128	497	464	157	446	480
129	445	447	158	446	481
130	el. 3	448	159	446	496
131	442	450	160	482	496
132	505D	449	161	454	496
133	505D	452	162	455	482
134	461	453	163	450	446
135	464	454	164	439	446
136	465	455	165	456	446
137	466	456	166	457	484
138	447	458	167	484	465
139	467	459	168	458	485
140	468	460	169	459	486
141	469	461	170	460	487
142	470	463	171	485	498
143	472	466	172	486	497
144	473	467	173		488
145	474	468	174		492

Gentili	Loeb/Page
175	489
176	490
177	(v. 471, 483)
178	493
179	—
180	495

ANACREON

Gentili	Loeb/Page
181	—
182	—
183	—
184	505D
185	—
186	Adesp. 978
187	505C
188	Adesp. 957
189	505D
190	501

ANACREONTEA

The numeration is that of Preisendanz, except that I have reunited 18(a) and (b) and dismembered 52 and 60.

The numeration of Bergk differs in the following instances, Bergk's number being shown in parentheses:

2(2A), 3(2B), 4(3), 5(4), 6(5), 7(6), 8(7), 9(8), 10(9), 11(10), 12(11), 13(12), 14(13), 15(14), 16(15), 17(16), 18(17, 18), 26(26A), 27(26B), 28(27A), 29(27B + C), 30(28), 31(29), 32(30), 33(31), 34(32) and similarly to 59(57), 60(58 + 59).

The numeration of West differs at 29, where he takes vv. 5–14 as a separate poem (29A); at 52, where my 52(a) and 52(b) are his 52 and 52A; and at 60(a) and 60(b), which he treats as a single poem (60). The fragments of the *Anacreontea* which are not in the Palatine ms. are numbered as follows in his edition:

fr. 1 = Anacr. 505(d) Page fr. 3 = Anacr. 62 Bergk
fr. 2 = Anacr. 60 Bergk fr. 4 = Anacr. 61 Bergk

CHORAL LYRIC POETRY

OLYMPUS
TO
ALCMAN

INTRODUCTION

Choral Lyric Poetry

The solo songs of Sappho, Alcaeus and Anacreon were performed by the poets themselves, singing to their own accompaniment on the lyre. Choral poetry is a more elaborate art-form and involves not only words and music but dance also. Pindar gave his singers the following text as the opening of one of his most splendid victory-odes: 'Golden lyre, rightful possession of Apollo and the violet-haired Muses, you are heeded by the dancer's step, that commencement of celebration, and your notes are obeyed by singers when with your throbbing you fashion the opening for the preludes that lead off the choral dance' (*Pyth.* 1. 1 ff.). The poet's responsibility was to provide the text and music and to devise the dance-movements which would interpret his words; he would train the choir if he lived in the same city and might travel from his home to prepare a performance. He might also provide the musical accompaniment on a large concert-lyre, and even if he did not—Alcman names three Phrygian pipers (109)—he probably had overall responsibility for the performance.

Choral poetry differed from monody in two other important ways: first, its metrical patterns were

261

always much more complex: Alcman used a repeated 14-line stanza in one song for a girls' choir, a 9-line stanza in another; and the poetry of Stesichorus and his successors shows a triadic structure, in which a strophe is followed by an antistrophe in the same metrical pattern, the antistrophe by an epode in a related but different rhythm; this threefold scheme is repeated several times. In comparison, the stanzas of solo song were short and simple. Second, the composers of choral lyric used an artificial language with a strong Doric flavour, whereas the monodists for the most part used their own dialect. The Doric element in Eumelus and Alcman needs no explanation, since those poets composed in the Peloponnese; Stesichorus lived in the Sicilian city of Himera, the inhabitants of which spoke a mixture of Ionic and Doric; there were Doric elements in the dialect of Boeotia where Pindar lived; what is remarkable is that Simonides and Bacchylides used Doric forms in their choral poetry although they were born in the Ionic-speaking island of Ceos.

The occasions of choral lyric were varied, as we gather from the catalogue of nine types attributed to Pindar: hymns, paeans, dithyrambs, prosodia or processional songs, partheneia or girls' songs, hyporchemata or dance-songs, encomia or eulogies, dirges and victory-odes. The paean and dithyramb, at least in their earliest forms, were performed in honour of Apollo and Dionysus respectively, while the hymn might be addressed to any god. The processional song happens to be represented by our earliest surviving fragment of choral lyric, two lines of a work composed in the eighth century by Eumelus of Corinth for a Messenian choir to perform on Delos, and our longest continuous portion of a partheneion is by the seventh-century poet Alcman, whose fame rested particularly on his composition of this genre for Spartan choirs. In the hyporchema, few examples of which survive from any period, the element of dance must have been important. The remaining three types, written to honour men, not gods, were developed later; Ibycus' poem written *c.* 525 in praise of Polycrates (282a) might be called an encomium, and the encomium and victory-ode are attested for Simonides; the dirge or formal lament, known from references in Homer, also found its most distinguished creator in Simonides.

Another genre, not attested for Pindar, was the hymenaeus or wedding song, mentioned by Homer in his description of the shield of Achilles (*Il.* 18. 491 ff.). It may have been an artistic development of the cry Ὑμὴν ὦ Ὑμέναιε, just as the paean had its origin in the shout ἰὴ Παιάν, the victory-ode in the triple καλλίνικε. In the case of the dithyramb we can trace something of the artistic development of the form: Archilochus in the mid-seventh century mentioned his ability to lead off 'the fair song of lord Dionysus, the dithyramb' when the wine had struck his wits like a thunderbolt (fr. 120); elsewhere we learn that he 'improvised' a song in honour of the god (fr. 251). Half-a-century later, Arion of Corinth seems to have organised the form: presumably he composed a work with the structure of a choral song by Eumelus or Alcman and trained a choir to perform it. Another century later the dithyramb was established in Athens, probably by Lasus of Hermione, and for some forty years (509–470) dithyrambic contests at the Athenian festivals of Dionysus attracted the greatest of the Greek poets, Simonides, Pindar and Bacchylides among them.

The early poets of choral lyric are all associated with the Peloponnese: Eumelus was Corinthian and composed for a Messenian choir; Terpander, Thaletas and Polymnestus came from various parts of Greece to Sparta, and Alcman composed for Spartan choirs. Arion was another Corinthian, Echembrotus was Arcadian; Sacadas came from Argos, Lasus from Hermione.

Olympus

The earliest names in the development of Greek song, Olen, Linus, Pamphos, Orpheus, Chrysothemis, Philammon, Thamyris, Eumolpus, Musaeus, belong to myth rather than to history: Olympus, the piper from Phrygia, has a stronger claim to be regarded as a historical figure, since he is set by the *Suda* in the reign of Midas (736–696 B.C.: test. 1), but there are difficulties in his case also. Authorities spoke of two Olympuses: it is possible that there was an earlier musician of prehistoric times as well as the eighth-century Olympus, but it may equally well be that there was only one Olympus to whom mythical material was attached—his association with Marsyas, who was flayed by Apollo, and his wrestling-match with Pan. Olympus was credited with the invention of new rhythms (test. 8), and Stesichorus was said to have been indebted to him (test. 3).

CHORAL LYRIC

Eumelus

Eumelus, a member of the ruling family of
Corinth, the Bacchiadae, is a historical figure. All
the indications of his date place him in the second
third of the 8th century B.C., and his poetry, mainly
epic, belongs therefore to the same period as the
Iliad. The fragment of his Delian processional song
for the Messenians is the earliest surviving remnant
of Greek lyric poetry.

Terpander

Terpander is in some ways as shadowy a figure as
Olympus, a convenient symbol for Asiatic musical
influence reaching Greece via Lesbos, for the ex-
cellence of music and poetry in the island which was
to produce Sappho and Alcaeus, and for the artistic
life of Sparta before the middle of the seventh cen-
tury. But his life is firmly linked with the Greek
festivals, both at Sparta, where he won a musical
contest in the newly established Carnea (test. 2), and
at Delphi, where he won four consecutive victories
(test. 6). The dates given for him are consistent with
each other, if Hellanicus (test. 5) is taken to mean
that Terpander was born in the time of Midas: the
date of his birth would then be some time before 696,
his Carnean victory belongs to 676–672, and he
might have lived as late as 640 (test. 4). If the detail
of the four Pythian victories is correct, his pro-
fessional life spanned twenty-four years, since in the
seventh century the Pythian festival was held only
once every eight years.

A famous citharode, remembered for the noble

simplicity of his compositions, he was regarded as an innovator in metre and music: for example, he was credited with the increase in the number of lyre-strings from four to seven (testt. 1, 14, fr. 6). The information about his nomes for cithara-song (testt. 18–20) is difficult to interpret: he seems to have established and named eight unchanging tunes to which he sang his own hexameter compositions and Homer's lines, perhaps even his settings of Spartan laws (test. 8). The various sections of the nome listed by Pollux (test. 20) might possibly reflect the pattern of a complete Terpandrean performance with 'beginning' (presumably the prelude in which he referred to or addressed a god as in fr. 2), 'downward-turn' or transition (brief, if we must reconcile it with fr. 8), 'navel' or centre (perhaps the Homeric or Terpandrean core), 'seal' (with Terpander's name and credentials) and 'epilogue'; but it may be wrong-headed even to attempt reconstruction along these lines.

Most of the fragments attributed to Terpander, whether by ancient writers or by modern scholars, are likely to be spurious. The sources are late and unreliable, and the content of a quotation (e.g. fr. 3) is sometimes hard to reconcile with a seventh-century date. A recently discovered papyrus (fr. 1) reminds us that the formidable Alexandrian scholar Aristarchus reckoned that he could identify a phrase of Terpander, and Plutarch seems to say that some of the poetry was extant in his time (fr. 7); but there is no evidence of a collection of his poems and none of formal study of them by the Alexandrians.

CHORAL LYRIC

Thaletas

Thaletas like Terpander belongs partly to the world of pre-history, partly to seventh-century Sparta. He is one of many musical and literary figures said to have been invited to Sparta, and he was thought to have introduced cretic rhythms from his home in Gortyn (testt. 8, 9). Late writers spoke of his paeans and hyporchemata (choral dance-songs) (testt. 7–10) but did not quote a single scrap. His choral songs were regarded as a stabilising influence on the Spartan character, and he was associated with the reformer Lycurgus (test. 6). The tale that he put an end to a plague was known in the fifth century B.C.: the poet Pratinas referred to it (test. 4).

Polymnestus

Polymnestus of Colophon is yet another example of a foreign musician invited to work in Sparta. He probably belonged to the middle of the seventh century: he is said to have composed hexameters on Thaletas (Thal. test. 5), and he in turn was mentioned by Alcman (test. 2). His importance was in the field of choral poetry for pipe accompaniment, and he is labelled the inventor of processional songs (test. 1), although Eumelus must have composed his famous one for the Messenians some three generations earlier. No fragment of his poetry survives, although Pindar is known to have quoted him (test. 7). His style is called noble like that of Terpander and Thaletas (Terp. test. 22); statements that his poetry was erotic or obscene are probably due to misinterpretation of a joke in Aristophanes (test. 8).

INTRODUCTION

Alcman

The debate on his birthplace—Sparta or Sardis—began at least as early as Aristotle (test. 8) and still continues. It is clear that the only valuable piece of internal evidence, fr. 16 ('he was no rustic . . . but from lofty Sardis'), did not refer unambiguously to Alcman himself, otherwise there could have been no doubt in the matter. On balance it is more likely that he was Spartan by birth, and that the story of his Lydian origin was due to the reluctance of later Greeks to believe that Sparta could ever have produced its own poets; but the debate is ultimately of little importance: what matters is that his work was composed for Spartan occasions, and that he was honoured in Sparta after his death (test. 14).

Alcman's dates are best determined by internal evidence. In 5 fr. 2 col. i 13 ff. he named or referred to King Leotychidas of Sparta, whose reign is dated approximately to the last quarter of the seventh century. If he applied the term δαίμων to him, as is possible, the king was dead when the song was composed, i.e. Alcman's life continued into the early sixth century. In fr. 157 he mentioned the Balearic Islands, which were not known to the Greeks before c. 640. These dates square well with the second offered by Eusebius, 609/8 (test. 10); and, since Alcman speaks of his old age (fr. 26), the synchronisation with king Ardys of Lydia (test. 1) and the earlier date offered by Eusebius (659/8) are not entirely ruled out.

His works, according to the entry in the *Suda*, were 'six books: lyric poetry and the *Diving Women*' (test. 1). We have references to all six books (frr. 1–3, 4C, 14–20), if we assume that 'book 2 of the partheneia' (fr. 16) is the second of the six. The nature of his *Diving Women*, Κολυμβῶσαι (testt. 1, 16, fr. 158), is unclear. He was most famous for his partheneia, written for girls' choirs in Sparta, but his wedding-hymns are attested (test. 3), and he may have composed other types of choral lyric (test. 15). The reference in the *Suda* to his amatory songs (test. 1) may be due simply to the erotic tone of his partheneia. He boasted about his wide-spread fame (fr. 148), but fate has been unkind to him: not one complete poem survives, and we are lucky to have the hundred fragmentary lines of the Louvre Partheneion (fr. 1), found on papyrus; apart from the papyrus scraps of another partheneion (fr. 3) we have no consecutive passage longer than six lines.

A difficult writer, Alcman attracted much scholarly attention. Chamaeleon may have composed a study *c*. 300 B.C. (frr. 39, 59), and in the following century the Athenian Philochorus (test. 23) and the Spartan Sosibius (frr. 94, 96, 100) both wrote works entitled *On Alcman*, the latter in at least three books. In the first century B.C. Cornelius Alexander (Polyhistor) wrote *On the Place-names in Alcman* (frr. 151, 153). The Louvre Partheneion was the subject of commentaries by at least five scholars, including the great Alexandrians Aristophanes of Byzantium and Aristarchus, and commentaries on other poems were written by Tyrannion and Theon (1st c. B.C./1st c. A.D.) and by Aristonicus and Ptolemaeus (see test. 23 n. 1).

SELECT BIBLIOGRAPHY
(Alcman)

Bergk, T. *Poetae Lyrici Graeci*, vol. iii [4], Leipzig, 1882

Bowra, C. M. *Greek Lyric Poetry from Alcman to Simonides* [2], Oxford, 1961

Calame, C. *Les Choeurs de jeunes filles en Grèce archaïque*: vol. i, *Morphologie, fonction religieuse et sociale*, vol. ii, *Alcman*, Rome, 1977; *Alcman: fragmenta edidit, veterum testimonia collegit*, Rome, 1983 (with full bibliography)

Campbell, D. A. *Greek Lyric Poetry: A Selection of Early Greek Lyric, Elegiac and Iambic Poetry*, London, 1967; *The Golden Lyre: The Themes of the Greek Lyric Poets*, London, 1983

Davison, J. A. *From Archilochus to Pindar*, London, 1968

Diehl, E. *Anthologia Lyrica Graeca*, vol. ii [2], Leipzig, 1942

Edmonds, J. M. *Lyra Graeca*, vol. i [2], London, 1928

Fränkel, H. *Early Greek Poetry and Philosophy*, trans. by M. Hadas and J. Willis, Oxford, 1975

Garzya, A. *Alcmane: I Frammenti*, Naples, 1954

Gerber, D. *Euterpe: An Anthology of Early Greek Lyric, Elegiac and Iambic Poetry*, Amsterdam, 1970

Page, D. L. *Alcman: The Partheneion*, Oxford, 1951; *Poetae Melici Graeci*, Oxford, 1962 (*P.M.G.*); *Lyrica Graeca Selecta*, Oxford, 1968 (*L.G.S.*); *Supplementum Lyricis Graecis*, Oxford, 1974 (*S.L.G.*)

Schneider, J. 'La Chronologie d'Alcman', *R.E.G.* 98 (1985) 1–64

West, M. L. 'Alcmanica', *C.Q.* 15 (1965) 188–202; 'Melica', *C.Q.* 20 (1970) 205–15

CHORAL LYRIC POETRY

OLYMPUS

TESTIMONIA VITAE ATQUE ARTIS

1 *Sud.* O 221 (iii 522 Adler)

Ὄλυμπος. Φρύξ, νεώτερος, αὐλητὴς γεγονὼς ἐπὶ
Μίδου τοῦ Γορδίου.

cf. O 219 Ὄλυμπος· Μαίονος, Μυσός, αὐλητὴς καὶ ποιητὴς μελῶν
καὶ ἐλεγείων, ἡγεμών τε γενόμενος τῆς κρουματικῆς μουσικῆς τῆς
διὰ τῶν αὐλῶν· μαθητὴς καὶ ἐρώμενος Μαρσύου, τὸ γένος ὄντος
Σατύρου, ἀκουστοῦ δὲ καὶ παιδὸς Ὑάγνιδος. γέγονε δὲ πρὸ τῶν
Τρωικῶν ὁ Ὄλυμπος, ἐξ οὗ τὸ ὄρος τὸ ἐν Μυσίᾳ ὀνομάζεται. O 220
Ὄλυμπος· ὁ τοὺς νόμους τῆς κιθαρῳδίας ἐνθεὶς καὶ διδάξας.

2 [Plut.] *Mus.* 5. 1132ef (p. 113 Lasserre, vi 3. 5
Ziegler)

Ἀλέξανδρος δ᾽ ἐν τῇ Συναγωγῇ τῶν περὶ Φρυγίας
(fr. 77 Jacoby) κρούματα Ὄλυμπον ἔφη πρῶτον εἰς
τοὺς Ἕλληνας κομίσαι, ἔτι δὲ καὶ τοὺς Ἰδαίους

OLYMPUS

LIFE AND WORKS

1 *Suda*, Olympus [1]

A Phrygian, the younger Olympus of the two, a piper; lived [2] in the time of Midas [3] son of Gordius.

[1] *Suda* (O 219) lists also 'Olympus, a Maeonian from Mysia, a piper and a composer of songs and elegiacs, the earliest performer of instrumental music for the pipes; pupil and favourite of Marsyas, who was a Satyr by birth and was the pupil and son of Hyagnis. Olympus lived before the Trojan Wars. The mountain in Mysia is named after him'; also (O 220) 'Olympus, who devised and taught the tunes of cithara-song'. The earlier Olympus, pupil of the Satyr Marsyas and wrestler with Pan (Plin. *N.H.* 36. 5. 35), is presumably fictitious; the view that there were two musicians of the name appears first in Pratinas (713(i) *P.M.G.*) and Glaucus of Rhegium.   [2] Less probably, 'born'.   [3] King of Phrygia (738–696 B.C.): cf. Terp. test. 5.

2 'Plutarch', *On Music*

Alexander [1] in his *Collected Materials on Phrygia* said that Olympus was the first to introduce instrumental music to Greece [2] along with the Idaean

[1] Alexander 'Polyhistor' (1st c. B.C.).   [2] Cf. Telestes *P.M.G.* 806, Eur. *I.A.* 576 ff., Pl. *Laws* 3. 677d, Str. 10. 3. 14.

GREEK LYRIC

Δακτύλους· Ὕαγνιν δὲ πρῶτον αὐλῆσαι, εἶτα τὸν
τούτου υἱὸν Μαρσύαν, εἶτ᾽ Ὄλυμπον.

3 [Plut.] *Mus.* 7. 1133d–f (p. 114 Lasserre, vi 3. 6s.
Ziegler)

. . . μεταβησόμεθα ἐπὶ [μόνους] τοὺς αὐλητικούς.
λέγεται γὰρ τὸν προειρημένον Ὄλυμπον, αὐλητὴν ὄντα
τῶν ἐκ Φρυγίας, ποιῆσαι νόμον αὐλητικὸν εἰς
Ἀπόλλωνα τὸν καλούμενον Πολυκέφαλον· εἶναι δὲ τὸν
Ὄλυμπον τοῦτόν φασιν ἕνα τῶν ἀπὸ τοῦ πρώτου
Ὀλύμπου τοῦ Μαρσύου, πεποιηκότος εἰς τοὺς θεοὺς
τοὺς νόμους· οὗτος γὰρ παιδικὰ γενόμενος Μαρσύου
καὶ τὴν αὔλησιν μαθὼν παρ᾽ αὐτοῦ, τοὺς νόμους τοὺς
ἁρμονικοὺς ἐξήνεγκεν εἰς τὴν Ἑλλάδα οἷς νῦν χρῶνται
οἱ Ἕλληνες ἐν ταῖς ἑορταῖς τῶν θεῶν. ἄλλοι δὲ
Κράτητος εἶναί φασι τὸν Πολυκέφαλον νόμον,
γενομένου μαθητοῦ Ὀλύμπου· ὁ δὲ Πρατίνας (fr. 713(i)
P.M.G.) Ὀλύμπου φησὶν εἶναι τοῦ νεωτέρου τὸν νόμον
τοῦτον.

τὸν δὲ καλούμενον Ἁρμάτειον νόμον λέγεται ποιῆσαι
ὁ πρῶτος Ὄλυμπος, ὁ Μαρσύου μαθητής. . . . ὅτι δ᾽
ἐστὶν Ὀλύμπου ὁ Ἁρμάτειος νόμος, ἐκ τῆς Γλαύκου
συγγραφῆς τῆς ὑπὲρ τῶν ἀρχαίων ποιητῶν (fr. 3
Müller) μάθοι ἄν τις, καὶ ἔτι γνοίη ὅτι Στησίχορος
ὁ Ἱμεραῖος οὔτ᾽ Ὀρφέα οὔτε Τέρπανδρον οὔτ᾽
Ἀρχίλοχον οὔτε Θαλήταν ἐμιμήσατο, ἀλλ᾽ Ὄλυμπον,
χρησάμενος τῷ Ἁρματείῳ νόμῳ καὶ τῷ κατὰ δάκτυλον

274

Dactyls [3]: Hyagnis, he says, was the first to play the pipes, then his son Marsyas,[4] then Olympus.

[3] Phrygian priests of Cybele.   [4] Cf. testt. 1, 12, 13, Pl. *Symp.* 215c, Str. 12. 8. 15, Ov. *Met.* 6. 392 ff., Paus. 10. 30. 9, Hyg. *Fab.* 165, 273; Apollodorus 1. 4. 2 makes Marsyas the son of Olympus.

3 'Plutarch', *On Music*

. . . I shall now pass to music for the pipes. The above-mentioned Olympus, one of the pipers from Phrygia, is said to have composed a pipe tune for Apollo, the so-called Many-headed nome. This Olympus, they say, was one of the descendants of the first Olympus,[1] Marsyas' pupil, who had composed his nomes in honour of the gods: this Olympus, who was the favourite of Marsyas and learned his piping from him, introduced to Greece the enharmonic [2] nomes which the Greeks now use in their festivals for the gods. Others say that the Many-headed nome is the work of Crates,[3] a pupil of Olympus, but Pratinas [4] says it is by the younger Olympus.

The so-called Chariot nome is said to have been composed by the first Olympus, pupil of Marsyas. . . . That it is by him can be gathered from Glaucus [5] *On the Ancient Poets*, where one can learn also that Stesichorus of Himera imitated not Orpheus nor Terpander nor Archilochus nor Thaletas but Olympus, using the Chariot nome and the dactylic

[1] Cf. test. 1.   [2] Cf. test. 5.   [3] Unknown.   [4] Lyric poet, early 5th c.   [5] Glaucus of Rhegium, late 5th c. scholar: see G. Huxley, *G.R.B.S.* 9 (1968) 47 ff.

GREEK LYRIC

εἴδει . . . ἄλλοι δέ τινες ὑπὸ τῶν Μυσῶν εὑρῆσθαι
τοῦτον τὸν νόμον· γεγονέναι γάρ τινας ἀρχαίους
αὐλητὰς Μυσούς.

4 [Plut.] *Mus.* 10. 1134e (p. 115 Lasserre, vi 3. 9
Ziegler)

ἐκ γὰρ τῆς Ὀλύμπου αὐλήσεως Θαλήταν φασὶν
ἐξειργάσθαι ταῦτα (sc. Παίωνα καὶ Κρητικὸν ῥυθμόν).

5 [Plut.] *Mus.* 11. 1134f–35c (p. 115 f. Lasserre, vi 3. 9s.
Ziegler)

Ὄλυμπος δέ, ὡς Ἀριστόξενός φησιν (fr. 83 Wehrli),
ὑπολαμβάνεται ὑπὸ τῶν μουσικῶν τοῦ ἐναρμονίου
γένους εὑρετὴς γεγενῆσθαι· τὰ γὰρ πρὸ ἐκείνου πάντα
διάτονα καὶ χρωματικὰ ἦν. ὑπονοοῦσι δὲ τὴν εὕρεσιν
τοιαύτην τινὰ γενέσθαι· ἀναστρεφόμενον τὸν Ὄλυμπον
ἐν τῷ διατόνῳ καὶ διαβιβάζοντα τὸ μέλος πολλάκις ἐπὶ
τὴν διάτονον παρυπάτην, τοτὲ μὲν ἀπὸ τῆς παραμέσης,
τοτὲ δ᾽ ἀπὸ τῆς μέσης, καὶ παραβαίνοντα τὴν διάτονον
λιχανόν, καταμαθεῖν τὸ κάλλος τοῦ ἤθους, καὶ οὕτως τὸ
ἐκ τῆς ἀναλογίας συνεστηκὸς σύστημα θαυμάσαντα καὶ
ἀποδεξάμενον, ἐν τούτῳ ποιεῖν ἐπὶ τοῦ Δωρίου
τόνου· . . .

τὰ μὲν οὖν πρῶτα τῶν ἐναρμονίων τοιαῦτα· ὕστερον
δὲ τὸ ἡμιτόνιον διῃρέθη ἔν τε τοῖς Λυδίοις καὶ ἐν τοῖς
Φρυγίοις. φαίνεται δ᾽ Ὄλυμπος αὐξήσας μουσικὴν τῷ

rhythm. . . . Others say that the nome was the invention of Mysians, since there were ancient Mysian pipers.

4 'Plutarch', *On Music*

For Thaletas [1] is said to have developed these, viz. the paeonic and cretic rhythms,[2] from the pipe music of Olympus.

[1] See Thaletas test. 8.   [2] The paeon has one long and three shorts, e.g. –∪∪∪ or ∪∪∪–, the cretic –∪–; both have 'five to the bar'.

5 'Plutarch', *On Music*

Olympus, as Aristoxenus [1] says, is supposed by musical authorities to have been the discoverer of the enharmonic genus,[2] everything before him having been diatonic or chromatic. They suspect that his discovery happened as follows: Olympus was working in the diatonic and often making his melody move to the diatonic parhypate (F), sometimes from the paramese (b), sometimes from the mese (a), by-passing the diatonic lichanos (G); and so he realised the beauty of the melody's character, and came in this way to admire and adopt the system founded on its analogy, composing with these intervals in the Dorian mode. . . .

These then were the first enharmonic compositions; later the semitone (F–E) was divided in both the Lydian and the Phrygian modes. Clearly

[1] Musical theorist, 4th c. B.C.   [2] I.e. the tetrachord a F E* E, where E* denotes the quarter-tone above E; the diatonic is a G F E.

ἀγένητόν τι καὶ ἀγνοούμενον ὑπὸ τῶν ἔμπροσθεν
εἰσαγαγεῖν, καὶ ἀρχηγὸς γενέσθαι τῆς Ἑλληνικῆς καὶ
καλῆς μουσικῆς.

6 [Plut.] *Mus.* 15. 1136c (p. 118 Lasserre, vi 3. 13
Ziegler)

Ὄλυμπον γὰρ πρῶτον Ἀριστόξενος ἐν τῷ πρώτῳ
περὶ μουσικῆς (fr. 80 Wehrli) ἐπὶ τῷ Πύθωνί φησιν
ἐπικήδειον αὐλῆσαι Λυδιστί.

7 [Plut.] *Mus.* 18. 1137ab (p. 118 f. Lasserre, vi 3. 14s.
Ziegler)

καὶ οἱ παλαιοὶ δὲ πάντες, οὐκ ἀπείρως ἔχοντες
πασῶν τῶν ἁρμονιῶν, ἐνίαις ἐχρήσαντο. οὐ γὰρ ἡ
ἄγνοια τῆς τοιαύτης στενοχωρίας καὶ ὀλιγοχορδίας
αὐτοῖς αἰτία γεγένηται, οὐδὲ δι' ἄγνοιαν οἱ περὶ
Ὄλυμπον καὶ Τέρπανδρον καὶ οἱ ἀκολουθήσαντες τῇ
τούτων προαιρέσει περιεῖλον τὴν πολυχορδίαν τε καὶ
ποικιλίαν. μαρτυρεῖ γοῦν τὰ Ὀλύμπου τε καὶ
Τερπάνδρου ποιήματα καὶ τῶν τούτοις ὁμοιοτρόπων
πάντων· τρίχορδα γὰρ ὄντα καὶ ἁπλᾶ, διαφέρει τῶν
ποικίλων καὶ πολυχόρδων, ὡς μηδένα δύνασθαι
μιμήσασθαι τὸν Ὀλύμπου τρόπον, ὑστερίζειν δὲ
τού⟨του⟩ τοὺς ἐν τῷ πολυχόρδῳ τε καὶ πολυτρόπῳ
καταγιγνομένους.

8 [Plut.] *Mus.* 29. 1141b (p. 124 Lasserre, vi 3. 24
Ziegler)

καὶ αὐτὸν δὲ τὸν Ὄλυμπον ἐκεῖνον, ᾧ δὴ τὴν ἀρχὴν
τῆς Ἑλληνικῆς τε καὶ νομικῆς μούσης ἀποδιδόασι, τό

Olympus advanced music by introducing something that was original and unknown to his predecessors, and was the founder of Greek, i.e. of beautiful, music.

6 'Plutarch', *On Music*

For Aristoxenus *On Music* Book 1 says that Olympus was the first to play on his pipes a lament for the Python [1] in the Lydian mode.

[1] The serpent of Delphi, killed by Apollo.

7 'Plutarch', *On Music*

Similarly it was not because they did not know all the modes that they used only some of them: it was not ignorance that caused their narrow range and their use of few notes or that made Olympus and Terpander and those who followed their chosen practice avoid the use of many notes and complexity. The compositions of Olympus and Terpander and all kindred spirits are the proof: they use three notes [1] and are simple, but they are superior to compositions that are complex and use many notes, so that no one can copy Olympus' style, and those who use many notes and a variety of scales fall short of him.

[1] a F E: see test. 5.

8 'Plutarch', *On Music*

Again, the famous Olympus, who is credited with the foundation of Greek and nomic music, is said to

GREEK LYRIC

τε τῆς ἁρμονίας γένος ἐξευρεῖν φασι, καὶ τῶν ῥυθμῶν
τόν τε προσοδιακόν, ἐν ᾧ ὁ τοῦ Ἄρεως νόμος, καὶ τὸν
χορεῖον, ᾧ πολλῷ κέχρηται ἐν τοῖς Μητρῴοις· ἔνιοι δὲ
καὶ τὸν βακχεῖον Ὄλυμπον οἴονται εὑρηκέναι.

9 [Plut.] *Mus.* 33. 1143a–c (p. 127 Lasserre, vi 3. 29
Ziegler)

τούτου δέ φαμεν αἰτίαν εἶναι σύνθεσίν τινα ἢ μῖξιν ἢ
ἀμφότερα. οἷον Ὀλύμπῳ τὸ ἐναρμόνιον γένος ἐπὶ
Φρυγίου τόνου τεθὲν παίωνι ἐπιβατῷ μιχθέν· τοῦτο γὰρ
τῆς ἀρχῆς τὸ ἦθος ἐγέννησεν ἐπὶ τῷ τῆς Ἀθηνᾶς νόμῳ·
προσληφθείσης γὰρ μελοποιίας καὶ ῥυθμοποιίας,
τεχνικῶς τε μεταληφθέντος τοῦ ῥυθμοῦ μόνον αὐτοῦ
καὶ γενομένου τροχαίου ἀντὶ παίωνος, συνέστη τὸ
Ὀλύμπου ἐναρμόνιον γένος. ἀλλὰ μὴν καὶ τοῦ
ἐναρμονίου γένους καὶ τοῦ Φρυγίου τόνου διαμενόντων
καὶ πρὸς τούτοις τοῦ συστήματος παντός, μεγάλην
ἀλλοίωσιν ἔσχηκε τὸ ἦθος· ἡ γὰρ καλουμένη ἁρμονία ἐν
τῷ τῆς Ἀθηνᾶς νόμῳ πολὺ διέστηκε κατὰ τὸ ἦθος τῆς
ἀναπείρας.

have invented the enharmonic genus [1] and among rhythms the prosodiac,[2] in which the nome of Ares is composed, and the choree,[3] of which he made much use in his compositions for the Great Mother. Some think Olympus also invented the bacchius.[4]

[1] See test. 5.   [2] Term applied to various dactylic lengths, e.g. $\cup|-\cup\cup|-\cup\cup|-$ [3] Term used of trochee ($-\cup$) or tribrach ($\cup\cup\cup$)   [4] $\cup--$, another rhythm with 'five in the bar': see test. 4.

9 'Plutarch', *On Music*

This (sc. the moral character of a piece of music), we say, is brought about by a combination or a blend of elements or by both. Take for example Olympus' setting of the enharmonic genus in the Phrygian mode and his blending of it with the paeon epibatos [1]: this is what created the moral character of the opening of the nome of Athena. For when you add the handling of the melody and rhythm and skilfully change the rhythm by itself so that it becomes trochaic instead of paeonic, then you have the enharmonic genus of Olympus. Moreover, if you keep the enharmonic genus and the Phrygian mode and the whole tetrachord system as well, the moral character can be much altered: for the so-called 'harmony' in the nome of Athena is very different in character from the introduction.

[1] A sequence of 5 long syllables.

10 Poll. 4. 78 (i 224 Bethe)

νόμοι δ' Ὀλύμπου καὶ Μαρσύου Φρύγιοι καὶ Λύδιοι,
ὁ δὲ Σακάδα νόμος Πυθικός, οἱ δὲ Εὐίου κύκλιοι, καὶ
Ὀλύμπου ἐπιτυμβίδιοι.

11 Ar. *Eq.* 7ss.

Οἰ. Α΄   ὦ κακόδαιμον, πῶς ἔχεις;
Οἰ. Β΄   κακῶς καθάπερ σύ.
Οἰ. Α΄   δεῦρο δὴ πρόσελθ', ἵνα
      ξυναυλίαν κλαύσωμεν Οὐλύμπου νόμον.
Οἰ. Α΄Β΄ μυμῦ μυμῦ μυμῦ μυμῦ μυμῦ μυμῦ.

12 Schol. ad loc. (p. 8 Mervyn Jones-Wilson)

. . . ὁ δὲ Ὄλυμπος μουσικὸς ἦν, Μαρσύου μαθητής·
ἔγραψε δὲ αὐλητικοὺς καὶ θρηνητικοὺς νόμους. ἄλλως·
. . . περὶ τὴν αὐλητικὴν ἄριστος, καὶ αὐτὸς
δυστυχήσας διὰ μουσικήν.

cf. Hsch. Ο 657 (ii 755 Latte) Ὀλύμπου νόμος· τῶν αὐλητικῶν
τις.

10 Pollux, *Vocabulary*

The nomes of Olympus and Marsyas were Phrygian and Lydian, that of Sacadas was Pythian, those of Euius cyclic, those of Olympus for performance at tombs.[1]

[1] Cf. test. 6.

11 Aristophanes, *Knights*

1st servant: Poor old fellow, how are you doing?
2nd servant: Badly, like yourself.
1st servant: Then come over here so that we can sob out a pipe duet together—a nome of Olympus.
　　　　　[They hum mournfully.]

12 Scholiast on the passage

Olympus was a musician, pupil of Marsyas. He composed nomes of lamentation for the pipes. He was the best player of the pipes, and he too came to grief because of music.[1]

[1] Like Marsyas, but the reference is not explained.

13 Plat. *Min*. 318b

Σω. τίς τῶν παλαιῶν ἀγαθὸς γέγονεν ἐν τοῖς αὐλητικοῖς νόμοις νομοθέτης; . . . ἆρ᾽ οὖν ὁ Μαρσύας λέγεται καὶ τὰ παιδικὰ αὐτοῦ Ὄλυμπος ὁ Φρύξ;

Ἑτ. ἀληθῆ λέγεις.

Σω. τούτων δὴ καὶ τὰ αὐλήματα θειότατά ἐστι, καὶ μόνα κινεῖ καὶ ἐκφαίνει τοὺς τῶν θεῶν ἐν χρείᾳ ὄντας· καὶ ἔτι καὶ νῦν μόνα λοιπά, ὡς θεῖα ὄντα.

14 Aristot. *Pol*. 1340a (p. 173s. Susemihl)

τοῦτο δ᾽ ἂν εἴη δῆλον, εἰ ποιοί τινες τὰ ἤθη γιγνόμεθα δι᾽ αὐτῆς. ἀλλὰ μὴν ὅτι γιγνόμεθα ποιοί τινες, φανερὸν διὰ πολλῶν μὲν καὶ ἑτέρων, οὐχ ἥκιστα δὲ καὶ διὰ τῶν Ὀλύμπου μελῶν· ταῦτα γὰρ ὁμολογουμένως ποιεῖ τὰς ψυχὰς ἐνθουσιαστικάς, ὁ δ᾽ ἐνθουσιασμὸς τοῦ περὶ τὴν ψυχὴν ἤθους πάθος ἐστίν.

13 Plato, *Minos*

Socrates: Who in the days of old was a good lawgiver in the laws [1] of pipe-playing? . . . Is it not Marsyas who is meant, and his favourite, Olympus the Phrygian?

Companion: That is correct.

Socrates: And their pipe music is most divine, and it alone stirs up and reveals those who are in need of the gods; and to this day it alone remains, since it is divine. [2]

[1] Socrates puns on νόμος, 'law' or 'tune'.   [2] Cf. Pl. *Ion* 533b, Luc. *Indoct.* 5, Ael. *V.H.* 13. 20.

14 Aristotle, *Politics*

This would be clear if our characters could be shown to be affected by music: but many instances do make this plain, and not least among them the tunes of Olympus; for they, it is generally agreed, make our souls excited, and excitement is a condition of the character of the soul.

EUMELUS

1 Clem. Alex. *Strom.* 1. 21. 131 (ii 82 Stählin)

Εὔμηλος δὲ ὁ Κορίνθιος πρεσβύτερος ὢν ἐπιβεβλη-
κέναι Ἀρχίᾳ τῷ Συρακούσας κτίσαντι.

2 Euseb. *Chron.*

(a) Ol. 5. 1 (p. 87 Helm, ii 80s. Schöne)
Eumelus poeta, qui *Bugoniam* et *Europiam*, et
Arctinus, qui *Aethiopidam* composuit, et *Ilii Persis*
agnoscitur.

(b) Ol. 9. 1 (p. 89 Helm, ii 82s. Schöne)
Eumelus Corinthius versificator agnoscitur et
Sibylla Erythraea.

EUMELUS

LIFE AND WORK [1]

1 Clement of Alexandria, *Miscellanies*

Eumelus the Corinthian, who was older (sc. than Callinus, Archilochus and Semonides), is said to have overlapped with Archias, the founder of Syracuse.[2]

[1] For the fragments of epic poems attributed to Eumelus, viz. *Corinthian History, Bugonia, Tales of Europa, Battle of the Titans, Homecomings*, see Kinkel *Epic. Gr. Fragm.* 185 ff., Jacoby *F. Gr. H.* iii B 378 ff. (with commentary p. 297 ff.); also T. J. Dunbabin, *J.H.S* 68 (1948) 66 ff., É. Will, *Korinthiaka* 124 ff., G. L. Huxley, *Greek Epic Poetry* 60 ff.   [2] Founded from Corinth *c.* 734 B.C.

2 Eusebius, *Chronicle* [1]

(a) Olympiad 5.1 (760/759 B.C.): Eumelus the poet, who composed the *Bugonia* and *Tales of Europa*, and Arctinus, who composed the *Aethiopis*, and *The Sack of Troy* are all well-known.

(b) Olympiad 9.1 (744/743 B.C.): Eumelus the Corinthian poet is well-known; also the Sibyl of Erythrae.

[1] See A. A. Mosshammer, *The Chronicle of Eusebius* 198–203.

3 Paus. 2. 1. 1 (i 107 Rocha-Pereira)

Εὔμηλός γε ὁ Ἀμφιλύτου τῶν Βακχιδῶν
καλουμένων, ὃς καὶ τὰ ἔπη λέγεται ποιῆσαι, φησὶν ἐν
τῇ Κορινθίᾳ συγγραφῇ—εἰ δὴ Εὐμήλου γε ἡ
συγγραφή— . . .

EUMELUS

3 Pausanias, *Description of Greece*

Eumelus, son of Amphilytus, one of the so-called Bacchids,[1] who is said to have composed the epic poems, states in his *History of Corinth*, if indeed it is his work,[2] that . . .

[1] I.e. the Bacchiads, the clan who ruled Corinth from *c.* 750 to *c.* 657 B.C.   [2] Cf. Paus. 4. 4. 1 below.

EUMELUS

FRAGMENTUM

1 (696 *P.M.G.*) (a) Paus. 4. 33. 2 (i 348 Rocha-Pereira)

ἄγουσι δὲ καὶ ἑορτὴν ἐπέτειον Ἰθωμαῖα, τὸ δὲ ἀρχαῖον καὶ ἀγῶνα
ἐτίθεσαν μουσικῆς· τεκμαίρεσθαι δ' ἔστιν ἄλλοις τε καὶ Εὐμήλου τοῖς
ἔπεσιν· ἐποίησε γοῦν καὶ τάδε ἐν τῷ προσοδίῳ τῷ ἐς Δῆλον·

> τῷ γὰρ Ἰθωμάτᾳ καταθύμιος ἔπλετο Μοῖσα
> ἁ καθαρὰ καὶ ἐλεύθερα σάμβαλ' ἔχοισα.

οὐκοῦν ποιῆσαί μοι δοκεῖ τὰ ἔπη καὶ μουσικῆς ἀγῶνα ἐπιστάμενος
τιθέντας.

2 καθαρὰ⟨ν κίθαριν⟩ suppl. Bergk   ἔχουσα codd., em. Dindorf

(b) Paus. 4. 4. 1 (i 278 Rocha-Pereira)

ἐπὶ δὲ Φίντα τοῦ Συβότα πρῶτον Μεσσήνιοι τότε τῷ Ἀπόλλωνι ἐς
Δῆλον θυσίαν καὶ ἀνδρῶν χορὸν ἀποστέλλουσι· τὸ δέ σφισιν ᾆσμα
προσόδιον ἐς τὸν θεὸν ἐδίδαξεν Εὔμηλος, εἶναί τε ὡς ἀληθῶς
Εὐμήλου νομίζεται μόνα τὰ ἔπη ταῦτα.

EUMELUS

PROCESSIONAL HYMN TO DELOS [1]

1 (a) Pausanias, *Description of Greece* (on Messenia)

They keep an annual festival, the Ithomaea, and in ancient times they used also to hold a contest in music. This can be proved by the lines of Eumelus among other things: at any rate he wrote the following in his Processional Hymn to Delos:

> For the god of Ithome [2] took pleasure in the Muse,
> the pure Muse [3] wearing her free sandals. [4]

I think he composed these lines because he knew that the Messenians held a music contest.

[1] See C. M. Bowra, *C.Q.* 57 (1963) 145 ff.   [2] Zeus.   [3] Or, supplementing the text, 'the Muse with her pure lyre'.   [4] The lines seem to indicate that Messenia's freedom is already threatened. The first quarrel with Sparta took place in the reign of Phintas (Paus. 4. 4. 1: see next note).

(b) Pausanias, *Description of Greece* (on Messenia)

In the time of Phintas,[1] son of Sybotas, the Messenians first sent a sacrifice and a chorus of men to Apollo at Delos. Their processional song to the god was taught them by Eumelus, and these lines are reckoned to be his only genuine work.

[1] Father of Androcles and Antiochus, who were kings of Messenia at the beginning of the first war (c. 740–720 B.C.). Eumelus may have named Phintas in his poem.

(c) Paus. 5. 19. 10 (ii 58s. Spiro)

τὸν μὲν δὴ τὴν λάρνακα εἰργασμένον ὅστις ἦν, οὐδαμῶς ἡμῖν δυνατὰ ἦν συμβαλέσθαι· τὰ ἐπιγράμματα δὲ τὰ ἐπ᾿ αὐτῆς τάχα μέν που καὶ ἄλλος τις ἂν εἴη πεποιηκώς, τῆς δὲ ὑπονοίας τὸ πολὺ ἐς Εὔμηλον τὸν Κορίνθιον εἶχεν ἡμῖν, ἄλλων τε ἕνεκα καὶ τοῦ προσοδίου μάλιστα ὃ ἐποίησεν ἐς Δῆλον.

EUMELUS

(c) Pausanias, *Description of Greece* (on Olympia)

I was quite unable to gather who had created the chest,[1] but the inscriptions on it could have been composed by someone else, and my inclination was to call them the work of Eumelus of Corinth, mainly on the strength of his Processional Hymn to Delos.[2]

[1] The 'Chest of Cypselus' in the temple of Hera.   [2] But the chest is dated to the late 7th or early 6th c.

TERPANDER

TESTIMONIA VITAE ATQUE ARTIS

1 *Sud.* T 354 (iv 527 Adler)

Τέρπανδρος· Ἀρναῖος, ἢ Λέσβιος ἀπὸ Ἀντίσσης, ἢ Κυμαῖος· οἱ δὲ καὶ ἀπόγονον Ἡσιόδου ἀνέγραψαν, ἄλλοι δὲ Ὁμήρου, Βοίου λέγοντες αὐτὸν τοῦ Φωκέως, τοῦ Εὐρυφῶντος, τοῦ Ὁμήρου· λυρικός, ὃς πρῶτος ἑπτὰ χορδῶν ἐποίησε τὴν λύραν καὶ νόμους λυρικοὺς πρῶτος ἔγραψεν, εἰ καί τινες Φιλάμμωνα θέλουσι γεγραφέναι.

2 Athen. 14. 635ef (iii 402 Kaibel)

ὅτι δὲ καὶ Τέρπανδρος ἀρχαιότερος Ἀνακρέοντος δῆλον ἐκ τούτων· τὰ Κάρνεια πρῶτος πάντων Τέρπανδρος νικᾷ, ὡς Ἑλλάνικος ἱστορεῖ ἔν τε τοῖς

TERPANDER

LIFE AND WORKS

BIOGRAPHY

1 *Suda,* Terpander

From Arne,[1] or from Antissa in Lesbos,[2] or from Cyme.[3] Some have made him a descendant of Hesiod, others of Homer, calling him son of Boeus of Phocis, son of Euryphon, son of Homer. A lyric poet, who first gave the lyre seven strings[4] and was the first to write lyric nomes,[5] though some attribute this to Philammon.

[1] Perhaps the Boeotian Arne: one of the cithara-nomes was called 'Boeotian' (test. 19), and Hesiod settled in Boeotia.   [2] His birthplace is usually given as Antissa (e.g. by Steph. Byz. s.v. Ἄντισσα) or Lesbos, but Diodorus 8. 28 (ap. Tzetz. *Chil.* 1. 388 ff.) calls him 'T. of Methymna'.   [3] Birthplace of Hesiod.   [4] Cf. testt. 14, 16, fr. 6.   [5] Cf. testt. 18–20.

CHRONOLOGY

2 Athenaeus, *Scholars at Dinner*

That Terpander too is earlier than Anacreon is clear from the following facts: Terpander was the first victor ever at the Carnea,[1] as Hellanicus[2]

[1] Spartan festival in honour of Apollo: cf. test. 10 n. 2.
[2] 5th c. B.C. historian and mythographer from Lesbos.

ἐμμέτροις Καρνεονίκαις κἀν τοῖς καταλογάδην (fr. 85a
Jacoby). ἐγένετο δὲ ἡ θέσις τῶν Καρνείων κατὰ τὴν
ἕκτην καὶ εἰκοστὴν ὀλυμπιάδα, ὡς Σωσίβιός φησιν ἐν
τῷ περὶ Χρόνων (fr. 3 Jacoby). Ἱερώνυμος δ᾽ ἐν τῷ
περὶ Κιθαρῳδῶν, ὅπερ ἐστὶ πέμπτον περὶ Ποιητῶν
(fr. 33 Wehrli), κατὰ Λυκοῦργον τὸν νομοθέτην τὸν
Τέρπανδρόν φησι γενέσθαι, ὃς ὑπὸ πάντων συμφώνως
ἱστορεῖται μετὰ Ἰφίτου τοῦ Ἠλείου τὴν πρώτην
ἀριθμηθεῖσαν τῶν Ὀλυμπίων θέσιν διαθεῖναι.

3 *Marm. Par.* Ep. 34 (p. 12 Jacoby)

ἀφ᾽ οὗ Τέρπανδρος ὁ Δερδένεος ὁ Λέσβιος τοὺς
νόμους τοὺ[ς κιθ]α[ρ]ῳδ[ικ]οὺς [ἐκαινοτόμ]ησε καὶ
τὴν ἔμπροσθε μουσικὴν μετέστησεν, ἔτη
ΗΗΗϜΔΔΔΙ, ἄρχοντος Ἀθήνησιν Δρωπίδου.

4 Euseb. *Chron.* Ol. 34.3[1] (p. 96 Helm, ii 88s. Schöne)

Terpander musicus insignis habetur.

[1] v. l. 34. 4.

records in his *Carnean Victors*, both the metrical and the prose versions; and the Carnea were established in the 26th Olympiad (676/672 B.C.), as Sosibius says in his work *On Chronology*. Secondly, Hieronymus[3] in his treatise *On Cithara-singers*, which is Book 5 of his work *On Poets*, says Terpander lived in the time of Lycurgus the lawgiver, who is universally agreed to have organized the first numbered Olympic Games[4] along with Iphitus of Elis.[5]

[3] 3rd c. B.C. philosopher and literary historian.   [4] I.e. in 776 B.C., but the date is at least a century too early for Terpander; for his alleged association with Lycurgus see also Plut. *Agis* 10.   [5] For the mistaken view that Terpander and Hipponax were contemporary see 'Plut.' *Mus.* 6.

3 *Parian Marble*

From the time when the Lesbian Terpander, son of Derdenes, introduced the new nomes of cithara-song and altered the earlier style of music 381 years[1]; Dropides was archon at Athens.

[1] I.e. 645/644 B.C., 381 years before 264/263.

4 Eusebius, *Chronicle*

Olympiad 34.3 (642/641 B.C.)[1]: the musician Terpander is regarded as famous.

[1] A variant reading gives 641/640. For the calculations of Eusebius see A. A. Mosshammer, *The Chronicle of Eusebius* 226 ff.

5 Clem. Alex. *Strom*. 1. 21. 131. 6 (ii 81 Stählin)

ναὶ μὴν καὶ Τέρπανδρον ἀρχαΐζουσί τινες·
Ἑλλάνικος γοῦν τοῦτον ἱστορεῖ κατὰ Μίδαν γεγονέναι
(fr. 85b Jacoby), Φανίας δὲ πρὸ Τερπάνδρου τιθεὶς
Λέσχην τὸν Λέσβιον Ἀρχιλόχου νεώτερον φέρει τὸν
Τέρπανδρον (fr. 33 Wehrli) . . .

6 [Plut.] *Mus*. 4. 1132e (p. 113 Lasserre, vi 3. 4s.
Ziegler)

ἔοικε δὲ κατὰ τὴν τέχνην τὴν κιθαρῳδικὴν ὁ
Τέρπανδρος διενηνοχέναι· τὰ Πύθια γὰρ τετράκις ἑξῆς
νενικηκὼς ἀναγέγραπται. καὶ τοῖς χρόνοις δὲ σφόδρα
παλαιός ἐστι· πρεσβύτερον γοῦν αὐτὸν Ἀρχιλόχου
ἀποφαίνει Γλαῦκος ὁ ἐξ Ἰταλίας ἐν συγγράμματί τινι
τῷ Περὶ τῶν ἀρχαίων ποιητῶν τε καὶ μουσικῶν· φησὶ
γὰρ (fr. 2 Müller) αὐτὸν δεύτερον γενέσθαι μετὰ τοὺς
πρώτους ποιήσαντας αὐλῳδίαν.

7 Ael. *V.H*. 12. 50 (p. 146 Dilts)

Λακεδαιμόνιοι μουσικῆς ἀπείρως εἶχον· ἔμελε γὰρ
αὐτοῖς γυμνασίων καὶ ὅπλων. εἰ δέ ποτε ἐδεήθησαν
τῆς ἐκ Μουσῶν ἐπικουρίας ἢ νοσήσαντες ἢ παρα-

5 Clement of Alexandria, *Miscellanies*

Some indeed make Terpander ancient: Hellanicus at any rate says that he lived in the time of Midas,[1] but Phanias,[2] putting Lesches of Lesbos earlier than Terpander, makes Terpander later than Archilochus [3] . . .

[1] Or 'was born . . .'; Midas' dates are 738–696 B.C.: cf. Olympus test. 1. [2] Phaenias of Eresus, literary historian (4th c. B.C.). [3] A.'s dates are *c*. 680–640 B.C.; see test. 6.

6 'Plutarch', *On Music*

Terpander appears to have excelled in the art of cithara-singing [1]: it is recorded that he won four successive victories at the Pythian Games. Moreover, he belongs to very early times: Glaucus of Italy [2] in a book *On the Ancient Poets and Musicians* makes him older than Archilochus, saying that Terpander came second after the first composers of song sung to the pipes.

[1] Cf. Themistius *Or*. 26. 316c. [2] See Olympus test. 3 n. 5.

LIFE

7 Aelian, *Historical Miscellanies* [1]

The Spartans had no literary skill, being concerned rather with gymnastics and military training. If ever they needed help from the Muses in sickness or madness or any other such civic disaster,

[1] Cf. Heraclides Lembus, *Excerpta Politiarum* (p. 373 Rose, p. 16 Dilts).

φρονήσαντες ἢ ἄλλο τι τοιοῦτον δημοσίᾳ παθόντες, μετ-
επέμποντο ξένους ἄνδρας οἷον ἰατροὺς ἢ ⟨καθαρτὰς⟩
κατὰ Πυθόχρηστον. μετεπέμψαντό γε μὴν Τέρπανδρον
καὶ Θαλήταν καὶ Τυρταῖον καὶ τὸν Κυδωνιάτην
Νυμφαῖον καὶ Ἀλκμᾶνα (Λυδὸς[1] γὰρ ἦν).

[1] Koraïs: αὐλώδης codd.

8 Clem. Alex. *Strom.* 1. 16. 78. 5 (ii 51 Stählin)

μέλος τε αὖ πρῶτος περιέθηκε τοῖς ποιήμασι καὶ
τοὺς Λακεδαιμονίων νόμους ἐμελοποίησε Τέρπανδρος ὁ
Ἀντισσαῖος.

9 *Sud.* M 701 (iii 370 Adler)

μετὰ Λέσβιον ᾠδόν· παροιμία λεγομένη ἐπὶ τῶν τὰ
δεύτερα φερομένων· οἱ γὰρ Λακεδαιμόνιοι τοὺς
Λεσβίους κιθαρῳδοὺς πρώτους προσεκαλοῦντο·
ἀκαταστατούσης γὰρ τῆς πόλεως αὐτῶν χρησμὸς
ἐγένετο τὸν Λέσβιον ᾠδὸν μεταπέμπεσθαι· οἱ δ᾽ ἐξ
Ἀντίσσης Τέρπανδρον ἐφ᾽ αἵματι φεύγοντα
μεταπεμψάμενοι ἤκουον αὐτοῦ ἐν τοῖς συσσιτίοις καὶ
κατεστάλησαν. ὅτι οἱ Λακεδαιμόνιοι στασιάζοντες
μετεπέμψαντο ἐκ Λέσβου τὸν μουσικὸν Τέρπανδρον, ὃς
ἥρμοσεν αὐτῶν τὰς ψυχὰς καὶ τὴν στάσιν ἔπαυσεν.

they would send for foreigners, doctors or purifiers, in accordance with a pronouncement from the Delphic oracle. For example, they sent for Terpander and Thaletas and Tyrtaeus and Nymphaeus of Cydonia and Alcman, who was a Lydian.

8 Clement of Alexandria, *Miscellanies*

Terpander of Antissa was the first to supply melody for his poems, and he set the laws of the Spartans to music.

9 *Suda* [1]: 'next to the Lesbian singer'

A proverbial expression for those who take second place, since the Lesbian cithara-singers were the first to be invited by the Spartans: when their city was in a state of unrest, they were told by the oracle to send for the Lesbian singer; so sending for Terpander, who was in exile from Antissa [2] because of a murder, they listened to him at their public dinners and were restored to calm. The [3] Spartans in time of civil strife sent to Lesbos for the musician Terpander, who brought their souls into harmony and

---

[1] So Photius *Lexicon* i 418. 7 ff. Naber; see also Aelius Dionysius (ap. Eust. *Il.* 741. 17) = Aristot. *Spartan Constitution* fr. 545 Rose, Philodemus *Mus.* i fr. 30. 31 ff., iv col. 19. 4 ff., 20. 1 ff. (the Epicurean Philodemus ridicules the story which had been transmitted by the Stoic Diogenes of Babylon: see von Arnim *Stoic. Vet. Fragm.* iii 232), Diodorus 8. 28 (ap. Tzetz. *Chil.* 1. 389 ff.), 'Plut.' *Mus.* 42 (= Thaletas test. 4), Zenobius *Cent.* 5. 9, Sappho 106.   [2] Or 'sending to Antissa for T., who was in exile . . .'.   [3] A second version of the story.

εἴποτε οὖν μετὰ ταῦτα μουσικοῦ τινος ἤκουον οἱ
Λακεδαιμόνιοι, ἔλεγον μετὰ Λέσβιον ᾠδόν.

10 *Anth. Pal.* 9. 488 (Τρύφωνος) (Page, *F.G.E.* 99ss.)

Τέρπης εὐφόρμιγγα κρέκων Σκιάδεσσιν ἀοιδὰν
κάτθανε νοστήσας ἐν Λακεδαιμονίοις,
οὐκ ἄορι πληγεὶς οὐδ᾽ οὖν βέλει, ἀλλ᾽ ἐνὶ σύκῳ
χείλεα. φεῦ, προφάσεων οὐκ ἀπορεῖ θάνατος.

11 [Plut.] *Mus.* 9. 1134b (p. 115 Lasserre, vi 3.8
Ziegler)

ἡ μὲν οὖν πρώτη κατάστασις τῶν περὶ τὴν μουσικὴν
ἐν τῇ Σπάρτῃ Τερπάνδρου καταστήσαντος γεγένηται.

12 Athen. 14. 635de (iii 402s. Kaibel)

ἀγνοεῖ δ᾽ ὁ Ποσειδώνιος ὅτι ἀρχαῖόν ἐστιν ὄργανον ἡ
μάγαδις, σαφῶς Πινδάρου λέγοντος τὸν Τέρπανδρον
ἀντίφθογγον εὑρεῖν τῇ παρὰ Λυδοῖς πηκτίδι τὸν
βάρβιτον (fr. 125 S.-M.)·
τόν ῥα Τέρπανδρός ποθ᾽ ὁ Λέσβιος εὗρεν
πρῶτος, ἐν δείπνοισι Λυδῶν

stopped their strife. So after that, whenever the Spartans listened to some musician, they said, 'Next to the Lesbian singer'.

10 *Palatine Anthology*: Tryphon

Terpes,[1] while singing to the strumming of his sweet lyre among the Sunshades,[2] died after returning to his home in Sparta. He was not struck by a sword nor by a missile: he died when he was struck on the lips by one single fig. Alas, Death is never at a loss for an occasion.

[1] Doubtfully equated with Terpander, e.g. by *Suda* Γ 315, where he is said to have choked when a fig was thrown in his mouth while he was singing.   [2] Tent-like structures used at the Carnea in Sparta (Athen. 4. 141 f).

MUSIC AND POETRY

11 'Plutarch', *On Music*

Now music was organized for the first time [1] by Terpander at Sparta.

[1] For the second 'organization' see Thaletas test. 7.

12 Athenaeus, *Scholars at Dinner*

Posidonius [1] does not realize that the magadis is an ancient instrument, although Pindar clearly says that Terpander invented the barbitos in answer to the Lydian pectis, 'the barbitos which once Terpander the Lesbian was the first to invent when he heard

[1] Philosopher and historian, 1st c. B.C.

ψαλμὸν ἀντίφθογγον ὑψηλᾶς ἀκούων πακτίδος.
πηκτὶς δὲ καὶ μάγαδις ταὐτόν . . .

13 [Plut.] *Mus.* 28. 1140f (p. 123 Lasserre, vi 3. 23 Ziegler)

οἱ γὰρ ἱστορήσαντες τὰ τοιαῦτα Τερπάνδρῳ μὲν τήν τε Δώριον νήτην προσετίθεσαν, οὐ χρησαμένων αὐτῇ τῶν ἔμπροσθεν κατὰ τὸ μέλος, καὶ τὸν Μιξολύδιον δὲ τόνον ὅλον προσεξευράσθαι λέγεται, καὶ τὸν τῆς ὀρθίου μελῳδίας τρόπον τὸν κατὰ τοὺς ὀρθίους πρός ⟨τε⟩ τῷ ὀρθίῳ ⟨καὶ τὸν⟩ σημαντὸν τροχαῖον. ἔ⟨τ⟩ι δέ, καθάπερ Πίνδαρός φησι (fr. 124d S.-M.), καὶ τῶν σκολιῶν μελῶν Τέρπανδρος εὑρετὴς ἦν.

14 Aristot. *Probl.* 920a (19. 32)

διὰ τί διὰ πασῶν καλεῖται, ἀλλ' οὐ κατὰ τὸν ἀριθμὸν δι' ὀκτώ, ὥσπερ καὶ διὰ τεττάρων καὶ διὰ πέντε; ἢ ὅτι ἑπτὰ ἦσαν αἱ χορδαὶ τὸ ἀρχαῖον, εἶτ' ἐξελὼν τὴν τρίτην Τέρπανδρος τὴν νήτην προσέθηκεν, καὶ ἐπὶ τούτου ἐκλήθη διὰ πασῶν, ἀλλ' οὐ δι' ὀκτώ· ἑπτὰ γὰρ ἦν.

at Lydian feasts the plucked strings of the lofty
pectis sounding in answer to it'[2]; and the pectis and
magadis are the same thing . . .

[2] I.e. in unison, the barbitos being probably an octave
lower; but Pindar may have meant 'sounding in answer to
the voice of the singer'.

13 'Plutarch', *On Music*

For those who have investigated these things have
credited Terpander with the invention of the Dorian
nete,[1] since his predecessors did not use it in their
melodies; and he is said to have invented the whole
Mixolydian mode[2] and the style of orthian melody
which uses the orthios foot,[3] and to have invented
also the marked trochee in addition to the orthios.
Also, as Pindar says, Terpander invented the music
of *scolia*.[4]

[1] The highest note of the scale: cf. test. 14.   [2] Invention
ascribed to Sappho in *Mus*. 16.   [3] $--\cup\cup$; for the marked
trochee see West, *Greek Metre* 55 f.   [4] Drinking songs.

14 Aristotle, *Problems*

Why is the diapason[1] so called and not named a
diocto ('eighth') after the number of notes, like the
diatessaron ('fourth') and the diapente ('fifth')? Is it
because there were originally seven strings, and
then Terpander removed *trite* and added *nete*, and in
his time it was called diapason and not diocto, since
there were seven notes?

[1] The octave, literally 'the interval of all the notes'.

15 Timoth. *Pers.* (*P.M.G.* 791) 221ss.

πρῶτος ποικιλόμουσος Ὀρ-
φεὺς ⟨χέλ⟩υν ἐτέκνωσεν
υἱὸς Καλλιόπα⟨s
⟩ Πιερίαθεν·
Τέρπανδρος δ' ἐπὶ τῷ δέκα
ζεῦξε μοῦσαν ἐν ᾠδαῖς·
Λέσβος δ' Αἰολία ν⟨ιν⟩ Ἀν-
τίσσᾳ γείνατο κλεινόν·
νῦν δὲ Τιμόθεος μέτροις
ῥυθμοῖς τ' ἑνδεκακρουμάτοις
κίθαριν ἐξανατέλλει . . .

16 [Plut.] *Mus.* 30. 1141c (p. 124 Lasserre, vi 3. 24
Ziegler)

οὗτος γάρ (sc. Τιμόθεος), ἑπταφθόγγου τῆς λύρας
ὑπαρχούσης ἕως εἰς Τέρπανδρον τὸν Ἀντισσαῖον,
διέρριψεν εἰς πλείονας φθόγγους.

17 Plut. *Inst. Lac.* 17 (238c, ii 209 Nachstädt)

εἰ δέ τις παραβαίνοι τι τῆς ἀρχαίας μουσικῆς, οὐκ
ἐπέτρεπον· ἀλλὰ καὶ τὸν Τέρπανδρον ἀρχαϊκώτερον
ὄντα καὶ ἄριστον τῶν καθ' ἑαυτὸν κιθαρῳδῶν καὶ
τῶν ἡρωικῶν πράξεων ἐπαινέτην, ὅμως οἱ ἔφοροι
ἐζημίωσαν καὶ τὴν κιθάραν αὐτοῦ προσεπαττάλευσαν
φέροντες, ὅτι μίαν μόνην χορδὴν ἐνέτεινε περισσοτέραν
τοῦ ποικίλου τῆς φωνῆς χάριν· μόνα γὰρ τὰ ἁπλούστερα
τῶν μελῶν ἐδοκίμαζον.

15 Timotheus, *The Persians*

First Orpheus of the intricate music, son of Calliope, begot the tortoise-shell lyre . . . from Pieria. After him Terpander yoked the Muse to ten songs [1]: Aeolian Lesbos bore him to give glory to Antissa. Now Timotheus with measures and rhythms of eleven strings brings the lyre to life . . .

[1] Perhaps 'to songs on ten strings', but cf. testt. 1, 14, 16, 17, fr. 6.

16 'Plutarch', *On Music*

For the lyre had seven notes as far back as the time of Terpander of Antissa,[1] but Timotheus took the plunge and increased the number.

[1] Cf. fr. 6, Pliny *N.H.* 7. 62. 204 (T. added three strings to the original four); Boethius *Mus.* 1. 20 says the number was suggested by the seven planets. But 'Plut.' *Mus.* 18 = Olympus test. 7 speaks of only three notes.

17 Plutarch, *Spartan Customs*

If anyone tried to break the rules of the old music in any way, they (sc. the Spartans) would not allow it. Even Terpander, one of the older musicians, the best cithara-singer of his day and a praiser of the deeds of the heroes, was none the less fined by the ephors, who took his lyre and nailed it to a wall, all because he fitted one extra string to give variety of sound: only the simpler type of melody met with their approval.

GREEK LYRIC

18 [Plut.] *Mus*. 3. 1132c (p. 112 Lasserre, vi 3. 3s. Ziegler)

καὶ γὰρ τὸν Τέρπανδρον ἔφη (sc. Ἡρακλείδης, fr. 157 Wehrli) κιθαρῳδικῶν ποιητὴν ὄντα νόμων, κατὰ νόμον ἕκαστον τοῖς ἔπεσι τοῖς ἑαυτοῦ καὶ τοῖς Ὁμήρου μέλη περιτιθέντα ᾄδειν ἐν τοῖς ἀγῶσιν. ἀποφῆναι δὲ τοῦτον λέγει ὀνόματα πρῶτον τοῖς κιθαρῳδικοῖς νόμοις.

19 [Plut.] *Mus*. 4. 1132d (p. 112s. Lasserre, vi 3. 4 Ziegler)

οἱ δὲ τῆς κιθαρῳδίας νόμοι πρότερον ⟨οὐ⟩ πολλῷ χρόνῳ τῶν αὐλῳδικῶν κατεστάθησαν ἐπὶ Τερπάνδρου· ἐκεῖνος γοῦν τοὺς κιθαρῳδικοὺς πρότερος ὠνόμασε, Βοιώτιόν τινα καὶ Αἰόλιον Τροχαῖόν τε καὶ Ὀξὺν Κηπίωνά τε καὶ Τερπάνδρειον καλῶν, ἀλλὰ μὴν καὶ Τετραοίδιον. πεποίηται δὲ τῷ Τερπάνδρῳ καὶ προοίμια κιθαρῳδικὰ ἐν ἔπεσιν.

18 'Plutarch', *On Music*

So, according to him (sc. Heraclides [1]), Terpander, a composer of nomes for cithara-singing, set to music in each nome his own hexameters [2] and Homer's and sang them in the contests; and he says that Terpander was the first to supply names [3] for the nomes of cithara-song.

[1] Heraclides Ponticus, 4th c. B.C. philosopher.   [2] Cf. Proclus *Chrest*. 45.   [3] See test. 19.

19 'Plutarch', *On Music*

The nomes sung to the cithara were established in the time of Terpander, shortly before those for the pipes: he at any rate gave them their names before the pipe-nomes got theirs, calling them Boeotian and Aeolian, Trochaios ('trochaic') and Oxys ('high-pitched'), Cepion [1] and Terpandrean, and also Tetraoidios ('four-songed'). [2] Terpander also composed hexameter preludes to be sung to the cithara. [3]

[1] Supposedly named after a favourite pupil (Pollux 4. 65, 'Plut.' *Mus*. 6).   [2] Pollux l.c. adds an eighth, the Orthios ('shrill') (cf. test. 13, fr. 2); see also Photius *Lexicon* ii 26. 13 f. Naber, *Suda* M 1279, N 478, O 575.   [3] Cf. fr. 8: fr. 2 might be an example; see also Ael. Aristid. *Or*. 46. 185 (ii 248 Dindorf) = 3. 231 Lenz-Behr.

20 Pollux 4. 66 (i 221 Bethe)

μέρη δὲ τοῦ κιθαρῳδικοῦ νόμου, Τερπάνδρου
κατανείμαντος, ἑπτά· ἀρχά, μεταρχά, κατατροπά,
μετακατατροπά, ὀμφαλός, σφραγίς, ἐπίλογος.

21 [Plut.] *Mus.* 5. 1132f (p. 113 Lasserre, vi 3. 5
Ziegler)

Ἀλέξανδρος δ' ἐν τῇ Συναγωγῇ τῶν περὶ Φρυγίας
(fr. 77 Jacoby) . . . ἔφη . . . ἐζηλωκέναι . . . τὸν
Τέρπανδρον Ὁμήρου μὲν τὰ ἔπη, Ὀρφέως δὲ τὰ μέλη.

22 [Plut.] *Mus.* 12. 1135c (p. 116 Lasserre, vi 3. 10s.
Ziegler)

ἔστι δέ τις καὶ περὶ τῶν ῥυθμῶν λόγος· γένη γάρ τινα
καὶ εἴδη ῥυθμῶν προσεξευρέθη, ἀλλὰ μὴν καὶ
μελοποιιῶν τε καὶ ῥυθμοποιιῶν. προτέρα μὲν γὰρ ἡ
Τερπάνδρου καινοτομία καλόν τινα τρόπον εἰς τὴν
μουσικὴν εἰσήγαγε· Πολύμνηστος δὲ μετὰ τὸν
Τερπάνδρειον τρόπον καινῷ ἐχρήσατο, καὶ αὐτὸς
μέντοι ἐχόμενος τοῦ καλοῦ τύπου, ὡσαύτως δὲ καὶ
Θαλήτας καὶ Σακάδας· καὶ γὰρ οὗτοι κατά γε τὰς
ῥυθμοποιίας καινοί, οὐκ ἐκβαίνοντες μέν⟨τοι⟩ τοῦ
καλοῦ τύπου.

20 Pollux, *Vocabulary*

The divisions of the nome for cithara-singing, as Terpander organized it, are seven in number: beginning, after-the-beginning, downward-turn, after-the-downward-turn, navel, seal and epilogue.[1]

[1] See B. A. van Groningen, *Mnem.* 4. 8 (1955) 177 ff.

21 'Plutarch', *On Music*

Alexander [1] in his *Collected Materials on Phrygia* said . . . that Terpander imitated the hexameters of Homer but the music of Orpheus.

[1] See Olympus test. 2.

22 'Plutarch', *On Music*

Something must be said also about rhythms, for new genera and species of rhythm were invented, and indeed of melodic and rhythmic composition. First of all, the originality of Terpander introduced a noble style into music [1]; while Polymnestus, after the introduction of this Terpandrean style, used a new one, although he too kept to the noble manner, as did Thaletas and Sacadas, who were innovators at least in rhythmic composition, but did not depart from the noble style.

[1] Cf. Olympus test. 7 and, for the 'simple' style of T.'s cithara-song, 'Plut.' *Mus.* 6.

23 Plut. *Lyc.* 28 (iii 2. 43 Ziegler)

διὸ καί φασιν ὕστερον ἐν τῇ Θηβαίων εἰς τὴν
Λακωνικὴν στρατείᾳ τοὺς ἁλισκομένους Εἵλωτας
κελευομένους ᾄδειν τὰ Τερπάνδρου καὶ Ἀλκμᾶνος καὶ
Σπένδοντος τοῦ Λάκωνος παραιτεῖσθαι, φάσκοντας οὐκ
ἐθέλειν τοὺς δεσποσύνους.

23 Plutarch, *Life of Lycurgus*

This is why they say that later, when the Thebans invaded Laconia [1] and told their Helot prisoners to sing the songs of Terpander or Alcman or Spendon the Laconian, the Helots declined, saying that their masters did not allow it.

[1] In 369 B.C.

TERPANDER

FRAGMENTA

1 (6 *S.L.G.*) P. Oxy. 2737 fr. 1 i 19–27 (v. Ar. fr. 590 K.-A.)

κύκνος ὑπὸ πτερύγων τοιόνδε [τι]·

τὸ μὲν Ἀριστάρχειον δο[κο]ῦν ὅτι Τερπάνδρου ἐστὶν [ἡ] ἀρχή, . . .
ἔστι δ᾽ ἐκ τῶν εἰς Ὅμη[ρ]ον ⟨ἀναφερομένων⟩ ὕμνων.

2 (697 *P.M.G.*) *Sud.* A 1701 (i 151s. Adler)

ἀμφιανακτίζειν· ᾄδειν τὸν Τερπάνδρου νόμον, τὸν καλούμενον
Ὄρθιον, οὗ τὸ (Kuster: ὁ αὐτῷ codd.) προοίμιον ταύτην τὴν ἀρχὴν
εἶχεν·

ἀμφί μοι αὖτε ἄναχθ᾽ ἑκατηβόλον ᾀδέτω ⟨ἀ⟩ φρήν.

cf. *Sud.* A 1700, schol. Ar. *Nub.* 595, Phot. *Lex.* s.v. (p. 99
Reitz.), al.

Hermann ex Ar. *Nub.*: αὐτὸν *Sud.* 1701: αὖτις schol. Ar., *Sud.*
1700 ἀ ci. Hermann, sed v. M.L. West, *C.Q.* 21 (1971)
307ss.

TERPANDER

1 Commentary on Aristophanes (2nd century A.D. papyrus)

The swan to the accompaniment of his wings (sings a song) such as this.

The view of Aristarchus [2] is that the beginning (sc. of the passage quoted from Aristophanes) is by Terpander, . . . but it comes from the hymns ascribed to Homer [Homeric hymn 21. 1].

[1] Mostly of doubtful authenticity: Page accepted only fr. 1; Wilamowitz regarded 6 and 7 as 3rd c. B.C. forgery. [2] The commentator gives alternative views of the source of Aristophanes' words, which may have been used by more than one poet: cf. Alcman 12B.

2 *Suda*

ἀμφιανακτίζειν [1]: to sing the nome of Terpander known as the Orthian,[2] the prelude of which began as follows:

About the far-shooting lord [3] let my heart sing again.

[1] Comic verb used by Cratinus (fr. 72 K.-A.) and Aristophanes (fr. 62 K.-A.) for the composition of hymnal preludes beginning ἀμφὶ . . . ἄνακτα, 'about the lord': see *Clouds* 595. Zenobius 5. 99 gives ἀλλά, ἄναξ, μάλα χαῖρε, 'Then fare thee very well, lord', as the opening of the cithara-singer's epilogue.   [2] See testt. 13, 19 n. 2.   [3] Apollo: cf. test. 2 n. 1.

GREEK LYRIC

3 (698 *P.M.G.*) Clem. Alex. *Strom.* 6. 11. 88. 2 (ii 475s. Stählin)

ἡ τοίνυν ἁρμονία τοῦ βαρβάρου ψαλτηρίου, τὸ σεμνὸν ἐμφαίνουσα τοῦ μέλους, ἀρχαιοτάτη τυγχάνουσα, ὑπόδειγμα Τερπάνδρῳ μάλιστα γίνεται πρὸς ἁρμονίαν τὴν Δώριον ὑμνοῦντι τὸν Δία ὧδέ πως·

> Ζεῦ, πάντων ἀρχά, πάντων ἀγήτωρ,
> Ζεῦ, σοὶ πέμπω ταύταν ὕμνων ἀρχάν.

cf. Arsen. 261 = Apostol. viii 29c

4 (adesp. 941 *P.M.G.*) *Anal. Gramm.* (6. 6 Keil)

σπονδεῖος δ᾽ ἐκλήθη ἀπὸ τοῦ ῥυθμοῦ τοῦ ἐν ταῖς σπονδαῖς ἐπαυλουμένου τε καὶ ἐπᾳδομένου, οἷον·

> σπένδωμεν ταῖς Μνάμας
> παισὶν Μούσαις
> καὶ τῷ Μουσάρχῳ
> Λατοῦς υἱεῖ.

5 (adesp. 1027c *P.M.G.*) D. H. *Comp.* 17 (vi 70 Usener-Radermacher)

ὁ δ᾽ ἐξ ἁπασῶν μακρῶν, μολοττὸν δ᾽ αὐτὸν οἱ μετρικοὶ καλοῦσιν, ὑψηλός τε καὶ ἀξιωματικός ἐστι καὶ διαβεβηκὼς ἐπὶ πολύ. παράδειγμα δὲ αὐτοῦ τοιόνδε·

> ὦ Ζηνὸς καὶ Λήδας κάλλιστοι σωτῆρες.

6 (5 Bergk) Str. 13. 2. 4 (iii 67 Kramer)

οὗτος μὲν οὖν (sc. Ἀρίων) κιθαρῳδός. καὶ Τέρπανδρον δὲ τῆς αὐτῆς μουσικῆς τεχνίτην γεγονέναι φασὶ καὶ τῆς αὐτῆς νήσου, τὸν πρῶτον ἀντὶ τῆς τετραχόρδου λύρας ἑπταχόρδῳ χρησάμενον, καθάπερ καὶ ἐν τοῖς ἀναφερομένοις ἔπεσιν εἰς αὐτὸν λέγεται·

316

TERPANDER

3 Clement of Alexandria, *Miscellanies*

Now the tuning of the barbarian harp [1] which brings out the solemn quality of the melody and is very ancient provides a pattern for Terpander above all, when he sings of Zeus to the Dorian tuning in something like these words:

> Zeus, beginning of all, leader of all, Zeus, to you I send this beginning of my hymns. [2]

[1] David's psaltery.   [2] Rejected by Wilam. and Page as later than 7th c.

4 *Grammatical Extracts*

The spondee (– –) was named after the rhythm played on pipes and sung at σπονδαί, 'libations', e.g.

> Let us pour libation to the Muses, the daughters of Memory, and to the leader of the Muses, Leto's son. [1]

[1] Apollo. Few scholars follow Bergk in ascribing frr. 4 and 5 to Terpander.

5 Dionysius of Halicarnassus, *On Literary Composition*

The rhythm consisting entirely of long syllables, called 'molossus' by the metricians (– – –), is lofty and dignified and has a long stride, e.g.

> (Sons) of Zeus and Leda, you handsome saviours. [1]

[1] The Dioscuri, Castor and Polydeuces. See fr. 4 n. 1.

6 Strabo, *Geography*

Now Arion was a cithara-singer. Terpander also, they say, practised the same kind of music and came from the same island (sc. Lesbos): he was the first to use the seven-stringed instead of the four-stringed lyre, as we are told in the hexameters attributed to him:

σοὶ δ' ἡμεῖς τετράγηρυν ἀποστέρξαντες ἀοιδὰν
ἑπτατόνῳ φόρμιγγι νέους κελαδήσομεν ὕμνους.

cf. Cleonid. *Introd. Harm.* 12 (p. 202 Jan, Euclid. viii 216
Menge), *Anecd. Par.* i 56 Cramer, Clem. Alex. *Strom.*
6. 16. 144. 1 (ii 505 Stählin)

1 ἡμεῖς τοι τ. ἀποστέρξαντες Cleonid.: ἀποστρέψαντες Str.

7 (6 Bergk) Plut. *Lyc.* 21. 4s. (iii 2. 34 Ziegler)

ὅλως δ' ἄν τις ἐπιστήσας τοῖς Λακωνικοῖς ποιήμασιν, ὧν ἔτι καθ'
ἡμᾶς ἔνια διεσῴζετο, καὶ τοὺς ἐμβατηρίους ῥυθμοὺς ἀναλαβών, οἷς
ἐχρῶντο πρὸς τὸν αὐλὸν ἐπάγοντες τοῖς πολεμίοις, οὐ κακῶς
ἡγήσαιτο καὶ τὸν Τέρπανδρον καὶ τὸν Πίνδαρον (fr. 199 S.-M.) τὴν
ἀνδρίαν τῇ μουσικῇ συνάπτειν. ὁ μὲν γὰρ οὕτως πεποίηκε περὶ τῶν
Λακεδαιμονίων·

ἔνθ' αἰχμά τε νέων θάλλει καὶ Μοῦσα λίγεια
καὶ Δίκα εὐρυάγυια, καλῶν ἐπιτάρροθος ἔργων.

cf. Arrian. *Tact.* 44. 3 (ii 176 Roos)

8 (7 Bergk) [Plut.] *Mus.* 6. 1133c (p. 113 Lasserre, vi 3. 6
Ziegler)

τὰ γὰρ πρὸς τοὺς θεοὺς ὡς βούλονται ἀφοσιωσάμενοι, ἐξέβαινον
εὐθὺς ἐπί τε τὴν Ὁμήρου καὶ τῶν ἄλλων ποίησιν. δῆλον δὲ τοῦτ' ἐστὶ
διὰ τῶν Τερπάνδρου προοιμίων.

9 (8 Bergk) Joh. Lyd. *Mens.* 4. 51 (p. 106 Wünsch)

Τέρπανδρός γε μὴν ὁ Λέσβιος Νύσσαν λέγει τετιθηνηκέναι τὸν
Διόνυσον . . .

TERPANDER

For you [1] we shall make new hymns resound on a lyre of seven notes, abandoning our love for the four-voiced song.

[1] Apollo? Cf. fr. 2, test. 2 n. 1.

7 Plutarch, *Life of Lycurgus*

In short, anyone who paid attention to the poetry of Sparta, some of which was still preserved in my time, and examined the marching rhythms they used when going against the enemy to pipe accompaniment, would decide that Terpander and Pindar were quite right to associate valour with music. The former says of Sparta,

There the spear of the young men flourishes and the clear-voiced Muse and Justice who walks in the wide streets, that helper in fine deeds. [1]

[1] The last phrase is in Arrian only.

8 'Plutarch', *On Music*

For they (sc. ancient cithara-singers from Terpander onwards) first performed their duty to the gods as they liked, then went straight on to the poetry of Homer and the rest. This is clear from the preludes of Terpander.

9 Johannes Lydus, *On the Months*

Terpander of Lesbos says Nyssa was the nurse of Dionysus. [1]

[1] She is named on an inscription in the theatre of Dionysus at Athens: see Keil *Philol.* 23 (1866) 608.

THALETAS vel THALES

TESTIMONIA VITAE ATQUE ARTIS

1 Diog. Laert. 1. 38 (i 16 Long)

γεγόνασι δὲ καὶ ἄλλοι Θαλαῖ, καθά φησι Δημήτριος ὁ Μάγνης ἐν τοῖς Ὁμωνύμοις, πέντε· . . . τρίτος ἀρχαῖος πάνυ, κατὰ Ἡσίοδον καὶ Ὅμηρον καὶ Λυκοῦργον.

2 [Plut.] *Mus.* 10. 1134d (p. 115 Lasserre, vi 3. 9 Ziegler)

Γλαῦκος (fr. 4 Müller) γὰρ μετ᾽ Ἀρχίλοχον φάσκων γεγενῆσθαι Θαλήταν . . .

3 [Plut.] *Mus.* 10. 1134e (p. 115 Lasserre, vi 3. 9 Ziegler)

πρεσβύτερον δὲ τῇ ἡλικίᾳ φησὶν ὁ Γλαῦκος (fr. 4 Müller) Θαλήταν Ξενοκρίτου γεγονέναι.

THALETAS OR THALES

LIFE AND WORKS

CHRONOLOGY [1]

1 Diogenes Laertius, *Life of Thales* (the philosopher)

There have been five other men called Thales, according to Demetrius of Magnesia in his *Men of the Same Name* . . . The third is very ancient, a contemporary of Hesiod, Homer and Lycurgus.[2]

[1] See also test. 7 nn. 2, 3.   [2] See also test. 6.

2 'Plutarch', *On Music*

For Glaucus,[1] alleging that Thaletas came after Archilochus, says . . .[2]

[1] See Olymp. test. 3.   [2] Continued at test. 8.

3 'Plutarch', *On Music*

Glaucus[1] says that Thaletas was older than Xenocritus.[2]

[1] See test. 2 n. 1.   [2] See test. 7.

4 [Plut.] *Mus.* 42. 1146b (p. 131 Lasserre, vi 3. 35 Ziegler)

ὅτι δὲ καὶ ταῖς εὐνομωτάταις τῶν πόλεων ἐπιμελὲς γεγένηται φροντίδα ποιεῖσθαι τῆς γενναίας μουσικῆς, πολλὰ μὲν καὶ ἄλλα μαρτύρια παραθέσθαι ἔστι, Τέρπανδρον δ᾽ ἄν τις παραλάβοι τὸν τὴν γενομένην ποτὲ παρὰ Λακεδαιμονίοις στάσιν καταλύσαντα, καὶ Θαλήταν τὸν Κρῆτα, ὅν φασι κατά τι πυθόχρηστον Λακεδαιμονίοις παραγενόμενον διὰ μουσικῆς ἰάσασθαι ἀπαλλάξαι τε τοῦ κατασχόντος λοιμοῦ τὴν Σπάρτην, καθάπερ φησὶ Πρατίνας (713 iii *P.M.G.*).

5 Paus. 1. 14. 4 (i 32 Rocha-Pereira)

Θάλης δὲ ὁ Λακεδαιμονίοις τὴν νόσον παύσας . . . ·
Θάλητα δὲ εἶναί φησι Γορτύνιον Πολύμναστος Κολοφώνιος ἔπη Λακεδαιμονίοις ἐς αὐτὸν ποιήσας.

6 Plut. *Lyc.* 4 (iii 2. 5 Ziegler)

ἕνα δὲ τῶν νομιζομένων ἐκεῖ σοφῶν καὶ πολιτικῶν χάριτι καὶ φιλίᾳ πείσας ἀπέστειλεν εἰς τὴν Σπάρτην, Θάλητα, ποιητὴν μὲν δοκοῦντα λυρικῶν μελῶν καὶ πρόσχημα τὴν τέχνην ταύτην πεποιημένον, ἔργῳ δ᾽ ἅπερ οἱ κράτιστοι τῶν νομοθετῶν διαπραττόμενον·

THALETAS

LIFE AND WORK [1]

4 'Plutarch', *On Music*

One could bring forward much evidence to show
that the best regulated cities have been careful to
pay attention to noble music, in particular the cases
of Terpander, who put an end to the civil strife which
had broken out in Sparta,[2] and of the Cretan Thale-
tas, who is said to have arrived in Sparta in ac-
cordance with an oracle and by means of his music
to have cured them and delivered Sparta from the
plague that gripped it, as Pratinas says.[3]

[1] See also Terp. test. 22. [2] See Terp. test. 9. [3] Cf.
Terp. test. 7, Philodemus *Mus.* i fr. 30. 23, 25, iv col. 18. 33 ff.,
19. 12 ff. (he discredits the story: cf. Terp. test. 9 n. 1),
Plutarch *Princ. Phil.* 4: Philodemus and Plutarch both say
that Thaletas, like Terpander, put an end to civil strife in
Sparta.

5 Pausanias, *Description of Greece*

Thales who stopped the plague for the Spartans
. . .: Polymnestus of Colophon, who composed
verses on Thales for the Spartans, says that he was
from Gortyn.

6 Plutarch, *Life of Lycurgus*

Lycurgus through favour and friendship per-
suaded one of the Cretans who had a high reputation
for wisdom and political ability to go off to Sparta:
this was Thales, who was ostensibly a composer of
songs for the lyre and used this art as a screen, but in
fact did the work of the best of the lawgivers; for his

GREEK LYRIC

λόγοι γὰρ ἦσαν αἱ ᾠδαὶ πρὸς εὐπείθειαν καὶ ὁμόνοιαν
ἀνακλητικοὶ διὰ μελῶν ἅμα καὶ ῥυθμῶν πολὺ τὸ
κόσμιον ἐχόντων καὶ καταστατικόν, ὧν ἀκροώμενοι
κατεπραΰνοντο λεληθότως τὰ ἤθη, καὶ συνῳκειοῦντο
τῷ ζήλῳ τῶν καλῶν ἐκ τῆς ἐπιχωριαζούσης τότε πρὸς
ἀλλήλους κακοθυμίας, ὥστε τρόπον τινὰ τῷ Λυκούργῳ
προοδοποιεῖν τὴν παίδευσιν αὐτῶν ἐκεῖνον.

7 [Plut.] *Mus.* 9. 1134bc (p. 115 Lasserre, vi 3. 8
Ziegler)

ἡ μὲν οὖν πρώτη κατάστασις τῶν περὶ τὴν μουσικὴν
ἐν τῇ Σπάρτῃ Τερπάνδρου καταστήσαντος γεγένηται·
τῆς δὲ δευτέρας Θαλήτας τε ὁ Γορτύνιος καὶ
Ξενόδαμος ὁ Κυθήριος καὶ Ξενόκριτος ὁ Λοκρὸς καὶ
Πολύμνηστος ὁ Κολοφώνιος καὶ Σακάδας ὁ Ἀργεῖος
μάλιστα αἰτίαν ἔχουσιν ἡγεμόνες γενέσθαι· τούτων γὰρ
εἰσηγησαμένων τὰ περὶ τὰς Γυμνοπαιδίας τὰς ἐν
Λακεδαίμονι λέγεται κατασταθῆναι, ⟨καὶ⟩ τὰ περὶ τὰς
Ἀποδείξεις τὰς ἐν Ἀρκαδίᾳ, τῶν τε ἐν Ἄργει τὰ
Ἐνδυμάτια καλούμενα. ἦσαν δ᾽ οἱ μὲν περὶ Θαλήταν τε
καὶ Ξενόδαμον καὶ Ξενόκριτον ποιηταὶ παιάνων . . .

---

test. 1); Xenocritus was said by Glaucus to have been
younger than Thaletas (test. 3); Sacadas did not win his
first Pythian victory till 586 (Paus. 10.7.3).   [4] See test. 8.

songs were exhortations to obedience and harmony,
composed moreover in melodies and rhythms that
were marked by great orderliness and tranquillity.
When they listened to them they became without
realising it quietened in their ways and united in
their enthusiasm for the good, giving up the mutual
ill-will that was endemic among them at the time. So
there is a sense in which Thales paved the way for
Lycurgus in his instruction of the Spartans.[1]

[1] Cf. Strabo 10. 4. 19, Plut. *Agis* 10, Aristot. *Pol.* 1274a. 26 ff.
(Aristotle rejects on chronological grounds the stories that
Lycurgus and Zaleucus were pupils of Thales and that
Onomacritus was his companion).

7 'Plutarch', *On Music*

Now music was organized for the first time by
Terpander at Sparta [1]; credit for the second organi-
zation is best given to Thaletas of Gortyn, Xeno-
damus of Cythera, Xenocritus of Locri, Polymnestus
of Colophon and Sacadas of Argos; for it is said that
it was on their suggestion that the festivals of the
Gymnopaediae [2] at Sparta, the Apodeixeis (Exhi-
bitions) in Arcadia and the so-called Endymatia
(Robings) at Argos were instituted.[3] Thaletas, Xeno-
damus and Xenocritus were composers of paeans[4]
. . .

[1] Terp. test. 11.   [2] Established in 668 to commemorate
Sparta's defeat by Argos at Hysiae in the previous
year.   [3] There are chronological difficulties over
this 'second organization': if Thaletas organized the first
Gymnopaediae, he was a contemporary of Terpander, and
according to one school Polymnestus (who is later than
Thaletas: test. 5) was also as early as Terpander (Polymn.

8 [Plut.] *Mus.* 10. 1134d (p. 115 Lasserre, vi 3. 9 Ziegler)

καὶ περὶ Θαλήτα δὲ τοῦ Κρητὸς εἰ παιάνων γεγένηται ποιητὴς ἀμφισβητεῖται. Γλαῦκος γὰρ (fr. 4 Müller) . . . μεμιμῆσθαι μὲν αὐτόν φησι τὰ Ἀρχιλόχου μέλη, ἐπὶ δὲ τὸ μακρότερον ἐκτεῖναι, καὶ παίωνα καὶ κρητικὸν ῥυθμὸν εἰς τὴν μελοποιίαν ἐνθεῖναι· οἷς Ἀρχίλοχον μὴ κεχρῆσθαι, ἀλλ' οὐδ' Ὀρφέα οὐδὲ Τέρπανδρον· ἐκ γὰρ τῆς Ὀλύμπου αὐλήσεως Θαλήταν φασὶν ἐξειργάσθαι ταῦτα καὶ δόξαι ποιητὴν ἀγαθὸν γεγονέναι.

9 Str. 10. 4. 16 (ii 408 Kramer)

ὡς δ' αὔτως καὶ τοῖς ῥυθμοῖς κρητικοῖς χρῆσθαι κατὰ τὰς ᾠδὰς συντονωτάτοις οὖσιν, οὓς Θαλήτα ἀνευρεῖν, ᾧ καὶ τοὺς παιᾶνας καὶ τὰς ἄλλας τὰς ἐπιχωρίους ᾠδὰς ἀνατιθέασι καὶ πολλὰ τῶν νομίμων.

10 Schol. Pind. *Pyth.* 2. 127 (ii 52s. Drachmann)

ἔνιοι μὲν οὖν φασι τὴν ἔνοπλον ὄρχησιν πρῶτον Κούρητας εὑρηκέναι καὶ ὑπορχήσασθαι, αὖθις δὲ Πύρριχον Κρῆτα συντάξασθαι, Θαλήταν δὲ πρῶτον τὰ εἰς αὐτὴν ὑπορχήματα· Σωσίβιος δέ (fr. 23 Jacoby), τὰ ὑπορχηματικὰ πάντα μέλη Κρηταϊκὰ λέγεσθαι.

THALETAS

8 'Plutarch', *On Music*

Whether Thaletas of Crete composed paeans is also disputed. For Glaucus [1] . . . says that Thaletas imitated Archilochus' songs but increased their length and also introduced into his music the paeonic (e.g. $-\cup\cup\cup$) and cretic ($-\cup-$) rhythms,[2] which Archilochus had not used nor Orpheus nor Terpander for that matter: Thaletas, they say, derived them from the pipe music of Olympus and so gained the reputation of an excellent poet.

[1] See test. 2.   [2] Appropriate to hyporchemata (test. 10).

9 Strabo, *Geography* (quoting Ephorus [1])

(The Cretan lawgiver ordered) likewise that they use in their songs the cretic rhythms, which are very vigorous and were invented by Thales, to whom they ascribe not only their paeans and other native songs but also many of their institutions.

[1] 4th c. historian (fr. 149 Jacoby).

10 Scholiast on Pindar

Now some say that the dance in armour was first invented and danced by the Curetes and that later on Pyrrhichus the Cretan organized it again, and that Thaletas was the first to compose the hyporchemata (choral dance-songs) for it; and Sosibius says all hyporchematic songs are called Cretan.

11 Athen. 15. 678bc (iii 499 Kaibel)

θυρεατικοί· οὕτω καλοῦνταί τινες στέφανοι παρὰ
Λακεδαιμονίοις, ὥς φησι Σωσίβιος ἐν τοῖς περὶ Θυσιῶν
(fr. 5 Jacoby) . . . φέρειν δ᾽ αὐτοὺς ὑπόμνημα τῆς ἐν
Θυρέᾳ γενομένης νίκης τοὺς προστάτας τῶν ἀγομένων
χορῶν ἐν τῇ ἑορτῇ ταύτῃ ⟦ὅτε καὶ τὰς Γυμνοπαιδιὰς
ἐπιτελοῦσιν⟧. χοροὶ δ᾽ εἰσὶν γ´, ὁ μὲν πρόσω παίδων, ⟨ὁ
δ᾽ ἐκ δεξιοῦ γερόντων⟩, ὁ δ᾽ ἐξ ἀριστεροῦ ἀνδρῶν,
γυμνῶν ὀρχουμένων καὶ ᾀδόντων Θαλητᾶ καὶ
Ἀλκμᾶνος ᾄσματα καὶ τοὺς Διονυσοδότου τοῦ
Λάκωνος παιᾶνας.

THALETAS

11 Athenaeus, *Scholars at Dinner*

Thyreatic: this is the Spartan term for certain garlands, according to Sosibius in his treatise *On Sacrifices*; . . . he says that they are worn to commemorate the victory in Thyrea (546 B.C.) by the leaders of the choruses that are organized at that Thyreatic festival [when they hold the Gymnopaediae also].[1] The choruses are three in number, boys in front, old men on the right, men on the left, dancing naked and singing songs by Thaletas and Alcman and the paeans of Dionysodotus the Spartan.

[1] Jacoby struck out this clause.

POLYMNESTUS

TESTIMONIA VITAE ATQUE ARTIS

1 [Plut.] *Mus.* 3. 1132c (p. 112 Lasserre, vi 3. 4 Ziegler)

ὁμοίως δὲ Τερπάνδρῳ Κλονᾶν, τὸν πρῶτον συστησάμενον τοὺς αὐλῳδικοὺς νόμους καὶ τὰ προσόδια, ἐλεγείων τε καὶ ἐπῶν ποιητὴν γεγονέναι, καὶ Πολύμνηστον τὸν Κολοφώνιον τὸν μετὰ τοῦτον γενόμενον τοῖς αὐτοῖς χρήσασθαι ποιήμασιν.

2 [Plut.] *Mus.* 5. 1133ab (p. 113 Lasserre, vi 3. 5 Ziegler)

μετὰ δὲ Τέρπανδρον καὶ Κλονᾶν ᾿Αρχίλοχος παραδίδοται γενέσθαι. ἄλλοι δέ τινες τῶν συγγραφέων Ἄρδαλόν φασι Τροιζήνιον πρότερον Κλονᾶ τὴν αὐλῳδικὴν συστήσασθαι μοῦσαν· γεγονέναι δὲ καὶ Πολύμνηστον ποιητήν, Μέλητος τοῦ Κολοφωνίου υἱόν, ὃν Πολύμνηστόν τε καὶ Πολυμνήστην νόμους ποιῆσαι . . . τοῦ δὲ Πολυμνήστου καὶ Πίνδαρος (fr. 188) καὶ ᾿Αλκμὰν (fr. 145) οἱ τῶν μελῶν ποιηταὶ ἐμνημόνευσαν.

POLYMNESTUS

LIFE AND WORKS

CHRONOLOGY [1]

1 'Plutarch', *On Music*

(Heraclides [2] says also that) like Terpander [3] Clonas, who was the first to compose nomes for pipe accompaniment and processional songs, wrote elegiac couplets and hexameters, and that Polymnestus of Colophon who came after him used the same metres.

[1] See also Thal. test. 7 with n. 3.　　[2] See Terp. test. 18 n. 1.　　[3] I.e. as Terpander composed nomes for cithara accompaniment, so Clonas (and Polymnestus) composed them for pipe accompaniment.

2 'Plutarch', *On Music*

Tradition has it that after Terpander and Clonas came Archilochus. But other historians say Ardalus of Troezen composed music for pipe accompaniment before Clonas, and that there was also a poet Polymnestus, son of Meles of Colophon, composer of the nomes Polymnestus and Polymnestes [1] . . . Polymnestus was mentioned by the lyric poets Pindar [2] and Alcman. [3]

[1] Text uncertain; this chronology would put P. before Archilochus.　　[2] Cf. test. 7.　　[3] Alcman may have died c. 590.

3 [Plut.] *Mus.* 8. 1134a (p. 114s. Lasserre, vi 3. 7s. Ziegler)

τόνων γοῦν τριῶν ὄντων κατὰ Πολύμνηστον καὶ Σακάδαν, τοῦ τε Δωρίου καὶ Φρυγίου καὶ Λυδίου . . .

4 [Plut.] *Mus.* 9–10. 1134cd (p. 115 Lasserre, vi 3. 8s. Ziegler)

οἱ δὲ περὶ Πολύμνηστον (ἦσαν ποιηταὶ) τῶν Ὀρθίων καλουμένων, οἱ δὲ περὶ Σακάδαν ἐλεγείων . . . καὶ Πολύμνηστος δ᾽ αὐλῳδικοὺς νόμους ἐποίησεν· εἰ δὲ τῷ Ὀρθίῳ νόμῳ ⟨ἐν⟩ τῇ μελοποιίᾳ κέχρηται, καθάπερ οἱ ἁρμονικοί φασιν, οὐκ ἔχομεν [[δ᾽]] ἀκριβῶς εἰπεῖν· οὐ γὰρ εἰρήκασιν οἱ ἀρχαῖοί τι περὶ τούτου.

5 [Plut.] *Mus.* 4. 1132d (p. 112 Lasserre, vi 3. 4 Ziegler)

οἱ δὲ νόμοι οἱ κατὰ τούτους, ἀγαθὲ Ὀνησίκρατες, αὐλῳδικοὶ ἦσαν· Ἀπόθετος, Ἔλεγοι, Κωμάρχιος, Σχοινίων, Κηπίων, Ἐπικήδειος [1] καὶ Τριμελής· ὑστέρῳ δὲ χρόνῳ καὶ τὰ Πολυμνήστεια καλούμενα ἐξευρέθη.

----
[1] τε καὶ Δεῖος codd.

3 'Plutarch', *On Music*

Since there were three tuning-systems in the time of Polymnestus and Sacadas,[1] the Dorian, the Phrygian and the Lydian, . . .

[1] This passage seems to make P. a contemporary of Sacadas, whose first Pythian victory was as late as 586.

MUSIC AND POETRY [1]

4 'Plutarch', *On Music* [2]

Polymnestus composed the so-called Orthian pieces,[3] Sacadas elegiacs . . . Polymnestus too composed nomes for pipe accompaniment. But whether he used the Orthios nome[4] in his melodic composition, as the writers on harmonics[5] claim, we cannot say for certain, for the ancients[6] have said nothing about this.

[1] See also Terp. test. 22, Thal. test. 5. [2] Continued from Thal. test. 7. [3] See Terp. test. 13 n. 3. [4] See Terp. test. 19 n. 2. [5] E.g. Archytas.. [6] I.e. the lyric poets.

5 'Plutarch', *On Music*

The nomes in the music of these poets (i.e. Clonas and Polymnestus), my good Onesicrates, were for pipe accompaniment: the Apothetos ('stored away for special occasions'), Elegoi ('laments'), Comarchius ('revel-leader's'), Schoinion ('rope'), Cepion,[1] Epicedius ('funereal') and Trimeles ('three-songed'). Later the so-called Polymnestian pieces were invented.[2]

[1] See Terp. test. 19 n. 1. [2] Terp. test. 19 follows.

6 [Plut.] *Mus.* 29. 1141b (p. 124 Lasserre, vi 3. 24 Ziegler)

Πολυμνήστῳ δὲ τόν θ᾽ ὑπολύδιον νῦν ὀνομαζόμενον τόνον ἀνατιθέασι, καὶ τὴν ἔκλυσιν καὶ τὴν ἐκβολὴν πολὺ μείζω πεποιηκέναι φασὶν αὐτόν.

7 Str. 14. 1. 28 (iii 109 Kramer)

λέγει δὲ Πίνδαρος καὶ Πολύμναστόν τινα τῶν περὶ τὴν μουσικὴν ἐλλογίμων (fr. 188)·
φθέγμα μὲν πάγκοινον ἔγνω-
κας Πολυμνάστου Κολοφωνίου ἀνδρός.

8 Cratinus fr. 338 K.-A.

καὶ Πολυμνήστει᾽ ἀείδει [1] μουσικήν τε μανθάνει.

[1] cf. Hesych. Π 2891 (iii 357 Schmidt) Πολυμνήστειον ᾁδειν· εἶδός τι μελοποιίας τὸ Πολυμνήστειον. ἦν δὲ Κολοφώνιος μελοποιὸς ὁ Πολύμνηστος, εὐμελὴς (cod. εὐημερής) πάνυ, Phot. *Lex.* s.v. Πολυμνήστει᾽ ἀείδειν (ii 98 Naber)

Ar. *Eq.* 1287

καὶ Πολυμνήστεια ποιῶν καὶ ξυνὼν Οἰωνίχῳ.

POLYMNESTUS

6 'Plutarch', *On Music*

To Polymnestus is ascribed the mode now called Hypolydian, and he is said to have greatly increased the *eklysis* and *ekbole*.[1]

[1] The lowering of pitch by three quarter-tones and its raising by five quarter-tones.

7 Strabo, *Geography* (on Colophon)

Pindar mentions a certain Polymnestus as one of the highly regarded figures in music: 'You know the utterance of Polymnestus, the man of Colophon, that is available to all.'

8 Cratinus

And he sings Polymnestian songs[1] and learns music.

[1] Hesychius: 'to sing the Polymnestian': the Polymnestian is a kind of musical composition. Polymnestus was a lyric poet of Colophon, very melodious (or 'cheerful').

Aristophanes, *Knights* (on Ariphrades, 'inventor of cunnilinctus')

And doing Polymnestian things[1] and consorting with Oeonichus.

[1] Presumably parody of Cratinus in the same metre, but the point of the joke is lost; perhaps P. and O. were both contemporary Athenians. Later commentators seem to have inferred wrongly that the poet P. behaved obscenely or that his songs were obscene: schol. Ar. ad loc., schol. Lucian (iv 235 Jacobitz), *Suda* on Ariphrades and Polymnestus.

ALCMAN

TESTIMONIA VITAE ATQUE ARTIS

1 *Sud.* A 1289 (i 117 Adler)

Ἀλκμάν· Λάκων ἀπὸ Μεσσόας· κατὰ δὲ τὸν
Κράτητα πταίοντα Λυδὸς ἐκ Σαρδέων· λυρικός, υἱὸς
Δάμαντος ἢ Τιτάρου. ἦν δὲ ἐπὶ τῆς κζ' Ὀλυμπιάδος,
βασιλεύοντος Λυδῶν Ἄρδυος, τοῦ Ἀλυάττου πατρός·
καὶ ὢν ἐρωτικὸς πάνυ εὑρετὴς γέγονε τῶν ἐρωτικῶν
μελῶν. ἀπὸ οἰκετῶν δέ· ἔγραψε βιβλία ἕξ, μέλη καὶ
Κολυμβώσας. πρῶτος δὲ εἰσήγαγε τὸ μὴ [1] ἑξαμέτροις
μελῳδεῖν. κέχρηται δὲ Δωρίδι διαλέκτῳ, καθάπερ
Λακεδαιμόνιοι. ἔστι δὲ καὶ ἕτερος Ἀλκμάν, εἷς τῶν
λυρικῶν, ὃν ἤνεγκεν ἡ Μεσσήνη. καὶ τὸ πληθυντικὸν
Ἀλκμᾶνες.

[1] μὴ secl. Haslam

Eusebius 222–5.   [5] See frr. 58 and 59(a) with the comment
of Archytas.   [6] Cf. test. 12.   [7] Cf. frr. 4C (n. 2), 158,
test. 16: was the *Diving Women* a component of the six
books, or should μέλη be altered to μελῶν to give 'six books
of lyric poetry and also the *Diving Women*'?   [8] Haslam
deletes μή to give 'in hexameter rhythms': cf. Terp.
test. 18.   [9] See Page, *Alcman: the Partheneion* 102–63, E.
Risch in *Mus. Helv.* 11 (1954) 20–37.   [10] See test. 29.

ALCMAN

LIFE AND WORKS

BIOGRAPHY

1 *Suda*, Alcman [1]

A Laconian from Messoa [2]: Crates [3] wrongly
makes him a Lydian from Sardis. A lyric poet; son of
Damas or Titarus. He was alive in the 27th Olympiad
(672/668 B.C.), when Ardys, father of Alyattes, was
King of Lydia. [4] He was extremely amorous and was
the first to write amatory songs. [5] His forebears were
household slaves. [6] He wrote six books: lyric poetry
and the *Diving Women*. [7] He was the first to intro-
duce the practice of singing poetry in rhythms other
than the hexameter. [8] He used the Dorian dialect, [9] as
Spartans do. There is also another Alcman, [10] one of
the lyric poets, who was brought by Messene. The
plural form is 'Alcmanes'.

---

[1] See J. A. Davison, *From Archilochus to Pindar* 173–87.
[2] One of the villages which comprised the town of
Sparta.   [3] Crates of Mallos, flor. 168 B.C., librarian of
Pergamum; for the controversy over the birthplace see
testt. 2–9.   [4] Ardys in fact ruled from *c.* 652 to *c.* 619 and
was father of Sadyattes and grandfather of Alyattes; for the
chronology see testt. 10–11, and for the synchronization of
A. and Ardys see A. A. Mosshammer, *The Chronicle of*

2 *Anth. Pal.* 7. 709 = Alexander Aetolus i Gow-Page

Σάρδιες, ἀρχαῖος πατέρων νομός, εἰ μὲν ἐν ὑμῖν
  ἐτρεφόμαν, κέρνας ἦν τις ἂν ἢ βακέλας
χρυσοφόρος ῥήσσων λάλα τύμπανα, νῦν δέ μοι ᾿Αλκμάν
  οὔνομα καὶ Σπάρτας εἰμὶ πολυτρίποδος,
καὶ Μούσας ἐδάην ῾Ελικωνίδας [1] αἵ με τυράννων
  θῆκαν Κανδαύλεω [2] μείζονα καὶ Γύγεω.

cf. Plut. *de exil.* 599e

[1] ῾Ελληνίδας Plut.   [2] Bentley: Δασκύλεω corrector, Plut.:
Δυσ- cod.

3 *Anth. Pal.* 7. 19 = Leonidas of Tarentum lvii Gow-
Page

τὸν χαρίεντ᾿ ᾿Αλκμᾶνα, τὸν ὑμνητῆρ᾿ ὑμεναίων
  κύκνον, τὸν Μουσέων ἄξια μελψάμενον,
τύμβος ἔχει, Σπάρτας μεγάλαν χάριν, ἔνθ᾿ [1] ὅ γε
  Λυδός [2]
ἄχθος ἀπορρίψας οἴχεται εἰς ᾿Αίδαν.

[1] Jacobs: εἴθ᾿ codd.   [2] Planudes, sed cf. test. 4: λοῖσθος
Pal., *Sud.* s.v.: λύσθος Pal. corrector

ALCMAN

2 *Palatine Anthology*: Alexander of Aetolia [2]

Sardis, ancient dwelling-place of my fathers, if I had been brought up in you I would have been an acolyte carrying the offering-dish or a eunuch-priest wearing gold ornaments, striking the noisy tambourine [3]; as it is, my name is Alcman, and I belong to Sparta with its many tripods,[4] and I have come to know the Muses of Helicon, who have made me greater than the despots Candaules or Gyges.[5]

[1] See test. 1, frr. 16, 24, 39 (n. 2), Terp. test. 7; also P.Oxy. 3542 (3rd c. A.D.): 'some say that D(amas), his father, moved from Lydia . . ., (having) with him (his son), still a child.' [2] The poem is quoted by Plutarch to illustrate the possibility of a happy exile. [3] In the service of Rhea. [4] Prizes in games. [5] Lydian kings with their capital in Sardis.

3 *Palatine Anthology*: Leonidas

Graceful Alcman, the swan who sang wedding-hymns,[1] whose song was worthy of the Muses, lies in this tomb; he was a great delight to Sparta, where the Lydian,[2] having thrown off his burden,[3] departed to Hades.

[1] V.1 = 159 *P.M.G.*: frr. 4C and 107 may be from wedding-hymns; see also M. W. Haslam, *Ox. Pap.* 45 (1977) 3. [2] Text uncertain: some authorities give 'where he at the end, having . . .'. [3] Presumably the burden of slavery: cf. testt. 1, 12.

4 *Anth. Pal.* 7. 18 = Antipater of Thessalonica xii Gow-Page

ἀνέρα μὴ πέτρῃ τεκμαίρεο· λιτὸς ὁ τύμβος
ὀφθῆναι, μεγάλου δ' ὀστέα φωτὸς ἔχει.
εἰδήσεις Ἀλκμᾶνα λύρης ἐλατῆρα Λακαίνης
ἔξοχον, ὃν Μουσέων ἐννέ' ἀριθμὸς ἔχει.
κεῖται δ' ἠπείροις διδύμαις ἔρις εἴθ' ὅ γε Λυδός
εἴτε Λάκων. πολλαὶ μητέρες ὑμνοπόλων.

5 Vell. Pat. 1. 18. 3 (p. 19 Stegmann de Pritzwald)

Alcmana Lacones falso sibi vindicant.

6 εἰς τοὺς ἐννέα λυρικούς 19s. (Schol. Pind. i 11 Drachmann)

Ἀλκμὰν ἐν Λυδοῖσι μέγα πρέπει· ἀλλὰ Δάμαντος
ἐστὶ καὶ ἐκ Σπάρτης, Δωρίδος ἁρμονίης.

7 Schol. B ad Alcm. 1. 58s. = P. Oxy. 2389 fr. 6 col. i 10–13

. . . . .][1] τοὺς [Ἰβην]ούς φησιν τῆς Λ[υδίας ἔθνος εἶ]ναι· [ἀπὸ τ]ούτου δὲ βούλετ[αι . . . . ὅτι] Λυ[δὸς ἦν] ὁ Ἀλκμάν.

[1] οὗτος]? Barrett

340

4 *Palatine Anthology*: Antipater of Thessalonica

Do not judge the man by the stone: his tomb is small to look at, but it holds the bones of a great man. You will recognize Alcman, outstanding striker of the Spartan lyre, one of the nine,[1] the Muses' number. Here he lies, source of dispute to two continents, whether he was Lydian or Spartan. Singers have many mothers.

[1] I.e. one of the Alexandrian canon of nine lyric poets.

5 Velleius Paterculus, *History of Rome*

Alcman is falsely claimed by the Spartans[1] as their own.

[1] Perhaps an allusion to the Spartan historian Sosibius (see fr. 94).

6 *On the Nine Lyric Poets* (quoted by Scholiast on Pindar)

Alcman shines strongly among the Lydians; but his father is Damas and he is from Sparta and his song is Dorian.

7 Scholiast B on Alcman 1. 58 f. (papyrus of 50–100 A.D.)

X[1] says (the Ibenians are a people) of (Lydia), and from this he is ready (to infer) that Alcman (was) Lydian.

[1] The space is too small for 'Crates' (see test. 1); perhaps 'he' with reference to Aristarchus.

GREEK LYRIC

8 P. Oxy. 2389 fr. 9 col. i 5ss. = fr. 13(a) *P.M.G.*

].[. . .]νος ἐχέγγυος [   ] βεβαιωτὴς ἂν
γένοι[το   ὅτι] Λάκων εἴη ὅτε φη[σί·   ]
ἀντίφαριν Λάκωνι τέ[κτονα πα]ρθενίων σοφῶν Ἀλκ-
μᾶ[νι   ω]ν τε μελέων ποτίφορον [   ].ον·
ἀλλ' ἔοικε Λυδὸν αὐ[τὸν νομί]ζειν ὅ τε Ἀριστοτέλης
καὶ [ὁ Κράτης σύ]μψηφοι ἀπατηθέντες [οὐκ ἦς]
ἀνὴρ ἀγρεῖος οὐδ[ὲ . . .

9 P. Oxy. 2506 fr. 1 col. ii = fr. 10(a) *P.M.G.*

. .] Φλε[ι]άσιος[Α]ἰσχύ[λ]ος ομ[.].α[
Λ]ακεδα[ι]μόνιον ἀ[ποφαί]νει τὸν Ἀλ[κμ]ᾶνα· [λέγει]
γὰρ ἐν τοῖς Ὑακιν[θίοις,] ἄκουσα τᾶν ἀηδ[όνων, ταὶ]
παρ' Εὐρώτα ῥ[οαῖσι] ταν Ἀμυκλα[   ]μεναι
τατ[   ]τον ἐννομω[   ]ουσαν αυτα.[   ]
ἀρεταν ταν[   ] που μέλεσι.[   ]ταλλαν
ταν τ.[   ] Ἀταρνίδα ἐν[.] ἐν γὰρ
τούτο[ις   ] γράφειν ταπ[   ] Ἀλκμᾶνος
. . .

ALCMAN

8 Commentary on Alcman's birthplace (same papyrus)

X[1] would be a reliable . . . authority that he (sc. Alcman) was Spartan, when he says, '. . . craftsman of skilled maiden-songs, rival to Spartan Alcman, and fitting . . . of . . . songs'; but it seems that Aristotle and (Crates?) agree in regarding him as Lydian, deceived (by the words), 'he was no rustic man nor . . .' [fr. 16].[2]

[1] Some lyric poet, perhaps Pindar.   [2] Similar material in P.Oxy. 2506 = fr. 13(c) and (d).

9 Commentary on the life of Alcman and others (papyrus of 1st or early 2nd century A.D.)

. . . the Phliasian[1] . . . Aeschylus . . . (he) shows that Alcman was a Spartan: for he says in his *Hyacinthia*,[2] 'I heard the nightingales, which by (the waters) of the Eurotas . . . the Amyclaean . . . best-governed . . .' . . . 'excellence . . .' somewhere in his songs . . . '. . . woman of Atarneus[3] . . .' For in these . . . to write . . . Alcman . . . (Xanthus?)[4]

[1] Presumably the scholar Aeschylus of Phlius mentioned by Xen. *Symp.* 4. 63; but perhaps the well-known 5th c. poets Pratinas of Phlius and Aeschylus.   [2] Name of the cult of Apollo and Hyacinthus at Amyclae, south of Sparta; it is not clear if the quotation is from Alcman himself.   [3] Same mysterious word in Schol. B on Alcm. 1. 60 ff.   [4] 5th c. Lydian historian.

(v. 24) Ξά]νθο[ς   ] . ια . ['Α].λκμ.[άν·
οὐδ]ὲ γὰρ ἄ[λ]λο τῶν ἐν Λ[υδοῖς πα]ραλέλ[οι]πεν οὐδ[ὲν
τῶν κα]τὰ μι[κρὸν] ἀξίων λό[γου γεγεν]ημένων· ἐστὶ
[δὲ] οὐδὲν [θα]υμ.[άσιον] ὡς Λακεδα[ι]μόνιοι τότ[ε]
ἐπέστησαν Λυδὸν ὄντα διδάσκαλον τῶν θυγατέρων καὶ
ἐφή[βω]ν πατρίο[ις] χοροῖς το[. . .].των [ἀ]γωνί-
σασθα[ι δ]ὲ μηδέπω [ἐᾶν?] καὶ νῦν ἔτι [ξε]νικῶι
κέχρη[ν]ται διδασκάλωι χο[ρῶν.   γ]ὰρ εἰ διὰ
[τ]ὴν σοφία[ν πο]λίτην ἐπ[ο]ιήσαντο, [ἄτοπόν] ἐστιν
ἑα[υ]τοῦ κατη[γορεῖν π]η⟨ι⟩(?) τοῖς ἄ[ισ]μασι τὸν
['Αλκμᾶ]να καὶ λέγειν ὅτι βά[ρβαρος] ἦν καὶ Λυδὸς
ὑπὲρ Λ[υδίας π]ατρίδος καὶ γέ[νους . . .

10(a) Euseb. *Chron.* Ol. 30. 3 (p. 94 Helm, ii 87 Schöne)

Alcmeon clarus habetur et Lesches Lesbius qui parvam fecit Iliadem.

(b) Euseb. *Chron.* Ol. 42. 4 (p. 98 Helm, ii 90s. Schöne)

Alcman, ut quibusdam videtur, agnoscitur.

. . . Alcman; for he has omitted nothing else about (Lydian) history that is in the least important.[5] It is not (surprising) that despite his Lydian origin Spartans at that date put him in charge of the traditional choruses of their daughters and young men . . . but did not yet (allow foreigners?) to compete, (since) even now they still use foreigners to train their choruses. For if the Spartans had made him a citizen because of his poetic skill, it is (strange) that Alcman should diffame himself in his songs and say that he was a barbarian and a Lydian on account of his (Lydian?) country and (race) . . .

[5] It seems that the historian of Lydia (Xanthus?) made no mention of Alcman, an argument from silence for his non-Lydian origin; the next sentence seems to assume his Lydian origin, though the next again argues against it.

CHRONOLOGY [1]

10 Eusebius, *Chronicle*

(a) Olympiad 30.3 (658/657)[2]: Alcmeon (i.e. Alcman) is considered famous together with Lesches of Lesbos, who composed the *Little Iliad*.

(b) Olympiad 42.4 (609/608): according to some, Alcman is well-known.

[1] See also test. 1.   [2] Cf. A. A. Mosshammer, *The Chronicle of Eusebius* 218. The Armenian version gives the year as 659/658.

11(a) *Sud.* Σ 1095 (Στησίχορος) (iv 433 Adler)

τοῖς δὲ χρόνοις ἦν νεώτερος ᾽Αλκμᾶνος τοῦ λυρικοῦ,
ἐπὶ τῆς λζ΄ ᾽Ολυμπιάδος γεγονώς.

(b) *Sud.* A 3886 (᾽Αρίων) (i 351 Adler)

γέγονε κατὰ τὴν λη΄ ᾽Ολυμπιάδα. τινὲς δὲ καὶ
μαθητὴν ᾽Αλκμᾶνος ἱστόρησαν αὐτόν.

12 Heraclid. Lemb. *Excerpt.* *Polit.* (p. 16 Dilts)
= Aristot. *Fragm.* p. 372 Rose

ὁ δὲ ᾽Αλκμὰν οἰκέτης ἦν ᾽Αγησίδου, εὐφυὴς δὲ ὢν
ἠλευθερώθη καὶ ποιητὴς ἀπέβη.

13 Arist. *Hist. An.* 556b–557a (ii 56 Louis)

οἱ δὲ φθεῖρες (sc. γίνονται) ἐκ τῶν σαρκῶν. γίνονται
δ᾽ ὅταν μέλλωσιν οἷον ἴονθοι μικροί, οὐκ ἔχοντες πύον·
τούτους ἄν τις κεντήσῃ, ἐξέρχονται φθεῖρες. ἐνίοις δὲ

11(a) *Suda*, Stesichorus

Stesichorus was later than the lyric poet Alcman, since he was born in the 37th Olympiad (632/628).[1]

(b) *Suda*, Arion

Arion was born in the 38th Olympiad (628/624).[2] Some said he was the pupil of Alcman.

[1] The *Suda* (test. 1) gives the conventional 40-year interval between the *floruit* of Alcman and the birth of Stesichorus. [2] Eusebius' date for Arion's *floruit* (Ol. 40.3 = 618/617) and his first date for Alcman's *floruit* (test. 10a) give the conventional 40-year gap between pupil and teacher.

ALLEGED SERVILE ORIGIN [1]

12 Heraclides Lembus, *On Constitutions*

Alcman was a household slave of Agesidas, but since he was talented he was set free, and he turned out to be a poet.

[1] See also test. 1.

DEATH

13 Aristotle, *History of Animals*

Lice are produced from flesh. When they are about to appear, a sort of small eruption forms, without pus; if this is pricked, lice come out. Some get this

τοῦτο συμβαίνει τῶν ἀνθρώπων νόσημα, ὅταν ὑγρασία
πολλὴ ἐν τῷ σώματι ᾖ· καὶ διεφθάρησάν τινες ἤδη
τοῦτον τὸν τρόπον, ὥσπερ Ἀλκμᾶνά τέ φασι τὸν
ποιητὴν καὶ Φερεκύδην τὸν Σύριον.

14 Paus. 3. 15. 2s. (i 237 Rocha-Pereira)

τοῦ Σεβρίου δέ ἐστιν ἐν δεξιᾷ μνῆμα Ἀλκμᾶνος
. . . · Ἑλένης δὲ ἱερὰ καὶ Ἡρακλέους, τῆς μὲν
πλησίον τοῦ τάφου τοῦ Ἀλκμᾶνος . . .

15 [Plut.] *Mus.* 17. 1136f (p. 118 Lasserre, vi 3. 14
Ziegler)

οὐκ ἠγνόει (sc. Πλάτων) δ' ὅτι πολλὰ Δώρια
παρθένεια ⟦ἄλλα⟧ Ἀλκμᾶνι καὶ Πινδάρῳ καὶ Σιμωνίδῃ
καὶ Βακχυλίδῃ πεποίηται, ἀλλὰ μὴν καὶ ὅτι προσόδια
καὶ παιᾶνες.

disease when there is much moisture in the body, and indeed people have died from it, the poet Alcman, they say, and Pherecydes of Syros.[1]

[1] Cf. Plin. *N.H.* 11.114, Helladius in Phot. *Library* 533a, where the three victims listed are the hero Acastus, Pherecydes and Sulla. Dissolute living was thought to aggravate phthiriasis (Plut. *Sulla* 36.5). O. Musso (*Prometheus* 1, 1975, 183 f.) argues that the text of Aristotle should read not 'the poet Alcman' but 'the physicist Alcmaeon', as in the *Excerpts* of pseudo-Antigonus (*Mir.* 88).

14 Pausanias, *Description of Greece*

On the right of the Sebrion [1] (in Sparta) is the monument of Alcman . . . There are sanctuaries of Helen [2] and of Heracles [3]: Helen's is near the tomb of Alcman . . .[4]

[1] Shrine of Sebrus, son of Hippocoon: see fr. 1.3.   [2] See fr. 21.   [3] See fr. 1 n. 2: Heracles killed Hippocoon and his sons.   [4] Continued at test. 22.

COMPOSITIONS [1]

15 'Plutarch', *On Music*

Plato was well aware that many maiden-songs in the Dorian mode were composed by Alcman, Pindar, Simonides and Bacchylides, in addition to processional-songs and paeans.

[1] See also testt. 1, 3, 9, frr. 158, 160 (= Thaletas test. 11). For references to books 1–6 see frr. 1–3, 4C, 14–20.

GREEK LYRIC

16 Ptolem. Heph. *Nov. Hist.* (ap. Phot. *Bibl.* 190. 151a Bekker, iii 64s. Henry)

τελευτήσαντος Δημητρίου τοῦ Σκηψίου τὸ βιβλίον Τέλλιδος πρὸς τῇ κεφαλῇ αὐτοῦ εὑρέθη· τὰς δὲ Κολυμβώσας Ἀλκμᾶνος [1] πρὸς τῇ κεφαλῇ Τυρονίχου [2] τοῦ Χαλκιδέως εὑρεθῆναί φασι . . .

[1] Casaubon: Ἀλκμάνους codd.   [2] Τυννίχου ci. Valesius, Naeke

17 Heph. *Sign.* 4 (p. 74 Consbruch)

ἡ δὲ διπλῆ ἡ ἔξω βλέπουσα παρὰ μὲν τοῖς κωμικοῖς καὶ τοῖς τραγικοῖς ἐστι πολλή, παρὰ δὲ τοῖς λυρικοῖς σπανία· παρὰ Ἀλκμᾶνι γοῦν εὑρίσκεται· γράψας γὰρ ἐκεῖνος δεκατεσσάρων στροφῶν ᾄσματα ⟦ ὧν ⟧ τὸ μὲν ἥμισυ τοῦ αὐτοῦ μέτρου ἐποίησεν ἑπτάστροφον, τὸ δὲ ἥμισυ ἑτέρου· καὶ διὰ τοῦτο ἐπὶ ταῖς ἑπτὰ στροφαῖς ταῖς ἑτέραις τίθεται ἡ διπλῆ σημαίνουσα τὸ μεταβολικῶς τὸ ᾆσμα γεγράφθαι.

ALCMAN

16 Ptolemy the Quail, *New History* (excerpted in Photius, *Library*)

When Demetrius of Scepsis died, the book of Tellis was found by his head; and they say that the *Diving Women* [1] of Alcman was found by the head of Tyronichus of Chalcis. [2]

[1] See test. 1, fr. 158.　　[2] Unknown; perhaps read 'Tynnichus of Chalcis', composer of a famous paean to Apollo (707 *P.M.G.*).

METRES [1]

17 Hephaestion, *On Critical Signs*

The outward-facing *diple* (>) [2] is common in comic and tragic texts but rare in lyric poets. It *is* found in Alcman, since he composed songs of fourteen strophes of which the first half consisted of seven strophes in the same metre, the other half of strophes in a different metre. So the *diple* is placed against the seven different strophes [3] to indicate the change of metre in the song.

[1] See also test. 1; for various dactylic and anapaestic lengths labelled 'Alcmanic' see 161(c) *P.M.G.*　　[2] A mark in the left margin used e.g. to indicate a new speaker in drama.　　[3] Presumably at the point where they begin.

18 Heph. *Ench*. 8. 4 (p. 25s. Consbruch)

τὸ μέντοι (sc. τὸ ἀναπαιστικὸν τὸ τετράμετρον
καταληκτικὸν εἰς συλλαβήν) τὸν σπονδεῖον ἔχον ἀλλὰ
μὴ τὸν ἀνάπαιστον παραλήγοντα εἰσὶν οἳ Λακωνικὸν
καλοῦσι, προφερόμενοι παράδειγμα τὸ

ἄγετ᾽ ὦ Σπάρτας ἔνοπλοι κοῦροι ποτὶ τὰν Ἄρεως
κίνασιν (= Carm. Pop. 857 *P.M.G.*),

ubi schol. A (p. 134 Consbruch) ἐπεὶ Ἀλκμὰν τούτῳ ἐχρήσατο·
οὗτος δὲ Λάκων. Cf. Choerobosc. (p. 234 Consbruch)

19 Heph. *Ench*. 8. 9 (p. 28 Consbruch) (de archebuleo)

τοὺς δὲ μετὰ τὸν πρῶτον πόδα τρεῖς οἱ μὲν ἐν
συνεχείᾳ γράψαντες τὸ μέτρον πάντως ἀναπαίστους
ἐφύλαξαν, Ἀλκμὰν δέ που καὶ σπονδείους
παραλαμβάνει.

20 Hsch. Κ 2939 (ii 487 Latte)

κλεψίαμβοι· Ἀριστόξενος, μέλη τινὰ παρὰ
Ἀλκμᾶνι.

21 [Plut.] *Mus*. 12. 1135c (p. 116 Lasserre, vi 3. 11 Ziegler)

ἔστι δὲ ⟨καί⟩ τις Ἀλκμανικὴ καινοτομία καὶ
Στησιχόρειος, καὶ αὐταὶ οὐκ ἀφεστῶσαι τοῦ καλοῦ.

ALCMAN

18 Hephaestion, *Handbook on Metres*

The catalectic anapaestic tetrameter with a spon-
dee instead of the anapaest in the second-last foot
some call 'Spartan', giving as an example, 'Come,
armed youths of Sparta, to the dance of Ares' (Pop.
Song 857).

Scholiast: since Alcman used it, and he was
Spartan.

19 Hephaestion, *Handbook on Metres*

In the archebulean[1] writers other than Alcman
made the second, third and fourth feet anapaestic
like the first, thus keeping the rhythm entirely ana-
paestic; but Alcman admits spondees somewhere.

[1] Four anapaests followed by a bacchius; see e.g. M. L.
West, *Greek Metre* 152.

20 Hesychius, *Lexicon*

Clepsiambi[1]: according to Aristoxenus, certain
songs (i.e. metres?) in Alcman.

[1] Used elsewhere of a type of stringed instrument. Bergk
thought that catalectic iambic trimeters (e.g. 19, 96) might
be meant.

21 'Plutarch', *On Music*

There is also a certain originality (sc. in metre) in
Alcman and Stesichorus, although their innovations
do not abandon the noble manner[1] either.

[1] I.e. the manner of Terpander.

22 Paus. 3. 15. 2 (i 237 Rocha-Pereira)

. . . Ἀλκμᾶνος, ᾧ ποιήσαντι ᾄσματα οὐδὲν ἐς ἡδονὴν αὐτῶν ἐλυμήνατο τῶν Λακώνων ἡ γλῶσσα, ἥκιστα παρεχομένη τὸ εὔφωνον.

23 *Sud.* Φ 441 (iv 736 Adler) = *F.Gr.H.* 328 T1, F91

Φιλόχορος· . . . ἔγραψεν . . . Περὶ Ἀλκμᾶνος.

ALCMAN

DIALECT [1]

22 Pausanias, *Description of Greece*

. . . Alcman,[2] the pleasure of whose songs was in no way spoiled by his use of the Spartan dialect, which is not in the least euphonious.

[1] See also test. 1. The Augustan scholar Tryphon wrote on A.'s dialect (*Sud.* T 1115).   [2] Continued from test. 14.

ANCIENT COMMENTATORS [1]

23 *Suda*, Philochorus [2]

He wrote . . . *On Alcman.*

[1] See also test. 1 n. 1 for Crates, frr. 94, 96, 100 for Sosibius, *On Alcman* in at least three books, frr. 39, 59 for a hypothetical *On Alcman* by Chamaeleon, frr. 151, 153 for Cornelius Alexander's *Place-names in Alcman.* Commentaries on the Louvre *Partheneion* (fr. 1) were written by Aristophanes of Byzantium, Aristarchus, Pamphilus, Sosiphanes and Stasicles: see the scholia there; Aristonicus and Ptolemaeus discussed fr. 3; one Dionysius wrote a commentary on Book 4 (see fr. 18). For Apollodorus of Athens see frr. 94, 100. The grammarians Theon and Tyrannion commented on fr. 5. 2 col. ii. Didymus may have posited 'the second Alcman' (see test. 29). See also test. 9 n. 1 for Aeschylus of Phlius. Aristotle (test. 8) and Aristoxenus (test. 20) knew his work.   [2] 3rd c. B.C. Athenian historian.

GREEK LYRIC

24 Athen. xiv 638e (iii 410 Kaibel)

καὶ ὁ τοὺς Εἵλωτας δὲ πεποιηκώς φησιν (Eup. fr. 148
K.-A.)·
τὰ Στησιχόρου τε καὶ Ἀλκμᾶνος Σιμωνίδου τε
ἀρχαῖον ἀείδειν. ὁ δὲ Γνήσιππος ἔστ᾽ ἀκούειν,
ὃς νυκτερίν᾽ εὗρε μοιχοῖς ἀείσματ᾽ ἐκκαλεῖσθαι
γυναῖκας ἔχοντας ἰαμβύκην τε καὶ τρίγωνον.

25 *Anth. Pal.* 9. 184. 9 = *F.G.E.* 1202

. . . θηλυμελεῖς τ᾽ Ἀλκμᾶνος ἀηδόνες . . .

26 *Anth. Pal.* 9. 571. 3 = *F.G.E.* 1206

. . . ἦν γλυκὺς Ἀλκμάν.

27 Stat. *Silv.* 5. 3. 146ss. (p. 121 Marastoni)

generosaque pubes
te monitore . . . discere . . .
. . . qua lege recurrat
Pindaricae vox flexa lyrae volucrumque precator
Ibycus et tetricis Alcman cantatus Amyclis . . .

ALCMAN

24 Athenaeus, *Scholars at Dinner*

The author [2] of the *Helots* says, 'To sing the songs of Stesichorus and Alcman and Simonides is old-fashioned; but we can all hear Gnesippus, who invented nocturnal serenades for adulterers to sing to their iambycé or triangle [3] when calling women from their houses.'

[1] See also test. 3, fr. 51, Terp. test. 23, Thal. test. 11.
[2] Eupolis, 5th c. comic poet.   [3] Types of lyre.

25 *Palatine Anthology* (anon.) [1]

. . . and you, Alcman's nightingales, tender singers,[2] . . .

[1] A prayer to the nine lyric poets.   [2] Or 'singers of women', with reference to the maiden-songs.

26 *Palatine Anthology* (anon.): *On the Nine Lyric Poets*

. . . Alcman was sweet.

27 Statius, *Silvae*

. . . and noble youths under your guidance [1] learned the rules which govern the recurrent rhythms of Pindar's lyre with its winding utterance, of Ibycus, who prayed to the birds, of Alcman, whose songs were sung by grim Amyclae [2] . . .

[1] Statius' father, who died in 19 A.D., was *grammaticus* of a school in Naples.   [2] A town near Sparta. Statius mentions Stesichorus and Sappho also.

357

28 *Anth. Pal.* 2. 393ss.

ἵστατο δ' Ἀλκμάων κεκλημένος οὔνομα μάντις·
ἀλλ' οὐ μάντις ἔην ὁ βοώμενος οὐδ' ἐπὶ χαίτης
δάφνης εἶχε κόρυμβον· ἐγὼ δ' Ἀλκμᾶνα δοκεύω,
ὃς πρὶν ἐυφθόγγοιο λύρης ἠσκήσατο τέχνην,
Δώριον εὐκελάδοισι μέλος χορδῇσιν ὑφαίνων.

29 P. Oxy. 2802 = 5 *S.L.G.*

. . . φληναφεῖ[. . . Δίδυ]μος ἐν γ' π(ερὶ) ε[. . .
ὅ]τι β' Ἀλκμᾶ[νες? . . . πρε]σβυτέρου περ[. . .
πρεσβ]ύτερος, ὁ δ(ὲ) ν[εώτερος? . . . τ]οῦ μὲν
πρεσ[βυτέρου . . . μ]εικρὸν ἀπω[. . .]λουμενου[
. . .]ν πατρίδος αὐτοῦ [. . . χρόν]ων καθ' οὓς
ἐγένε[το . . .] παιδείας δ(ὲ) φη(σιν) Ἀρη[. . .]τικὴν
ἱστορίας . . . [Ἀλκ]μὰν ὥστε Μου[σαῖος π]ρὸ αὐτοῦ
πολὺ γε[. . .]τερος δ(ὲ) . . .

post ed. pr. (Lobel) suppl. K. Tsantsanoglou, *Hellenica* 26
(1973) 107ss.

ALCMAN

28 *Palatine Anthology*: Christodorus, *Description of Statues in Baths of Zeuxippus* [1]

One called Alcmaeon the seer [2] stood there; but he was not the celebrated seer: he had no cluster of laurel-berries on his hair. I think he was Alcman, who formerly practised the art of the melodious lyre, weaving a Dorian song on his tuneful strings.

[1] In Constantinople.   [2] From Argos, son of Amphiaraus, seer in mythology.

A SECOND ALCMAN?

29 Papyrus (150–200 A.D.): commentary on Alcman

. . . (Didymus?) [1] talks nonsense in Book 3 of his *Concerning* . . . (when he says) that two Alcmans [2] . . . older . . . older, the other younger . . . (of) the older . . . a little . . . his native land . . . the times at which he lived; Are- says of his training . . . stories . . . Alcman, so that (Musaeus?) [3] who lived long before him . . .

[1] The prolific Alexandrian scholar (1st c. B.C.).   [2] See end of test. 1.   [3] The mythical singer.

ALCMAN

1 P. Louvr. E 3320 [1]

>] Πωλυδεύκης·
> οὐκ ἐγὼ]ν Λύκαισον ἐν καμοῦσιν ἀλέγω
> Ἐνα]ρσφόρον τε καὶ Σέβρον ποδώκη
>]ν τε τὸν βιατὰν
> 5]. τε τὸν κορυστὰν
> Εὐτείχη] τε Ϝάνακτά τ᾽ Ἀρήιον
>]ά τ᾽ ἔξοχον ἡμισίων·

[1] cf. Clem. Alex. *Protr.* 36, schol. ibid. (i 308 Staehlin); schol.
Pind. *Ol.* 11. 15a (i 346 Drachmann) καὶ Ἀλκμάν (Ἀλκαῖος
codd.)· οὐκ ἐγὼ Λύκον ἐν Μούσαις ἀλέγω (vid. v. 2); Cramer
Anecd. Oxon. i 159 εἰ οὖν ἐστιν Εὐτείχης ὄνομα κύριον παρ᾽
Ἀλκμᾶνι, Εὐτείχη τ᾽ ἄνακτ᾽ ἀρήιον . . . (cf. Hdn. i 81. 33,
ii 99. 31 Lentz, schol. A Hom. *Il.* 16. 57c, iv 172ss. Erbse)
(vid. v. 6); Hsch. N 516 (ii 711 Latte) Νηρεύς· θαλάσσιος δαίμων.
Ἀλκμὰν καὶ Πόρκον ὀνομάζει (vid. v. 19); *Et. Mag.* 783. 20, *Et.
Sym.* (cod. V ibid. Gaisford), *Et. Gen.* (p. 45 Calame) s.v.
ὑποπτέρων ὀνείρων (vel sim.), Hdn. ii 237. 11 Lentz (vid. v. 49);
Hdn. π.μ.λ. β´ 36 (ii 942. 9 Lentz: cf. i 392. 35) τὸ φάρος . . .
οὐδέτερον, ὁπότε σημαντικὸν τοῦ ἱματίου ἢ καὶ τοῦ ἀρότρου, ὡς καὶ
παρ᾽ Ἀλκμᾶνι, ἀλλὰ καὶ παρ᾽ Ἀντιμάχῳ (fr. 119 Wyss) (vid.
v. 61); schol. Lips. Hom. *Il.* 5. 266 (i 243 Bachmann), Eust. *Il.*
546. 29 φησὶ γὰρ ὁ γραμματικὸς Ἀριστοφάνης (fr. 33 Slater) τὸ
ἀμύνεσθαι . . . τίθεσθαι καὶ ἀντὶ ψιλοῦ τοῦ ἀμείψασθαι. φέρει γὰρ
χρῆσιν ἔκ τε Ἀλκμάνος τό· οὐ γὰρ πορφύρας τόσος κόρος ὥστ᾽
ἀμύνασθαι (cf. v. 64s.); *Et. Mag.* 134.25, *Et. Sym.* (cod. V
Gaisford), *Et. Gen.* (p. 15 Calame) σιοειδὴς σιειδὴς συγκοπῇ τοῦ
ο̄ (vid. v.71).

2 e schol. Pind. suppl.　　　3 suppl. Bergk　　　6 ex *Anecd.
Oxon.* suppl.

ALCMAN

Frr. 1–13 together with 18 are papyrus finds, frr. 14–157 are the book-quotations.

1–4C are papyrus fragments of the text of Alcman.

1 The Louvre partheneion (1st c. A.D. papyrus) [1]

. . . Polydeuces [2]: I do not reckon Lycaethus [3] among the dead but Enarsphorus and swift-footed Sebrus and . . . the violent [4] and . . . the helmeted and Euteiches and lord Areius and . . . outstanding among demigods;

[1] Found at Saqqâra in 1855, first published by Egger in 1863. Grammarians and others refer to various lines of the poem, ascribing them to Alcman: the scholiast on Pindar and Herodian and others give garbled versions of vv. 2 and 6; Hesychius reports that Alcman gave the name Porcus to Nereus, the sea-god (see v. 19); others discuss the words ὑποπετριδίων (49), φάρος (61), ἀμύνασθαι (cf. 65), σιειδής (71).
[2] Perhaps 35 lines are missing from the beginning of the poem. A. lists the dead sons of Hippocoon, mythical king of Sparta, who had exiled his younger brother Tyndareus, father of Castor and Polydeuces; he was attacked by Heracles, apparently in collaboration with Tyndareus and his sons, and was killed together with his sons, of whom A. names ten; Heracles established Tyndareus as king, instructing him to hold the kingship in his family until the return of the Heraclidae. Heracles is not mentioned in the extant lines; but when Clement of Alexandria quotes Sosibius to the effect that Heracles was wounded by the sons of Hippocoon, the scholiast reports, 'Alcman mentions it in Book 1.' According to the same scholiast, Euphorion in his *Thrax* made the sons of Hippocoon 'rival suitors' of Castor and Polydeuces: this may be relevant to v. 16 ff.   [3] A distant cousin of the sons of Hippocoon: see scholia A.   [4] For supplementation of the missing names see Page, *Alcman* 27–9.

καὶ   ]ν τὸν ἀγρέταν
     ] μέγαν Εὔρυτόν τε
10 Ἄρεος ἂν] πώρω κλόνον
Ἄλκωνά] τε τὼς ἀρίστως
οὐδ᾽ ἀμῶς] παρήσομες·
κράτησε γ]ὰρ Αἶσα παντῶν
καὶ Πόρος] γεραιτάτοι,
15 λύθη δ᾽ ἀπ]έδιλος ἀλκά.
μή τις ἀνθ]ρώπων ἐς ὡρανὸν ποτήσθω
μηδὲ πη]ρήτω γαμῆν τὰν ᾿Αφροδίταν
Κυπρίαν Ϝ]άν[α]σσαν ἤ τιν᾽
     ] ἢ παῖδα Πόρκω
20 εἰναλίω· Χά]ριτες δὲ Διὸς δόμον
ἀμφιέπου]σιν ἐρογλεφάροι·

     ]τάτοι
     ]τα δαίμων
     ]ι φίλοις
25   ἔδ]ωκε δῶρα
     ]γαρέον
     ]ώλεσ᾽ ἤβα
     ]ρονον
     μ]αταίας
30   ]έβα· τῶν δ᾽ ἄλλος ἰῶι
     ]μαρμάρωι μυλάκρωι
     ]. εν ᾿Αΐδας
     ]αυτοι
     ]᾿πον· ἄλαστα δὲ
35 Ϝέργα πάσον κακὰ μησαμένοι.

8 Bergk: -όταν pap.   10–11 suppl. Bergk   12–18 suppl.
Blass   15 λύθη δ᾽ Penwill   20 suppl. Crusius, Blass
21 suppl. exempli gratia Page   25 ἔδωκε vel δέδωκε
28 θρόνον vel χρόνον   35 εργα pap.

ALCMAN

and great . . . , gatherer (of the army), and Eurytus in the hurly-burly (of blind Ares?) and Alcon, finest warriors, we shall by no means pass over: Fate and Poros,[5] those ancient ones, conquered them all, and their valour which was without foundation [6] collapsed. Let no man fly to heaven or attempt to marry Aphrodite, the (Cyprian) queen, nor some . . . nor a daughter of Porcus [7] (of the sea) . . . ; it is the Graces [8] with love in their eyes who (frequent?) the house of Zeus; . . . god . . . to friends . . . gave gifts . . . youth lost . . . throne [9] . . . vain . . . went; one of them (died) [10] by an arrow, (another) by a marble millstone . . . Hades . . . ; and unforgettably they suffered, since they plotted evil.

[5] The Contriver? See fr. 5. 2 col. iii.   [6] Cf. Pindar's ἀδαμαντο-πέδιλος, 'with foundation of adamant'.
[7] Probably a Laconian sea-god (Page l.c. 38 ff.).
[8] Worshipped in Sparta along with Castor and Polydeuces; see also fr. 62.   [9] Or 'time'.   [10] A. seems to have moved to a new example of hybris, probably the fighting of the Giants against the Gods.

ἔστι τις σιῶν τίσις·
ὁ δ' ὄλβιος, ὅστις εὔφρων
ἀμέραν [δι]απλέκει
ἄκλαυτος· ἐγὼν δ' ἀείδω
40 Ἀγιδῶς τὸ φῶς· ὁρῶ
F' ὥτ' ἄλιον, ὅνπερ ἇμιν
Ἀγιδὼ μαρτύρεται
φαίνην· ἐμὲ δ' οὔτ' ἐπαινῆν
οὔτε μωμήσθαι νιν ἁ κλεννὰ χοραγὸς
45 οὐδ' ἁμῶς ἐῆι· δοκεῖ γὰρ ἤμεν αὔτα
ἐκπρεπὴς τὼς ὥπερ αἴτις
ἐν βοτοῖς στάσειεν ἵππον
παγὸν ἀεθλοφόρον καναχάποδα
τῶν ὑποπετριδίων ὀνείρων.

50 ἦ οὐχ ὁρῆις; ὁ μὲν κέλης
Ἐνητικός· ἁ δὲ χαίτα
τᾶς ἐμᾶς ἀνεψιᾶς
Ἀγησιχόρας ἐπανθεῖ
χρυσὸς [ὡ]ς ἀκήρατος·
55 τό τ' ἀργύριον πρόσωπον,
διαφάδαν τί τοι λέγω;
Ἀγησιχόρα μὲν αὔτα·
ἁ δὲ δευτέρα πεδ' Ἀγιδὼ τὸ Fεῖδος
ἵππος Ἰβηνῶι Κολαξαῖος δραμήται·

---

39 ἀκλαυστος pap., corr. Wilamowitz   41 F' Diels: scriba
quid voluerit incertum   43 φαίνεν, επαινέν pap.
44 μωμέσθαι pap.   45 δοκεει pap.   είμεν, η suprascr.,
pap.   46 ωιπερ pap.   51 ενετικος, ─‖─ suprascr., pap.:
corr. Diels   58 ἀγιδὼι ἁ ειδος pap.   59 ειβηνωι, δραμείται
pap.

There is such a thing as the vengeance of the gods:
that man is blessed who devoutly [11] weaves to the
end the web of his day unweeping.

And so I sing of the brightness of Agido: I see her
like the sun, which Agido summons to shine on us as
our witness; but our illustrious choir-leader [12] by no
means allows me either to praise or to fault her [13];
for she herself seems pre-eminent, just as if one were
to put a horse among grazing herds, a sturdy,
thunderous-hoofed prize-winner, one of those seen in
rock-sheltered dreams. Why, don't you see? The
race-horse is Venetic [14]; but the hair of my cousin
Hagesichora has the bloom of undefiled gold, and
her silver face—why do I tell you openly? This is
Hagesichora here; and the second in beauty after
Agido will run like a Colaxaean horse against an
Ibenian [15]; for the Pleiads,[16] as we carry a plough [17]

---

[11] Or 'cheerfully'.   [12] Presumably Hagesichora, whose
name means Choir-leader; so at 84. Agido seems to be
her principal assistant in the rites.   [13] I.e. Agido.
[14] From the northern Adriatic (mod. Venice); the race-
horse must be Agido.   [15] I.e. Agido has no close rival:
the Colaxaean horse may be from Scythia (see Bolton,
Aristeas 43), the swifter Ibenian from Lydia.   [16] Subject
of much controversy: probably the Pleiads (or Doves) are
a rival choir, and the imagery of fighting (63), protection
(65), guarding (77) and peace (91) refers to their com-
petition. Others take the Pleiads to be the star-group,
hurrying the singers at the approach of dawn or of the
ploughing-season. Others again follow the Scholiast and
take the Pleiads (or doves) to be Hagesichora and Agido;
in their view the military imagery is erotic.   [17] So
Sosiphanes (schol.); the word usually means 'robe'.

60 ταὶ Πεληάδες γὰρ ἇμιν
  Ὀρθρίαι φᾶρος φεροίσαις
  νύκτα δι᾽ ἀμβροσίαν ἅτε σήριον
  ἄστρον ἀυηρομέναι μάχονται.

  οὔτε γάρ τι πορφύρας
65 τόσσος κόρος ὥστ᾽ ἀμύναι,
  οὔτε ποικίλος δράκων
  παγχρύσιος, οὐδὲ μίτρα
  Λυδία, νεανίδων
  ἰανογ[λ]εφάρων ἄγαλμα,
70 οὐδὲ ταὶ Ναννῶς κόμαι,
  ἀλλ᾽ οὐ[δ᾽] Ἀρέτα σιειδής,
  οὐδὲ Σύλακίς τε καὶ Κλεησισήρα,
  οὐδ᾽ ἐς Αἰνησιμβρ[ό]τας ἐνθοῖσα φασεῖς·
  Ἀσταφίς [τ]έ μοι γένοιτο
75 καὶ ποτιγλέποι Φίλυλλα
  Δαμαρ[έ]τα τ᾽ ἐρατά τε Ϝιανθεμίς·
  ἀλλ᾽ Ἁγησιχόρα με τηρεῖ.

  οὐ γὰρ ἀ κ[α]λλίσφυρος
  Ἁγησιχ[ό]ρ[α] πάρ᾽ αὐτεῖ,
80 Ἀγιδοῖ [δ᾽ ἴκτ]αρ μένει
  θωστήρ[ιά τ᾽] ἄμ᾽ ἐπαινεῖ;
  ἀλλὰ τᾶν [εὐχάς], σιοί,
  δέξασθε· [σι]ῶν γὰρ ἄνα
  καὶ τέλος· [χο]ροστάτις,
85 Ϝείποιμί κ᾽, [ἐ]γὼν μὲν αὐτὰ

60 πελειάδες pap. 62 σιριον, σειριον suprascr. ut
videtur 63 αυειρ- pap. 76 ιανθ- pap. 77 τείρει
pap.(?), schol. B 80 fortasse [δὲ π]αρμένει 82 suppl.
Blass 85 ειποιμι pap.

to Orthria,[18] rise through the ambrosial night like the star Sirius and fight against us.

For abundance of purple is not sufficient for protection, nor intricate snake of solid gold, no, nor Lydian headband, pride of dark-eyed girls, nor the hair of Nanno, nor again godlike Areta nor Thylacis and Cleësithera; nor will you[19] go to Aenesimbrota's[20] and say, 'If only Astaphis were mine, if only Philylla were to look my way and Damareta and lovely Ianthemis'; no, Hagesichora guards me.[21] For is not fair-ankled Hagesichora present here? Does she not remain (near) Agido and commend our festival? Come, you gods, accept their (prayers): to the gods belong fulfilment and accomplishment. Choir-leader,—if I may speak—I am myself only a girl

---

[18] Goddess of the Morning Twilight, called 'Dawn-goddess' at v. 87: see n. 22. Some read ὀρθρίαι as an adjective, 'for the Pleiads in the morning twilight, as we carry a plough, rise ...'.   [19] Feminine.   [20] Trainer of the four girls? Or a dispenser of love-potions?   [21] Others read τείρει and translate, 'H. wears me out (with love)'.

παρσένος μάταν ἀπὸ θράνω λέλακα
γλαύξ· ἐγὼ[ν] δὲ τᾶι μὲν Ἀώτι μάλιστα
Ϝανδάνην ἐρῶ· πόνων γὰρ
ἇμιν ἰάτωρ ἔγεντο·
90 ἐξ Ἀγησιχόρ[ας] δὲ νεάνιδες
ἰρ]ήνας ἐρατ[ᾶ]ς ἐπέβαν.

τῶ]ι τε γὰρ σηραφόρωι
αὐ]τῶς εδ[
τ[ῶι] κυβερνάται δὲ χρὴ
95 κ[ἠ]ν νᾶϊ μάλιστ᾽ ἀκούην·
ἁ δὲ τᾶν Σηρην[ί]δων
ἀοιδοτέρα μ[ὲν οὐχί,
σιαὶ γάρ, ἀντ[ὶ δ᾽ ἕνδεκα
παίδων δεκ[ὰς ἅδ᾽ ἀείδ]ει·
100 φθέγγεται δ᾽ [ἄρ᾽] ὥ[τ᾽ ἐπὶ] Ξάνθω ῥοαῖσι
κύκνος· ἁ δ᾽ ἐπιμέρωι ξανθᾶι κομίσκαι

desunt iv versus

88 ἀνδ- pap.   91 suppl. Page   93 suppl. Blass.
97 suppl. Weil 98 e schol. suppl. 99 suppl. Wilamowitz,
Blass   100 suppl. Blass   105 in marg. coronis

screeching pointlessly, an owl from a rafter; but even
so I long to please Aotis [22] most of all, for she proved
the healer of our sufferings [23]; but it was thanks to
Hagesichora that girls trod the path of lovely
peace. [24]

For (like) the trace-horse [25] . . . , and in a ship too
one must obey the helmsman most of all; and she is of
course (not) more melodious than the Sirens, for they
are goddesses; but this our choir of ten sings as well
as [26] eleven girls: why, its song is like that of a swan
on the waters of the Xanthus; and she [27] . . . her
lovely yellow hair . . . [28]

[22] Presumably 'Dawn-goddess' and to be equated with
Orthria (61), but not securely identified: suggestions are
Artemis, Helen, Phoebe (for whom see fr. 8). [23] Not
understood: perhaps a metaphorical reference to the
arduous preparations for a previous festival and
competition, rather than to a disaster such as sickness or
war. [24] Perhaps victory in a competition, but see
n. 16. [25] Presumably Hagesichora guides the choir as
the trace-horse and helmsman direct chariot and
ship. [26] Or 'instead of' (Schol.). [27] Hagesichora
again? [28] The poem ends four lines later.

GREEK LYRIC

Schol. A (P. Louvr. E 3320)

v. 2 ὅτι τοιαύτη ἡ διάν(οια)· τὸν Λύκαιον οὐ συγκαταριθμ(ῶ) τ[οῖς]
α... ['Ιπποκων]τίδαις . . . ἔσται οὐ μόνον τὸν Λύκαι(ον) ἀλλ[ὰ] καὶ
τοὺς λο[ι]ποὺς Δηρίτιδας οὓς ⟨οὐκ⟩ (Pavese) ἐπ' ὀνόματος λέγει

v. 6 Φερεκ(ύδης) ἕνα τ(ῶν) Ἱπποκωντιδ(ῶν) 'Αρήιτον· μή[π]οτ'
οὖν κ(αὶ) ὧδε σὺν τῶ[ι τ̄] δεῖ γρ(άφειν) ἢ τ(ὸν) 'Αρήιτον ὁ 'Αλκμ(ὰν)
'Αρήιον

v. 14 ὅτι τὸν Πόρον εἴρηκε τὸν αὐτὸν τῶι ὑπὸ τοῦ 'Ησιόδο(υ)
μεμυθολογημένωι Χάει

v. 32 'Αριστο(φάνης) (fr. 384A Slater) 'Αΐδας, Πάμφιλο(ς)
Αΐδας

v. 37 αἱ π(ρὸς) τῆ(ς) 'Αγιδοῦς . . . . . .

v. 38 'Αρί(σταρ)χ(ος) ὅ[δ' ὄλβιος]

v. 42 ἐντεῦθεν αἱ π(ρὸς) τῆς 'Αγησιχόρ(ας) παρα[. . . .].ουσι

v. 48 αἱ π(ρὸς) τῆ(ς) 'Αγιδο(ῦς) τοῦτ[ο . . . .] οτα αἱ π(ρὸς) τῆ(ς)
'Αγησιχό(ρας)

v. 49 ὅτι τὰ θαυμαστὰ καὶ τερατώδη οἱ ποιηταὶ εἰώθα(σι) τοῖς
ὀνείροις προσάπτειν κ(αὶ) παρομοιοῦν διὰ τὸ φαίνεσθαι κατὰ τὸ[ν]
ὄνειρον τοιαῦτα· ὑ[πο]π[ετρ]ιδίο(υς) εἴρηκε ὡς ὑπὸ π[έ]τρα(ι)
οἰκοῦντα(ς) ἐν α.... τόπω(ι)· παραγρά(φει) δὲ Ὅμη(ρον) ὡς ἐν τῆ(ι)
'Οδυσσέαι (24. 11s.)

v. 59 τα γένη ἐστὶν . . . . .ικῶν ἵππων[.].[ ]Εἰβην( ) . . . .
[.] . . . . . αζειαγ[. . .] . . .την

v. 61 sup. voc. φάρος: αροτο

370

ALCMAN

Scholia A (in Louvre papyrus) [1]

v. 2 the sense is this: I do not number Lycaeus with the sons of Hippocoon . . . will be not only Lycaeus but also Derites' other sons, whom he does not mention by name.[2]

[1] The word ὅτι, used to introduce some of the scholia, indicates that a critical sign has been placed in the margin of the text 'because . . .'.   [2] Derites was a cousin of Oebalus, father of Tyndareus and Hippocoon (Paus. 7.18.5).

v. 6 Pherecydes makes Areitus one of Hippocoon's sons, so perhaps here also it should be written with the letter t; either that or Alcman called Areitus Areius.

v. 14 he has identified Poros with the god called Chaos by Hesiod in his mythologising [*Theog.* 116, 123].

v. 32 Aristophanes reads Ἀίδας (with three syllables), Pamphilus Αἶδας (with two).

v. 37 The girls beside Agido . . .

v. 38 Aristarchus reads ὅδ' ὄλβιος, 'this man is blessed'.

v. 42 Next, the girls beside Hagesichora . . .

v. 48 The girls beside Agido . . . this . . . those beside Hagesichora.

v. 49 The poets are accustomed to ascribe and compare to dreams things that are wonderful and prodigious, since that is how they appear in the dream. He has called dreams 'rock-sheltered' since they dwell under a rock in a . . . place. He is copying Homer: cf. *Odyssey* [24.11f.],[1] 'and they went past the streams of Ocean and the White Rock, past the gates of the Sun and the land of Dreams.'

[1] The Homeric passage is irrelevant.

v. 59 The breeds are . . . of . . . horses . . . Eibenian . . .

v. 61 (over the word φᾶρος) plough.

GREEK LYRIC

v. 60ss. Ἀριστο(φάνης) ὀρθίαι. φᾶρος· Σωσιφάνης ἄροτρον. ὅτι τὴν [Ἀγι]ζὼ καὶ Ἀγησιχόραν περιστεραῖς εἰκάζουσι

v. 64ss. . . . διδάσκαλος . . . ις τ' ἀριθμ' τ' ι̅β̅ πρωτοσ
. . . . οὐδὲ ταὶ Ναν[νῶς κόμαι] . . . . .Ἀρέτα . . . . .
Θυλακίς τ(ε) κ(αὶ) Κλεησισήρα[. . . τ]ε κ(αὶ) Ἀσταφὶς . . . . . .
κ(αὶ) Φίλυλλα κ(αὶ) Δαμαρέτα κ(αὶ) Ἰανθεμ[ίς

v. 79 ἀν(τὶ) αὐτοῦ. Στασικλεῖ . . .

v. 81 θωστήρεια ἑορτ[ή

v. 83 ὅτι τὸ ἄνα ἄνυσις

v. 88 ἀρέσκειν ἐπιθυμῶ

v. 95 ναῒ ναὶ Ἀρι . . .

v. 98 ενδ . . . τα . . [. . . .]δ° εἴρηκε ἀλλὰ διὰ τὸ τὸν χορὸν ὅτε μὲν ἐξ
ι̅α̅ παρθένων ὅτε δὲ ἐκ ι̅· φη(σὶν) οὖν τὴν χορηγὸν ἐπαινῶν ἀντὶ ι̅α̅
ἄιδειν ι̅· ἐξῆν γὰρ α. ἀριθμὸν εἰπεῖν . . . . . εἴπερ οὐκ ἐβούλετο τὸν
ἀριθ[μ(ὸν) τ(ῶν)] παρθένων . . . αι Ολυμπι . . . ι̅θ̅ εξην . . .

ALCMAN

v. 60 ff. (at foot of column) Aristophanes reads 'to Orthia'.[1] φᾶρος: 'plough', according to Sosiphanes. They compare Agizo (sic) and Hagesichora to doves.

[1] I.e. the plough in his view is brought to the Spartan goddess Orth(e)ia; but see Page, *Alcman* 77 f. For the text of the scholia here see E. G. Turner, *Greek Manuscripts of the Ancient World* 44.

v. 64 ff. . . . chorus-trainer . . . the number of twelve . . . the first . . . nor the hair of Nanno . . . Areta . . . Thylacis and Cleësithera and Astaphis . . . and Philylla and Damareta and Ianthemis

v. 79 (αὐτεῖ) for αὐτοῦ, 'here'. Stasicles . . .

v. 81 θωστήρια: ἑορτή, 'festival'

v. 83 ἄνα is ἄνυσις, 'accomplishment'

v. 88 'I wish to please'

v. 95 νᾶϊ: νᾶι (i.e. monosyllabic) according to Ari(stophanes of Byzantium) [1]

[1] Or Ari(starchus).

v. 98 (Eleven?) . . . he has said (? not because . . . ?) but because the chorus was sometimes of eleven girls, sometimes of ten; so he says (in praise of) the chorus-leader that ten sing instead of eleven; for he might have mentioned the number . . . since he did not want . . . the number of the girls . . . Olymp-[1] . . . it was possible . . . nineteen . . .

[1] Perhaps a reference to the Festival of Hera at Olympia, at which two choruses of girls performed (Paus. 5. 16. 2).

GREEK LYRIC

Schol. B (P. Oxy. 2389)

fr. 6 col. i (v.58s.)] ς ἵππος Κολαξαῖος [.................]
οὕτως ἡ Ἀγιδὼ προ[............. δευ]τέρα κατὰ τὸ εἶδος
[........] ἵππος Κολ[αξαῖος πρὸ]ς Ἰβηνὸν [...... Κολ]αξαίου
δ.[..............] ο[....... Ἰβ]ηνοῦ. πε[ρὶ δὲ τοῦ γένο]υς τῶν
[ἵππω]ν Ἀρίσταρχος ο[ὕτως ἱστορ]εῖ· ἀμ[φότερ]α ταῦτα γένη ἵπ[πων
ἐξωτι]κά, λέ[γεται] δὲ ἀμφοτέρω[ν διαπρε]πόντων [προφ]έρειν τὸν
[Ἰ]βην[όν..... δὲ] τοὺς [Ἰβην]ούς φησιν τῆς Λ[υδίας ἔθνος εἶ]ναι,
[ἀπὸ τ]ούτου δὲ βούλετ[αι .... ὅτι] Λυ[δὸς ἦν] ὁ Ἀλκμάν.
Σω[σίβιος δ᾽ ἕτερ]ον [Ἰβηνῶ]ν ἔθνος ἀποφ[αίνει ....].ρι[..
....]κεισθαι, προσα[γόμενος ..].δο[... μ]άρτυν. περὶ δὲ τῶ[ν
Κολαξαί]ων [Εὔδοξο]ς ὁ Κν[ίδι]ος δια...... τὸν Πόντον τουτ.[

fr. 6 col. ii (v. 60ss.) ... εἰρημέν [   ] τὴν Ἀγιδὼ [   ]
αὐταῖς ὀρ[   ] δὲ τοῦτο λ.[... πλεο]νάκις εἴσα[...
Ἀ]ταρνίδες [...] . .. τὰς [δὲ Πλειάδας Πελειάδας φη]σὶν καθάπερ
[καὶ Πίνδαρος   ὀρει]ᾶν γε Πελει[άδων μὴ τηλόθεν Ὀαρίωνα]
νεῖσθαι· ἐὰν [...] οὕτως ἀκοῦσα[ι   ἥ τε Ἀγησιχό]ρα καὶ ἡ
Ἀγιδὼ. [   ] οὖσαι τὸ τοῦ σιρ[ίου ἄστρον   ] μαχόμεναι
πε[   ] πλειάδων τὸ α[   ] γὰρ ὡς πελει[άδες   ]ρουσιν
πα.[   ] v. 62s.   ]πειν τι· εἶναι γὰρ [νύκτα δι᾽
ἀμβρο]σίαν ἀντίστροφο[ν τῶι   κανα]χάποδα ὥστε
ηλ[   ]λείπειν· τιμων[   ]ν ἄστρον ἄτε σ[ίριον
κατὰ] λόγον τοιοῦτον [   ] ἡμᾶς περὶ τῆς [...]
.. νου ἀστρ[

ALCMAN

Scholia B (in Oxyrhynchus papyrus) (50–100 A.D.)

fr. 6 col. i (on v. 58 ff.) Colaxaean horse . . . thus Agido . . . second in respect of her beauty . . . Colaxaean horse . . . against an Ibenian; Colaxaean . . . Ibenian. And concerning the breed of the horses Aristarchus speaks as follows: both these breeds of horses (are foreign). But it is said that although both are eminent the Ibenian is better. (He) [1] says (the Ibenians are a people) of (Lydia), and from this he is ready (to infer) that Alcman was Lydian. But Sosibius shows that a second race of Ibenians is situated . . . ,[2] adducing X [3] as his witness. Concerning the Colaxaeans (Eudoxus) [4] the Cnidian . . . they (dwell near) the Black Sea [5] . . .

[1] Aristarchus? See test. 7.   [2] In a Celtic area (see Steph. Byz. on Ἰβαῖοι).   [3] Herodotus? If so, there seems to be a mistake.   [4] Or Ctesias.   [5] Hdt. 4. 5, 7 speaks of a Scythian king called Colaxais.

fr. 6 col. ii (on vv. 60–63) . . . said . . . Agido . . . to them [1] . . . this . . . more often . . . Atarnides [2] . . . He calls the Pleiads Peleiads as does Pindar, *Nem.* 2. 11 f.[3] If . . . , (one must) understand it as follows: . . . Hagesichora and Agido . . . being . . . the star of Sirius . . . fighting . . . of Pleiads . . . as Pleiads [1] . . . νύκτα . . . μάχονται (vv. 62 f.). (They say that in the above something is missing), for the words νύκτα δι' ἀμβροσίαν correspond with (ἀεθλοφόρον) καναχάποδα (v. 48) [4] so that [5] . . . ; honour . . . star like Sirius . . . by such reasoning . . . us about the . . . star . . .

[1] It seems that Hagesichora and Agido are being equated with the Pleiads as in schol. A.   [2] 'Women of Atarneus' is obscure: there was an Atarneus on the coast of Asia Minor opposite Lesbos. See also fr. 10(a).   [3] Other examples, including Simon. 555, in Athen. 11. 490 f.   [4] V. 62 corresponds metrically with v. 48, but the argument is not clear.   [5] There may be a reference here to the words 'like the sun' in v. 41.

GREEK LYRIC

fr. 7 col. i (a) (v. 73ss.) . . . Φίλυλλα Δαμαρέ[τα   ]· καθ’
ὑπόθεσιν ταύ[την   τ]ῆς Αἰνησιμβρό[τας   ]βου[

(b) (v. 75ss.) . . . ἵ]να βλέπηι[τὰς λ]οιπὰς παρθ[ένους . . .
vv. 77–9: ο]ὐχ ὡς νῦν μὴ παρού[σης μέμνηται τ]ῆς Ἀγησιχόρας, ἀλλὰ
[. . . . .]ται ὅτι ἐὰν εἴ[σ]ω τῆ[ς Αἰνησιμβρότας ἔλ]θηις
οὐδεμίαν [τοιαύτην δυνήσει εὑ]ρεῖν πα[ρθ]ένο[ν ἀλλὰ μόνη
Ἀγησιχόρα μ]ε τείρ[ει . . .

2 P. Oxy. 2389 fr. 3(a) 3–7

 ]σιοῖσι π[ᾶσι κἀνθρώποισί τ’ αἰδ]οιεστάτοι
ν[αί]οισι νέ[ρθεν γᾶς ἀειζώοι σι]όδματο[ν τ]έγος
Κά[στωρ τε πώλων ὠκέων] δματῆ[ρε]ς [ἱ]ππότα[ι
 σοφοὶ
καὶ Πωλυδεύκης] κυδρός.

suppl. Lobel praeter   1 πᾶσι Barrett, 2 νέρθεν γ. ἀ. Page
(ναίοισιν ἐ[ν φίλαις Σεράπναισιν] Barrett): cf. schol. Eur. *Troad.*
210 (ii Schwartz)

[Hdn.] *Fig.* 61 (*Rhet. Gr.* viii 606 Walz)

 Ἀλκμανικὸν δὲ τὸ μεσάζον τὴν ἐπαλλήλων ὀνομάτων ἢ ῥημάτων
θέσιν πληθυντικοῖς ἢ δυϊκοῖς ὀνόμασιν ἢ ῥήμασι . . . πλεονάζει δὲ
τοῦτο τὸ σχῆμα παρ’ Ἀλκμᾶνι τῷ λυρικῷ, ὅθεν καὶ Ἀλκμανικὸν
ὠνόμασται. εὐθὺς γοῦν ἐν τῇ δευτέρᾳ ᾠδῇ παρείληπται· Κάστωρ . . .
κυδρός.

cf. schol. Pind. *Pyth.* 4. 318b (ii 141 Drachmann), schol. Hom.
Od. 10. 513 (ii 476 Dindorf), Eust. *Od.* 1667. 34.

ALCMAN

fr. 7 col. i (on v. 73 ff.)

(a) . . . Philylla and Damareta . . . ; on this hypothesis . . .
of Aenesimbrota . . .

(b) (in order that) she may see [1] . . . the other girls . . .
'But Hagesichora wears me out': (i.e. oppresses me with
love). 'But Hagesichora wears me out. For fair-ankled
Hagesichora is not present here': he does not mention
Hagesichora as being not present (with the others) now but
says that if you go inside Aenesimbrota's (you will be able to
find) no girl (like her, but Hagesichora alone) wears me
out. [2]

[1] With reference to ποτιγλέποι (75)?   [2] Page suggests that
in this explanation αὐτεῖ ('here', v. 79) is wrongly taken to
refer to Aenesimbrota's house. Other scraps of this papyrus
seem to comment on v. 82 f. and perhaps on 38 and 100.

2 Papyrus (50–100 A.D.) [1]

Most worthy of reverence from all gods and men,
they dwell in a god-built home (beneath the earth,
always alive?), [2] Castor—tamers of swift steeds,
skilled horsemen—and glorious Polydeuces.

[1] The papyrus scraps are supplemented from 'Herodian' and
Et. Gen.; see also fr. 12. 8 f.   [2] Or (in their beloved
Therapne?).

'Herodian', *On Figures of Speech*

The Alcmanic figure is the one which inserts plural or
dual nouns or verbs between (singular) nouns or verbs
which belong together . . . This figure is used to excess in
the lyric poet Alcman, [1] so that it is called Alcmanic. There
is no need to go further than the second ode [2] for an
example: 'Castor . . . Polydeuces'.

[1] But this is his only extant example.   [2] Presumably the
second poem of Book 1.

GREEK LYRIC

Et. Gen. (p. 18 Calame)

. . . καὶ τὸ αἰδοιέστατοι (-τον Β) ὡς παρ᾽ Ἀλκμᾶνι, οἷον· σιοῖσι
κἀνθρώποισιν αἰδοιέστατοι.

cod. A συοῖσι κἀνθρ. αἰδ.   cod. B ναοῖσιν ἀνθρ. αἰδ. (cf. v. 2)

cf. fr. 12. 8s.

3 P. Oxy. 2387

fr. 1   Μώσαι ᾽Ολ]υμπιάδες, περί με φρένας
      ἱμέρωι νέα]ς ἀοιδᾶς
      πίμπλατ᾽· ἰθύ]ω δ᾽ ἀκούσαι
      παρσενηΐ]ας ὀπός
   5 πρὸς αἰ]θέρα καλὸν ὑμνιοισᾶν μέλος
      ].οι
      ὕπνον ἀ]πὸ γλεφάρων σκεδ[α]σεῖ γλυκύν
      ]ς δέ μ᾽ ἄγει πεδ᾽ ἀγων᾽ ἴμεν
      ᾆχι τά]χιστα κόμ[αν ξ]ανθὰν τινάξω.

   10   ]. σχ[ἀπ]αλοὶ πόδες

fr. 3 col. ii

   61 λυσιμελεῖ τε πόσωι, τακερώτερα
      δ᾽ ὕπνω καὶ σανάτω ποτιδέρκεται·
      οὐδέ τι μαψιδίως γλυκ[ῆα κ]ήνα·

      Ἀ[σ]τυμέλοισα δέ μ᾽ οὐδὲν ἀμείβεται,
   65 ἀλλὰ τὸ]ν πυλεῶν᾽ ἔχοισα
      [ὥ] τις αἰγλά[ε]ντος ἀστήρ
      ὠρανῶ διαιπετής
      ἢ χρύσιον ἔρνος ἢ ἀπαλὸ[ν ψίλ]ον
      ∴.]ν

ALCMAN

Etymologicum Genuinum (on superlatives in -έστατος)

αἰδοιέστατοι is also found, as in Alcman: 'most worthy . . . men'.

3 Papyrus (end of 1st c. B.C. or beginning of 1st c. A.D.)

fr. 1 Olympian [1] (Muses, fill) my heart (with longing for a new) song: I (am eager) to hear the (maiden) voice of girls singing a beautiful melody (to the heavens). . . . : (it?) will scatter sweet (sleep) from my eyes and leads me to go to the assembly (of Antheia?),[2] (where) I shall (rapidly) shake my yellow hair . . . soft feet [3] . . .

fr. 3 . . . cold . . .
. . . and with limb-loosening desire, and she looks (at me?) more meltingly than sleep or death, and not in vain [4] is she sweet. But Astymeloisa makes no answer to me; no, holding the garland,[5] like a bright star of the shining heavens or a golden branch or soft down

---

[1] The opening lines may have been sung by a solo singer introducing the song of the whole choir. [2] Hera of the Flowers? See n. 5. [3] A reference to dancing? 50 verses are missing here, except for the adjective 'cold', which is mentioned in a marginal note. [4] Text and sense uncertain. [5] Pamphilus in Ath. 15. 678a says that the word (also in fr. 60) is used of a garland offered by Spartans to Hera.

379

70   ]. διέβα ταναοῖς πο[σί·
   καλλίκ]ομος νοτία Κινύρα χ[άρ]ις
   ἐπὶ π]αρσενικᾶς χαίταισιν ἴσδει·

   ἦ μὰν ’Α]στυμέλοισα κατὰ στρατόν
   ἔρχεται   ] μέλημα δάμωι
75   ]μαν ἐλοῖσα
          ]λέγω·
        ]εναβαλ’ α[ἴ] γὰρ ἄργυριν
   ]. [.]ία
          ]α ἴδοιμ’ αἴ πως με . . ον φιλοῖ
80 ἆσ]σον [ἰο]ῖσ’ ἀπαλᾶς χηρὸς λάβοι,
   αἶψά κ’[ἐγὼν ἰ]κέτις κήνας γενοίμαν·

   νῦν δ’ [   ]δα παῖδα βα[θ]ύφρονα

   παιδι.[   ]μ’ ἔχοισαν
   ]. ·ε̣[   ]. ν ἀ παίς
85   ]χάριν·

fr. 3 col. iii: notandi v. 98 ὀλκ[,   v. 115 ἴστε̣[,   v. 116 οἶδε[.

omnia suppl. ed. pr. (Lobel) praeter 1–5 (e.g.), 9 ἇχι, 65 τὸ]ν, 71 καλλίκ]ομος, 73s. (e.g.), 81 ἐγὼν Page, 80 Barrett, Peek. 8 ’Ανθεία]ς? Barrett   9 τά]χιστα Barrett: μά]λιστα Lobel 34 marg. schol. κ]ρυερα ψυχρα   68 Paus. 3. 19. 6 ψίλα καλοῦσιν οἱ Δωρεῖς τὰ πτέρα   72 -ᾶς? Page: -ᾶν pap. (ante correct.?)   77 βάλ’ vel ἀβάλ’ Lobel   79 μεσ̣ι̣ο̣ν̣ ut vid.

Schol. (in marg. sup. script.)

[π]αρεγγράφ(εται) ἐν [το]ῖς ἀντιγρά(φοις) αὕτη [κἀν τῶι] πέμπτωι καὶ ἐν ἐκείνωι [ἐν μὲν τῶι] ’Αρ(ιστο)νί(κου) περιεγέγρα(πτο), ἐν δὲ τῶι Πτολ(εμαίου) ἀπερ[ί]γρα(πτος) ἦν.

380

. . . she passed through with her long feet; . . . giving beauty to her tresses, the moist charm of Cinyras [6] sits on the maiden's hair. (Truly) Astymeloisa (goes) through the crowd the darling of the people [7] . . . taking . . . I say; . . . if only . . . a silver cup . . . I were to see whether perchance she were to love me.[8] If only she came nearer and took my soft hand, immediately I would become her suppliant. As it is, . . . a wise girl . . . girl . . . me having . . . the girl . . . grace . . . [9]

[6] I.e. Cyprian perfumed oil: Cinyras was a mythical king of Cyprus.   [7] Her name means 'darling of the city'.   [8] The connection of the clauses is uncertain.   [9] The papyrus has the beginnings of another 30 lines: v. 98 may have the word 'nightingale(s)', vv. 115 and 116 seem to begin, 'you know' and '(s)he knows'. The poem had at least 126 verses, i.e. 14 stanzas.

Scholiast (in the upper margin of the papyrus)

This ode is wrongly inserted in the exemplars in the fifth book also, and in that book it was bracketed [1] in Aristonicus' exemplar but not bracketed in Ptolemaeus'.

[1] To denote exclusion. The scholiast maintains that the poem belongs to Book 1, not to Book 5. An Aristonicus and Ptolemaeus, father and son, are known as scholars from Ath. 11. 481d, schol. *Il.* 4. 423, *Sud.* A3924, Π3036.

fr. 4: 2]αιόλαν.[,   3]τακομέ[ν- ,   4]ῆρά νυν[,
6]νυμφᾶ[,   7 ἀ]είσεν[

fr. 11: 2,3 πήρα[τα . . . εὐρυστέρν[ω,   4 ἄμευσα[

fr. 13: 5 ἀσανα[

fr. 17: 3]δόμοισιν[6 σιοκ.[7 τ]ηλυγετωι.[

fr. 21: 3]φοιβ[

fr. 23: 2 εὐρυ]χόρω δ' Ἀσίας[?   3 πυρός?
4 πολλά   5]ἄστη καὶ φ[6 Μαιόν[?

4 P. Oxy. 2388

fr. 1   ].[.]ναὶ.[
                   ]αλλονεραιοφ[
                   ]ωτα δ' ἐγίνετ[
                 σαυ]μαστὰ δ' ἀνθ[ρώποισ(ι)
            5 γαρύματα μαλσακὰ [
              νεόχμ' ἔδειξαν τερπ[
              ποικίλα φ.[.]ρα[.].αι·[
              ἆ δ' ἱππέω[ν
              Κλησιμβ[ρότα   ἠ-
           10 βῶσα τεμε[
              κληνὸν β[
              οὐδ' ἀ[.].ιο[

4, 9 suppl. ed. pr. (Lobel)

fr. 4 [1]:　2 flashing,　3 melting,　4 So then . . . ?
6 brides, 7 sang

fr. 11: 2–3 the limits of the wide-breasted (earth),
4 passed through

fr. 13: 5 Athena [2]

fr. 17: 3 house　6 god-　7 beloved (child)?

fr. 21: 3 Phoebus [3]?

fr. 23: 2 spacious Asia?　3 fire?　4 many　5 cities
and　6 Maeonia(n) [4]?

[1] These fragments are not from the Astymeloisa poem.
[2] Or 'immortal'.　[3] Or 'Phoebe'?　[4] Maeonia was a
district in Lydia.

---

4 Papyrus (150–200 A.D.)

fr. 1 . . . (other?) . . . (became?) . . . and wonderful
soft utterances they [1] revealed new to men . . .
delight . . . intricate . . . ; and she . . . of horsemen
. . . Clesimbrota . . . being young . . . glorious . . .
nor . . .

[1] Alcman's predecessors? He mentioned Polymnestus once
(fr. 145).

fr. 3: 2 τἄλλοτρ[4 ἴδμεν . [5 οιος ἦ . [

fr. 4: 4]πολεμ[5] . γ' αἴδη[λ-

fr. 5: 3 ἀκό]λουσον   4s. Δυμαί[ναις . . . φιλο-
πλ]οκάμοις   7 σ]άλπιγξ

fr. 6: 2]χοραγοι[9]π' ἵππωνεα[11]μεῖον · [

fr. 8: 4 Σ]εράπνα[

4A P. Oxy. 2443 fr. 1 + 3213

          ]εφ . [. . . .]ουδεις . [
          ]φρασάμαν μόνος [
          ]ε Ποσειδᾶνος χα[.] .
10   ] . ος
       μα. Λευκοθεᾶν ἐρατὸν τέμενος
       ἐκ Τρυγεᾶν ἀνιών, ἔχον
       δὲ σίδας δύω γλυκήας.

       ταὶ δ' ὅτε δὴ ποταμῶι καλλιρρόωι
15   ἀράσαντ' ἐρατὸν τελέσαι γάμον
       καὶ τὰ παθῆν ἃ γυναιξὶ καὶ ἀνδρά[σι
       φίλτ]ατα κωριδίας τ' εὐνᾶς [τυ]χῆν[,

v. M. L. West, *Z.P.E.* 26 (1977) 38s. Suppl. ed. pr. (Lobel)
praeter 17 φίλτ]ατα Brown   11 ἱκό]μαν Brown

ALCMAN

fr. 3: 2 possessions of others, 4 we know, 5 what (he) was like

fr. 4: 4 war, 5 destructive

fr. 5: 3 follower, 4 f. curl-loving Dymainai,[1] 7 war-trumpet

fr. 6: 2 choir-leaders, 9 horse(s), 11 smaller

fr. 8: 4 Therapne

[1] Same expression in Euphorion fr. 47. Hesychius explains Dyme as 'a tribe and place in Sparta' and Dymainai (s.v. Δύσμαιναι) as 'the choir-girls in Sparta in the worship of Dionysus'. See also 5 fr. 2 col. ii, 10(b) (where the Dymainai may be the choir who are addressing their leader) and 11.

4A Papyrus (2nd c. A.D.)

. . . no-one . . . I[1] planned . . . alone . . . of Poseidon . . . (I came to) the lovely sanctuary of the Leucotheae[2] by going up from Trygeae, and I carried two sweet pomegranates; and when they had prayed to the fair-flowing river that they achieve lovely wedlock and experience those things that are (dearest) to women and men and find a lawful marriage-bed, . . .

[1] The speaker is male, 'they' of v. 14 are female. A. L. Brown, *Z.P.E.* 32 (1978) 36–8, notes similarities with Homer's account of the meeting of Odysseus and Nausicaa and her companions (see especially *Od.* 5. 441 ff., 6. 85, and cf. fr. 81). [2] The Nereids; Ino Leucothea had helped Odysseus (*Od.* 5. 333 ff.).

4B P. Oxy. 2801 (= 3 *S.L.G.*)

>] ἐπακουσομε]
>   σ]άλος οἷά τ' α[] . . . [
> 5] ὑμνίομες ἀπίαισ[
>   ] . πον . ς ευρ[

suppl. ed. pr. (Lobel)   6 πονός, deleto altero ο

4C P. Oxy. 3209

fr. 1
>] κλέος φερ[
>] σκαίροισα τ[
>] . . . [. .]ερ[
>]ὂ δ' εὐθὺς . [
>   .] . . . . [
>]ἀχὼ δ' ἀφ' ὑψηλῶ[
>]δόμων ἀπ' ἄκρω[ν

'Αλκμᾶνος μελῶν ϛ'

fr. 2: 1 νεβρῶ(ι)   7 ἀγερωχ[10]ἐκ Σπάρ[τας?

fr. 3: 1]α κυν.[2]φοβω[

fr. 4: 3]ς γαμ[5]κᾱλον[

suppl. ed. pr. (Haslam)

ALCMAN

4B Papyrus (early 2nd c. A.D.)

. . . (we?) shall hear . . . offspring as . . . we sing (with?) kindly . . .

4C Papyrus (100–150 A.D.)

fr.1:. . .bring( )fame. . .frisking [1]. . .and he at once . . .shout from the high. . .from the housetops [2]. . .

fr. 2:   1 fawn   7 proud [3]   10 from Sparta(?)

fr. 3:   1 dog(?)   2 fear

fr. 4:   3 marriage   5 beautiful

---

[1] Feminine singular participle.   [2] The poem, possibly a wedding-song, ended in this line, as did Book 6 of Alcman's songs according to the end-title in the papyrus.   [3] Cf. Eust. *Il.* 314. 43, 'the word ἀγέρωχος means "proud", as in Alcman': also at 5 fr. 1(b), 10(b).

5 P. Oxy. 2390

fr. 1 (a) 3 τ]οῦ Πολυδεύ[κεος 5 Κάστ]ωρ ἕως τοῦ 7s. ἀπέ-
φευγ- 8 ἔβλαψεν 9 Π]ολυδεύκης 10 κασιγ]νηταν σα[

(b) 4]αγερωχε 5 Πλε]ιστοδίκη? 6] . βλεφαρων

(c) 2 τ(ὴν) τῶν Φοιβα[ί]ων ἑο[ρτήν 3]ς τὴν τῶν Φοιβαίω[

suppl. ed.pr. (Lobel)

fr. 2 col. ii

. . . οὐδ . [   ] παρασταθεῖσαν [   ] τὴν Ἀφροδίτην.
Θέων [καὶ Τ]υραννίων ἀναγινώσκου[σι χρυσῷ] κατὰ γενικήν,
ἵν᾽ ἦι· οὐδὲ εἷς [σε μέμ]ψεται πλησίον χρυσοῦ στᾶσαν οὐ[δὲ]
ἐ[ξελ]έγξει σε χρυσός, ἀλλὰ διοίσεις αὐτόν.
  οὐ γὰρ πολυπήμων Κά[λα]ισος ἀνὴρ πεδ᾽ ἀνδρῶν
οὐ[δ᾽] ἄγριος· ἐ[κ] τοῦ ἐναντίου τὸ ἐναντίον. οὐκ ἐστὶ πολυπήμων ὁ
Κάλαισο[ς ἀ]λλ᾽ εὐδαίμων οὐδ᾽ ἄγριος ἀλλὰ ἥμερος.
  νῦν δ᾽ ἴομες τῶ δαίμονος ἔω(ς) τοῦ παι[δῶν] ἀρίσταν·
Λεωτυχίδας [Λ]ακεδαι[μονί]ων βασιλεύς. ἄδηλον δὲ [τίνος ἐστὶ
θ]υγάτηρ ἢ Τιμασιμβρότα [καὶ τίς ὁ υἱὸς] καὶ τίνος.

ALCMAN

Frr. 5–13 are papyrus fragments of commentaries on Alcman's poetry and life.

5 Papyrus (2nd c. A.D.)

fr. 1 (a)   3 of Polydeuces   5 'Castor' as far as   7 f. (were?) fleeing   8 (he? Polydeuces?) harmed   9 Polydeuces   10 sisters [1]

(b)   4 proud man!   5 Pleistodice?   6 eyelids

(c)   2, 3 the festival of the Phoebaea [2]

[1] Presumably the daughters of Leucippus, Phoebe and Hilaeira, who were carried off by Castor and Polydeuces: see fr. 8.   [2] A festival of Phoebe? See A. F. Garvie, *C.Q.* 59 (1965) 185–7.

fr. 2 col. ii

nor . . . standing beside . . . Aphrodite. Theon [1] . . . and Tyrannion [2] read χρυσῶ ('gold') in the genitive to give the meaning, 'Nor will anyone find fault with you [3] if you stand near gold, nor will gold show you up, but you will surpass it.'

For Calaesus is not a man of much hurt among men nor savage: opposite is used to express opposite: Calaesus is not 'of much hurt' but prosperous,[4] not savage but civilised.

But now let us go (trusting in the power?) of the god as far as best [5] of (his) children: Leotychidas is king of Sparta, but it is unclear (whose) daughter Timasimbrota (is and who is the son) and whose (son he is).

[1] Augustan grammarian.   [2] Another grammarian, either the Elder, Cicero's contemporary, or his pupil, the Younger. [3] Feminine.   [4] This explanation is improbable; Alcman must have meant 'not hurtful nor savage'.   [5] Feminine adjective.

φυὰν δ' ἔοικεν [Εὐρυκρατέος π]αιδὶ ξανθῶι
Πολυδώ[ρ]ω[ι· Ἱπποκρατίδας] Λεωτυχίδα υἱός ἐστι τοῦ
[Λακεδαιμονίων] βασιλέ[ω]ς· [το]ῦ δ' Εὐρυκ[ρ]ά[τους υἱὸς
Πολύδ]ωρος καὶ Τιμ[ασιμ]βρότα θυγά[τηρ.

Μῶ]σα, λίσσομαί τ[ε σι]ῶν μάλιστα· [τὰς Μο]ύσας ὑπὲρ
[τῆς θυγ]ατρὸς (?) τῆς τ[ῶν   ]ντιδων· φυλ[ικὸς δὲ χ]ορός (ἐστι)
Δύμα[ς· . . . . . .]τρα Δύμα[ινα· ἐν δ]ὲ ταύτηι τῆι ὠιδ[ῆι 'Αλ]κμὰν
φυσ[ικός (ἐστι)· ἐ]κθησ[ό]μεθα δὲ [τὰ δ]οκοῦντα ἡ[μῖν μ]ετὰ τὰς τῶν
λοιπῶ[ν πεί]ρας. Γῆς [μὲν] Μούσα[ς] θυγατέρας ὡς Μίμνερμ[ος
.]τας ἐγε[νεαλόγησε . . .

390

In build (she) is like the yellow-haired Polydorus, child (of Eurycrates): (Hippocratidas) is the son of Leotychidas, king (of Sparta), but Eurycrates' (son) is Polydorus, and Timasimbrota is his daughter.[6]

Muse, I beseech you most (among the gods): (he invokes) the Muses on behalf of the daughter of the -ntidae [7]); and it is the tribal chorus of Dyme: -tra [8] is a girl from Dyme. In this song Alcman is cosmogonist: we shall set out our opinions [9] following the attempts of the others. He made the Muses the daughters of Earth,[10] as Mimnermus [fr. 13 West] does.

[6] The commentator seems to have quoted a passage from elsewhere in the poem to solve his difficulty over the identity of Timasimbrota. The relevant royal family trees are:

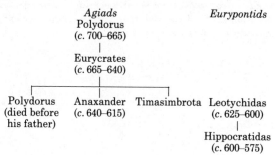

Agiads
Polydorus
(*c*. 700–665)
|
Eurycrates
(*c*. 665–640)
|

Polydorus (died before his father) — Anaxander (*c*. 640–615) — Timasimbrota — Leotychidas (*c*. 625–600) | Hippocratidas (*c*. 600–575)

Eurypontids

[7] The name of her family, conceivably Eurypontidae, the royal house.   [8] The chorus-leader? For Dyme see 4 fr. 5 n. 1.   [9] See col. iii below.   [10] As suited a poem concerned with cosmogony: the present poem may be the source of fr. 67. For the usual genealogy see frr. 3. 1, 8. 9 ff., 27, 28.

col. iii

. . . πάντων . . . [θέ]τις.

ἐκ δὲ τῶ π[ρέσγυς Πόρος Τέκμωρ τε· τέ]κμωρ ἐγένετο
τ[ῶι πόρωι ἀκόλουθον] μο[.] ἐντεῦθεν ει.[   ] πόρον ἀπὸ τῆς
πορί[μο]υ [πάντων ἀρχῆς]. ὡς γὰρ ἤρξατο ἡ ὕλη κατασκευα[σθῆναι],
ἐγένετο πόρος τις οἰονεὶ ἀρχή· π[οιεῖ] οὖν ὁ Ἀλκμὰν τὴν ὕλην
πάν[των τετα]ραγμένην καὶ ἀπόητον· εἶτα [γενέ]σθαι τινά φησιν τὸν
κατασκευά[ζοντα] πάντα, εἶτα γενέσθαι [πό]ρον, τοῦ [δὲ πό]ρου
παρελθόντος ἐπακολουθῆ[σαι] τέκμωρ· καὶ ἔστιν ὁ μὲν πόρος οἷον
ἀρχή, τὸ δὲ τέκμωρ οἰονεὶ τέλος. τῆς θέτιδος γενομένης ἀρχὴ καὶ
τέ[λ]ο[ς ἅμ]α πάντων ἐγένε[τ]ο, καὶ τὰ μὲν πάντα [ὁμο]ίαν ἔχει τὴν
φύσιν τῆι τοῦ χαλκοῦ ὕληι, ἡ δὲ θέτις τ[ῆι] τοῦ τεχνίτου, ὁ δὲ πόρος
καὶ τὸ τέκμωρ τῆι ἀρχῆι καὶ τῶι τέλει. πρέσγυ[υς] δὲ ἀντὶ τοῦ
πρεσβύτης.

καὶ τρίτος σκότος· διὰ τὸ μηδέπω μήτε ἥλιον μήτε σε[λ]ήνην
γεγονέναι, ἀλλ᾽ ἔτι ἀδιάκριτ[ο]ν εἶναι [τ]ὴν ὕλην· ἐγένοντο οὖν ὑπὸ
τ[α]ὐτὸ πόρος καὶ τέκμωρ καὶ σκότ[ος].[

ALCMAN

col. iii

. . . of all . . . (Thetis?).

After that, ancient Poros and Tekmor[11]: Tekmor came into being after Poros . . . thereupon . . . (called him) Poros since (the beginning 'provided' all things?); for when the matter[12] began to be set in order, a certain Poros came into being as a beginning. So Alcman (represents) the matter of all things as confused and unformed. Then he says that one came into being who set all things in order, then that Poros came into being, and that when Poros had passed by Tekmor followed. And Poros is as a beginning, Tekmor like an end. When Thetis[13] had come into being, a beginning and end of all things came into being (simultaneously), and all things[14] have their nature resembling the matter of bronze, while Thetis has hers resembling that of the craftsman, Poros and Tekmor resembling the beginning and the end. He uses the word 'ancient' (πρέσγυς) for 'old'.

And the third, darkness: since neither sun nor moon had come into being yet, but matter was still undifferentiated. So (at the same moment?) there came into being Poros and Tekmor and darkness.[15]

---

[11] See J. L. Penwill, *Apeiron* 8 (1974) 13 ff.: Poros, the Contriver at 1. 14, may here be rather the 'Passage' created between Heaven and Earth; Tekmor is probably 'Ordinance'.   [12] The commentator uses an Aristotelian term in his explanation: so with 'beginning' and 'end'. [13] Not the sea-goddess, but 'Creation' (=Attic θέσις: cf. 20. 1 ἔσηκε, probably from this poem).   [14] By 'all things' he means the ὕλη, 'matter'.   [15] This explanation seems wrong-headed: darkness is third not to Poros and Tekmor but to 'day and moon', as is shown by the longer quotation which follows.

393

ἀμάρ] τε καὶ σελάνα καὶ τρίτος (pap. -ον) σκότος ⟨ἕως⟩
τοῦ μαρμαρυγας· ἀμαρ οὐ ψιλῶς ἀλλὰ σὺν ἡλίωι· τὸ μὲν πρότερον
ἦν σκότος μόνον, μετὰ δὲ ταῦτα διακριθέ[ντο]ς αὐτοῦ . . .

post ed. pr. (Lobel), Page, Barrett suppl. M. L. West (*C.Q.* 57, 1963, 156; 59, 1965, 188ss.), F. D. Harvey (*J.H.S.* 87, 1967, 62ss.)

fr. 29. 5 τίν

fr. 30. 2 κυ[δάσδεν

fr. 34. 7s. ᾿Αλκμ[ὰν . . . ἐ]ν τῶι α´

fr. 49 col. i   1 Κρί[ωι   2 Πέρσῃ[ν   7 Ε]ὔβοιαν
12]βριαρε
col. ii   4 γαρυσεσ.[6 γαμον.[11 ἐν β´ πα[13 γενεά

6 P. Oxy. 2391

fr. 4:   2]αργυρου[4]φατὶ φιλέν[5]φησινηφιλ[

fr. 9: 4 γλυκεω[

fr. 10: 1 Φ]ίλυλλ[α- ?

fr. 11: 5 Κ]υπριδ[

fr. 21(a):   2].πενθερο[4]ος κεῖθι δὴ σ[5]οο ᾿Αλκαῖ(ος)[
(b):   7]τεθνηώτων   8]συνουσίαν γα[9 τ]ὰς ᾿Αμύκλας κα[
10].δρομον φυλα[(c):   2]γλυκηα[

Day and moon and the third, darkness (as far as) flashing(s) [16]: 'day' does not mean simply 'day', but contains the idea of the sun. Previously there was only darkness, and afterwards, when it had been differentiated, (light came into being).

[16] Perhaps of the stars.

fr. 29. 5 to you

fr. 30. 2 to revile [1]

fr. 34. 7 f. Alcman . . . in book 1

fr. 49 col. i   1 Crius [2]   2 Perses   7 Euboea 12 Briareus [3]

col. ii   4 speech   6 marriage   11 in book 2 of the (Partheneia)   13 family

[1] The commentator gives the meaning ($\kappa\alpha\kappa\iota\zeta\epsilon\iota\nu$).   [2] The Titan, father of Perses (Hes. *Theog.* 375 f.).   [3] Or Obriareus, one of the Hundred-handed (*Theog.* 149, 617).

6 Papyrus (1st c. A.D.)

fr. 4:   2 silver   4, 5 (s)he says (s)he loves

fr. 9:   4 sweet

fr. 10:   1 Philylla (?)

fr. 11:   5 Cyprian

fr. 21(a)   2 father-in-law   4 there indeed   5 Alcaeus (?) (b)   7 of the dead   8 society   9 Amyclae   10 running . . . tribe   (c)   2 sweet

7 P. Oxy. 2389 fr. 1

```
    . . . ]κῶμα σιῶν·        κω]μα θεῶν δ' εἴρη[ται
    . . . ] ἀσανάτας τελε[τὰς        ]
    ἐτάρφθεν  φρέ[να(ς)      ] ὁ Μενέλαος [      ]α.δ.[
    . . . . . α]ὐτὸν τιμᾶ[σθαι ἐν ταῖς Θεράπ]ναις μετὰ τῶν Διὸς κού[ρων
    ]κος ἐν τῆι Πελο[ποννήσωι      ]σ[.]αι 'Ελένη καὶ[      ]λεγο[
    ]ω . . . [.] .αφα[ρητιαδ-?      ]. μετ' αὐτ[ο]ῦ δ[ὲ      ]ν ἐν
    Θεράπναις [τιμ]ὰς ἔχουσι·
    πο[λλὰ] δ' ἐμνάσαντ' οσ[            ]αν ἀπήρ[ι]τον
    Β[α]κχῶν Καδ[μ-              ]. σε ν[ί]καν· ἀμφίβ[ολ]ον
    πότ[ερον      ]. ουσα . . [      τ]ῶν ἔργων [ἐμ]νήσθη[σαν      ]ασαν[
    ὔ]βριος ἀντ' ὀλοᾶς καὶ ἀτα[σθαλίας
```

fere omnia suppl. ed. pr. (Lobel)   sup. vers. ult. schol.
] . ως οἱ Διὸς κο[ῦ]ρ[οι] Ἅιδου . [

Schol. Eur. *Tro.* 210 (ii 353 Schwarz)

οἰκητήριόν φασι τὰς Θεράπνας τῶν Διοσκούρων παρόσον ὑπὸ τὴν
γῆν τῆς Θεράπνας εἶναι λέγονται ζῶντες, ὡς 'Αλκμὰν φησι.

Harp. s.v. Θεράπναι (i 151 Dindorf)

. . . τόπος ἐστὶν ἐν Λακεδαίμονι Θεράπναι, οὗ μνημονεύει καὶ
'Αλκμὰν ἐν α΄.

ALCMAN

7 Papyrus (50–100 A.D.)

. . . the sleep of the gods [1]: he uses σιῶν for θεῶν, 'of the gods'.

. . . immortal rites:

they were delighted in their hearts: . . . Menelaus . . . that he is honoured in Therapne with the Dioscuri . . . in the Peloponnese . . . Helen and . . . (the sons of Aphareus?) [2] . . . (with him?) . . . have honours in Therapne.

and often they remembered all the . . . boundless . . . of the Cadmaean Bacchae [3] . . . (victory?): it is uncertain whether . . . they remembered the deeds . . .

in return for destructive brutality and wickedness [4]:

[1] After death the Dioscuri (Castor and Polydeuces) lived on alternate days below the earth (in a 'sleep') and on Olympus (Pind. *Nem.* 10. 80 ff.); the rites which gave them pleasure were their worship at Therapne, where Menelaus and Helen were also worshipped.   [2] Lynceus and Idas, who fought the Dioscuri over the daughters of Leucippus and killed Castor (Pind. 1.c.).   [3] Relevance unknown.
[4] The scholiast's note above this line suggests that the Dioscuri are still the subject.

Scholiast on Euripides

They call Therapne the dwelling-place of the Dioscuri inasmuch as they are said to be alive underground in Therapne, as Alcman says.

Harpocration, *Lexicon of the Ten Attic Orators*

Therapne: a place in Laconia mentioned by Alcman in book 1.[1]

[1] See also 14(b).

8 P. Oxy. 2389 fr. 4 col. ii

1 ἀν]δροδάμα[2 Φοίβη κα[ὶ Ἰλάειρα   3]ται Ἀπόλλ[ων-
4]στροφε τον[5 συλληπτικ[6 θεῶν[

9ss. Μῶσαι μ[ακαίραι, τὰς Δὶ Μν]αμοσύνα μ[ι]γεῖσα
π.[. . . . .] . ς   ἐγέννατο   . . . μα[. . . .
. . . .]ρ θνατ[ο]ῖσι τέρψι[ν

post ed. pr. (Lobel) suppl. Barrett

9 P. Oxy. 2389 fr. 23

3 σφυ[

9A P. Oxy. 3210

fr. 1:   9 Σαπφώ   10 διὰ δυεῖν φωνηέν[των   11 σύμφωνα . .
λήγει   12s. Σαπφὼ διὰ [φωνη]έντων ἓν σύμφωνον   15 περ[ὶ]
τοῦ κνῖσα ῥητέον [ὅτι (?)   16 φησιν ὅτι παρὰ τον

fr. 2:   3 Ἀρχ]ιδαμ[6]Ἀρχιδ[9 παρὰ τὴν γα[10]ἅτερ
τοῦ ι (?) γράφεσθαι   11 (ἀν)ακολο]ύθως (?) ἐστὶν γαιο[16 αι εἰς η
23 εὐθεῖαν (vel Ὀρθείαν?)   24 φω[σφορ- (?)   25]ρχες ἕως
ἑωσφό[ρ- (?)   26 [α]παλω (?)

fr. 3:   3 Ἀσκαλαφ[7 μάχεσθαι

suppl. ed. pr. (Haslam)

ALCMAN

8 Same papyrus

. . . man-taming . . . Phoebe and (Hilaeira) [1] . . .
(Apollo?) [2] . . . comprehensive(ly) . . . of gods . . .
(Blessed) [3] Muses, (whom) Memory bore (to Zeus)
having lain (with him) . . . (delight to mortals?) . . .

[1] The daughters of Leucippus, abducted by Castor and
Polydeuces.   [2] According to the *Cypria* they were the
daughters of Apollo (Paus. 3. 16. 1).   [3] The commentator
begins a new poem; a title, which mentioned the sons of
Tyndareus (Castor and Polydeuces), has been cancelled in
the papyrus.

9 Same papyrus

(Alcman used a word beginning σφυ-)

9A Papyrus (50–100 A.D.)

The commentary, part of the same ms. as P. Oxy. 2389 frr.
1–34, mentions Sappho in connection with vowels and
consonants and seems to discuss the word κνῖσα ('smell of
roasting meat') (fr. 1); Archidamus(?), [1] then the form of a
compound word beginning γαι-/γα- ('earth-'), then perhaps
the word ἑωσφό[ρος ('dawn-bringer', i.e. the Morning Star)
and conceivably Ortheia (fr. 2); Ascalaphus [2] and fighting
(fr. 3).

[1] It is only the probable mention of this Spartan king, two
generations before Leotychidas, that suggests that Alcman
is the subject of the commentary.   [2] Son of Ares and
Astyoche, killed at Troy (*Il.* 13. 518 f., 15. 110 ff.).

10(a) = test. 9

(b) P. Oxy. 2506 fr. 5 col. ii

. . . ἀλλὰ ἀγ[ένειος   τὴν ἡ]λικίαν ὁ ['Αγ]η[σ]ί[δαμος   ]ς
Δ[ι]οσκού[ρ]ων κα[   ]ανάγει πρὸς τὸ χ[ρ]ῶμ[α . . . . .]
ἐλεφάντινο[ν . . .] προσονο[μ]άζειν·

τὺ δ[. . .]λαις ἄρχε ταῖς Δυμαί[ναις] Τυνδαρι-
δαιενα[   ]εσα[   ]εν αἰχμᾶι, σιοφιλὲς χο[ρα]γὲ
'Αγησίδαμε κλε[νν]ὲ Δαμοτιμίδα· καὶ μικρ[ὸν π]ροελθὼν
περὶ τῆ[ς] ἡλ[ικίας] αὐτοῦ λέγει καὶ τό[δε·

.γερώχως κήρατῶς χο[ρα]γώς· αὐτοὶ γὰρ ἁμέων
ἅλι[κ]ες νεανίαι φίλοι τε κἀγ[έ]νει[οι κ]ἀνύπανοι· αὐτόν
τε γὰρ [τὸ]ν 'Αγησ[ί]δαμον ἀγένει[ον] ἀποφα[ίνει   ]ν
συν[. .].δεδει[   ] αὐτῶι [   ]τον πω[γων-

suppl. et emend. ed. pr. (Page); v. R. Führer, Z.P.E. 11 (1973)
130.

11 P. Oxy. 2389 fr. 35

. . . παρσεν[· . . .]ωιδαιδ[. . . εἰσ[ή]κται ἐν
Πιτά[νηι . . . νῦν γὰρ ἐπι . . . Δυμαι[ν . . .].νταν . . .].ς δ(ὲ)
τὰς Μού[σας . . . τὰς παρθέ[νους . . . Πρατίνο]υ τοῦ Φλ[ειασίου] ?
. . . π[ολ]λάκις δ(ὲ) [Δ]υμαιν[ῶν παρθένοι ἀφί]κοντο ε[ἰς] τὴν
Πιτά[ν]ην συγ[χορεύσουσαι τ]αῖς Πιτανάτισι.
. .ἐ]πέων[. . .]ισαι ἐν τη[ι Πι]τάνηι σ.[. . .]τα Σαρδ[. . .
]ν τὰς εὑ[ρ]έσεις [. . . . . . . .τ]οὐ[ς] ὕμνου[ς] κ(αὶ) τὰ ἔπ[η . .]τε τὸ
μέλο[ς κ(αὶ) τὴ]ν λέξιν.
ἐπέων π[τεροέντω]ν· ὡς Ὅμη(ρος), ἔπεα πτερό[εντα.
κἀμὰ πα[ίγνια πα]ρσένω[ν] μάλι[σ]τ' ἀείσατ[ε · . . .

10(a) = test. 9

(b) Papyrus (1st or early 2nd c. A.D.)

. . . but beardless . . . his youth Hagesidamus . . . of the Dioscuri . . . refers . . . to the colour . . . to call . . . 'ivory'.[1]

And you, god-loved choir-leader Hagesidamus, glorious son of Damotimus, lead the Dymainai [2] . . . Tyndarid(ae) [3] . . . the spear: and a little later he says this also about his youth:

proud (?) and lovely choir-leaders [4]; for our young comrades themselves (are) dear and beardless and without hair on the lip: for he shows that both Hagesidamus himself is beardless . . . him . . . beard . . .

[1] I.e. Alcman used 'ivory' of the colour.   [2] See 4 fr. 5 n. 1. Beardless Hagesidamus seems to be leader of a girls' choir.   [3] With reference to Castor and Polydeuces. [4] Masculine, object of a verb which has not been quoted. Text and metre of both quotations are uncertain.

11 Papyrus (50–100 A.D.?)

girl(s): . . . has been introduced in Pitane [1] . . . ; for now . . . girls of Dyme . . . the Muses . . . the girls . . . (Pratinas of Phlius?) [2] . . . and often girls from Dyme came to Pitane to join (in choirs) with the girls of Pitane.

of words: . . . in Pitane . . . (Sardis?) . . . the discoveries . . . the songs and the verses and the melody and the diction.

of winged words: as in Homer.

and sing most of all the (playful songs) of us girls:

[1] One of the villages and tribes of Sparta; for Dyme see 4. fr. 5 n. 1.   [2] Bold supplement, but Pratinas wrote a play called *Dymainai*.

.... · ἦσαν] δ(ὲ) μάχιμοι [οὐ μόνοι οὗτοι ἀλλὰ κ(αὶ) οἱ ἐν]
Ἰων[ί]αι κ(αὶ) ἐν Θεσσα[λίαι......... Μο]λοσσοὶ δ(ὲ) τῆς
Ἠπείρ[ου πάλαι κατεστρέψαν]το Χάονας Θεσπρω[τοὺς Ὀρέστας (?)
Κασσω]παίους. οἱ δὲ Χαλκ[ιδεῖς.............]. εἰσὶ δὲ καὶ ἐπὶ
Θράικη[ς................] Θεοπομπ( ) ἐστι κ(αὶ) Αἰτω[λι
..............οἱ] γ(ὰρ) Αἰτωλοὶ πάντες [εἰσὶ μάχιμοι. ταύτης
δ(ὲ)] τῆς Αἰτωλικῆς Χαλκ[ίδος Ὅμη(ρος) μνημονεύ]ει λέγω(ν)
Χαλκίδα τ' ἀγ[χίαλον. τοὺς δ(ὲ) Χαλκι]δεῖς [το]ὺς ἐν Εὐβοίαι [

post ed. pr. (Lobel) retract. et suppl. Barrett.

12 P. Oxy. 2393

4 σιόφιν[·
6s. αἰχμα[τ]ὰς στρατ[ός· πολεμι]κὸν ἄθρο[ι]σμα
8s. σιόδματον τέγ[ος· τῶν Δι]οσκούρων ο[ἰκία

suppl. ed. pr. (Lobel), Page

12A P. Oxy. 2737 fr. 1 col. ii 18s.=1 *S.L.G.* (v. Ar. fr. 590 K.-A.)

χρυσοκόμα φιλόμολπε· Ἀλκμᾶνος ἡ ἀρχή.

. . . (these [3] were not the only ones who were) warlike: those in Ionia and Thessaly [4] . . . were also. The Molossians (once conquered) the Chaonians, Thesprotians, (Orestians?) and Cassopaeans of Epirus. The Chalcidians . . . There are Chalcidians also on the coast of Thrace [5] . . . Theopompus [6] . . . and also Aetolia(ns) . . . For the Aetolians are all (warlike. This) Aetolian Chalcis (is mentioned by Homer) in the words 'Chalcis by the sea' (*Il.* 2. 640). The Chalcidians in Euboea . . .

[3] Alcman seems to have spoken of 'warlike Chalcidians and Molossians'.   [4] Known from Strabo 644 and Dionysius the Guide 496 respectively. [5] The inhabitants of Chalcidice.   [6] Known to have mentioned the tribes of Epirus and also Chalcis and Chalcidice.

12 Papyrus (2nd c. A.D.): part of a lexicon

from the god(s) [1]:
spearman host: hostile gathering
god-built home [2]: house of the Dioscuri

[1] The form has the epic case-suffix -$\phi\iota(\nu)$.   [2] See fr. 2; presumably the other two entries are from earlier lines in the poem.

12A Papyrus (late 2nd c. A.D.): commentary on Aristophanes

Golden-haired song-lover [1]: the beginning (sc. of Aristophanes' stanza) belongs to Alcman.

[1] Opening words of a hymn to Apollo?

12B P. Oxy. 2737 fr. 1 col. i 19–27 = 6 *S.L.G.* (v. Ar. fr. 590 K.-A.)

κύκνος ὑπὸ πτερύγων τοιόνδε [τι]· τὸ μὲν ᾿Αριστάρχειον δο[κο]ῦν ὅτι Τερπάνδρου ἐστὶν [ἡ] ἀρχή, Εὐφρόνιος δὲ ὅτι ἐκ [τ]ῶν ῎Ι[ω]νος μελῶν, ὁ δὲ τὴν [π]αραπλοκὴν ὅτι ἐκ τῶν ᾿Αλ[κ]μᾶνος· ἔστι δ᾿ ἐκ τῶν εἰς ῞Ομη[ρ]ον ⟨ἀναφερομένων⟩ ὕμνων.

12C P. Oxy. 2812 fr. 1(a) col. i = 4 *S.L.G.*

7]. αι ᾿Αλκμὰ(ν)   8s. πε]ρὶ τοῦ Γα[νυμήδους?   9 ο]ὐκ ἦνθεν

13(a) = test. 8

(b) P. Oxy. 2506 fr. 4 10–15

. . . ἐμπε]ριπλέκει, ἐζ[ήτησε γὰρ ὧσ]περ ἔφην ἤδ[η   διαλλατ]τούσαις καὶ μὴ [κοιναῖς ἰστο]ρίαις χρῆσθαι κ[. . . . .] ἐστὶ περὶ ᾿Αλκμ[ᾶνος

(c) fr. 5 col. 1(b) 3–5

᾿Αλκ]μᾶνα[   ]ς· οὐδὲ [Θεσσαλὸς γένος ἀλλὰ] Σαρδί[ων ἀπ᾿ ἀκρᾶν

(d) fr. 17. 5–8

]εκτον ὅτι . . . ᾿Αλκ]μὰν ἐν Λυδοῖς . . .]σαι το[ῦ] μέλους . . .]ς κλ[ε]ιναὶ Σάρ[διες

suppl. ed. pr. (Page)

ALCMAN

12B Same commentary

The swan to the accompaniment of his wings (sings a song) such as this: the view of Aristarchus is that the beginning (sc. of the Aristophanic stanza) is by Terpander [fr. 1], Euphronius thinks it is from Ion's songs, the author of the *Paraploke* [1] thinks it comes from Alcman's songs; but it comes from the hymns ascribed to Homer [Homeric hymn 21. 1].

[1] Unknown; the translated title may be *Quotation*.

12C Papyrus (1st c. A.D.): commentary on a tragedy

. . . Alcman . . . concerning (Ganymede?) [1] . . . he did not go . . .

[1] The tragedy deals with the action of Poseidon and Apollo at Troy.

13(a) = test. 8

(b) Papyrus (1st or early 2nd c. A.D.): commentary on the life and work of Alcman and others

. . . introduces complications, for he sought, as I have said already, to use different stories, not ordinary ones . . . is . . . concerning Alcman . . .

(c) Same papyrus

. . . Alcman . . . nor Thessalian by race, but from lofty) Sardis [1]

(d) Same papyrus

. . . that . . . Alcman among the Lydians . . . (of) his song . . . famous Sardis . . .

[1] Cf. fr. 16.

14 Syrian. in Hermog. (i 61 Rabe) = Max. Plan., *Rhet. Gr.*
v 510 Walz

ἡ μὲν οὖν στροφή ἐστιν ἡ πρώτη τιθεμένη περίοδος ἐκ δυεῖν ἢ
πλειόνων κώλων ὁμοίων ἢ ἀνομοίων συγκειμένη, ὡς παρὰ ᾿Αλκμᾶνι
[fr. 27] . . . , ἐξ ἀνομοίων δὲ ὡς τόδε·

(a) Μῶσ᾽ ἄγε Μῶσα λίγηα πολυμμελές
αἰὲν ἀοιδὲ μέλος
νεοχμὸν ἄρχε παρσένοις ἀείδην.

cf. Ap. Dysc. *Synt.* 1. 3 (p. 3 Uhlig), schol. Callim. fr. 1. 42 (i 7
Pfeiffer), *Et. Mag.* 589. 47, Erotian. s.v. νεοχμόν (p. 99 Klein)

2 αἰεναοιδὲ ci. Bergk

Prisc. *de metr. Ter.* 24 (iii 428 Keil)

Simonides et Alcman in iambico teste Heliodoro non
solum in fine ponunt spondeum sed etiam in aliis locis:
Simonides [fr. 533]; Alcman autem in primo catalecticum
trimetrum fecit habentem in quarto loco modo iambum
modo spondeum, sic:

(a) νεοχμὸν ἄρχε παρσένοις ἀείδην.
(b) καὶ ναὸς ἁγνὸς εὐπύργω Σεράπνας:

hic quarto loco spondeum habet; similiter

(c) χέρρονδε κωφὸν ἐν φύκεσσι πίτνει

quarto loco spondeum posuit (nam φυ producitur) teste
Heliodoro, qui ait Simonidem hoc frequenter facere.

(b) Hermann: ἁγνᾶς codd.   (c) Page: χερσάνδε codd. (cf.
Hsch. χέρρον· τὴν χέρσον γῆν. Λάκωνες)

ALCMAN

Frr. 14–157 are book-quotations; 14–20 are assigned to numbered books.

14 Syrianus on Hermogenes, *On Kinds of Style*

Now the strophe, the period which stands first,[1] consists of two or more cola (metrical phrases), which may be similar or dissimilar: similar as in Alcman [fr. 27], dissimilar as in this example:

(a) Come, Muse, clear-voiced Muse of many songs, singer always, begin a new [2] song for girls to sing.

[1] I.e. before antistrophe and epode.   [2] According to Erotianus Alcman uses the adjective in book 1. The newness may lie in the metre.

Priscian, *On the Metres of Terence*

In their iambic lines Simonides and Alcman, according to Heliodorus, place a spondee not only at the end but in other positions also: Simonides [fr. 533]; Alcman in book 1 composed catalectic trimeters with sometimes an iamb, sometimes a spondee in the fourth position, as follows:

(a) = begin a new (song) for girls to sing [1];

(b) and the holy temple of well-towered Therapne,[2]

which has a spondee in the fourth position; so in

(c) (the wave?) falls mutely on the land [3] among the seaweed,

he put a spondee in the fourth position—for the first syllable of φύκεσσι is long—according to Heliodorus, who says Simonides often does this.

[1] Regular iambic trimeter catalectic.   [2] See fr. 7 and Harpocration cited there.   [3] If all the lines come from the same poem, the beach may be that of Pephnos, where the Dioscuri were said to have been born (fr. 23).

15 Heph. *Ench.* 1. 3 (p. 2 Consbruch)

γίνεται δὲ τοῦτο κατὰ πέντε τρόπους· ἤτοι γὰρ λήξει εἰς δύο σύμφωνα, οἷον Τίρυνς κτλ [adesp. 1043 *P.M.G.*],

καὶ κῆνος ἐν σάλεσσι πολλοῖς ἥμενος μάκαρς ἀνήρ

cf. Ap. Dysc. *Pron.* 75b (i 59 Schneider), 74a (i 58) ἀλλὰ καί Ἀλκμὰν πρώτῳ μάκαρς ἐκεῖνός φησί, schol. Dion. Thrac. (p. 346 Hilgard)

κείμενος Heph. cod. I

16 Steph. Byz. s.v. Ἐρυσίχη (i 281s. Meineke)

Ἐρυσίχη· πόλις Ἀκαρνανίας ἥτις ὕστερον Οἰνιάδαι ὠνομάσθη . . . τὸ ἐθνικὸν Ἐρυσιχαῖος, περὶ οὗ πολὺς λόγος τοῖς ἀρχαίοις· ὁ τεχνικὸς γὰρ καὶ Ἡρωδιανός φησιν [i 130s., ii 874 Lentz] ὅτι σεσημείωται τὸ Ἐρυσίχαιος προπαροξυνόμενον ἐν τοῖς ἐθνικοῖς· μήποτε οὖν τὸ χαῖον ἐγκεῖσθαι, ὅ ἐστιν ἡ βουκολικὴ ῥάβδος, καὶ τὸν ἐρύσω μέλλοντα. διχῶς οὖν ἔσται, ὡς ἔστι δῆλον παρ' Ἀλκμᾶνι ἐν ἀρχῇ τοῦ δευτέρου τῶν παρθενείων ᾀσμάτων· φησὶ γάρ·

> οὐκ ἦς ἀνὴρ ἀγρεῖος οὐ-
> δὲ σκαιὸς οὐδὲ †παρὰ σοφοῖ-
> σιν† οὐδὲ Θεσσαλὸς γένος,
> Ἐρυσιχαῖος οὐδὲ ποιμήν,
> ἀλλὰ Σαρδίων ἀπ' ἀκρᾶν.

εἰ γὰρ τῷ Θεσσαλὸς γένος συναπτέον, ἐθνικόν ἐστι καὶ προπερισπάσθω, Ἡρωδιανὸς ἐν ταῖς καθόλου προσῳδίαις [i 131 Lentz] καὶ Πτολεμαῖος ἔφη· εἰ δὲ τῷ οὐδὲ ποιμὴν συνάψειέ τις, λέγων τὸ οὐδὲ ποιμὴν ἢ ἐρυσίχαιος, πρόδηλον ὡς προπαροξυνθήσεται καὶ δηλοῖ τὸν βουκόλον ἢ τὸν αἰπόλον, πρὸς ὃ τὸ ποιμὴν ἁρμόδιον ἐπαχθήσεται.

vv. 1–4 Steph., 4–5 Strabo 10. 2. 22. Cf. test. 8, *Anecd. Oxon.* (i 10 Cramer) et *Et. Mag.* 180.27 s.v. Ἀχαιός, Chrysipp. π. ἀποφ. 21 (*S.V.F.* ii 57 Arnim), schol. Ap. Rhod. 4.972 (p. 300 Wendel)

1 ἦς Chrysipp.: εἶς Steph. ἄγριος Steph., P. Oxy. 2389 (= test. 8) ante corr.: ἀγροῖκος Chrysipp. 2s. παρ'

ALCMAN

15 Hephaestion, *Handbook on Metres*

This (sc. the lengthening of syllables 'by position') occurs in five different ways: either the syllable will end in two consonants, as with 'Tiryns', [anon. fragment] or μάκαρς,[1] 'blessed':

> and he sitting, blessed man,[2] amid much good cheer . . .

[1] Apollonius Dyscolus says Alcman used μάκαρς ἐκεῖνος, 'blessed he', in book 1.   [2] Perhaps of the deified Heracles.

16 Stephanus of Byzantium, *Lexicon of Place-names*

Erysiche: a city of Acarnania, later named Oeniadae . . . The ethnic adjective is Ἐρυσιχαῖος, 'Erysichaean', about which the ancients had much to say: the grammarian Herodian says that Ἐρυσίχαιος, so accented, is marked in texts as being an exception among ethnic adjectives, so perhaps, he says, it is made up of χαῖον, 'a cowman's stick', and the future of ἐρύω, 'drag': it will therefore be ambiguous, as is evident in Alcman at the beginning of book 2 of the partheneia, for he says,

> he was no rustic man nor clumsy (not even in the view of unskilled men?) nor Thessalian by race nor an Erysichaean shepherd: he was from lofty Sardis.[1]

For if the adjective is to be linked with 'Thessalian by race', it is an ethnic adjective and should be accented Ἐρυσιχαῖος, as Herodian in his *Universal Prosody* and Ptolemaeus said; but if it is linked with 'nor a shepherd', i.e. 'nor a shepherd or erysichaean', clearly it will be accented ἐρυσίχαιος and indicates 'cowman' or 'goatherd', next to which the word 'shepherd' will be aptly introduced.

[1] This is the passage which was taken, rightly or wrongly, to prove the Lydian origin of Alcman: see test. 8, fr. 13(c)(d).

ἀσόφοισιν Welcker   4 Hartung: οὐδ' 'E. οὐδὲ π. codd.

409

GREEK LYRIC

17 Athen. x 416cd (ii 405s. Kaibel)

καὶ ᾿Αλκμὰν δ᾽ ὁ ποιητὴς ἑαυτὸν ἀδηφάγον εἶναι παραδίδωσιν ἐν τῷ τρίτῳ διὰ τούτων·

καί ποκά τοι δώσω τρίποδος κύτος
ᾧ κ᾽ ἐνὶ ⟨   ⟩λέ᾽ ἀγείρῃς.
ἀλλ᾽ ἔτι νῦν γ᾽ ἄπυρος, τάχα δὲ πλέος
ἔτνεος, οἷον ὁ παμφάγος ᾿Αλκμὰν
5 ἠράσθη χλιαρὸν πεδὰ τὰς τροπάς·
οὔτι γὰρ ἀδὺ τετυγμένον ἔσθει,
ἀλλὰ τὰ κοινὰ γάρ, ὥπερ ὁ δᾶμος,
ζατεύει.

cf. Aelian. *V.H.* 1. 27 (p. 11 Dilts)

2 ⟨σιτί᾽ ἀολ⟩λέ᾽ Crusius, Jurenka   5 Casaubon: χαιερον παιδα codd. 6 e.g. Page: οὐ τετυμμένον codd. 7 Casaubon: καινὰ codd.

18 P. Oxy. 2392

Διονυσίου ἐπο.[   ] ᾿Αλκμᾶνος μελ[ῶ]ν δ᾽ ὑπ(όμνημα)

19 Athen. iii 110f, 111a (i 254 Kaibel)

μακωνίδων δ᾽ ἄρτων μνημονεύει ᾿Αλκμὰν ἐν τῷ ε᾽ οὕτως·

κλίναι μὲν ἑπτὰ καὶ τόσαι τραπέσδαι
μακωνιᾶν ἄρτων ἐπιστεφοίσαι
λίνω τε σασάμω τε κἠν πελίχναις
†πεδεστε† χρυσοκόλλα.

ἐστὶ ⟨δὲ⟩ βρωμάτιον διὰ μέλιτος καὶ λίνου.

cf. Hsch. s.v. χρυσοκόλλα.

2 Chantraine et Irigoin: μακωνίδων codd.   4 fort. πλέεσσι Page

410

ALCMAN

17 Athenaeus, *Scholars at Dinner*

Even the poet Alcman puts his gluttony on record in these lines from book 3:

and some day I shall give you a great tripod bowl,[1] in which you may collect (provisions packed together?). It has still not been over a fire, but soon it will be full of pea-soup, the kind that Alcman, who eats everything, loves hot after the solstice: he eats no (sweet confections?) but looks for common fare like the people.[2]

[1] A prize he hopes to win and present to the choir or choir-leader.   [2] Continued at fr. 20.

18 Papyrus (2nd c. A.D.)[1]

The commentary of Dionysius[2] on book 4 of Alcman's songs.

[1] The title at the end of a roll.   [2] Unknown, unless he is the Dionysius of Sidon mentioned in *Et. Mag.* in connection with 1. 49 (ὑποπετριδίων) or Dionysius of Thrace, grammarian of 2nd c. B.C.

19 Athenaeus, *Scholars at Dinner*

Poppy-seed loaves are mentioned by Alcman in book 5[1] in these words:

Seven couches and as many tables laden with poppy-seed loaves and linseed and sesame,[2] and chrysocolla in (full?) bowls.[3]

Chrysocolla is a dish made of honey and linseed.[4]

[1] Or book 6 (Haslam, *Ox. Pap.* 45, 1977, 3 n. 2).
[2] Presumably loaves sprinkled with these.   [3] Perhaps from the same poem as fr. 96.   [4] Same explanation in Hesychius. Cf. the provisions taken by divers to the Spartans trapped on Sphacteria (Thuc. 4. 26. 8).

411

GREEK LYRIC

20 Athen. x 416d (ii 406 Kaibel)

κἀν τῷ ε′ δὲ ἐμφανίζει αὐτοῦ τὸ ἀδηφάγον λέγων οὕτως·

> ὥρας δ' ἔσηκε τρεῖς, θέρος
> καὶ χεῖμα κὠπώραν τρίταν
> καὶ τέτρατον τὸ Ϝῆρ, ὄκα
> σάλλει μέν, ἐσθίην δ' ἄδαν
> οὐκ ἔστι.

2 anon.: χειμάχωι· παραν cod.   3s. edd. vett.: τοηροκας ἀλλ'
εἰ μὲν ἐσθειεν cod.

21 Paus. 1. 41.4 (i 95 Rocha-Pereira)

. . . Μεγαρέως δὲ Τίμαλκον παῖδα τίς μὲν ἐς Ἄφιδναν ἐλθεῖν
μετὰ τῶν Διοσκούρων ἔγραψε; πῶς δ' ἂν ἀφικόμενος ἀναιρεθῆναι
νομίζοιτο ὑπὸ Θησέως, ὅπου καὶ Ἀλκμὰν ποιήσας ᾆσμα ἐς τοὺς
Διοσκούρους, ὡς Ἀθήνας ἕλοιεν καὶ τὴν Θησέως ἀγάγοιεν μητέρα
αἰχμάλωτον, ὅμως Θησέα φησὶν αὐτὸν ἀπεῖναι;

Schol. A Hom. *Il.* 3. 242 (i 153 Dindorf)

Ἑλένη ἁρπασθεῖσα ὑπὸ Ἀλεξάνδρου, ἀγνοοῦσα τὸ συμβεβηκὸς
μεταξὺ τοῖς ἀδελφοῖς Διοσκούροις κακόν, ὑπολαμβάνει δι' αἰσχύνης
αὐτῆς μὴ πεπορεῦσθαι τούτους εἰς Ἴλιον, ἐπειδὴ προτέρως ὑπὸ
Θησέως ἡρπάσθη, καθὼς προείρηται. διὰ γὰρ τὴν τότε γενομένην
ἁρπαγὴν Ἄφιδνα πόλις Ἀττικῆς πορθεῖται καὶ τιτρώσκεται
Κάστωρ ὑπὸ Ἀφίδνου τοῦ τότε βασιλέως κατὰ τὸν δεξιὸν μηρόν. οἱ
δὲ Διόσκουροι Θησέως μὴ τυχόντες λαφυραγωγοῦσι τὰς Ἀθήνας. ἡ
ἱστορία παρὰ τοῖς Πολεμωνίοις (?) ἢ τοῖς Κυκλικοῖς καὶ ἀπὸ μέρους
παρὰ Ἀλκμᾶνι τῷ λυρικῷ.

412

ALCMAN

20 Athenaeus, *Scholars at Dinner* [1]

And in book 5 also he reveals his gluttony in the following words:

and he created three seasons, [2] summer and winter and the third, autumn, and spring as a fourth, when things grow but there is not enough to eat.

[1] The passage follows fr. 17.   [2] The lines may be from the poem on cosmogony (5 fr. 2 col. iii). For another possible quotation from book 5 see fr. 48.

21–25 are concerned with the Dioscuri, as are 2, 7, 14(b).

21 Pausanias, *Description of Greece*

. . . but who wrote that Timalcus, the son of Megareus, went to Aphidna with the Dioscuri [1]? And how could he be thought to have been killed on his arrival by Theseus, when Alcman in a song he composed to the Dioscuri tells how they conquered Athens and carried off Theseus' mother as their prisoner but says that Theseus himself was absent.

[1] Pausanias is expressing his disagreement with a story told in Megara. When Theseus kidnapped Helen, her brothers the Dioscuri went to Aphidna in N.E. Attica and carried off Theseus' mother in reprisal.

Scholiast on Homer, *Iliad* 3. 242

Helen, carried off by Paris, has no knowledge of the disaster that has overtaken her brothers the Dioscuri in the meantime, but imagines that they have not come to Troy because they are ashamed of her: she had previously been carried off by Theseus, as has been said already. On account of that incident Aphidna, a city in Attica, was sacked and Castor was wounded in the right thigh by Aphidnus, king at that time. The Dioscuri having failed to get hold of Theseus plundered Athens. The story is in (Polemon?) or the cyclic poems and in part in the lyric poet Alcman.

22 Hsch. A 7622

'Ασαναίων πόλιν· τὰς 'Αφίδνας.

Palmer: 'Ασανέων cod.　　Alcmani trib. O. Mueller

23 Paus. 3. 26. 2 (i 268 Rocha-Pereira)

Θαλαμῶν δὲ ἀπέχει σταδίους εἴκοσιν ὀνομαζομένη Πέφνος ἐπὶ θαλάσσῃ. πρόκειται δὲ νησὶς πέτρας τῶν μεγάλων οὐ μείζων, Πέφνος καὶ ταύτῃ τὸ ὄνομα. τεχθῆναι δὲ ἐνταῦθα τοὺς Διοσκούρους φασὶν οἱ Θαλαμᾶται. τοῦτο μὲν δὴ καὶ 'Αλκμᾶνα ἐν ᾄσματι οἶδα εἰπόντα. τραφῆναι δὲ οὐκέτι ἐν τῇ Πέφνῳ φασὶν [1] αὐτούς, ἀλλὰ Ἑρμῆν τὸν ἐς Πελλάναν κομίσαντα εἶναι.

[1] φησὶν ci. Siebelis

24 Him. *Or.* 39. 2 (p. 160 Colonna)

'Αλκμὰν δὲ ⟨ὁ⟩ τὴν Δώριον λύραν Λυδίοις κεράσας ᾄσμασιν ἐτύγχανε μὲν διὰ τῆς Σπάρτης εἰς Διὸς Λυκ⟨α⟩ίου κομίζων ᾄσματα· οὐ μὴν παρῆλθε τὴν Σπάρτην πρὶν καὶ αὐτὴν τὴν πόλιν καὶ Διοσκόρους ἀσπάσασθαι.

25 Schol. Bern. ad Verg. *Geo.* 3. 89

Amycla urbs in Peloponneso: equos autem a Neptuno Iunoni datos Alcman lyricus dicit Cyllarum et Xanthum, quorum Polluci Cyllarum, Xanthum fratri eius concessum esse dictum est; Cyllarus enim equus fuit Pollucis.

cf. Serv. Dan. ad loc. (iii 1. 283 Thilo-Hagen)

ALCMAN

22 Hesychius, *Lexicon*

city of the Asanaioi [1]: Aphidnae.

[1] Alcman's form of 'Athenians'.

23 Pausanias, *Description of Greece*

Two-and-a-half miles from Thalamae is a place on the coast called Pephnos.[1] Off it lies an island no bigger than a big rock, and it too is called Pephnos. The people of Thalamae say the Dioscuri were born there. I know that Alcman said so in a song; but they say [2] that they were brought up not on Pephnos but at Pellana,[3] and that it was Hermes who took them there.

[1] On the shore of the gulf of Messene.   [2] Perhaps read 'he says'.   [3] 16 miles N.W. of Sparta.

24 Himerius, *Oration*

Alcman, who mingled the Dorian lyre with Lydian songs, happened to be carrying songs through Sparta to the temple of Zeus Lycaeus [1]; but he did not pass Sparta before greeting both the city itself and the Dioscuri.

[1] In Arcadia.

25 Scholiast on Virgil, *Georgics* ('such was Cyllarus, subdued by the reins of Amyclaean Pollux')

Amycla is a city in the Peloponnese; the horses given to Juno by Neptune are called Cyllarus and Xanthus by the lyric poet Alcman: Cyllarus was said to have been given [1] to Pollux, Xanthus to his brother; for Cyllarus belonged to Pollux.

[1] By Juno, according to another scholiast on the passage, who adds, 'as unimportant Greek poets tell'; cf. frr. 2, 76, Stes. 178.

26 Antig. Caryst. *Mir.* 23 (27) (p. 8 Keller)

τῶν δὲ ἀλκυόνων οἱ ἄρσενες κηρύλοι καλοῦνται. ὅταν οὖν ὑπὸ τοῦ γήρως ἀσθενήσωσιν καὶ μηκέτι δύνωνται πέτεσθαι, φέρουσιν αὐτοὺς αἱ θήλειαι ἐπὶ τῶν πτερῶν λαβοῦσαι. καὶ ἔστι τὸ ὑπὸ τοῦ Ἀλκμᾶνος λεγόμενον τούτῳ συνῳκειωμένον· φησὶν γὰρ ἀσθενὴς ὢν διὰ τὸ γήρας καὶ τοῖς χοροῖς οὐ δυνάμενος συμπεριφέρεσθαι οὐδὲ τῇ τῶν παρθένων ὀρχήσει·

οὔ μ' ἔτι, παρσενικαὶ μελιγάρυες ἱαρόφωνοι,
γυῖα φέρην δύναται· βάλε δὴ βάλε κηρύλος εἴην,
ὅς τ' ἐπὶ κύματος ἄνθος ἅμ' ἀλκυόνεσσι ποτῆται
νηλεὲς ἦτορ ἔχων, ἁλιπόρφυρος ἱαρὸς ὄρνις.

cf. Ap. Dysc. *Coni.* 522 (i 254 Schneider), *Et. Gen.* (p. 19 Calame), *Et. Mag.* (+ *Et. Sym.*) 186. 39 s.v. βάλε, *Anecd. Oxon.* (i 264s. Cramer), Hdn. (i 108 Lentz), *Anecd. Gr.* (ii 946 Bekker)=schol. Dion. Thrac. (p. 279 Hilgard), *Sud.* K 1549 (iii 112 Adler)=schol. Ar. *Av.* 299 (p. 73 White), schol. Ar. *Av.* 250 (p. 60s. White), Phot. *Lex.* s.v. ὄρνις (ii 28 Naber), Athen. ix 374d (v. fr. 40 inf.)

1 ἱερό- Antig.: ἱμερό- ci. Barker   4 ἀδεὲς Phot.: νηδεὲς Boissonade: νηλεγὲς Bergk   Hecker: εἴαρος Antig., Athen., Phot.

27 Heph. *Ench.* 7. 4 (p. 22 Consbruch)

Ἀλκμὰν δὲ καὶ ὅλας στροφὰς τούτῳ τῷ μέτρῳ κατεμέτρησε·

Μῶσ' ἄγε Καλλιόπα, θύγατερ Διός,
ἄρχ' ἐρατῶν Fεπέων, ἐπὶ δ' ἵμερον
ὕμνῳ καὶ χαρίεντα τίθη χορόν.

cf. 4. 1 (p. 13 Consbruch), epitom. 8 (p. 361), Syrian. *in Hermog.* (i 61 Rabe)=Max. Plan., *Rhet. Gr.* v 510 Walz, Arsen.=Apostol. xi 94a (ii 540 Leutsch-Schneidewin)

ALCMAN

26–41 deal with Alcman's songs and with the Muses.

26 Antigonus of Carystus, *Marvels*

Male halcyons are called ceryli.[1] When they become weak from old age and are no longer able to fly, the females carry them, taking them on their wings.[2] What Alcman says is connected with this: weak from old age and unable to whirl about with the choirs and the girls' dancing, he says,

No longer, honey-toned, strong-voiced[3] girls, can my limbs carry me.[4] If only, if only I were a cerylus, who flies along with the halcyons over the flower of the wave[5] with resolute heart, strong,[6] sea-blue bird.

[1] Both mythical seabirds, sometimes identified with the kingfisher.   [2] This marvel is contradicted by Alcman's text.   [3] Or 'holy-voiced'.   [4] The lines may be part of a solo hexameter prelude to a choral song: cf. Terp. test. 19.   [5] Aristophanes adapts this line in *Birds* 250 f.   [6] Perhaps 'holy': cf. Simon. 508. 4 ff.; probably not 'sea-blue bird of Spring'.

27 Hephaestion, *Handbook on Metres*

Alcman put whole strophes in this metre (viz. dactylic tetrameter acatalectic)[1]:

Come, Muse, Calliope, daughter of Zeus, begin the lovely verses; set desire on the song and make the choral dance graceful.

[1] See also fr. 14.

GREEK LYRIC

28 Schol. A Hom. *Il.* 13. 588 (iii 512 Erbse)

τῇ φι παραγωγῇ ὁ ποιητὴς κατὰ τριῶν κέχρηται πτώσεων, ἐπὶ γενικῆς δοτικῆς αἰτιατικῆς· . . . ἐπὶ δὲ κλητικῆς Ἀλκμὰν ὁ μελοποιὸς οὕτως·

Μῶσα Διὸς θύγατερ λίγ' ἀείσομαι † ὠρανίαφι †,

ἐστὶ γὰρ οὐρανία.

cf. schol. Lips. Hom. *Il.* 2. 233 (i 102 Bachmann), Ap. Dysc. *Adv.* 575 (i 165 Schneider), *Anecd. Oxon.* (i 293 Cramer), *Et. Gud.* 411. 16, *Et. Mag.* (+ *Et. Sym.*) 800. 10

29 Achill. *in Arat.* 1 (p. 82 Maass)

ἐγκαλοῦσι δὲ αὐτῷ τὴν ἐκ πρόθεσιν ἀντὶ τῆς ἀπὸ παρειληφότι· ἔδει γὰρ (φασίν) εἰπεῖν ἀπὸ Διός. ἀγνοοῦσι δὲ ὅτι καὶ Πίνδαρος κατεχρήσατο τῷ ἔθει τούτῳ λέγων [*Nem.* 2. 1–3] καὶ Ἀλκμάν·

ἐγὼν δ' ἀείσομαι
ἐκ Διὸς ἀρχομένα.

Valckenaer: ἐγὼ δὲ ἀεί σοι με ἐκ Δ. ἀρχόμενα cod.

30 Ael. Aristid. *Or.* 28. 51 (ii 158 Keil)

ἀκούεις δὲ τοῦ Λάκωνος λέγοντος εἰς αὐτόν τε καὶ τὸν χορόν·

ἁ Μῶσα κέκλαγ', ἁ λίγηα Σηρήν.

. . . προστίθει δὲ κἀκεῖνο, ὅτι αὐτῆς τῆς Μούσης δεηθεὶς κατ' ἀρχὰς ὁ ποιητής, ἵν' ἐνεργὸς ὑπ' αὐτῆς γένοιτο, εἶτα ὥσπερ ἐξεστηκὼς φησὶν ὅτι τοῦτο ἐκεῖνο ⟨ὁ⟩ χορὸς αὐτὸς ἀντὶ τῆς Μούσης γεγένηται.

31 Eust. *Od.* 1547. 60

λέγει δὲ καὶ Ἀλκμάν·
τὰν Μῶσαν καταυσεῖς

ἀντὶ τοῦ ἀφανίσεις.

cf. Hsch. Κ 93 καθαῦσαι· ἀφανίσαι.

418

ALCMAN

28 Scholiast on Homer

The ending -φι is used by Homer in three cases, genitive, dative and accusative . . . ; Alcman the lyric poet has it in the vocative, thus:

Muse, daughter of Zeus, I shall sing clearly, (heavenly one?).[1]

For ὡρανίαφι is οὐρανία, 'heavenly one'.

[1] Most modern scholars reject the vocative form.

29 Achilles, *Commentary on Aratus* ('From Zeus let us begin')

They find fault with Aratus for using the preposition ἐκ instead of ἀπό ('from'); but they are ignorant of the fact that Pindar too has this usage [*Nem.* 2. 1–3], and Alcman:

and I shall sing beginning [1] from Zeus.

[1] Feminine participle: a girl or girls' choir is singing.

30 Aelius Aristides, *On a Remark made in Passing*

And you hear the Spartan saying to himself and the choir:

The Muse cries out, that clear-voiced Siren.

. . . Add this point too, that the poet, having in the first place requested the Muse herself, so that he might become active under her influence, goes on to say as though he has changed his mind that the choir itself instead of the Muse has become what he says.[1]

[1] I.e. that his choir has been his source of inspiration.

31 Eustathius on *Od.* 5. 490 (αὔω, 'kindle')

And Alcman says,

you will destroy the Muse,

using καταύω for ἀφανίζω ('destroy').

419

GREEK LYRIC

32 Phot. s.v. (p. 654 Porson, ii 268 Naber)

⟨ψιλεύς· ἐπ᾽ ἄκρου χοροῦ ἱστάμενος. ὅθεν καὶ

φιλόψιλος

παρ᾽ Ἀλκμᾶνι, ἡ φιλοῦσα ἐπ᾽ ἄκρου⟩ χοροῦ ἵστασθαι.

cf. *Sud.* Ψ 101 (iv 846 Adler), unde Phot. suppl. Porson;
Hsch. Ψ 197 (iv 311 Schmidt) ψιλεῖς· οἱ ὕστατοι χορεύοντες.

33 Anon. I *in Arat.* (p. 91 Maass)

εἰσὶν οὖν τέσσαρες σφαῖραι, ἃ στοιχεῖα καλοῦσιν οἱ παλαιοὶ διὰ τὸ
στοίχῳ καὶ τάξει ἕκαστον αὐτῶν ὑποκεῖσθαι, ὥς που καὶ Ἀλκμὰν

ὁμοστοίχους

ἐκάλεσε τὰς ἐν τάξει χορευούσας παρθένους.

34 Schol. Theocr. *argum. carm.* 12 (p. 249s. Wendel)

ἐπιγράφεται μὲν τὸ εἰδύλλιον Ἀίτης, γέγραπται δὲ Ἰάδι
διαλέκτῳ. ὁ δὲ λόγος ἐκ τοῦ ποιητικοῦ προσώπου πρὸς ἐρώμενον.
ὅθεν καὶ τὸ ἐπίγραμμα Ἀίτης, ἐπειδὴ τοὺς ἐρωμένους ἀίτας ἔνιοι
καλοῦσιν, ὡς Θεσσαλοί. καὶ γὰρ Ἀλκμὰν τὰς ἐπεράστους κόρας
λέγει

ἀίτας.

cf. schol. Theocr. (p. 251 Wendel), ubi Ἀλκμὰν δὲ τὰς ἀίτας
χορδὰς ἀπεράστους φησίν codd., *Et. Gud.* s.v. ἀίτιας (i 58 di
Stefani), *Et. Mag.* 43. 40 s.vv. ἀίτιας χορδάς, Hdn. (i 105, ii 296
Lentz), *Anecd. Oxon.* (ii 173 Cramer)

Ahrens: ἀίτας codd.

420

ALCMAN

32 Photius, *Lexicon*

ψιλεύς: standing at the edge of the choir. Whence

edge-loving

in Alcman: she who loves to stand at the edge of the choir.[1]

[1] Hesychius explains the plural as 'those who dance at the end'. But there was also a word ψῖλον, the Doric form for πτίλον, 'down, feathers': Alcman's adjective might have meant 'down-loving'.

33 Anonymous commentator on Aratus (introduction)

So there are four spheres [viz. earth, water, air, aether], which the ancients call στοιχεῖα ('elements') since each of them lies in a row (στοῖχος) or line, just as Alcman somewhere called the girls dancing in line ὁμό-στοιχοι,

all in one row.

34 Scholiast on Theocritus 12

The idyll is entitled ᾿Αίτης and is written in the Ionic dialect. The speech is addressed by the poet in his own name to a beloved boy, whence the title ᾿Αίτης, since some people, the Thessalians for example, call a beloved boy an ἀίτης. Alcman uses ἀίτιες for

darling girls.[1]

[1] C. Gallavotti, *Q.U.C.C.* 27 (1978) 183 ff. argues that the scholiast wrote χορδάς, not κόρας, so that Alcman sang of his 'darling lyre-strings'.

35 *Et. Mag.* 486. 38

καλά· τὸ καλά παρὰ τῷ ᾿Αλκμᾶνι κάλλα ἐστίν, οἷον·
κάλλα μελισδομέναι.

cf. *Et. Gen.* (p. 31 Calame), *Anecd. Par.* (iv 63 Cramer), Ap.
Dysc. *Adv.* 565 (i 155 Schneider)

36 Ap. Dysc. *Pron.* 118c (i 93 Schneider)

ἀμές Δώριον. ᾿Αλκμάν·
ὡς ἀμὲς τὸ καλὸν μελίσκον.
οὐκ ἐπίληπτος δὲ ἡ τάσις.

37 Ap. Dysc. *Pron.* 123b (i 96s. Schneider)

ἡ ἀμίν Δωρικὴ συστέλλει τὸ ι, ἐν οἷς ἐγκλινομένη προπερισπᾶται·
(a)   αἰ γὰρ ἀμιν
τούτων μέλοι,

ὀξυνομένη τε
(b) ἀμὶν δ᾿ ὑπαυλησεῖ μέλος,
᾿Αλκμάν.

38 Ap. Dysc. *Pron.* 121b (i 95 Schneider)

ἡ ἀμῶν παρὰ Δωριεῦσι καὶ σύναρθρον γενικὴν σημαίνει ἀκόλουθον
τῇ ἀμός. τῇ μέντοι διαιρέσει ἡ πρωτότυπος διαλλάσσει τῆς κτητικῆς,
οὐκέτι τὸ αὐτὸ ἀναδεχομένης. ᾿Αλκμάν·
ὅσσαι δὲ παῖδες ἀμέων
ἐντί, τὸν κιθαριστὰν
αἰνέοντι.

ALCMAN

35 *Etymologicum Magnum*

καλά ('beautifully'): the form in Alcman is κάλλα, e.g.
singing [1] beautifully.

[1] Feminine plural participle, used of a girls' choir.

36 Apollonius Dyscolus, *Pronouns*

The form ἀμές ('we') is Doric, as in Alcman:
as we (sing?) the beautiful song.
And the accent on ἀμές is quite correct.

37 Apollonius Dyscolus, *Pronouns*

Doric ἀμίν (= ἡμῖν, 'to us') shortens the ι when it is enclitic
and has the circumflex on the first syllable (ἇμιν), as in
  (a) If only these were of interest to us!
and when it has the acute on the last syllable (ἀμίν), as in
  (b) and to our song he will pipe an accompaniment.
So Alcman.

38 Apollonius Dyscolus, *Pronouns*

The form ἀμῶν in Doric signifies a possessive genitive ('of
our') that corresponds to ἀμός ('our'). The original pronoun
('of us') differs from the possessive in its diaeresis (ἀμέων)
and does not admit the same form (ἀμῶν). So Alcman:
and all the girls among us praise the lyre-player.[1]

[1] Alcman himself?

GREEK LYRIC

39 Athen. ix 389f, 390a (ii 350 Kaibel)

καλοῦνται δ' οἱ πέρδικες ὑπ' ἐνίων κακκάβαι, ὡς καὶ ὑπ' Ἀλκμᾶνος λέγοντος οὕτως·

    Ϝέπη τάδε καὶ μέλος Ἀλκμὰν
    εὗρε γεγλωσσαμέναν
    κακκαβίδων ὄπα συνθέμενος,

σαφῶς ἐμφανίζων ὅτι παρὰ τῶν περδίκων ᾄδειν ἐμάνθανε. διὸ καὶ Χαμαιλέων ὁ Ποντικὸς (fr. 24 Wehrli) ἔφη τὴν εὕρεσιν τῆς μουσικῆς τοῖς ἀρχαίοις ἐπινοηθῆναι ἀπὸ τῶν ἐν ταῖς ἐρημίαις ᾀδόντων ὀρνίθων.

1 Bergk: ἔπη γε δὲ codd.   2 Meineke, Marzullo: εὕρετε γλωσσαμενον codd.   3 Schneidewin: ὄνομα codd.

40 Athen. ix 374d (ii 318 Kaibel)

οἱ δὲ Δωριεῖς λέγοντες ὄρνιξ τὴν γενικὴν διὰ τοῦ χ λέγουσιν ὄρνιχος. Ἀλκμὰν δὲ διὰ τοῦ ς τὴν εὐθεῖαν ἐκφέρει [fr. 26. 4] καὶ τὴν γενικήν

    Ϝοῖδα δ' ὀρνίχων νόμως
    παντῶν.

1 Hermann: δι' ὀρνίχων codd.

41 Plut. Lyc. 21. 6 (iii 2. 34 Ziegler)

μουσικωτάτους γὰρ ἅμα καὶ πολεμικωτάτους ἀποφαίνουσιν αὐτούς·

    ῥέπει γὰρ ἄντα τῶ σιδάρω τὸ καλῶς κιθαρίσδην,

ὡς ὁ Λακωνικὸς ποιητὴς εἴρηκε.

cf. Plut. de Alex. fort. 335a (ii 2. 96 Nachstädt)

Scaliger: ἔρπει codd.

424

ALCMAN

39 Athenaeus, *Scholars at Dinner*

Some writers call partridges *caccábae*, as does Alcman when he says,

These words and melody Alcman invented by ob-serving [1] the tongued cry of partridges (*caccabídes*).[2] He makes it clear that he learned to sing from the partridges. That is why Chamaeleon of Pontus said that the invention of music was devised by the ancients from the birds singing in lonely places.

[1] Perhaps 'by organising', i.e. by putting into words; see B. Gentili, *Studi . . . in onore di Vittorio de Falco*, Naples, 1971, 59–67.   [2] The species in question is the chukar partridge (*Alectoris chukar*), which calls *kakkabi*; since the bird is found in Asia Minor and the eastern Aegean islands but not to the west, the passage may be evidence that Alcman grew up in Lydia, not in Sparta: see K. Borthwick ap. W. G. Arnott, *C.Q.* 27 (1977) 337 n. 1.

40 Athenaeus, *Scholars at Dinner*

The Doric form of the word ὄρνις, 'bird', is ὄρνιξ, genitive ὄρνιχος. But Alcman shows the nominative ὄρνις (fr. 26. 4) and the genitive plural ὀρνίχων:

and I know the tunes of all birds.

41 Plutarch, *Life of Lycurgus*

They (viz. Terpander fr. 7 and Pindar fr. 199) show that the Spartans were at the same time very musical and very warlike;

for when weighed against the steel fine lyre-playing tips the scales,

as the Spartan poet has said.

GREEK LYRIC

42 Athen. ii 39a (i 90 Kaibel)

οἶδα δ᾽ ὅτι ᾿Αναξανδρίδης (ii 160 Kock) τὸ νέκταρ οὐ ποτὸν ἀλλὰ τροφὴν εἶναι λέγει θεῶν . . . καὶ ᾿Αλκμὰν δέ φησι τὸ

νέκταρ ἔδμεναι

αὐτούς.

cf. Eust. *Od.* 1633. 1

43 Ap. Dysc. *Pron.* 64b (i 50s. Schneider)

οἱ αὐτοὶ Δωριεῖς ἐγώνγα καὶ ἐγώνη·
       οὐ γὰρ ἐγώνγα, Ϝάνασσα, Διὸς θύγατερ,

᾿Αλκμάν.

44 Schol. Ar. *Pac.* 457 (p. 185 Dübner)

πρὸς τοὺς οἰομένους τῶν νεωτέρων τὸν αὐτὸν εἶναι ῎Αρεα καὶ ᾿Ἐννάλιον, κατ᾽ ἐπίθετον . . . ᾿Αλκμᾶνα δὲ λέγουσιν ὁτὲ μὲν τὸν αὐτὸν λέγειν ὁτὲ δὲ διαιρεῖν.

45 Ap. Dysc. *Pron.* 105a (i 82 Schneider)

ὀρθοτονεῖται δὲ (sc. τοί) καὶ παρ᾽ ᾿Αλκμᾶνι συνήθως Δωριεῦσιν·

Ϝάδοι Διὸς δόμῳ χορὸς ἁμὸς καὶ τοί, Ϝάναξ.

Hartung: ὁ χορὸς codd.   Maittaire: τοί γ᾽ αναξ codd.

46 Heph. *Ench.* 12. 2 (p. 37s. Consbruch)

Καὶ ὅλα μὲν οὖν ᾄσματα γέγραπται ἰωνικά, ὥσπερ ᾿Αλκμᾶνι·

Ϝέκατον μὲν Διὸς υἱὸν τάδε Μῶσαι κροκόπεπλοι.

---

[1] Apollo.

426

ALCMAN

42–67 deal with the gods.

42 Athenaeus, *Scholars at Dinner*

I know that Anaxandrides [1] says that nectar is the food, not the drink, of the gods . . . ; and Alcman too says that they

eat nectar.

[1] Middle Comedy playwright.

43 Apollonius Dyscolus, *Pronouns*

The same Dorians have ἐγώνγα and ἐγώνη (in addition to ἐγών, for ἐγώ, 'I'), as in Alcman:

For I, lady, daughter of Zeus,[1] . . . not . . .

[1] An address to Athena or Artemis or the Muse.

44 Scholiast on Aristophanes, *Peace* ('Not to Ares, and not to Enyalius either')

Directed against those moderns who think that Ares is the same as Enyalius, which is taken to be an epithet for him . . . They say that Alcman sometimes identifies them, sometimes distinguishes between them.

45 Apollonius Dyscolus, *Pronouns*

The pronoun τοί ('to you') is treated as non-enclitic by Alcman in the usual Doric manner:

May our choir be pleasing to the house of Zeus and to you, lord.[1]

[1] Apollo? Cf. 12A.

46 Hephaestion, *Handbook on Metres*

Whole songs have been writen in ionics, e.g. by Alcman:

The saffron-robed Muses (taught?) these things to the far-shooting son of Zeus.[1]

GREEK LYRIC

47 Ap. Dysc. *Coni.* 490 (i 223s. Schneider) = *Anecd. Gr.* (ii 490 Bekker)

ἆρα· οὗτος κατὰ πᾶσαν διάλεκτον, ὑπεσταλμένης τῆς κοινῆς καὶ Ἀττικῆς, ἦρα λέγεται . . . παρ᾽ Ἀλκμᾶνι·

ἦρα τὸν Φοῖβον ὄνειρον εἶδον;

48 Ap. Dysc. *Pron.* 96b (i 75 Schneider)

ἡ σέο μεταβάλλει τὸ σ εἰς τὸ τ παρὰ Δωριεῦσιν. Ἀλκμὰν ἐν ε΄·

Λατοΐδα, τέο δ᾽ ἀρχ⟨όμεν⟩ος χορόν

ἐν ε΄ Hermann: ἐμὲ codd.   West: δ᾽ αχοσχορον codd.

49 Ap. Dysc. *Adv.* 563 (i 153 Schneider) = *Anecd. Gr.* (ii 563 Bekker)

πρόσθεν πρόσθα· καὶ παρ᾽ Ἀλκμᾶνι οὕτω δεκτέον τὴν συναλοιφήν·

πρόσθ᾽ Ἀπόλλωνος Λυκήω

Bast: προς cod.

50 Heph. *Ench.* 14. 6 (p. 46 Consbruch)

ἀπ᾽ ἐλάσσονος δὲ ἐπιωνικὸν τρίμετρον ἀκατάληκτόν ἐστι παρ᾽ Ἀλκμᾶνι, ὃ τὴν μὲν πρώτην ἔχει ἰαμβικὴν ἑξάσημον ἢ ἑπτάσημον, τὰς δὲ ἑξῆς δύο ἰωνικὰς ἑξασήμους καθαράς, οἷον·

(a) περισσόν· αἱ γὰρ Ἀπόλλων ὁ Λύκηος
(b) Ἰνὼ σαλασσομέδοισ᾽ ἂν ἀπὸ μασδῶν

(b) Porson: σαλασσομέδοισὰν cod. A: σάλας· ὀμέδοισαν cod. I

428

ALCMAN

47 Apollonius Dyscolus, *Conjunctions*

In every dialect except the Koine (Common) and Attic ἆρα (interrogative particle) has the form ἦρα [1]; . . . in Alcman,

Then did I see Phoebus in a dream?

[1] In fact ἦρα = ἦ ἄρα.

48 Apollonius Dyscolus, *Pronouns*

The pronoun σέο ('of you') changes the σ to τ in Doric: e.g. Alcman (in Book 5?):

Son of Leto, (beginning with?) you (I . . . ?) the choir

49 Apollonius Dyscolus, *Adverbs*

(In Aeolic and Doric) πρόσθεν ('before') is πρόσθα. In Alcman that is how the elision (πρόσθ') should be understood:

before Lycean [1] Apollo.

[1] The wolf-god, or the god born in Lycia.

50 Hephaestion, *Handbook on Metres*

The epionic *a minore* trimeter acatalectic is in Alcman: the first metron is iambic, either (a) ∪–∪– or (b) ––∪–, the other two are pure ionic, ∪∪––: e.g.

(a) . . . excessive; if only [1] Lycean Apollo . . . ,

(b) Ino, queen of the sea, whom [2] from her breast . . .

[1] Or 'for if'. [2] Perhaps 'whom they declare to have thrown from her breast the baby Melicertes': Ino in flight from her husband Athamas threw herself and her child into the sea.

GREEK LYRIC

51 [Plut.] *Mus.* 14. 1136b (p. 117 Lasserre, vi 3. 12 Ziegler)

ἄλλοι δὲ καὶ αὐτὸν τὸν θεόν φασιν αὐλῆσαι, καθάπερ ἱστορεῖ ὁ
ἄριστος μελῶν ποιητὴς Ἀλκμάν.

52 Schol. Theocr. 5. 83 (p. 170s. Wendel)

τὰ δὲ Κάρνεα· Πράξιλλα μὲν ἀπὸ Κάρνου φησὶν ὠνομάσθαι τοῦ
Διὸς καὶ Εὐρώπης υἱοῦ, ὃς ἦν ἐρώμενος τοῦ Ἀπόλλωνος· Ἀλκμὰν δὲ
ἀπὸ Καρνέου τινὸς Τρωϊκοῦ.

53 Schol. Townl. Hom. *Il.* 21. 485 (v 238 Erbse)

θήρας ἐναίρειν· φονεύειν ἢ σκυλεύειν. περιάπτεται γὰρ νεβρίδας.
Ἀλκμάν·

Ϝεσσαμένᾳ πέρι δέρματα θηρῶν.

Hartung: παρά cod.

54 Eust. *Od.* 1618. 28

κατὰ δὲ τὴν παρὰ Ἡρωδιανῷ (ii 646 Lentz) Ἀλκμανικὴν χρῆσιν
καὶ Ἀρτέμιδος Ἀρτέμιτος, οἷον·

Ἀρτέμιτος θεράποντα.

55 Str. 8. 3. 8 (ii 110s. Kramer)

ποιητικῷ δέ τινι σχήματι συγκαταλέγειν τὸ μέρος τῷ ὅλῳ φασὶ τὸν
Ὅμηρον, ... · καὶ Ἀλκμὰν δέ·

Κύπρον ἱμερτὰν λιποῖσα καὶ Πάφον περιρρύταν.

cf. Eust. *Il.* 305. 34

ALCMAN

51 'Plutarch', *On Music*

Others say that the god himself (sc. Apollo) played the pipes [1]: Alcman, for example, best of lyric poets, tells us so.

[1] And not the lyre only.

52 Scholiast on Theocritus

The Carnea [1]: Praxilla [fr. 753 *P.M.G.*] says the festival took its name from Carnus, Apollo's beloved boy, son of Zeus and Europa, but Alcman says it was named after a certain Trojan Carneus.

[1] Dorian festival of Apollo.

53 Scholiast on Homer

θῆρας ἐναίρειν: to kill or skin wild animals; for she (sc. Artemis) fastens fawnskins about herself: cf. Alcman,

to her, clad in the skins of wild animals.

54 Eustathius on *Odyssey* 9. 112 (θέμιστες)

. . . and in the passage of Alcman cited by Herodian Ἀρτέμιδος ('of Artemis') has the form Ἀρτέμιτος:

servant of Artemis.[1]

[1] For Artemis see also 55, 170.

55 Strabo, *Geography*

They say that Homer by a poetic figure gives the part alongside the whole . . . ; so Alcman has

leaving [1] lovely Cyprus and Paphos,[2] wave-washed on all sides.

[1] An invocation to Aphrodite.   [2] Paphos is a city of Cyprus.

GREEK LYRIC

Men. Rh. π. ἐπιδ. (p. 8s. Russell-Wilson)

. . . μέτρον μέντοι τῶν κλητικῶν ὕμνων ἐν μὲν ποιήσει
ἐπιμηκέστερον. ἀναμιμνήσκειν (Nitsche: ἅμα μὲν P) γὰρ πολλῶν
τόπων ἐκείνοις ἔξεστιν, ὡς παρὰ τῇ Σαπφοῖ καὶ τῷ Ἀλκμᾶνι
πολλαχοῦ εὑρίσκομεν. ὁ μὲν (Nitsche: τὴν μὲν P) γὰρ Ἄρτεμιν ἐκ
μυρίων ὀρέων, μυρίων δὲ πόλεων, ἔτι δὲ ποταμῶν ἀνακαλεῖ, ἡ δὲ
(Nitsche: τὴν δὲ P) Ἀφροδίτην ⟨ἐκ⟩ Κύπρου, Κνίδου, Συρίας,
πολλαχόθεν ἀλλαχόθεν ἀνακαλεῖ.

56 Athen. xi 498f–499a (iii 100 Kaibel)

Ἀσκληπιάδης δ' ὁ Μυρλεανὸς ἐν τῷ περὶ τῆς Νεστορίδος φησὶν
ὅτι τῷ σκύφει καὶ τῷ κισσυβίῳ τῶν μὲν ἐν ἄστει καὶ μετρίων οὐδεὶς
ἐχρῆτο, συβῶται δὲ καὶ νομεῖς καὶ οἱ ἐν ἀγρῷ, ὡς ὁ Εὔμαιος. καὶ
Ἀλκμὰν δέ φησι·

> πολλάκι δ' ἐν κορυφαῖς ὀρέων, ὄκα
> σιοῖσι Ϝάδη πολύφανος ἑορτά,
> χρύσιον ἄγγος ἔχοισα, μέγαν σκύφον,
> οἷά τε ποιμένες ἄνδρες ἔχοισιν,
> 5 χερσὶ λεόντεον ἐν γάλα θεῖσα
> τυρὸν ἐτύρησας μέγαν ἄτρυφον Ἀργειφόντᾳ.

cf. Ael. Aristid. *Or*. 41. 7 (ii 331 Keil) λεόντεον γάλα ἀμέλγειν
ἀνέθηκέν τις αὐτῷ (sc. Διονύσῳ) Λακωνικὸς ποιητής, gramm.
anon. Hamburg. (*Rh. Mus*. 10, 1856, 256), Hsch. A 8163
(i 276 Latte)

5 Hermann; ἐπαλαθεισα codd.   6 Bergk: ἀργειοφόντᾳ codd.

ALCMAN

Menander, *On Display Oratory*

Hymns of invocation are longer in poetry, for poets can mention many locations, as we often find in Sappho and Alcman: he(?) summons Artemis from thousands of mountains and cities, from rivers too, and she(?) summons Aphrodite from Cyprus, Cnidos, Syria and many other places.[1]

[1] Text doubtful: see Russell-Wilson ad loc.: the distinction made between Sappho and Alcman is uncertain, and it is possible that 'Alcman' should be replaced by 'Anacreon'; cf. Sa. test. 47.

56 Athenaeus, *Scholars at Dinner*

Asclepiades of Myrlea in his work *On Nestor's Cup* says that the σκύφος and κισσύβιον (types of cup) were used not by city-dwellers and well-to-do people but by swineherds, shepherds and country-dwellers like Eumaeus (*Od.* 14. 112 f.). Alcman also says,

Often among the mountain-peaks, when the festival with its many torches gives pleasure to the gods, you [1] held a golden vessel, a great cup (σκύφος), such as shepherds hold, and putting into it with your hands the milk of a lioness you made a great firm cheese for the Slayer of Argus.[2]

[1] Addressed to a Bacchant, a female votary of Dionysus. According to Aristides, 'a Spartan poet' attributed to Dionysus the power of milking lionesses.   [2] Hermes, who was represented on the throne of Apollo at Amyclae carrying the child Dionysus to heaven (Paus. 3. 18. 11).

57 Plut. *Qu. Conv.* 659b, iii 10. 3 (iv 115s. Hubert)

τοῦτο δὲ καὶ τὸν ἀέρα πάσχοντα θεωροῦμεν· δροσοβολεῖ γὰρ ταῖς πανσελήνοις μάλιστα διατηκόμενος, ὥς που καὶ Ἀλκμὰν ὁ μελοποιὸς αἰνιττόμενος τὴν δρόσον ἀέρος θυγατέρα καὶ σελήνης·

> οἷα Διὸς θυγάτηρ Ἔρσα τράφει
> καὶ Σελάνας.

cf. *aet. phys.* 24, 918a (v 3. 21 Hubert-Pohlenz), *de fac. in orbe lun.* 25, 940a (v 3. 75 H.-P.), Macrob. *Sat.* 7. 16. 31 (i 461 Willis), Com. Natal. *Myth.* iii 255. 1

2 καὶ σελάνας δίας *aet. phys.*

58 Heph. *Ench.* 13. 6 (p. 42 Consbruch)

δύναται δὲ καὶ μέχρι τοῦ ἑξαμέτρου προκόπτειν τὸ μέτρον διὰ τὸ τὸ τριακοντάσημον μὴ ὑπερβάλλειν, καὶ εἴη ἂν ἑξάμετρον καταληκτικὸν τὸ καλούμενον ⟨. . .⟩ τὸ τοῦ Ἀλκμᾶνος ἐκ μόνων ἀμφιμάκρων·

> Ἀφροδίτα μὲν οὐκ ἔστι, μάργος δ' Ἔρως οἷα ⟨παῖς⟩
> παίσδει,
> ἄκρ' ἐπ' ἄνθη καβαίνων, ἃ μή μοι θίγῃς, τῶ
> κυπαιρίσκω.

cf. Apostol. *Cent.* iv 62b (ii 322 Leutsch-Schneidewin)

1 suppl. Bentley

59 Athen. xiii 600f (iii 324 Kaibel)

Ἀρχύτας δ' ὁ ἁρμονικός, ὥς φησι Χαμαιλέων (fr. 25 Wehrli), Ἀλκμᾶνα γεγονέναι τῶν ἐρωτικῶν μελῶν ἡγεμόνα καὶ ἐκδοῦναι πρῶτον μέλος ἀκόλαστον †ὄντα καὶ περὶ τὰς γυναῖκας καὶ τὴν τοιαύτην Μοῦσαν εἰς τὰς διατριβάς†· διὸ καὶ λέγειν ἔν τινι τῶν μελῶν·

(a) > Ἔρως με δηὖτε Κύπριδος Ϝέκατι
> γλυκὺς κατείβων καρδίαν ἰαίνει.

ALCMAN

57 Plutarch, *Table-Talk*

We observe this happening to the air also: it sheds dew especially at the full moon when it melts, as the lyric poet Alcman says somewhere when he talks in riddling fashion of the dew as daughter of air and moon:

such things as are nurtured by Dew, daughter of Zeus and Selene.

58 Hephaestion, *Handbook on Metres*

The metre (sc. paeonic) can reach hexameter length, since that still does not exceed the equivalent of thirty short syllables; and Alcman's line, composed only of the cretic ($-\cup-$), will be a hexameter catalectic, the so-called . . . [1]:

Aphrodite it is not, but wild Eros playing like the boy he is, coming down over the flower-tips—do not touch them, I beg you!—of the galingale.[2]

[1] Name missing.   [2] See P. E. Easterling, *P.C.P.S.* 20 (1974) 37–41.

59 Athenaeus, *Scholars at Dinner*

According to Chamaeleon, Archytas, the expert on harmonics,[1] says that Alcman led the way in erotic songs and was the first to make public a licentious song (since in his way of life he was undisciplined in the matter of women and of such poetry?)[2]; and that that was why he said in one of his songs,

(a) At the command of the Cyprian,[3] Eros once again pours sweetly down and warms my heart.

[1] Presumably the Pythagorean mathematician of 4th c. B.C.
[2] Text corrupt.   [3] Aphrodite, mother of Eros.

GREEK LYRIC

λέγει δὲ καὶ ὡς τῆς Μεγαλοστράτης οὐ μετρίως ἐρασθεὶς ποιητρίας μὲν οὔσης δυναμένης δὲ καὶ διὰ τὴν ὁμιλίαν τοὺς ἐραστὰς προσελκύσασθαι· λέγει δ᾽ οὕτως περὶ αὐτῆς·

(b) τοῦτο Ϝαδειᾶν ἔδειξε Μωσᾶν
δῶρον μάκαιρα παρσένων
ἁ ξανθὰ Μεγαλοστράτα.

(b) 1 Wilamowitz: Μοῦσαν ἔδειξε codd.

60 Athen. xv 680f–681a (iii 506 Kaibel)

μνημονεύει αὐτοῦ (sc. τοῦ ἑλιχρύσου) Ἀλκμὰν ἐν τούτοις·
καὶ τὶν εὔχομαι φέροισα
τόνδ᾽ ἑλιχρύσω πυλεῶνα
κήρατῶ κυπαίρω.

cf. Eust. *Od.* 1648. 7, Didym. ad Hom. *Il.* 21. 351

Casaubon, Boissonade, Welcker: πυλεω ακηράτων κυπερω codd.

61 Eust. *Il.* 1154.25

Ἄκμων δὲ ὅτι καὶ ὁ τοῦ Οὐρανοῦ, ὡς ἐρρέθη, λέγεται πατὴρ διὰ τὸ ἀκάματον τῆς οὐρανίου κινήσεως . . . καὶ ὅτι Ἀκμονίδαι οἱ Οὐρανίδαι, δηλοῦσιν οἱ παλαιοί. ὡς δὲ Ἄκμονος (cod.: Ἄκμων Bergk) ὁ οὐρανὸς ὁ Ἀλκμάν, φασίν, ἱστορεῖ.

And he speaks as having fallen wildly in love with Megalostrate, a poetess but able to attract her lovers by her conversation; he speaks as follows about her:

(b) This gift of the sweet Muses was displayed by one blessed among girls, the yellow-haired Megalostrata.[4]

[4] Perhaps lines of Alcman which gave evidence of his alleged passion for the girl have been lost; on the whole passage see B. Marzullo, *Helikon* 4 (1964) 297–302.

60 Athenaeus, *Scholars at Dinner*

Alcman mentions the gold-flower in these lines:

And to you [1] I pray, bringing [2] this garland of gold-flower and lovely galingale.

[1] To Hera: see fr. 3 n. 5.   [2] Fem. sing. participle: a girl or girls' choir is singing.

61 Eustathius on *Iliad* 18. 476 (ἄκμων, 'anvil')

The father of Heaven (Uranus), as was said already, is called Acmon because heavenly motion is untiring (ἀκάματος); and the sons of Uranus are Acmonidae: the ancients make these two points clear. Alcman, they say, tells that the heaven belongs to Acmon.[1]

[1] Or 'that Uranus is son of Acmon'. Bergk emended the text to read 'that Uranus is Acmon', which squares with Eust. 1150.59, 'the father of Cronus is Acmon'. See *R.E.* s.v. Akmon 1.

GREEK LYRIC

62 Paus. 3. 18. 6 (i 246 Rocha-Pereira)

ἐς Ἀμύκλας δὲ κατιοῦσιν ἐκ Σπάρτης ποταμός ἐστι Τίασα·
θυγατέρα δὲ νομίζουσιν εἶναι τοῦ Εὐρώτα τὴν Τίασαν, καὶ πρὸς αὐτῇ
Χαρίτων ἐστὶν ἱερὸν Φαέννας καὶ Κλητᾶς, καθὰ δὴ καὶ Ἀλκμὰν
ἐποίησεν. ἱδρύσασθαι δὲ Λακεδαίμονα Χάρισιν ἐνταῦθα ⟨τὸ⟩ ἱερὸν
καὶ θέσθαι τὰ ὀνόματα ἥγηνται.

63 Schol. min. Hom. *Il.* 6. 21, *Atti d. R. Acc. Naz. Lincei*
1931, ser. vi, vol. iv p. 384 (de Marco).

οἱ δὲ πολλὰ γένη νυμφῶν, ὥς φησιν Ἀλκμάν·

Ναΐδες τε Λαμπάδες τε Θυιάδες τε,

Θυιάδες μὲν αἱ συμβακχεύουσαι Διονύσῳ καὶ συνθυίουσαι, τουτέστι
συνεξορμοῦσαι· Λαμπάδες δὲ αἱ σὺν Ἑκάτῃ δᾳδοφοροῦσαι καὶ
συλλαμπαδεύουσαι.

64 Plut. *de fort. Rom.* 4, 318a (ii 2. 49 Nachst.-Siev.-Titch.)

οὐ μὲν γὰρ ἀπειθής (sc. ἡ Τύχη), κατὰ Πίνδαρον (fr. 40 Snell),
οὐδὲ δίδυμον στρέφουσα πηδάλιον, ἀλλὰ μᾶλλον

Εὐνομίας ⟨τε⟩ καὶ Πειθῶς ἀδελφὰ
καὶ Προμαθήας θυγάτηρ,

ὡς γενεαλογεῖ Ἀλκμάν.

1 τε add. Bergk

438

ALCMAN

62 Pausanias, *Description of Greece*

On the way down to Amyclae from Sparta there is a river called the Tiasa; they believe that Tiasa was a daughter of Eurotas. Near the river is a sanctuary of the Graces, Phaenna and Cleta, as Alcman said in his poetry. They think it was Lacedaemon who established the sanctuary there for the Graces and gave them their names.

63 Scholiast on *Iliad* 6. 21 ('nymph')

Some say there are many kinds of nymphs, e.g. Alcman:
> Naiads [1] and Lampads and Thyiads,

Thyiads being those who revel and go wild, i.e. go out of their minds, with Dionysus, Lampads those who carry torches and lights with Hecate.

[1] Nymphs of rivers and springs.

64 Plutarch, *On the Fortune of the Romans*

For Fortune is not 'inflexible', as Pindar has it, nor 'plying a double steering-paddle'; rather she is
> sister of Good Order (Eunomia) and Persuasion and daughter of Foresight,

as in Alcman's account of her lineage.

GREEK LYRIC

65 Schol. A (i 36 Dindorf) D Gen. (p. 9 Nicole) Hom. *Il.*
1. 222

οὕτως δαίμονας καλεῖ τοὺς θεοὺς ἤτοι ὅτι δαήμονες . . . ἢ ὅτι
διαιτηταί εἰσι καὶ διοικηταὶ τῶν ἀνθρώπων, ὡς Ἀλκμὰν ὁ λυρικός
φησιν·

† οἴεθεν † πάλως ἔπαλε δαιμονάς τ' ἐδάσσατο·

τοὺς μερισμούς, τὰς διαιρέσεις αὐτῶν.

cf. *Anecd. Oxon.* (iv 409 Cramer), *Anecd. Gr.* (p. 409
Matranga)

οἰόθεν ci. Page   Bergk: πάλοις, πάλλοις, πάλιν codd.
Ursinus: ἔπαλλε(ν), ἔπαλαν codd.   Nauck: δαίμονάς τ' codd.

66 Tzetz. in Hom. *Il.* 1. 4 (p. 65 Hermann)

Θαλῆς, Πυθαγόρας, Πλάτων τε καὶ οἱ Στωικοὶ διαφορὰν ἴσασι
δαιμόνων τε καὶ ἡρώων. δαίμονας γὰρ φάσκουσιν ἀσωμάτους εἶναι
οὐσίας, ἥρωας δὲ ψυχὰς σωμάτων διαζυγείσας. Ὀρφεὺς δὲ καὶ
Ὅμηρος Ἡσίοδός τε καὶ Ἀλκμὰν ὁ λυροποιὸς καὶ οἱ ἄλλοι ποιηταὶ
ἀλληνάλλως ταῦτα ἐκδέχονται.

67 Diod. Sic. 4. 7. 1 (i 404 Vogel)

ταύτας γὰρ (sc. τὰς Μούσας) οἱ πλεῖστοι τῶν μυθογράφων καὶ
μάλιστα δεδοκιμασμένοι φασὶ θυγατέρας εἶναι Διὸς καὶ Μνημοσύνης.
ὀλίγοι δὲ τῶν ποιητῶν, ἐν οἷς ἐστι καὶ Ἀλκμάν, θυγατέρας
ἀποφαίνονται Οὐρανοῦ καὶ Γῆς.

cf. schol. Pind. *Nem.* 3. 16b (iii 43 Drachmann)

ALCMAN

65 Scholiast on *Iliad* 1. 222 ('to join the other gods')

Homer calls the gods δαίμονες like this either because they are knowledgeable (δαήμονες) . . . or because they are arbitrators (διαιτηταί) and controllers of men, as Alcman the lyric poet says:

(alone?) he shook the lots and made the distributions (δαιμονάς),

i.e. their apportionments or shares.

66 Tzetzes on *Iliad* 1. 4 ('heroes')

Thales, Pythagoras, Plato and the Stoics know of a distinction between *daimones* (gods, spirits) and heroes (demigods). *Daimones*, they say, are bodiless beings, whereas heroes are souls separated from bodies. Orpheus, Homer, Hesiod, Alcman the lyric poet and the rest of the poets show no regularity in their acceptance of all this.

67 Diodorus Siculus, *World History*

Most of the mythographers, including those of the highest reputation, say that the Muses are the daughters of Zeus and Mnemosyne (Memory); but one or two of the poets, Alcman among them, make them the daughters of Uranus and Ge (Heaven and Earth).[1]

[1] See fr. 5 col. ii (end) with n. 10.

68 Choerob. in Theodos. (i 123 Hilgard +)

ἰστέον δὲ ὅτι . . . τὸ Αἶας τὸ παρ' Ἀλκμᾶνι ἔχομεν σεσημειωμένον ὡς συστέλλον τὸ α· ἐκεῖνος γὰρ συνέστειλεν αὐτὸ εἰπών·

δουρὶ δὲ ξυστῷ μέμανεν Αἶας αἱματῇ τε Μέμνων.

ἐστὶ δὲ τροχαϊκὸν τὸ μέτρον . . .

cf. Hdn. (i 525. 30 Lentz +), Anecd. Oxon. (iii 283 Cramer), Et. Gen. (p. 24 Calame), Drac. Straton. (p. 12 Hermann)

Hiller-Crusius: αἱματά codd.

69 Et. Gen. (p. 36 Calame)

μέγας· μήγας ὁ μὴ ὢν ἐν τῇ γῇ ἀλλ' ὑπερέχων αὐτῆς. τὸ δὲ †μὴ† Ἀλκμὰν εἶπε·

†με δ' αὖτε† φαίδιμος Αἶας

μέγ' αὐχεῖ ci. Stanford (Hermath. 97, 1963, 107)

70 Ap. Dysc. Pron. 106bc (i 83 Schneider)

ἡ σέ ὁμοίως πρὸς πάντων κοινή. Δωριεῖς διὰ τοῦ τ . . .

(a) πρὸς δέ τε τῶν φίλων

Ἀλκμάν· καὶ ἔτι μετὰ τοῦ ι

(b) τεὶ γὰρ Ἀλεξάνδρῳ δαμάσαι

καὶ ἔτι κοινῶς

(c) σὲ γὰρ ἄζομαι.

cf. Ap. Synt. β' 89, 100 (pp. 193, 203 Uhlig)

ALCMAN

68–79 deal with heroes (in alphabetical order).

68 Choeroboscus, *On the Canons of Theodosius*

Note that we find Αἴας ('Ajax') marked as exceptional for
its short α in Alcman: for he shortened the α when he said,

Ajax raves with sharpened spear and Memnon is
thirsty for blood.

The metre is trochaic . . .[1]

[1] Which proves that the second syllable of Αἴας is short. See
Page, *Alcman* 131 ff.

69 *Etymologicum Genuinum* s.v. μέγας ('great')

The 'great' man is the one who is not on the ground but
towers over it.[1] Alcman said . . .

(great?)[2] . . . glorious Ajax

[1] Fancifully derived from μή ('not') and γῆ ('earth').
[2] Text corrupt.

70 Apollonius Dyscolus, *Pronouns*

The form σέ ('you') is likewise common to all Greeks.
Dorians have the form τέ . . .

(a) (I beg?) you by your friends[1]

in Alcman; also the form τεί:

(b) for to subdue you to Alexander[2] . . .

and also the common form σέ:

(c) For I respect you.[3]

[1] Translation insecure without context.   [2] Addressed to
Achilles, who was killed by Paris?   [3] Perhaps cf. *Od.*
6. 168, where Od. speaks similar words to Nausicaa.

71 Schol. A Hom. *Il*. 3. 250 (i 154 Dindorf)

Λαομεδοντιάδη· μήτηρ Πριάμου, ὥς φησι Πορφύριος ἐν τῷ περὶ τῶν παραλελειμμένων τῷ ποιητῇ ὀνομάτων, κατὰ μὲν Ἀλκμᾶνα τὸν μελοποιὸν Ζευξίππη, κατὰ δὲ Ἑλλάνικον Στρυμώ.

72 Plut. *de malign. Herod*. 14, 857ef (v 2. 2. 14 Häsler)

καίτοι τῶν παλαιῶν καὶ λογίων ἀνδρῶν οὐχ Ὅμηρος οὐχ Ἡσίοδος οὐκ Ἀρχίλοχος οὐ Πείσανδρος οὐ Στησίχορος οὐκ Ἀλκμὰν οὐ Πίνδαρος Αἰγυπτίου ἔσχον λόγον Ἡρακλέους ἢ Φοίνικος, ἀλλ᾽ ἕνα τοῦτον ἴσασι πάντες Ἡρακλέα τὸν Βοιώτιον ὁμοῦ καὶ Ἀργεῖον.

73 *Epim. Hom.* (*Anecd. Oxon.* i 418 Cramer) (ad voc. ὕπαιθα)

λέγεται δὲ καὶ ἄνευ τῆς θα παρὰ Ἀλκμᾶνι καὶ σημαίνει τὸ πρότερον·

†ὁπότε ὑπὸ τοῦ Ἱππολόχου κλέος δ᾽ ἔβαλλον
οὐ νῦν ὑπεστάντων†

ἀντὶ τοῦ πρότερον· βαρύνεται.

οἵ τότ᾽ ὑπ᾽ Ἱππολόχῳ ci. Page   ⟨Δορυ⟩κλέος τ᾽ ci. Bergk

74 *Epim. Hom.* (*Anecd. Oxon.* i 159s. Cramer)

καὶ ὁ μὲν ποιητὴς τὴν ἄρχουσαν συστέλλει ἐν τῷ ἔσκεν, ὁ δὲ Ἀλκμὰν φυλάττει·

ἦσκε τις Καφεὺς Ϝανάσσων·

τινὲς δύο μέν φασι, ἦς ἀντὶ τοῦ ἦν Δωρικῶς καὶ κε σύνδεσμος· οἱ ⟨δὲ⟩ Δωριεῖς ἢ μετὰ τοῦ ν λέγουσιν ἢ τροπῇ τοῦ ε εἰς κα.

Neumann: σκαφεὺς cod.

ALCMAN

71 Scholiast on *Iliad* 3. 250 (Priam, son of Laomedon)

Priam's mother, says Porphyry in his treatise *On the names omitted by Homer*, was Zeuxippe according to the lyric poet Alcman, Strymo according to Hellanicus.

72 Plutarch, *On the malice of Herodotus*

And yet among the story-tellers of ancient times neither Homer nor Hesiod nor Archilochus nor Peisander nor Stesichorus nor Alcman nor Pindar made any mention of an Egyptian or Phoenician Heracles [1]: they all know this single Heracles, who is both Boeotian and Argive.[2]

[1] See Hdt. 2. 43 f. [2] Prince of Tiryns (near Argos) but born in Thebes in Boeotia. Cf. frr. 1 n. 2, 15 n. 2, 87(a).

73 *Homeric Parsings* (on ὕπαιθα, 'under')

The word is also found without the *-θα* in Alcman in the sense of 'previously' and is accented ὑπαί:

(who were then driven back by Hippolochus and Dorycles, who previously had not resisted?) [1]

[1] Text corrupt.

74 *Homeric Parsings* (on ἔσκε, 'was')

Homer shortens the first vowel in his form ἔσκε, but Alcman keeps it long (ἦσκε):

There was a certain Cepheus ruling . . . [1]

Some say there are two words, the Doric ἦς for ἦν ('was') and the 'conjunction' κε; but the Dorians have either κεν or κα.

[1] Text uncertain. There was a king of Tegea called Cepheus.

445

75 Aelian. *V.H.* 12. 36 (p. 141 Dilts)

ἐοίκασιν οἱ ἀρχαῖοι ὑπὲρ τοῦ ἀριθμοῦ τῶν τῆς Νιόβης παίδων μὴ συνάδειν ἀλλήλοις. Ὅμηρος μὲν ἓξ λέγει ⟨ἄρρενας⟩ καὶ τοσαύτας κόρας, Λᾶσος δὲ δὶς ἑπτὰ λέγει, Ἡσίοδος δὲ ἐννέα καὶ δέκα . . . · Ἀλκμὰν δὲ καʹ (Haslam: ⟨δὲ⟩ δέκα Page) φησί, Μίμνερμος εἴκοσι καὶ Πίνδαρος τοσούτους.

76 Aelian. *H.A.* 12. 3 (iii 10 Scholfield)

Ὁμήρῳ μὲν οὖν φωνὴν Ξάνθῳ τῷ ἵππῳ δόντι συγγνώμην νέμειν ἄξιον, ποιητὴς γάρ· καὶ Ἀλκμὰν δὲ μιμούμενος ἐν τοῖς τοιούτοις Ὅμηρον οὐκ ἂν φέροιτο αἰτίαν, ἔχει γὰρ ἀξιόχρεων †ἐς αἰδῶ† τὴν πρωτίστην τόλμαν.

77 Schol. A Hom. *Il.* 3. 39 (i 365 Erbse)

δύσπαρι· ἐπὶ κακῷ ὠνομασμένε Πάρι, κακὲ Πάρι. καὶ Ἀλκμὰν φησιν·

Δύσπαρις Αἰνόπαρις κακὸν Ἑλλάδι βωτιανείρᾳ.

cf. Eust. *Il.* 379.34.

78 *Et. Gen.* (p. 40 Calame) = *Et. Mag.* 663.54

Περίηρς· ἐκ τοῦ Περιήρης, ἀποβολῇ τοῦ η,

Περίηρς·

ταύτῃ ἐάν σοι προστεθῇ παρ' Ἀλκμᾶνι ὅτι κλῖνον αὐτό, μὴ κλίνῃς· οὐ γὰρ ἀκολουθεῖ ἡ κατάληξις, εἰ γένοιτο Περιήρους, πρὸς τὴν Περίηρς εὐθεῖαν. περὶ Παθῶν.

cf. schol. Dion. Thrac. (p. 346.20 Hilgard)

ALCMAN

75 Aelian, *Historical Miscellanies*

The ancients seem to be at loggerheads over the number of Niobe's children. Homer says six males and six females (*Il.* 24. 603), Lasus says twice seven (706 *P.M.G.*), Hesiod nineteen (fr. 183 M.-W.) . . . , Alcman twenty-one,[1] Mimnermus (fr. 19 West) and Pindar (fr. 52n Snell) twenty.

[1] So Haslam (*Rh. Mus.* 119, 1976, 192); with Page's text, 'ten'. See also A. Allen, *Rh. Mus.* 117, 1974, 358 f. and Sappho 205.

76 Aelian, *On the Nature of Animals*

When Homer attributes speech to the horse Xanthus (*Il.* 19. 404 ff.), he deserves our forgiveness: he is a poet, after all; and when Alcman copies Homer in this,[1] he will not be blamed: he has Homer's original boldness as sufficient excuse.

[1] Cf. fr. 25.

77 Scholiast on *Iliad* 3. 39 (Hector's insult to his brother)

'Paris the Evil': Paris named for disaster, disastrous Paris; Alcman has

Paris the Evil, Paris the Grim, a disaster for Greece, that nurse of men.

78 *Etymologicum Genuinum* s.v. Periers

From Perieres [1] with loss of the e,

Periers;

if you are told to decline it in this form in Alcman's manner, decline to do so: for if you were to offer Περιήρους as genitive, that ending does not square with the nominative Περίηρς. From Herodian, *On Inflexions* (i 246, ii 252 Lentz).

[1] Father of Tyndareus, Icarius, Aphareus and Leucippus (Stes. 227).

GREEK LYRIC

79 Schol. Pind. *Ol.* 1. 91a (i 37s. Drachmann)

καὶ ᾿Αλκαῖος δὲ καὶ ᾿Αλκμὰν λίθον φασὶν ἐπαιωρεῖσθαι τῷ
Ταντάλῳ· (Alc. fr. 365)· ὁ δὲ ᾿Αλκμὰν οὕτως·

†ἀνὴρ δ᾿ ἐν ἀσμένοισιν ἀλιτηρὸς ἦστ᾿ ἐπὶ
θάκας κατὰ πέτρας ὀρέων μὲν οὐδὲν δοκέων δέ†

cf. Eust. *Od.* 1701. 23

οὕτως· ci. Bergk: ὅκως, ὅπη codd.   1 ἐν ἀρμ- ci. Bergk: φθι-
μένοισιν vel ἐνέροισιν subiacere ci. Ursinus   ἀλιτρὸς ci.
Bergk   2 θάκοις ci. Heyne: θάκω Bergk

80 Schol. T Hom. *Il.* 16. 236 (iv 223 Erbse)

καὶ ᾿Αλκμὰν γάρ φησι·
καί ποκ᾿ ᾿Οδυσσῆος ταλασίφρονος ὦατ᾿ ἑταίρων
Κίρκα ἐπαλείψασα·
οὐ γὰρ αὐτὴ ἤλειψεν, ἀλλ᾿ ὑπέθετο ᾿Οδυσσεῖ.

1 Schneidewin: ὦτά θ᾿ cod.   2 ἐπάλειψε(ν) ci. Heyne (ἐπή-)

81 Schol. Hom. *Od.* 6. 244s. (p. 314 Dindorf)

αἱ γὰρ ἐμοὶ τοιόσδε πόσις κεκλημένος εἴη / ἐνθάδε ναιετάων· ἄμφω
μὲν ἀθετεῖ ᾿Αρίσταρχος, διστάζει δὲ περὶ τοῦ πρώτου, ἐπεὶ καὶ
᾿Αλκμὰν αὐτὸν μετέβαλε παρθένους λεγούσας εἰσάγων
Ζεῦ πάτερ, αἰ γὰρ ἐμὸς πόσις εἴη.

448

ALCMAN

79 Scholiast on Pindar, *Olympian* 1. 57 (Tantalus and the stone)

Alcaeus and Alcman say that a stone hangs over Tantalus, Alcaeus (fr. 365), Alcman as follows:

a sinner, he sat among agreeable things [1] on a seat under a rock, seeing nothing, but supposing that he did.

[1] Or 'among the dead'? The text is uncertain throughout.

80–86 are or may be connected with Odysseus; see also 4A with notes, 70(c). See P. Janni, La cultura di Sparta arcaica, Ricerche II (Rome 1970).

80 Scholiast on *Iliad* 16. 236 [1]

And so Alcman says,

And once Circe anointing [2] the ears of the companions of stout-hearted Odysseus . . .

For she did not anoint them herself: it was her suggestion to Odysseus. [3]

[1] Achilles speaks of 'my prayer', when in fact it was his mother's (*Il.* 1. 503).   [2] Or 'anointed'.   [3] *Od.* 12. 47.

81 Scholiast on *Odyssey* 6. 244f. ('If only such a man were called my husband, dwelling here!') [1]

Aristarchus rejects both lines; but he has doubts about the first, since it was reshaped by Alcman, who made girls say,

Father Zeus, if only he were my husband!

[1] Nausicaa to her attendants about Odysseus; cf. 7. 311.

82 Athen. ix 373de (ii 316 Kaibel)

ὅτι δὲ καὶ ἐπὶ τοῦ πληθυντικοῦ ὄρνις λέγουσι πρόκειται τὸ
Μενάνδρειον μαρτύριον (sup. 373c). ἀλλὰ καὶ Ἀλκμάν πού φησι·

λῦσαν δ' ἄπρακτα νεάνιδες ὥ-
τ' ὄρνις Ϝιέρακος ὑπερπταμένω.

1 δῦσαν ci. Jacobs

83 Cyrill. *lex.* (*Anecd. Par.* iv 181 Cramer)

εἴκω· τὸ ὑποχωρῶ. ἔνθεν καὶ τὸ οἶκος εἰς ὃν ὑποχωροῦμεν, ὡς
Ἀλκμάν·

τῷ δὲ γυνὰ ταμία σφεᾶς ἔειξε χώρας.

cf. Ap. Dysc. *Pron.* 142b (i 112 Schneider)

Bergk: τό δε γυναι τάμιας *Anecd. Par.*   φέας εἶξε *Anecd.
Par.*: σφεασε, ειξεν Ap. Dysc.

84 Eust. *Il.* 110.35

μονῆρες δὲ ἐν θηλυκοῖς ἡ χείρ, ἢ κλίνεται διχῶς, ποτὲ μὲν διὰ τοῦ ε
. . . . , ποτὲ δὲ διὰ τῆς ει διφθόγγου, ποτὲ δὲ κατὰ Ἡρωδιανὸν
(ii 356, 645, 748 Lentz) καὶ μετατεθείσης αὐτῆς εἰς η, ᾧ μαρτυρεῖ,
φησίν, Ἀλκμάν ἐν τῷ

ἐπ' ἀριστερὰ χηρὸς ἔχων.

⟨Ἄρκτον δ'⟩ ἐπ' ἀρ. suppl. Bergk

ALCMAN

82 Athenaeus, *Scholars at Dinner*

That they also use the plural form ὄρνις ('birds') is shown by the testimony of Menander (frr. 155–6 Körte-Thierfelder); but Alcman too says somewhere,

The girls scattered, their task unfinished,[1] like birds when a hawk flies over them.

[1] Text uncertain; perhaps 'sank down helplessly'; cf. *Od.* 6. 138 of Nausicaa's companions at the sight of the naked Odysseus, 'they fled this way and that'.

83 Cyril, *Lexicon*

εἴκω ('yield'): 'withdraw'; whence οἶκος ('house'), since we withdraw to it: cf. Alcman:

And to him the house-keeper yielded her place.[1]

[1] Editors compare *Od.* 7. 175 of Odysseus at the palace of Alcinous, 'and a revered housekeeper brought bread and put it before him'. See also fr. 88.

84 Eustathius on *Iliad* 1. 323

χείρ ('hand') is unique among feminine nouns: it is declined in two different ways, sometimes with ε (χερ-) . . . , sometimes with the diphthong ει (χειρ-), and sometimes according to Herodian with the ει changed to η (χηρ-), for which he cites Alcman:

keeping on his left hand.[1]

[1] Or 'on my left hand'; same phrase in *Od.* 5. 277 of Odysseus sailing towards the land of the Phaeacians with the Bear on his left hand.

85 Ap. Dysc. *Pron.* 139bc (i 109 Schneider)

πλεῖστα γοῦν ἔστι παρ' ἑτέροις εὑρεῖν. σφέτερον πατέρα ἀντὶ τοῦ ὑμέτερον, ἀντὶ τοῦ τεά τὸ κήδεα λέξον ἑά παρὰ Καλλιμάχῳ καὶ πάλιν παρ' αὐτῷ ἀντὶ τοῦ σφωϊτέρου. Ἀλκμάν·

(a) ὑμέ τε καὶ σφετέρως ἵππως

(b) σφεὰ δὲ †ποτὶ† γούνατα πίπτω.

(b) δὴ ποτὶ ci. Lobel: δὲ προτὶ Bekker

86 *Epim. Hom.* (*Anecd. Oxon.* i 343 Cramer) s.v. πλεῖτε

καὶ πλῆτρον τὸ πηδάλιον, καὶ ὑποκοριστικῶς εἶπεν Ἀλκμὰν
πλήθριον.

87 Ap. Dysc. *Synt.* 4. 61 (p. 483s. Uhlig)

ἀπειράκις γὰρ τὰ Δωρικὰ διὰ ψιλῶν ἀντιστοίχων τὰς συναλιφὰς ποιεῖται·

(a) κὼ τοξότας Ἡρακλέης

(b) κάλλιστ' ὑπαυλῆν

(c) κὰ μεγασθενὴς Ἀσαναία

(d) Μελάμποδά τ' Ἀρπόλυκόν τε

(e) ἄρχοι μὲν γὰρ †κοθρασιων†

(e) κὼ θρασίων Bekker, Ahrens, Bergk: κ' ὁ θρασίων Hiller-Crusius, Diehl

ALCMAN

85 Apollonius Dyscolus, *Pronouns*

Very many usages (sc. of the possessive adjective) can be found in other writers: σφέτερον πατέρα (Hes. *Op.* 2) for 'your father', ἑός for τεός, 'your', in Callimachus (fr. 472 Pfeiffer), 'tell your anxieties', and again in him τεός for σφωίτερος ('your', dual). Alcman [1] has

   (a) both you and your horses,[2]

   (b) and I fall at your knees.[3]

[1] Both of Alcman's adjectives are probably dual, although that in (b) may be singular.   [2] Addressed to the Dioscuri? Cf. frr. 2, 25.   [3] Perhaps addressed to Arete (and Alcinous?): cf. *Od.* 7.146 f., where Odysseus says, 'Arete . . . , I come to your husband and to your knees, having suffered much.'

86 *Homeric Parsings* (on *Od.* 3. 71 πλεῖτε, 'you sail')

And πλῆτρον is a term meaning πηδάλιον; Alcman used the diminutive form πλήθριον,

steering-paddle.

87 Apollonius Dyscolus, *Syntax*

For time and time again Doric [1] runs syllables together by using the corresponding unaspirated consonant (i.e. κ τ π, not χ θ φ):

   (a) and the bowman Heracles

   (b) to accompany most beautifully on the pipes

   (c) and mighty Athena

   (d) and Melampus and Harpolycus [2]

   (e) for (the bolder would rule?)

[1] The ms. has 'Alcman's' in the margin opposite the examples.   [2] Melampus was a famous seer; but Hyginus *fab.* 181 names Melampus and Harpalicus (Blackfoot and Snatcher) as two of the hounds of Actaeon.

88 Ap. Dysc. *Pron.* 143b (i 112 Schneider)

πάλιν δὴ ὁ Ἀλκμὰν τὸ σφεᾶς ἀντὶ ἑνικοῦ ἔταξε καὶ τὸ
σφοῖς ἀδελφιδεοῖς
κᾶρα καὶ φόνον

2 Bast: κάραν cod.

89 Apollon. Soph. *Lex.* (p. 101 Bekker, 488s. de Villoison)

Ὅμηρος δὲ ἅπαξ πᾶν θηρίον. ἔνιοι δὲ θῆρας μὲν καὶ θηρία λέγουσι
λέοντας καὶ παρδάλεις καὶ λύκους καὶ πάντα τὰ παραπλήσια τούτοις,
ἑρπετὰ δὲ πάλιν κοινῶς τὰ γένη τῶν ὄφεων, κνώδαλα δὲ τὰ θαλάσσια
κήτη, φαλαίνας καὶ ὅσα τοιαῦτα, καθάπερ καὶ Ἀλκμὰν διαστέλλει
λέγων οὕτως·

εὕδουσι δ' ὀρέων κορυφαί τε καὶ φάραγγες
πρώονές τε καὶ χαράδραι
φῦλά τ' ἑρπέτ' ὅσα τρέφει μέλαινα γαῖα
θῆρές τ' ὀρεσκῷοι καὶ γένος μελισσᾶν
5 καὶ κνώδαλ' ἐν βένθεσσι πορφυρέας ἁλός·
εὕδουσι δ' οἰωνῶν φῦλα τανυπτερύγων.

1s. de Villoison: φάλαγγες πρώτονέστέ cod. 3 ὕλα ci.
Pfeiffer   φῦλά τε del. West (*Greek Metre* 52)   τε ἑρπετά θ'
ὅσα cod.   ὅσσα Bergk

ALCMAN

88 Apollonius Dyscolus, *Pronouns*

Again, Alcman used σφεᾶς for the singular ('her', not 'their', at fr. 83); so with σφός, 'his':

(bringing?) fate and death to his nephews.[1]

[1] Of Danaus or Atreus? For the expression cf. *Il.* 2. 352.

89–90 describe scenes of nature.

89 Apollonius the Sophist, *Homeric Lexicon* (on κνώδαλον)

Homer uses the word once only (*Od.* 17. 317) and means by it any wild animal; others use θῆρες and θηρία ('wild animals') for lions, leopards, wolves and suchlike, ἑρπετά ('creeping things') as a general term for the different kinds of snakes, κνώδαλα for sea-monsters, whales and the like. This is the distinction made by Alcman when he says,

And the mountain-peaks are asleep and the ravines, the headlands and the torrent-beds, all the creeping tribes[1] that the black earth nourishes, the wild animals of the mountains, the race of bees and the monsters in the depths of the surging sea; and the tribes of long-winged birds are asleep.[2]

[1] Or '. . . the torrent-beds, the forest and all the creeping things'.   [2] The continuation may have been, 'but X is not asleep'; or Alcman may be setting the scene for the epiphany of a god.

90 Schol. Soph. *O.C.* 1248 (p. 53 de Marco)

τὰ ἀπὸ τῶν ὀρῶν φησι τῶν προσαγορευομένων ῾Ριπῶν. τινὲς δὲ οὕτω καλοῦσι, ῾Ρίπαια ὄρη. λέγει δὲ αὐτὰ ἐννύχια διὰ τὸ πρὸς τῇ δύσει κεῖσθαι. μέμνηται δὲ καὶ ᾿Αλκμὰν λέγων οὕτως·

> ῾Ρίπας, ὄρος ἀνθέον ὕλᾳ,
> νυκτὸς μελαίνας στέρνον.

1 Lobeck: ἔνθεον codd.   2 Triclinius: στέρνων codd.

91 Athen. xv 682a (iii 508 Kaibel)

τῶν δὲ καλχῶν μέμνηται καὶ ᾿Αλκμὰν ἐν τούτοις·

> χρύσιον ὅρμον ἔχων ῥαδινᾶν πετάλοις ἴσα καλχᾶν.

Dalecamp, Bergk: ῥαδινὰν πετάλοισι κάλχαν codd.

92 Athen. i 31cd (i 72s. Kaibel)

᾿Αλκμὰν δέ που

(a) ἄπυρον Ϝοῖνον

καὶ

(b) ἄνθεος ὄσδοντα

φησὶ τὸν ἐκ

(c) Πέντε Λόφων,

ὅς ἐστι τόπος Σπάρτης ἀπέχων στάδια ἑπτά, καὶ τὸν ἐκ Δενθιάδων, ἐρύματός τινος, καὶ τὸν ἐξ Οἰνοῦντος καὶ τὸν ἐξ ᾿Ονόγλων καὶ

ALCMAN

90 Scholiast on Sophocles, *Oedipus at Colonus* 1248 ('from night-wrapped Rhipae')

He is speaking of the mountains called Rhipae: some in fact call them 'the Rhipaean mountains'. He speaks of them as 'night-wrapped' because they are situated in the west.[1] Alcman mentions them in these words:

Rhipae, mountain blossoming with forest, breast of black night.

[1] Sophocles clearly thinks of them as in the north, as do other Greek and Latin writers: see Bolton, *Aristeas* 39 ff. with n. 4.

91–101 deal with feasting, food and wine; cf. 17, 19.

91 Athenaeus, *Scholars at Dinner*

Calchae[1] are mentioned by Alcman in these words:

wearing[2] a golden chain (like?) petals of slender calchae.[3]

[1] Purple flowers.   [2] The participle is masc. sing.   [3] I.e., as bright as petals . . . ? Text and translation uncertain.

92 Athenaeus, *Scholars at Dinner*

Alcman somewhere uses the expressions
> (a) wine unfired

and
> (b) smelling of flowers

of the wine from
> (c) Five Crests,

a place just under a mile from Sparta, and of the wines from Denthiades, a fortress, Carystus near the Arcadian border,

Σταθμῶν. χωρία δὲ ταῦτα κεῖται πλησίον Πιτάνης. φησὶν οὖν·

(d) †οἶνον δ' Οἰνουντιάδα ἢ Δένθιν ἢ Καρύστιον
ἢ Ὄνογλιν ἢ Σταθμίταν†

καὶ τὸν ἐκ Καρύστου, ὅς ἐστι πλησίον Ἀρκαδίας (haec post ἐρύματός τινος transp. Porson)· ἄπυρον δὲ εἶπε τὸν οὐχ ἡψημένον· ἐχρῶντο γὰρ ἐφθοῖς οἴνοις.

cf. Strab. 10.1.6, Steph. Byz. s.v. Κάρυστος, Eust. Il. 281.10, Od. 1449.12, 1633.51, Hsch. s. vv. Δένθις, Καρύστιος, Οἰνούσιος, Ὄνιγλιν

93 Ammon. Diff. 244 (p. 64 Nickau)

ἴκες δὲ τὰ διεσθίοντα τοὺς ὀφθαλμοὺς τῶν ἀμπέλων· Ἀλκμάν·
καὶ ποικίλον ἴκα τὸν ὀφθαλμῶν
†ἀμπέλων† ὀλετῆρα.

2 ἀμπελίνων ci. Bergk: del. Schneidewin

P. Med. inv. 72. 10

5   ]αδυ ἱστοπέδαις
      ]ναῒ ἁμᾶ κέλομαι
  καὶ ποίκιλον] ἴκα τὸν ὀ-
8 φθαλμῶν ἀπα]λῶν ὀλετῆρα, Ϝάναξ

Schol. v. 7 ὀρνέου..μ.[ὁ]φθαλμὸν τῆς ἀμ[πέ]λ[ου

94 Athen. iii 114f–115a (i 263 Kaibel)

αἱ δὲ παρ' Ἀλκμᾶνι θριδακίσκαι λεγόμεναι αἱ αὐταί εἰσι ταῖς Ἀττικαῖς θριδακίναις. λέγει δὲ οὕτως ὁ Ἀλκμάν·
θριδακίσκας τε καὶ κριβανωτώς.

458

Oenus, Onogli and Stathmi: these places [1] are near Pitana. He says, then,

    (d) and wine of Oenus or Denthian or Carystian or Onoglian or Stathmite.

By 'unfired' he meant 'not mulled'—they used to mull their wines.

[1] The last three? None of the sites is identified, but Denthiades is probably Dentheliades on the Messenian frontier, and the river Oenus joins the Alpheus from the N.E. just N. of Sparta.

93 Ammonius, *On Similar but Different Words*

ἴκες are the creatures that eat through vine-buds: Alcman has

    and the many-coloured *ix*,[1] destroyer of vine-buds.

[1] Probably a bird: W. G. Arnott ap. S. Daris, *Actes XVe Congr. papyr.* ii. 9, n. 3, suggests the rose-coloured starling, *Sturnus roseus*.

Papyrus (Augustan era)

    . . . mastholds . . . ship . . . at the same time I bid (you) . . . and the (many-coloured) *ix*, destroyer of (tender?) buds, lord.[1]

Scholiast at v. 7: (kind?) of bird . . . bud of the vine

[1] The papyrus scrap, published by Daris in 1979 (loc. cit.), sets the fragment in an unexpected context and presents textual difficulties.

94 Athenaeus, *Scholars at Dinner*

    The cakes called *thridakiskai* by Alcman are the same as the Attic *thridakinai* ('lettuce-cakes'). Alcman speaks of
        lettuce-cakes and pan-cakes.

GREEK LYRIC

Σωσίβιος δ' ἐν γ' περὶ 'Αλκμᾶνος (F.Gr.H. 595 F6) κριβάνας φησὶ
λέγεσθαι πλακοῦντάς τινας τῷ σχήματι μαστοειδεῖς.

xiv 646a (iii 427 Kaibel)

κριβάνας πλακοῦντάς τινας ὀνομαστικῶς 'Απολλόδωρος (F. Gr.
H. 244 F255) παρ' 'Αλκμᾶνι. ὁμοίως καὶ Σωσίβιος ἐν γ' περὶ
'Αλκμᾶνος τῷ σχήματι μαστοειδεῖς εἶναι φάσκων αὐτούς, χρῆσθαι δ'
αὐτοῖς Λάκωνας πρὸς τὰς τῶν γυναικῶν ἐστιάσεις, περιφέρειν τ'
αὐτοὺς ὅταν μέλλωσιν ᾄδειν τὸ παρεσκευασμένον ἐγκώμιον τῆς
Παρθένου αἱ ἐν τῷ χορῷ ἀκόλουθοι.

95 Athen. iv 140c (i 318 Kaibel)

ἔτι φησὶν ὁ Πολέμων καὶ τὸ δεῖπνον ὑπὸ τῶν Λακεδαιμονίων
ἄικλον προσαγορεύεσθαι, παραπλησίως ἁπάντων Δωριέων οὕτως
αὐτὸ καλούντων. 'Αλκμὰν μὲν γὰρ οὕτω φησί·

(a) κἠπὶ τᾷ μύλᾳ δρυφῆται κἠπὶ ταῖς συναικλίαις,

οὕτω τὰ συνδείπνια καλῶν. καὶ πάλιν·

(b) αἶκλον 'Αλκμάων ἁρμόξατο.

Sosibius [1] in book 3 of his work *On Alcman* says *kribanai* ('pan-cakes') is the name for certain cakes shaped like breasts.

Apollodorus [2] says that *kribanai* is a special name for cakes in Alcman; similarly Sosibius in book 3 of his work *On Alcman*, who says they are shaped like breasts and used by Spartans for their women's festivals; he says they carry them round when the followers in the choir are going to sing the song of praise prepared in honour of the Maiden. [3]

[1] 3rd c. B.C. Spartan historian.   [2] 2nd c. B.C. Athenian scholar.   [3] Artemis?

95 Athenaeus, *Scholars at Dinner*

Moreover, Polemon [1] says that the evening meal is called *aiklon* by the Spartans, and that all Dorians alike use this name. Alcman says,

(a) (mourns?) [2] both at the mill and at the communal suppers,

using the term *syn-aiklia* for the shared evening meals. And again,

(b) Alcman prepared a supper for himself.

[1] Early 2nd c. B.C. antiquarian from Ilium.   [2] 'Is mourned?' Sense much disputed: see L. Massa Positano, *P.P.* 1 (1946) 367–9.

461

GREEK LYRIC

96 Athen. xiv 648b (iii 433 Kaibel)

πολτοῦ δὲ μνημονεύει ᾽Αλκμὰν οὕτως·

   ἤδη παρεξεῖ πυάνιόν τε πολτὸν
   χίδρον τε λευκὸν κηρίναν τ᾽ ὀπώραν.

ἐστὶ δὲ τὸ πυάνιον, ὥς φησι Σωσίβιος, πανσπερμία ἐν γλυκεῖ
ἡψημένη. χίδρον δὲ οἱ ἐφθοὶ πυροί. κηρίναν δὲ ὀπώραν λέγει τὸ μέλι.

cf. Eust. *Od.* 1563. 1, 1735. 51

97 Schol. Hom. *Od.* 23. 76 (p. 717 Dindorf)

ὁ δὲ ᾽Αλκμὰν καὶ τὰς γνάθους

                        μάστακας

φησὶ παρὰ τὸ μασᾶσθαι.

98 Str. x 4. 18 (ii 410 Kramer)

τὰ δὲ συσσίτια ἀνδρεῖα παρὰ μὲν τοῖς Κρησὶν καὶ νῦν ἔτι καλεῖσθαι
(sc. φησὶν ῎Εφορος, *F.Gr.H.* 70 F149), παρὰ δὲ τοῖς Σπαρτιάταις
μὴ διαμεῖναι καλούμενα ὁμοίως ⟨ὡς⟩ πρότερον· παρ᾽ ᾽Αλκμᾶνι γοῦν
οὕτω κεῖσθαι·

   θοίναις δὲ καὶ ἐν θιάσοισιν
ἀνδρείων παρὰ δαιτυμόνεσσι πρέπει παιᾶνα κατάρχην.

2 Ursinus: πρέπε codd.

99 Athen. iii 81d (i 189 Kaibel)

Κυδωνίων δὲ μήλων μνημονεύει Στησίχορος (fr. 187 *P.M.G.*)
. . . καὶ ᾽Αλκμάν.

ALCMAN

96 Athenaeus, *Scholars at Dinner*

Porridge is mentioned by Alcman in these words:

Soon he [1] will provide bean porridge and white frumenty and the waxen harvest.[2]

Puanion,[3] according to Sosibius,[4] is mixed seeds boiled in raisin-syrup. 'Frumenty' is boiled wheaten-grains. By 'waxen harvest' he means honey.

[1] Some link the lines with fr. 20 and take Zeus to be the subject; Wilamowitz suggested that 96 and 19 belong to the same poem. [2] Or 'wax-like fruit'. [3] An adjective in Alcman, it should mean 'bean' porridge, according to Hesychius. The mixed seeds may include peas, lentils, lupins, vetch; see P. Cartledge, *Sparta and Lakonia* 175. [4] See 94 n. 1.

97 Scholiast on *Odyssey* 23. 76 (μάσταξ, 'mouth')

Alcman uses the plural for

jaws,

from μασᾶσθαι, 'to chew'.

98 Strabo, *Geography*

Ephorus [1] says that in Crete the public messes are still called *andreia* ('men's halls') but that in Sparta they did not keep the old name attested by Alcman in the lines,

And at the meals and banquets of the messes it is right to strike up the paean in the presence of the feasters.

[1] Historian, 4th c. B.C.

99 Athenaeus, *Scholars at Dinner*

Cydonian apples [1]

are mentioned by Stesichorus . . . and by Alcman.

[1] Quinces; Cydonia is in N.W. Crete.

GREEK LYRIC

100 Athen. iii 81f (i 189s. Kaibel)

Ἕρμων δ᾽ ἐν Κρητικαῖς Γλώσσαις κοδύμαλα καλεῖσθαί φησι τὰ κυδώνια μῆλα. Πολέμων δ᾽ ἐν ε᾽ τῶν πρὸς Τίμαιον ἄνθους γένος τὸ κοδύμαλον εἶναί τινας ἱστορεῖν. Ἀλκμὰν δὲ τὸ στρουθίον μῆλον, ὅταν λέγῃ

μεῖον ἢ κοδύμαλον.

Ἀπολλόδωρος δὲ καὶ Σωσίβιος τὸ κυδώνιον μῆλον ἀκούουσιν. ὅτι δὲ διαφέρει τὸ κυδώνιον μῆλον τοῦ στρουθίου σαφῶς εἴρηκε Θεόφραστος ἐν β᾽ τῆς ἱστορίας.

101 Athen. xiv 636f–637a (iii 405s. Kaibel)

καὶ Ἀλκμὰν δέ φησιν·

μάγαδιν δ᾽ ἀποθέσθαι.

102 *Epim. Hom.* (*Anecd. Oxon.* i 60 Cramer)

. . . παρὰ τὴν Δωρίδος διάλεκτον τροπὴ γίνεται τοῦ η εἰς α μακρόν· . . . ἐὰν δὲ ὦσιν ἐκ τοῦ ε, οὐκέτι· ἔλατος ἱππήλατος. Ἀλκμάν·

λεπτὰ δ᾽ ἀταρπὸς †ἀνηλὴς† δ᾽ ἀνάγκα,

ἐκ γὰρ τοῦ ἐλεεινή.

νηλεὴς Bergk: ἀνηλεὴς Schneidewin

ALCMAN

100 Athenaeus, *Scholars at Dinner*

Hermon [1] in his *Cretan Glossary* says that *kodymala* is a name for quinces. Polemon [2] in book 5 of his *Reply to Timaeus* says that according to some writers the *kodymalon* is a kind of flower. Alcman uses the term of the *struthium* [3] when he says,

> smaller than a medlar.

Apollodorus and Sosibius [4] take it to mean quince here, but Theophrastus in book 2 of his *Enquiry into Plants* (2. 2. 5) says clearly that the quince is different from the *struthium*.

[1] Or Hermonax, unknown; see *R.E.* s.v. Hermonax (3).
[2] See 95 n. 1.   [3] Theophrastus implies that the quince (Cydonian apple) is an inferior kind of *struthium*, which may be a medlar.   [4] See 94 nn. 1, 2.

101 Athenaeus, *Scholars at Dinner* (on musical instruments)

Alcman also says,

> and to set aside the magadis. [1]

[1] A kind of stringed instrument; see Anacr. 374.

102–126 are miscellaneous quotations with consecutive words (in alphabetical order of the sources).

102 *Homeric Parsings* (on ἀνήκεστος)

In the Doric dialect η is changed to long α; . . . but not if the η is derived from ε: ἔλατος gives ἱππ-ήλατος (not ἱππ-άλατος). Alcman has

> and narrow is the path, pitiless the necessity, [1]

with ἀνηλής [2] (not ἀναλής) ('pitiless'), since it comes from ἐλεεινή ('pitiable').

[1] Doubtless the path of life and the necessity of death.
[2] The form must be emended to correct the metre.

103 Ap. Dysc. *Pron.* 136bc (i 107 Schneider)

Αἰολεῖς μετὰ τοῦ F κατὰ πᾶσαν πτῶσιν καὶ γένος· Σαπφώ (fr. 164). καὶ Ἀλκμὰν δὲ συνεχῶς αἰολίζων φησί·

τὰ Fὰ κάδεα.

Bergk: τα εα cod.

104 Ap. Dysc. *Adv.* 566 (i 156 Schneider)

ἑξῆς ῥητέον ἐστὶ καὶ περὶ τοῦ ῥά. Ἀλκμάν·

τίς κα, τίς ποκα ῥᾷ ἄλλω νόον ἀνδρὸς ἐνίσποι;

Bergk, Bekker: τίς ἂν τίς . . . ἄλλα . . . ἐπίσποι cod.

105 Ap. Dysc. *Synt.* 3. 31 (p. 298 Uhlig)

. . . ἡ εὐκτική, ὡς ἔχει τὸ παρ᾽ Ἀλκμάνι·

νικῶ δ᾽ ὁ κάρρων.

106 Ael. Aristid. *Or.* 28.54 (ii 159 Keil)

ἀλλαχῇ δὲ οὕτω σφόδρα ἔνθεος γίγνεται (sc. ὁ Ἀλκμάν) ὥστε φαίης ἂν ὅτι οὐδ᾽ οὑτωσὶ κατὰ τὸ ῥῆμα ἔνθεός ἐστιν, ἀλλ᾽ αὐτὸ δὴ τοῦτο ὥσπερ θεὸς τῶν ἀπὸ μηχανῆς λέγει·

Fείπατέ μοι τάδε, φῦλα βροτήσια.

ALCMAN

103 Apollonius Dyscolus, *Pronouns*

The Aeolians spell ὅς ('his', 'her' etc.) with digamma in all cases and genders: cf. Sappho (fr. 164); Alcman too, who constantly uses aeolic forms,[1] says,

> his (her) cares.

[1] See Page, *Alcman* 155 f.

104 Apollonius Dyscolus, *Adverbs*

Next I must discuss [1] the form ῥᾴ ('easily'). Alcman has

> Who, who could ever tell easily the mind of another man?

[1] He notes the long α as anomalous in adverbs.

105 Apollonius Dyscolus, *Syntax*

. . . the optative [1] νικῷ, as in Alcman:

> and may the better man win!

[1] Distinguished by the iota from νικῶ, 'I conquer', and νικῶ, 'be conquered'.

106 Aelius Aristides, *On a Remark made in Passing*

Elsewhere [1] Alcman becomes so inspired (ἔνθεος) that you might declare that it is not so much a case of inspiration in the literal sense of his having a god in him as of his making a pronouncement like one of your 'gods from a machine':

> Tell me this, you mortal tribes.

[1] This passage follows fr. 148.

107 Ael. Aristid. *Or.* 45. 32 (ii 40s. Dindorf) = 2. 129 (i 2. 184 Lenz-Behr)

τί δὲ ὁ τῶν παρθένων ἐπαινέτης τε καὶ σύμβουλος λέγει ὁ Λακεδαιμόνιος ποιητής (viz. ὁ 'Αλκμάν, schol.);

Πολλαλέγων ὄνυμ' ἀνδρί, γυναικὶ δὲ Πασιχάρηα.

πολλά, φησίν, ὁ ἀνὴρ λεγέτω, γυνὴ δὲ οἷς ἂν ἀκούσῃ χαιρέτω.

108 Ael. Aristid. *Or.* 46. 206 (ii 272 Dindorf) = 3. 294 (i 2. 391 Lenz-Behr)

ἀλλ' ὅμως ἐῶ ταῦτα Πλάτωνος χάριν. ἔστω τὸ γειτόνημα ἁλμυρόν, ὥς φησιν (*Leg.* 705a).

Schol. ad loc. (iii 635 Dindorf)

'Αλκμὰν ὁ λυρικὸς τοῦτο εἶπεν·

ἁλμυρὸν τὸ γειτόνημα·

ἀντὶ τοῦ τὶ κακόν ἐστι γείτονα ἔχειν τὴν θάλασσαν.

cf. Arsen. = Apostol. *Cent.* ii 23 (ii 271s. Leutsch-Schneidewin) ἁλμυρὸν γειτόνημα ἔμβλεπε πόρρω . . .· ἐχρήσατο δὲ ταύτῃ (sc. τῇ λέξει) καὶ 'Αλκμὰν ὁ λυρικός.

ALCMAN

107 Aelius Aristides, *In Defence of Oratory*

And what does the praiser and counsellor of the girls, the Spartan poet, have to say?

Say-much is the man's name, Happy-with-all the woman's.[1]

He means, 'let the man say much and the woman be happy with whatever she hears.'

[1] Regarded by some as part of a wedding-hymn; if so, satirical: the woman's name, like Pasiphile in [Archilochus] 331 West, suggests promiscuity, so the man's may be Protest-much (Garzya) or even Collect-much (McKay, *Mnem.* 27, 1974, 413 f.).

108 Aelius Aristides, *In defence of the Four*

Nevertheless I allow this in favour of Plato; I grant the 'briny neighbourhood', as he puts it (*Laws* 705a).

Scholiast:
Alcman the lyric poet said this:

the neighbourhood is briny.

He meant, 'It is a bad thing to have the sea as a neighbour.'[1]

[1] Arsenius gives a proverb, 'Look from a distance on a briny neighbourhood', and says that Alcman used the expression.

109 Athen. xiv 624b (iii 376 Kaibel)

ταύτην δὲ τὴν ἁρμονίαν (sc. τὴν Φρυγιστί) Φρύγες πρῶτοι εὗρον
καὶ μετεχειρίσαντο. διὸ καὶ τοὺς παρὰ τοῖς Ἕλλησιν αὐλητὰς
Φρυγίους καὶ δουλοπρεπεῖς τὰς προσηγορίας ἔχειν, οἷός ἐστιν ὁ παρὰ
Ἀλκμᾶνι

Σάμβας

καὶ

Ἄδων

καὶ

Τῆλος,

παρὰ δὲ Ἱππώνακτι (fr. 118 West) Κί⟨κ⟩ων καὶ Κώδαλος καὶ
Βάβυς.

110 Choerob. in Theodos. (ii 343s. Hilgard)

. . . οἶκα, ὃ σημαίνει τὸ ὡμοίωμαι, ὡς παρὰ Ἀλκμᾶνι·

οἶκας μὲν ὡραίῳ λίνῳ,

ἀντὶ τοῦ ὡμοίωσαι.

cf. Choerob. ii 107 Hilgard, *Anecd. Oxon.* (i 287, iv 368, 415
Cramer), Hdn. (ii 796, 837 Lentz), *Anecd. Gr.* (iii 1294, 1404
Bekker)

οἶκας vel εἶκας codd.

111 *Et. Gen.* (p. 19 Calame)

βάλε· ἀντὶ τοῦ ἀβάλε, οἷον [Alcm. fr. 26. 2]· ὁ δὲ ⟨αὐτὸς⟩
Ἀλκμὰν τὸ ἀβάλε, οἷον·

ἀβάλε καὶ νοέοντα.

cf. schol. Marc. ad Dion. Thrac. (p. 431 Hilgard)

112 *Et. Gen.* (p. 17 Calame) = *Et. Mag.* 171.7

αὐσίον· καὶ ὁ μὲν Ἴβυκος αὔσιον λέγει (293 *P.M.G.*), ὁ δὲ
Ἀλκμὰν ταυσία, οἷον

†ταυσία παλλακίω.†

ALCMAN

109 Athenaeus, *Scholars at Dinner*

The Phrygians were the first to discover and use this tuning (i.e. the Phrygian). That (says Theophrastus) is why the pipers in Greek circles have Phrygian names appropriate to slaves, as in Alcman,[1]

Sambas

and

Adon

and

Telus,

and in Hipponax Cicon and Codalus and Babys.

[1] Cf. 126.

110 Choeroboscus, *On the Canons of Theodosius*

. . . οἶκα, which means 'I am like', as in Alcman,[1]

You are like ripe flax.

[1] Ascription doubtful, since the verb form is Ionic (Page, *Alcman* 108).

111 *Etymologicum Genuinum*

βάλε: for ἀβάλε ('if only'), as in [Alcm. fr. 26. 2]; Alcman also has ἀβάλε, as in

if only . . . both wise . . . !

112 *Etymologicum Genuinum*

αὐσίον ('vain'): Ibycus uses αὖσιον (293 *P.M.G.*). Alcman has ταυσία:

vain (are my many journeys?).

471

GREEK LYRIC

ὁ δὲ ποιητὴς κατὰ διάστασιν καὶ τροπὴν τοῦ α εἰς η, οἷον· τηϋσίην ὁδόν (*Od.* 3. 316)· οὐδεὶς γὰρ τὸν σχηματισμὸν αὐτοῦ κατώρθωσεν. ἐγὼ δὲ ἡγοῦμαι ὅτι πρῶτον τὸ παρ' Ἰβύκῳ, δεύτερον τὸ παρὰ Ἀλκμᾶνι, τρίτον τὸ παρὰ Ὁμήρῳ κατὰ διάστασιν. οὕτως Ἡρωδιανὸς περὶ Παθῶν (ii 176 Lentz).

ταύσια πολλὰ κίω Sitzler, Hiller

113 *Et. Gen.* (p. 45 Calame)

ὑλακόμωροι· ὑλακτικοί· . . . τῇ ὑλακῇ ὡροῦντες, ὅ ἐστιν ὀξείᾳ χρώμενοι· καὶ Ἀλκμάν·

†μελισκόνα τὸν ἀμόρη†

cf. 36 τὸ καλὸν μελίσκον

114 *Et. Gen.* (p. 33 Calame) = *Et. Mag.* 506.20 = *Et. Gud.* 316.42

Κέρκυρ· . . . Ἀλκμάν φησι·

καὶ Κέρκυρος ἀγήται,

ἀπὸ εὐθείας τῆς Κέρκυρ, ἀλλ' οὐκ εἴρηται . . . · οὕτως Ἡρωδιανός.

115 *Et. Gen.* (p. 39 Calame) = *Et. Mag.* 620. 35

ὄκκα δὴ γυνὰ εἴην

παρὰ Ἀλκμᾶνι. τὸ ὅτε ὄκα λέγεται, εἶτα διπλα(σιασμῷ) ὄκκα. περὶ Παθῶν (Hdn. i 495, ii 302, 559).

cf. Ap. Dysc. *Adv.* 606 (i 193 Schneider)

Ett. ὄκκα δὲ τύνη εἴην: Ap. ὄκκα δὴ γυνή

ALCMAN

Homer has it with diaeresis and *a* changed to *η*: *τηϋσίην ὁδόν*
('vain journey': *Od.* 3.316)—no one has corrected his form
of the word. I think that Ibycus' was the original form,
Alcman's next, Homer's with diaeresis third. So Herodian,
On Inflexions (ii 176 Lentz).

113 *Etymologicum Genuinum*

ὑλακόμωροι [1]: fond of barking; . . . keeping guard with
their barking; that is, giving a piercing [2] bark; Alcman has

(piercing song?)

[1] Homeric epithet for dogs.   [2] *μόρος* is said to be Cyprian
for 'sharp'.

114 *Etymologicum Genuinum*

Κέρκυρ ('Corcyraean'): Alcman says,

and leads a Corcyraean,

from the nominative Κέρκυρ, which is not found. . . . So
Herodian (ii 212 Lentz).

115 *Etymologicum Genuinum*

whenever I was a woman [1]

in Alcman. The form *ὅτε* ('when') is pronounced *ὅκα* and
then doubles the *κ*. Herodian, *On Inflexions* (i 495, ii 302,
559 Lentz).

[1] Text and translation insecure.

GREEK LYRIC

116 *Et. Gen.* (p. 39 Calame) = *Et. Mag.* 622.44 = *Et. Sym.* (cod. V Gaisford)

ἐκ δὲ τοῦ ὀλοός γίνεται ἡ κλητικὴ ὦ ὀλοέ, καὶ κατὰ συγκοπὴν ὀλέ· ἐὰν δὲ ὀλός ἡ εὐθεῖα, ἡ κλητικὴ γίνεται ὀλέ, οἷον·

> ἔχει μ᾽ ἄχος, ὦ ὀλὲ δαῖμον.

τοῦτο περὶ Παθῶν Ἡρωδιανός (ii 250 Lentz).

cf. *Anecd. Oxon.* (ii 461s. Cramer), schol. A Hom. *Il.* 10. 134 (τὸ Ἀλκμανικόν· ἔχει . . . δαῖμον), *Anecd. Oxon.* i 442, Hdn. (i 154 Lentz)

ὦλοὲ, ὦ ᾽λοὲ ci. edd.

117 Eust. *Il.* 1147. 1

ἐπεί, φησί (sc. Δίδυμος), λῆδος τὸ πρωτότυπον, ὃ Δωριεῖς λᾶδός φασιν, ὡς Ἀλκμάν·

> λᾶδος Ϝημένα καλόν,

ὅ ἐστι λήδιον ἐνδεδυμένη εὐειδές.

118 Eust. *Od.* 1787. 40

περὶ δὲ τοῦ εἴην εἴης εἴη γράψας ὁ Ἀλεξανδρεὺς Ἡρακλείδης . . . γράφει οὕτω· λέγουσιν οἱ Αἰολεῖς ἐκ τοῦ φιλῶ μετοχὴν φίλεις καὶ τοῦ φρονῶ φρόνεις καὶ εὐκτικὰ τούτων φιλείη καὶ φρονείη . . . μήποτε οὖν καὶ τὸ εἴη ῥῆμα Αἰολικόν ἐστιν ἀπὸ τῆς εἰς μετοχῆς, ἧς κλίσιν παρὰ τοῖς ποιηταῖς εἰπὼν φυλάττεσθαι παράγει χρῆσιν ἐξ Ἀλκμάνος τὸ

> ἔστι παρέντων μνᾶστιν † ἐπιθέσθαι†,

οὐ κατὰ ἔξαρσιν, φησί, τοῦ ο ἀπὸ τοῦ παρεόντων, ἀλλ᾽ ἐκ τοῦ εἰς ἔντος Αἰολικοῦ.

ALCMAN

116 *Etymologicum Genuinum*

From ὀλοός ('destructive') comes the vocative ὀλοέ and by syncope ὀλέ; but if the nominative is ὀλός, the vocative is ὀλέ, as in

> Distress grips me, you destructive god.[1]

This is in Herodian, *On Inflexions* (ii 250 Lentz).

[1] Ascribed to Alcman in *Anecdota Oxoniensia*.

117 Eustathius on *Iliad* 18. 352 ('fine linen')

For according to Didymus the original form of λῃδίον ('light summer dress') is λῆδος, called λᾶδος by the Dorians, as in Alcman:

> wearing[1] a beautiful dress,

i.e. clad in a handsome summer dress.

[1] The participle is fem. sing.: perhaps of a choir-girl (cf. 1. 64 ff.).

118 Eustathius on *Od.* 15. 435 (εἴη, 'might be')

On the optative εἴη Heraclides of Alexandria[1] . . . writes as follows: the Aeolians have the participles φίλεις from φιλῶ, φρόνεις from φρονῶ, and as the optatives of these φιλείη and φρονείη; so perhaps the verb form εἴη is Aeolic, derived from the participle εἴς, 'being': he says that this declension is observed in the poets and adduces an example from Alcman:

> we may (preserve?) the memory of those who were present.

The form παρ-έντων, he says, comes not from παρ-εόντων with the ο removed but from the Aeolic εἴς, gen. ἔντος.

[1] Heraclides Lembus, Alexandrian scholar of 2nd c. B.C.

119 Heph. *Ench*. 7. 3 (p. 22 Consbruch)

τῷ δὲ ἐφθημιμερεῖ Ἀλκμάν (sc. δακτυλικῷ χρῆται)·

> ταῦτα μὲν ὣς κεν ὁ δᾶμος ἅπας

cf. schol. B in Heph. (p. 273 Consbruch)

Page: ὡς ἂν ὁ δῆμος codd.

120 Hdn. π. μον. λέξ. β 44. 3 (ii 949 Lentz)

τὰ εἰς ζω λήγοντα ῥήματα ὑπὲρ δύο συλλαβὰς βαρύτονα οὐδέποτε τῷ ε παραλήγεσθαι θέλει . . . σημειῶδες ἄρα παρ᾽ Ἀττικοῖς καὶ τοῖς Ἴωσι λεγόμενον διὰ τοῦ ε τὸ πιέζω, ὥσπερ καὶ παρὰ τῷ ποιητῇ. προσέθηκα δὲ καὶ τὰς διαλέκτους, ἐπεὶ παρ᾽ Ἀλκαίῳ (fr. 422) διχῶς λέγεται, παρὰ δὲ Ἀλκμᾶνι διὰ τοῦ α·

> τῷ δὲ † σηομυνθια κατ᾽ αν κάρραν μάβως † ἐπίαζε.

σκόλλυν θεὰ (leg. θιὰ, σιὰ) Bergk   κατὰν κάρραν (vel κὰτ τὰν, κόρραν) Page

120A Hdn. π. μον. λέξ. a 9. 32 (ii 915 Lentz)

Εὐρυπῶν· Ἀλκμ(άν)·

> οἶσι δ᾽ Εὐρυπῶν

Nauck: ἀλκμοῖς ἤδε ῥυπῶν cod.

476

ALCMAN

119 Hephaestion, *Handbook on Metres*

Alcman[1] uses the hephthemimeral [2] dactylic line:

these things as the whole people would . . .

[1] Ascribed to Anacreon by Wilamowitz.   [2] I.e. consisting of three-and-a-half feet.

120 Herodian, *On Anomalous Words* (on πιέζω, 'press')

Paroxytone verbs in -ζω with more than two syllables never have ε in the penultimate syllable . . . So πιέζω with its ε in Attic and Ionic as in Homer is remarkable. I have added the dialects, since in Alcaeus (fr. 422) the word is used in two forms (πιέζω and πιάζω) and Alcman has πιάζω:

(the goddess . . . was tugging his hair down from his head?) [1]

[1] Of Athena beheading a giant, or accosting a hero as at *Il.* 1. 197? Text very uncertain.

120A [1] Herodian, *On Anomalous Words* (on proper names in -ῶν)

Eurypon: Alcman,

and those to whom Eurypon [2] . . .

[1] See Bergk iii 78, Edmonds fr. 163, S. Nannini, *Q.U.C.C.* 22 (1976) 69.   [2] Founder of the Spartan royal family of Eurypontids.

GREEK LYRIC

121 Prisc. *Inst. Gramm.* i 21 (ii 16 Keil)

inveniuntur etiam pro vocali correpta hoc digamma illi
usi, ut Ἀλκμάν·

$$καὶ \ χεῖμα \ πῦρ \ τε \ δάϜιον.$$

est enim dimetrum iambicum, et sic est proferendum Ϝ ut
faciat brevem syllabam.

cf. i 22 (ii 17 Keil)

122 Schol. A Hom. *Il.* 12. 66 (iii 312 Erbse)

προπερισπαστέον δὲ τὸ στεῖνος. οὐδετέρως γὰρ ἐξενήνεκται, πᾶν δὲ
οὐδέτερον εἰς ος λῆγον ἐν ὀνόμασι βαρύνεσθαι θέλει. οὕτως οὖν καὶ
μακρός ὀξύνομεν ἀρσενικὸν ὑπάρχον. εἰ δὲ οὐδέτερον γένοιτο,
βαρύνεται. οὕτως καὶ τὸ κλειτός. οὐδέτερον γὰρ γενόμενον βαρύνεται
παρ' Ἀλκμᾶνι·

$$† τῶ \ ἐν † \ Θεσσαλίῳ \ κλήτει.$$

cf. Hdn. (i 393, ii 81 Lentz), *Sud.* κλῆτος· δόξα

ἐν τῷ ε΄ ci. Schneidewin: ἐν τῷ· Dindorf: τῶν ἐν Θεσσαλίᾳ
Bergk

123 Schol. BT Hom. *Il.* 22. 305 (v 323s. Erbse)

ἀλλὰ μέγα ῥέξας· λείπει ἀγαθόν. Ἀλκμάν·

$$μέγα \ γείτονι \ γείτων.$$

478

ALCMAN

121 Priscian, *Grammar* (on digamma)

They are found using this digamma to give a shortened vowel, as in Alcman:

> and storm and destructive fire.[1]

For the line is iambic dimeter, and the digamma must be introduced in such a way as to create a short syllable (Ϝι).[2]

[1] Perhaps 'both winter and destructive heat'.   [2] Elsewhere he says that the digamma is introduced to avoid hiatus.

122 Scholiast on *Iliad* 12. 66 (στεῖνος, 'narrow place')

The word στεῖνος must have the accent on the first syllable, for it has been used as a neuter noun (from adjective στεινός, 'narrow'), and all neuter nouns ending in -ος are accented before the last syllable. So we give μακρός, masculine adjective, an acute accent on the last syllable, but when it becomes the neuter noun the first syllable is accented (τὸ μάκρος). So with κλειτός, 'famous': when it becomes a neuter noun, τὸ κλεῖτος, 'fame', the first syllable is accented in Alcman:

> (Thessalian?) fame.[1]

[1] Text uncertain. Cf. 16. 3 for the insulting force of 'Thessalian'.

123 Scholiast on *Iliad* 22. 305

'but having done a great thing': the word 'good' is omitted. So in Alcman:

> Neighbour is a great thing for neighbour.

GREEK LYRIC

124 Schol. Hom. *Od.* 3. 171 (i 134s. Dindorf) = *Anecd. Par.* (iii 433 Cramer)

νησίδιον μικρὸν πρὸ τῆς Χίου ἐστὶ τὰ Ψύρα, ἀπέχον Χίου σταδίους ὀγδοήκοντα, ἔχον λιμένα νεῶν εἴκοσι. Ἀλκμάν·

πάρ τ' ἱαρὸν σκόπελον παρά τε Ψύρα
τὸν Διόνυσον ἄγοντες,

οἷον ἐν μηδενὶ αὐτὸν τιθέμενοι· διὰ τὸ λυπρὸν τῆς νήσου.

cf. Eust. *Od.* 1462.46, Cratin. fr. 347 K.-A., Steph. Byz. s.v. Ψύρα (i 704 Meineke)

Buttmann: παρά τε ἱερὸν codd.

125 Schol. Pind. *Isthm.* 1. 56 (iii 205s. Drachmann)

ὁ πονήσαις δὲ νόῳ καὶ προμάθειαν φέρει· . . . Ἀλκμάν·

πῆρά τοι μαθήσιος ἀρχά.

126 Str. xii 8. 21 (ii 586s. Kramer)

λέγεται δέ τινα φῦλα Φρύγια οὐδαμοῦ δεικνύμενα, ὥσπερ οἱ Βερέκυντες. καὶ Ἀλκμὰν λέγει·

Φρύγιον αὔλησε μέλος τὸ Κερβήσιον,

καὶ βόθυνός τις λέγεται Κερβήσιος ἔχων ὀλεθρίους ἀποφοράς· ἀλλ' οὗτός γε δείκνυται, οἱ δ' ἄνθρωποι οὐκέθ' οὕτω λέγονται.

Κερβήσιον ci. Ursinus (cf. Hsch. Κιρβιαῖον· ἔθνος ἐχόμενον Λυδῶν)

127 Hsch. A 21 (i 4 Latte)

ἀάνθα·

εἶδος ἐνωτίου παρὰ Ἀλκμᾶνι ὡς Ἀριστοφάνης (Bergk: ἢ Ἀριστοφάνει codd., καὶ Ἀριστοφάνει Pearson) (v. fr. 422 Slater)

cf. Zonar. ap. *Anecd. Par.* (iv 84 Cramer)

480

ALCMAN

124 Scholiast on *Odyssey* 3. 171

Psyra is a small islet ten miles off Chios with a harbour
for twenty ships. Alcman has

taking Dionysus to the holy rock, to Psyra,[1]

in other words, considering him of no account, since the
island is a wretched place.

[1] It is not certain that the words 'taking Dionysus' belong
to Alcman; Stephanus of Byzantium cited the phrase
'taking Dionysus to Psyra' from the comic poet Cratinus
(fr. 347 K.-A.). A proverb, 'Dionysus to Psyra', was said
(with strange logic) to be applicable to people not drinking
at a party, since Psyra could not produce wine.

125 Scholiast on Pindar *Isthmian* 1. 40.

'he who has toiled wins foresight for his mind': . . .
Alcman has

Experience is the beginning of learning.

126 Strabo, *Geography*

Some Phrygian tribes are mentioned by writers but
nowhere to be seen, for example, the Berecyntians. And
Alcman says,

he piped a Phrygian tune,[1] the Cerbesian,

and Cerbesian is the name of a pit which gives off deadly
effluvia; but although it at least can be seen, the people are
no longer called Cerbesians.

[1] Cf. 109.

127–147 are isolated words (in alphabetical order).

127 Hesychius, *Lexicon* (on ἀάνθα)

A kind of

earring

in Alcman, according to Aristophanes.[1]

[1] Perhaps 'and in Aristophanes (the comic poet)'.

GREEK LYRIC

128 *Et. Gen.* (p. 47 Calame) = *Et. Mag.* 22.30 = *Et. Sym.* (cod. V Gaisford)

ὁ δὲ Ἡρωδιανὸς λέγει (ii 256 Lentz) ὅτι παράγωγόν ἐστιν ἀπὸ τοῦ ἄγος ἀγίζω καὶ κατὰ συγκοπὴν ἄζω . . . πόθεν δὲ δῆλον; ἐκ τοῦ τὸν Ἀλκμᾶνα εἰπεῖν

$$\dot{\alpha}\gamma\acute{\iota}\sigma\delta\epsilon\omicron$$

ἀντὶ τοῦ ἄζεο.

129 *Epim. Hom.* (*Anecd. Oxon.* i 55 Cramer)

ἀγαθόν· . . . ἀπλοῦν δὲ εἰ παρὰ τὸ ἀγάζω ἐστί, τὸ θαυμάζω, ὅπερ παρὰ ἀγῶ· ἐστὶν δὲ παρ' Ἀλκμᾶνι

$$\alpha\dot{\upsilon}\tau\grave{o}\nu \dagger \dot{\alpha}\gamma\hat{\alpha}\dagger,$$

ἀφ' οὗ καὶ ἄγημι καὶ ἄγαμαι.

leg. ἀγῇ?

130 *Et. Mag.* 228. 38

γεργύρα· ζήτει εἰς τὸ γόργυρα. ὁ δὲ Ἀλκμὰν διὰ τοῦ ε

$$\gamma\acute{\epsilon}\rho\gamma\upsilon\rho\alpha$$

φησί.

cf. Hdn. (ii 487 Lentz), *Anecd. Gr.* (i 233 Bekker)

131 Schol. Lucian. *Anachars.* 32 (p. 170 Rabe)

$$\gamma\acute{\epsilon}\rho\rho\omicron\nu\cdot$$

. . . Ἀλκμὰν δὲ ἐπὶ τῶν οἰστῶν τέθεικε τὴν λέξιν.

132 Schol. Vat. in Dion. Thrac. *Gramm.* (p. 281 Hilgard) = *Anecd. Gr.* (ii 949 Bekker)

τὰ δὲ εἰς αν βαρύνεται, λίαν ἄγαν πέραν . . . · τὸ

$$\delta\omicron\acute{\alpha}\nu$$

παρὰ Ἀλκμᾶνι Δωρικῶς ὀξύνεται, γεγονὸς οὕτως· δήν, δάν, δοάν.

leg. δϝάν vel δοϝάν?

ALCMAN

128 *Etymologicum Genuinum*

Herodian (ii 256 Lentz) says that ἁγίζω ('make sacred') is derived from ἄγος ('source of religious fear') and by syncope becomes ἄζω . . . The proof? Alcman's use of ἀγίσδεο for ἄζεο,

> revere.

129 *Homeric Parsings* (on ἀγαθόν)

The adjective is simple, not compound, if it comes from ἀγάζω, 'I marvel', which is derived from ἀγῶ; this verb is in Alcman:

> adores him,

and from it come ἄγημι and ἄγαμαι.

130 *Etymologicum Magnum*

γεργύρα· see under γόργυρα. Alcman has γέργυρα with the ε,

> drain.[1]

[1] Underground drain for carrying off rain-water.

131 Scholiast on Lucian, *Anacharsis* (γέρρον, a Scythian shield)

Alcman uses the word of

> arrows.

132 Scholiast on Dionysius of Thrace

Words ending in -αν are accented on the first syllable, e.g. λίαν, ἄγαν, πέραν . . . ; δοάν,

> for a long time,

in Alcman has the Doric acute accent on the last syllable, being formed from δήν through δάν.

133 *Et. Gud.* 395. 51 Sturz

μνήμη· . . . 'Αλκμὰν δέ, φασί,

δόρκον

αὐτὴν καλεῖ· βλέπομεν γὰρ τῇ διανοίᾳ τὰ ἀρχαῖα.

φρασίδορκον pro φασὶ δόρκον ci. O. Mueller, παλίδορκον Emperius

134 *Et. Gen.* (p. 27s. Calame) (s.v. ἐνστραφεός)

τὸ δὲ

ζάτραφα

παρὰ 'Αλκμᾶνι κανονιστέον κατὰ μεταπλασμὸν ἀπὸ τοῦ ζάτροφον.

135 *Et. Mag.* 420. 48

ἥδυμος· . . . τὸ συγκριτικὸν ἡδυμώτερος, καὶ 'Ιωνικῶς ἡδυμέστερος . . . · τὸ δὲ ὑπερθετικὸν

Ϝαδυμέστατον

'Αλκμὰν ἔφη.

ἡδυ- codd.

136 *Epim. Hom.* (*Anecd. Oxon.* i 190 Cramer)

ἡσί· . . .

ἠτί

δὲ λέγει 'Αλκμὰν ἀντὶ τοῦ ἡσίν.

137 Schol. Callim. fr. 384. 1 Pfeiffer = P. Oxy. 2258 C fr. 2(a) 25

ποιητικὸ(ν) δὲ τὸ ἀπὸ συνδέσμου ἄρχεσθ(αι). 'Αλκμάν·

κ(αὶ) δ' αὖ με . [

δ' αὖ = δὴ αὖ (Lobel)   fort. μετ[

ALCMAN

133 *Etymologicum Gudianum*

μνήμη, 'Memory': . . . Alcman, they say, calls her

big-eyed,[1]

since we 'see' the past by our thinking.

[1] Or 'A. calls Memory "the one who sees with her mind's eye".'

134 *Etymologicum Genuinum*

In Alcman ζάτραφα,

well-nourished,[1]

is to be classified as a metaplasm of ζάτροφον.

[1] Neuter plural. Cf. Homer's ζατρεφής.

135 *Etymologicum Magnum*

The comparative of ἥδυμος is ἡδυμώτερος and in Ionic ἡδυμέστερος . . . ; Alcman used the superlative Ϝαδυμέστατον,

most pleasant.

136 *Homeric Parsings* (on *Iliad* 1. 528 ἦ, 'he spoke')

. . . Alcman uses ἠτί instead of ἠσί,

says.[1]

[1] This passage follows Sa. 109.

137 Scholiast on Callimachus, *The Victory of Sosibius*

To begin with a conjunction (καί, 'and') is a poetic device. Alcman has

And once again . . .

GREEK LYRIC

138 *Epim. Hom.* (*Anecd. Oxon.* i 55 Cramer)

ἀγαθόν· . . . Τρύφων δὲ οὕτως· τὰ εἰς ος τριγενῆ παραλήγοντα τῷ
α καὶ ἔχοντα ἐν τῇ τρίτῃ ἀπὸ τέλους συλλαβῇ α ὀξύνεται· μαδαρός
πλαδαρός ἀγανός . . . · σεσημείωται τὸ κάρχαρος· . . . καὶ τὸ
θηλυκὸν παρ' Ἀλκμᾶνι·

$$καρχάραισι \ φωναῖς.$$

Schneidewin: καρχάρεσσι cod.

139 Eust. *Il.* 756. 30

. . . ἀντιθέσει τοῦ ν εἰς λ, ᾧ ἀντιστοιχοῦσι Δωριεῖς ἐν τῷ φίλτατος
φίντατος, ἦλθεν ἦνθεν . . . , κέλετο

$$κέντο$$

παρὰ Ἀλκμᾶνι.

140 *Et. Gen.* (p. 33 Calame)=*Et. Mag.* 506.18

$$κερκολύρα·$$

οὕτως ὁ Ἀλκμὰν ἐχρήσατο ἀντὶ τοῦ κρεκολύρα. Περὶ Παθῶν.

cf. Zonar. 1190, *Sud.* κερκόλυρα· ὄνομα τόνου (Bergk: τόπου
codd.)

141 *Et. Gen.* (p. 36 Calame)

$$λιγύκορτον$$

πάλιν παρ' Ἀλκμᾶνι ἔχεις ἀντὶ τοῦ λιγύκροτον ὑπερθέσει τοῦ ρ.

Miller: λιγύκρυτον (in marg. λιγύκυρτον) πάλιν . . . ἀντὶ τοῦ
λιγύκυρτον cod.

ALCMAN

138 *Homeric Parsings* (on ἀγαθόν)

Tryphon [1] writes as follows: adjectives in -ος with all three genders and with α in the second-last and third-last syllables have acute accent on the last syllable: μαδαρός, πλαδαρός, ἀγανός . . . The adjective κάρχαρος, 'sharp', is marked in our texts as exceptional . . . The feminine is in Alcman:

> with sharp voices.

[1] Grammarian in the reign of Augustus.

139 Eustathius on *Iliad* 9. 364 (ἔρρων)

. . . by the change from ν to λ, the same substitution as the Dorians make in saying φίντατος for φίλτατος, ἦνθεν for ἦλθεν, . . . κέντο for κέλετο,

> he ordered,

in Alcman.

140 *Etymologicum Genuinum*

κερκολύρα: so in Alcman instead of κρεκολύρα,

> resounding lyre. [1]

So Herodian, *On Inflexions*.

[1] κερκολύρα should mean tailed lyre (or shuttle lyre?); κρεκολύρα is presumably the later form, coined from κρέκειν, 'strike with a plectrum'; cf. Zonaras, *Lexicon*.

141 *Etymologicum Genuinum*

Again in Alcman you have λιγύκορτον instead of λιγύκροτον,

> clear-struck, [1]

with the ρ transposed.

[1] Perhaps of the clear notes of a lyre.

GREEK LYRIC

142 Cod. Coisl. 394 (ap. Reitzenstein, *Ind. Lect. Rost.* 1890–91 p. 6: cf. *Rh. Mus.* 43. 451 n. 2)

ὁλκάς·

πλοῖον. καὶ παρὰ ᾽Αλκμᾶνι ἀηδών (ἀειδῶν cod.). καὶ Σειρήν (Voss: εἰρήνη cod.) . . .

cf. Hsch. s.v.

143 Schol. A Hom. *Il.* 17. 40 (iv 338 Erbse)

τὰ γὰρ εἰς -τις λήγοντα θηλυκὰ δισύλλαβα, μὴ ὄντα ἐπιθετικά, παραληγόμενα δὲ τῷ ο ἤτοι μόνῳ ἢ σὺν ἑτέρῳ φωνήεντι ὀξύνεσθαι θέλει, κοιτίς Προιτίς φροντίς,

οὐτίς

τὸ ζῷον παρ᾽ ᾽Αλκμᾶνι.

cf. Hdn. i 103, ii 104 Lentz

144 *Et. Gen.* (p. 41 Calame)

πείρατα (Miller: πήρατα codd.)· πέρατα. καὶ παρ᾽ ᾽Αλκμᾶνι

πήρατα.

περὶ Παθῶν.

Page: πέρασα cod. A: om. cod. B

145 [Plut.] *Mus.* 5. 1133ab (p. 113 Lasserre, vi 3. 5 Ziegler)

τοῦ δὲ Πολυμνήστου καὶ Πίνδαρος (fr. 188 Snell) καὶ ᾽Αλκμὰν οἱ τῶν μελῶν ποιηταὶ ἐμνημόνευσαν.

146 *Sud.* X 326 (iv 808 Adler)

χθονία· . . . καὶ παρ᾽ ᾽Αλκμᾶνι δέ, ὅτε φησὶ

χθόνιον τέρας

ἐπὶ τῆς ῎Εριδος, τινὲς ἀντὶ τοῦ στυγνὸν ἐδέξαντο, ἔνιοι δὲ ἀντὶ τοῦ μέγα· ἐπεὶ πρὸς αὐτὴν λέγει.

ALCMAN

142 Cyril, *Lexicon*

ὁλκάς: a boat. In Alcman,
nightingale.
Also Siren . . .

143 Scholiast on *Iliad* 17. 40 (Φρόντις)

Disyllabic feminine words (so long as they are not adjectives) ending in -τις and having ο either by itself or with another vowel in the second-last syllable are accented with acute on the last syllable: κοιτίς, Προιτίς, φροντίς, and οὐτίς, the animal,[1] in Alcman.

[1] Not identified. The bustard was ὠτίς.

144 *Etymologicum Genuinum*

πείρατα: πέρατα,
limits.
In Alcman, πήρατα.[1] [Herodian,] *On Inflexions.*

[1] Cf. 3 fr. 11. 2.

145 'Plutarch', *On Music*

Polymnestus [1]
was mentioned by the lyric poets Pindar (fr. 188 Snell) and Alcman.

[1] See Polymn. test. 2.

146 *Suda* (on χθονία, 'infernal')

In Alcman, when he says of Strife
infernal monster,
some have taken it to mean 'loathsome', while others take it in the sense of 'great', since he is addressing Strife.

489

GREEK LYRIC

147 Schol. A Hom. *Il.* 12. 137 (iii 327s. Erbse)

αὔας· . . . ἴσως δὲ βεβαρυτόνηται, ἐπεὶ καὶ τὸ ναῦος ἐβαρύνετο καὶ τὸ Τραῦος κύριον καὶ τὸ

ψαῦος

παρ' Ἀλκμᾶνι.

cf. Hdn. (i 109 Lentz)

φαῦος Edmonds

148 Ael. Aristid. *Or.* 28. 54 (ii 159 Keil)

ἑτέρωθι τοίνυν καλλωπιζόμενος (sc. ὁ Ἀλκμάν) παρ' ὅσοις εὐδοκιμεῖ, τοσαῦτα καὶ τοιαῦτα ἔθνη καταλέγει ὥστ' ἔτι νῦν τοὺς ἀθλίους γραμματιστὰς ζητεῖν οὗ γῆς ταῦτ' εἶναι, λυσιτελεῖν δ' αὐτοῖς καὶ μακράν, ὡς ἔοικεν, ἀπελθεῖν ὁδὸν μᾶλλον ἢ περὶ τῶν Σκιαπόδων ἀνήνυτα πραγματεύεσθαι.

Str. 1. 2. 35 (i 65 Kramer)

Ἡσιόδου δ' οὐκ ἄν τις αἰτιάσαιτο ἄγνοιαν Ἡμίκυνας λέγοντος καὶ Μακροκεφάλους καὶ Πυγμαίους (fr. 153 M.-W.). οὐδὲ γὰρ αὐτοῦ Ὁμήρου ταῦτα μυθεύοντος, ὧν εἰσι καὶ οὗτοι οἱ Πυγμαῖοι, οὐδ' Ἀλκμᾶνος

Στεγανόποδας

ἱστοροῦντος, οὐδ' Αἰσχύλου Κυνοκεφάλους καὶ Στερνοφθάλμους καὶ Μονομμάτους.

cf. Str. 7. 3. 6, *Anecd. Oxon.* (iii 370 Cramer)

ALCMAN

147 Scholiast on *Iliad* 12. 137 (αὖας, 'dried')

Perhaps it has been accented on the first syllable on the analogy of ναῦος (=ναϝός, 'temple') and the proper name Τραῦος and ψαῦος [1] in Alcman.

[1] Meaning unknown. Edmonds read φαῦος, i.e. φάϝος, φῶς, 'light'.

148–157 are on peoples and places (in alphabetical order after 148).

148 Aelius Aristides, *On a Remark made in Passing* [1]

Elsewhere when Alcman brags about the number of people among whom he has a high reputation, he lists so many and such obscure races that the wretched school-teachers are still trying to discover where on earth they are; they would do better to go on a long journey, if you ask me, instead of worrying pointlessly about those

Shadow-foots.[2]

[1] Followed by fr. 106.   [2] Cf. scholiast on Ar. *Birds* 1553: they went on all fours and raised one gigantic foot to provide shelter from the sun in their flat country. Stephanus of Byzantium calls them an Ethiopian race, citing Hecataeus, *Journey round Egypt*.

Strabo, *Geography*

But no one could accuse Hesiod of ignorance [1] when he mentions the Half-dogs and Long-heads and Pygmies (fr. 153 M.-W.), nor Homer himself when he tells these tales, including the one about the Pygmies (*Il.* 3. 2 ff.), nor Alcman when he talks of the

Umbrella-foots,

nor Aeschylus with his Dog-heads, Chest-eyes and One-eyes.

[1] As did Apollodorus, *On the Catalogue of Ships*, citing Eratosthenes with approval (Strabo 7. 3. 6).

GREEK LYRIC

149 Steph. Byz. (p. 40 Meineke)

Αἰγιαλός· . . . τὸ ἐθνικὸν Αἰγιαλεύς . . . τὸ θηλυκὸν Αἰγιάλεια
καὶ
Αἰγιαλίς

παρὰ ᾽Αλκμᾶνι.

cf. Hdn. (i 90 Lentz)

150 Steph. Byz. (p. 97 Meineke)

᾽Αννίχωρον·

μέμνηται ᾽Αλκμάν. οἱ οἰκοῦντες ᾽Αννίχωροι καὶ ᾽Αννίχωρες, πλησίον
Περσῶν κείμενοι.

cf. Hdn. (i 49, 388 Lentz)

151 Steph. Byz. (p. 109 Meineke)

᾽Αράξαι ἢ ῎Αραξοι·

ἔθνος ᾽Ιλλυρίας, ὡς ᾽Αλέξανδρος Κορνήλιος ἐν τῷ περὶ τῶν παρ᾽
᾽Αλκμᾶνι τοπικῶς εἰρημένων (F.Gr.H. 273 F95).

152 Steph. Byz. (p. 129 Meineke)

῎Αρυββα· τὸ ἐθνικὸν
᾽Αρύββας·

οὕτω γὰρ ᾽Αλκμάν.

cf. Hdn. (i 53 Lentz)

ἀρ- et ἀρρ-, -υβ- et -υββ- codd.

492

ALCMAN

149 Stephanus of Byzantium, *Places and Peoples*

Aegialus [1]: . . . The ethnic name is Αἰγιαλεύς . . . The feminine is Αἰγιάλεια and in Alcman Αἰγιαλίς,

woman of Aegialus.

[1] Ancient name for Achaea, the north Peloponnesian coast (αἰγιαλός).

150 Stephanus of Byzantium, *Places and Peoples*

Annichorum:

mentioned by Alcman. The inhabitants are Annichori or Annichores, and they live near the Persians.

151 Stephanus of Byzantium, *Places and Peoples*

Araxae or Araxi:

a people of Illyria, according to Cornelius Alexander [1] in his work *On the Place-names in Alcman*.

[1] 'Polyhistor', prolific Roman scholar, 1st c. B.C.

152 Stephanus of Byzantium, *Places and Peoples*

Arybba [1]: the ethnic name is Ἀρύββας,

Arybban,

for that is how Alcman has it.

[1] A king of Epirus was called Arybbas (Paus. 1. 11. 1, Plut. *Pyrrh.* 1).

GREEK LYRIC

153 Steph. Byz. (p. 136 Meineke)

Ἀσσός·

. . . Ἀλέξανδρος δ' ὁ Κορνήλιος ἐν τῷ περὶ τῶν παρ' Ἀλκμᾶνι τοπικῶς ἱστορημένων (*F.Gr.H.* 273 F 96) Μιτυληναίων ἄποικον ἐν τῇ Μυσίᾳ φησὶν Ἀσσόν, ὅπου ὁ σαρκοφάγος γίνεται λίθος.

154 Steph. Byz. (p. 198s. Meineke)

Γάργαρα· πόλις τῆς Τρῳάδος ἐπὶ τῇ ἄκρᾳ τῆς Ἴδης Παλαι-γάργαρος καλουμένη, ἣν Αἰολικὴν ὀνομάζει Στράβων (13. 1. 5) καὶ Ἑκαταῖος (*F.Gr.H.* 1 F 224). Ἀλκμὰν δὲ θηλυκῶς

τὴν Γάργαρον

φησίν· ἐν ᾗ κατῴκουν Λέλεγες.

cf. Hdn. (i 194, 385 Lentz)

155 Steph. Byz. (p. 212 Meineke)

Γραικός, ὁ Ἕλλην, ὀξυτόνως, ὁ Θεσσαλοῦ υἱός, ἀφ' οὗ Γραικοί οἱ Ἕλληνες . . . .

Γραῖκες

δὲ παρὰ Ἀλκμᾶνι αἱ τῶν Ἑλλήνων μητέρες, καὶ παρὰ Σοφοκλεῖ ἐν Ποιμέσιν (fr. 518 Pearson). ἔστι δὲ ἢ μεταπλασμὸς ἢ τῆς Γραῖξ εὐθείας κλίσις ἐστίν.

cf. Hdn. (i 397 Lentz)

ALCMAN

153 Stephanus of Byzantium, *Places and Peoples*

Assus:

. . . Cornelius Alexander[1] in his work *On the Place-names in Alcman* says that Assus,[2] where the limestone is found, was a Mytilenaean colony[3] in Mysia.

[1] See 151 n. 1.   [2] In the Troad, facing south to Lesbos; Stephanus says it was 'near Atarneus': cf. schol. B on fr. 1. 60 ff.   [3] Strabo 13. 1. 58 says it was colonized from Methymna.

154 Stephanus of Byzantium, *Places and Peoples*

Gargara: a city in the Troad[1] on the promontory of Ida, known as Palaegargarus (Old Gargara), described as an Aeolian city by Strabo and Hecataeus. Alcman uses a feminine form Γάργαρος,

Gargarus.

Leleges used to live there.

[1] Between Assus and Atarneus: see 153.

155 Stephanus of Byzantium, *Places and Peoples*

Graecus: the Hellene, when accented on the last syllable (Γραικός): the son of Thessalus, after whom the Hellenes are called Graeci . . . The form Γραῖκες,

Graeces,

in Alcman refers to the mothers of the Hellenes; also in Sophocles, *Shepherds*.[1] Either it is a metaplasm, or it is formed from the nominative singular Γραῖξ.

[1] See Pearson on Soph. fr. 518.

156 Steph. Byz. (p. 339 Meineke)=Hdn. (i 26 Lentz: cf. ii 527)

Ἰσσηδόνες· ἔθνος Σκυθικόν. Ἑκαταῖος Ἀσίᾳ (*F.Gr.H.* 1 F193).
Ἀλκμὰν δὲ μόνος
Ἐσσηδόνας
αὐτούς φησιν. εὑρίσκεται δὲ ἡ δευτέρα παρ᾽ ἄλλοις διὰ τοῦ ε.
Ἐσσηδ-, Ἀσσεδ-, Ἀσεδ- codd.

157 Steph. Byz. (p. 525 Meineke)=Hdn. (i 270 Lentz)

Πιτυοῦσσαι· νῆσοι διάφοροι, ἃς
Πιτυώδεις
καλεῖ Ἀλκμάν.
cf. Eust. *Il.* 355. 45

158 *Sud.* A 1289 (i 117 Adler)
ἔγραψε βιβλία ἕξ, μέλη καὶ Κολυμβώσας.

159 *Anth. Pal.* 7. 19. 1 = test. 3

160 Athen. 15. 678bc = Thaletas test. 11

161 = testt. 17–20

ALCMAN

156 Stephanus of Byzantium, *Places and Peoples*

Issedones: a Scythian tribe. So Hecataeus in his *Asia*. Alcman alone calls them

Essedones.[1]

In other writers it is found with a short e in the second syllable.

[1] Aristeas said that he visited them: see Bolton, *Aristeas* 5 with nn. 2, 3; 39 ff., West, *C.Q.* 15 (1965) 193.

157 Stephanus of Byzantium, *Places and Peoples*

Pityussae: various islands, called

Pityodeis [1]

by Alcman.

[1] The Balearic Islands off the Spanish coast; see West, *C.Q.* 15 (1965) 193.

158–161 give miscellaneous information about Alcman's songs.

158 *Suda*, Alcman = test. 1

He wrote six books: lyric poetry and the *Diving Women.*[1]

[1] Or *Swimming Women*, a mysterious title, also in test. 16; see J. A. Davison, *From Archilochus to Pindar* 182 f., G. Huxley, *G.R.B.S.* 5 (1964) 26–28.

159 *Palatine Anthology*: Leonidas = test. 3

160 Athenaeus, *Scholars at Dinner* = Thaletas test. 11

161 = testt. 17–20 (on Alcman's metres)

GREEK LYRIC

162 P. Oxy. 2394

fr. 1

(a) col. i (a) 1 ὁ]μάλικᾰς
    4 πλο]υσίαι

(b) col. ii 5 παπτα[ιν-
    6 αἶψ' ἀνεχω[ρ
    7 παρὰ πυθμ[εν-
    8 σχεδον
    10 καλωσϋ[
    11 σιγαλ[όεις, sim.
    13 ἤἶσα[ν

schol. (a) i (a) 5 οὐ διὰ τὴν ἀντίστροφο[ν

fr. 2

<table>
<tr><td>(a)</td><td>(c)</td></tr>
<tr><td></td><td>] φοινικεα [</td></tr>
<tr><td>]αιτα κόμ[ας</td><td>ἀ]ναδήματα[</td></tr>
<tr><td>]ας τε καλ[ὰς</td><td>π]λείας μύρου[</td></tr>
<tr><td>]α πὰρ πυκ[ινὰ]ς</td><td>θέσαν ἰτέα[ς</td></tr>
<tr><td>5 ἐλε]φαντιν . . [</td><td></td></tr>
<tr><td>ἀθ]ύρματα κ[</td><td></td></tr>
<tr><td>]νων [</td><td></td></tr>
<tr><td>παρ]σενισκ[αι</td><td></td></tr>
<tr><td>]ᾰ [</td><td></td></tr>
<tr><td>10]πόδας[</td><td></td></tr>
<tr><td>]κάτω κεφ[αλ-</td><td></td></tr>
<tr><td>]ες ὕδωρ [</td><td></td></tr>
<tr><td>τα]νυσιπτέρ[</td><td></td></tr>
</table>

suppl. ed. pr. (Lobel)   fr. 2 (a) cum (c) ita coniungend. ci.
ed. pr.

ALCMAN

162–177 are fragments of uncertain authorship.

162 Papyrus (late 2nd or 3rd c. A.D.) [1]

fr. 1 (a) . . . (companions) of the same age . . . wealthy (girls?) . . .

(b) . . . look about . . . (were?) immediately return-ing . . . (to? from? at?) the base . . . near . . . beautiful(ly) . . . shining . . . (they) were going . . .

fr. 2 . . . crimson . . . hair . . . hairbands . . . and beautiful . . . full of perfume . . . put tightly-woven willows on . . . ivory . . . adornments . . . young girls . . . feet . . . down from the head . . . water . . . long-winged . . .

---

[1] Content and Doric features suggest Alcman; for difficulties see Page, *C.R.* 73 (1959) 21. The scholiast at 1(a) i(a) 5 suggests that some conclusion is being drawn from the repeated metrical pattern. See also Lobel in *Ox. Pap.* 45, p. 17 f.

GREEK LYRIC

163 Athenag. *Leg. pro Christ.* 14 (vii 62, 64 Otto = p. 15 Schwartz)

Ἀθηναῖοι μὲν Κελεὸν καὶ Μετάνειραν ἵδρυνται θεούς, . . . Σάμιοι Λύσανδρον ἐπὶ τοσαύταις σφαγαῖς καὶ τοσούτοις κακοῖς, Ἀλκμὰν καὶ Ἡσίοδος Μήδειαν †ἧ†, Νιόβην Κίλικες, . . . Ἀμίλκαν Καρχηδόνιοι.

ἀλκμὰν καὶ ἡσίοδος ex ἀμίλκαν καρχηδόνιοι ortum ci. Page

164 Schol. in Ael. Arist. *Or.* 46. 138. 4 (iii 490 Dindorf)

ὁ Κρὴς δὴ τὸν πόντον· . . . παροιμία ἐπὶ τῶν εἰδότων μέν, προσποιουμένων δ' ἀγνοεῖν. . . . λέγεται δὲ καὶ ἡ παροιμία καὶ οὕτως· ὁ Σικελὸς τὴν θάλατταν. . . . Ἀλκμὰν δὲ ὁ λυρικὸς μέμνηται τῆς παροιμίας.

cf. Arsen. = Apostol. *Cent.* xiii 6 (ii 571 Leutsch-Schneidewin), Zen. v 30 (i 131 L.-S.) (μέμνηται ταύτης Ἀλκαῖος), cod. Athoum ap. Miller, *Mélanges* 360.

165 Eust. *Od.* 1648. 6

λέγει (sc. Ἡρακλείδης . . . ὡς) ἐκ τοῦ κτείνω κταίνω Δωρικώτερον παρὰ Ἀλκαίῳ.

παρὰ Ἀλκμᾶνι ci. Lobel.

166 Hsch. A 2979 (i 105 Latte)

ἀλιάποδα·

τὸν κέπφον, ἢ θαλάττιον ὄρνιν ⟨Ἀχαιὸς (fr. 54 Nauck) καὶ Ἀλκμάν (Musurus: Ἀλκμας cod.)⟩

Ἀχ. καὶ Ἀλκμ. transtul. ex A 2984 Schmidt, Latte

167 Hsch. B 713 (i 330 Latte)

βλῆρ·

δέλεαρ. τὸ δὲ αὐτὸ καὶ αἴθμα. παρὰ †Ἀλκμαιων† ἡ λέξις.

Ἀλκμᾶνι Meineke: Ἀλκαίῳ (fr. 404A) Schow

500

ALCMAN

163 Athenagoras, *Embassy for the Christians* ·

The Athenians have established Celeus and Metanira as gods, . . . the Samians Lysander despite all his murders and crimes, Alcman and Hesiod [1] Medea, the Cilicians Niobe, . . . the Carthaginians Hamilcar.

[1] The poets' names are unexpected in a list of ten peoples; but Hesiod regards Medea as immortal (*Theog.* 992).

164 Scholiast on Aelius Aristides, *In defence of the Four*

'The Cretan and the sea': . . . . a proverb used of people who know but pretend not to know . . . ; it exists also in the form 'the Sicilian and the sea . . .' The lyric poet Alcman [1] mentions the proverb.

[1] Zenobius says 'Alcaeus mentions this proverb': see Sappho or Alcaeus 15 (vol. i, p. 445).

165 Eustathius on *Odyssey* 10. 72

Heraclides says that from κτείνω comes the more Doric form κταίνω, 'kill', in Alcaeus. [1]

[1] Lobel conjectured 'in Alcman'.

166 Hesychius, *Lexicon*

ἀλιάποδα:

stormy petrel,
a sea-bird. Achaeus and (Alcman?). [1]

[1] The words 'bird. Achaeus and (Alcman?)' are wrongly attached to the entry on ἀλιβάπτοις, 'sea-dipped, purple', and are transferred here by the editors of Hesychius.

167 Hesychius, *Lexicon*

βλῆρ:

bait,
like αἶθμα. The word is in Alcman(?). [1]

[1] Or Alcaeus (fr. 404A).

GREEK LYRIC

168, 169 Ap. Dysc. *Pron.* 68b (p. 54 Schneider)

ἡ γὰρ τύ ὀρθῆς τάσεως οὖσα εὐθεῖαν σημαίνει παρὰ Δωριεῦσι·

κaὶ τὺ Διὸς θύγατερ μεγαλόσθενες (169),

ἐγκλινομένη δὲ αἰτιατικήν·

καί τυ φίλιππον ἔθηκεν (168).

cf. *Synt.* β′ 77 (p. 183, p. 184 Uhlig)

170 *Et. Gen.* (p. 43 Calame)

ῥύτειρα· παρὰ τὸ ἐρύω ἐρυτήρ, καὶ ῥύτειρα ἀποβολῇ τοῦ ε·

Ἄρταμι, ῥύτειρα τόξων.

171 *Et. Sym.* (cod. V ap. *Et. Mag.* 116. 22)

τὸ δὲ ἀειδέμεναι ποιητικὴ παραγωγή, οὐ Δωρικὴ διάλεκτος. τὸ γὰρ Λακωνικόν ἐστιν ἀείδην ἢ ἀείδεν·

μηδ' ἔμ' ἀείδην ἀπέρυκε.

cf. *Anecd. Par.* (iii 297 Cramer), Hdn. (ii 354 ad fr. 568 Lentz)

μηδέ μ' edd.   Bergk: ἀείδειν pro ἀείδην utroque loco *Et. Sym.*

172 Hsch. E 2958 (ii 97 Latte)

Ἐνετίδας πώλους στεφανηφόρους·

ἀπὸ τῆς περὶ τὸν Ἀδρίαν Ἐνετίδος. διαφέρει γὰρ ἐκεῖ.

Musurus: στεφαενιφόρω cod.   πώλως στεφαναφόρως ci. Bergk: ἐν Στεφανηφόρω Livadaras

502

ALCMAN

168, 169 Apollonius Dyscolus, *Pronouns*

For when the pronoun τύ, 'you', has the acute accent, it is in the nominative case in Doric:

and you, mighty daughter of Zeus (169);

but when it is enclitic, it is accusative:

and made you a horse-lover (168).

170 *Etymologicum Genuinum* on ῥύτειρα

From ἐρύω, 'draw', comes ἐρυτήρ, 'he who draws', and with loss of the ε ῥύτειρα, 'she who draws':

Artemis,[1] drawer of the bow.

[1] Vocative case; cf. 53–55.

171 *Etymologicum Symeonis*

The infinitive ἀειδέμεναι, 'to sing', is a creation of the poets, not Doric usage; for the Laconian form is ἀείδην or ἀείδεν:

and do not prevent me from singing.[1]

[1] Attributed to Alcman by Bergk.

172 Hesychius, *Lexicon*

garland-winning Venetic foals [1]:

from Venetis on the Adriatic coast; for that breed is outstanding.

[1] Cf. 1. 50 f. with n. 14; attributed to Alcman by Bergk. But N. A. Livadaras (*Rh. Mus.* 115, 1972, 197–9) makes a strong case for reading 'Venetic foals: in the *Garland-wearer . . .*', i.e. in the *Hippolytus* of Euripides: see *Hipp.* 231.

173 Choerob. *de paeon.* (Consbruch *Hephaestion* p. 247)

Ἡλιόδωρος δέ φησι κοσμίαν εἶναι τῶν παιωνικῶν τὴν κατὰ πόδα τομήν, . . . οἷον·

οὐδὲ τῷ Κνακάλῳ
οὐδὲ τῷ Νυρσύλα.

174 Heph. *Ench.* 4. 3 (p. 13s. Consbruch)

βραχυκατάληκτα δὲ καλεῖται ὅσα ἀπὸ διποδίας ἐπὶ τέλους ὅλῳ ποδὶ μεμείωται, οἷον ἐπὶ ἰαμβικοῦ·

ἄγ᾽ αὖτ᾽ ἐς οἶκον τὸν Κλεησίππω,

ἐνταῦθα γὰρ ὁ σιππω ποὺς ἀντὶ ὅλης ἰαμβικῆς κεῖται διποδίας.

cf. epitom. Heph. (p. 361 C.)

αὖτε Ϝοῖκον ci. Wilamowitz, qui versum Alcmani attribuit

175 Hsch. Σ 165 (iv 9 Schmidt)

σάνδυξ· δένδρον θαμνῶδες, οὗ τὸ ἄνθος χροιὰν κόκκῳ ἐμφερῆ ἔχει, ὡς Σωσίβιος (*F.Gr.H.* 595 F18).

176 Schol. Theocr. 5. 92 (p. 174 Wendel)

Σωσίβιος δὲ (*F.Gr.H.* 595 F24) Λάκωσι τὰς ἀνεμώνας φαινίδας καλεῖσθαί φησι.

177 Hsch. Ι 60, 61 (ii 343 Latte)

ἰανοκρήδεμνος, ἰανόκροκα

ALCMAN

173 Choeroboscus, *On the paeonic rhythm*

Heliodorus [1] says that end of foot [2] regularly corresponds with end of word in paeonics . . . , e.g.

nor from [3] Cnacalus [4] nor from Nyrsylas. [5]

[1] Writer on metre, 1st c. A.D. [2] Cretic ($-\cup-$). [3] Or 'of'. [4] Mountain at Caphyae in Arcadia, where Artemis was worshipped (Paus. 8. 23. 4). Bergk ascribed the fragment to a hymn to Artemis by Alcman; cf. Menander at fr. 55. [5] Unknown.

174 Hephaestion, *Handbook on Metres*

Brachycatalectic is the name given to lines which end with a dipody shortened by a whole foot, e.g. in an iambic line [1]

Off again to the house of Cleësippus!

For in that line the foot -σιππω takes the place of a whole iambic dipody.

[1] Iambic trimeter brachycatalectic: see West, *Greek Metre* 53.

175 Hesychius, *Lexicon*

σάνδυξ: a bushy tree, the flower of which has a colour like that of kermes oak gall (i.e. scarlet): so Sosibius. [1]

[1] See 94 n. 1.

176 Scholiast on Theocritus 5. 92 ('anemone')

Sosibius says that anemones are called *phainides* ('shining ones') by the Laconians.

177 Hesychius, *Lexicon*

        (a) with dark headdress,
        (b) dark-threaded (?) [1]

[1] Wilamowitz ascribed both adjectives to Alcman; Taillardat (*Rev. Phil.* 27, 1953, 131 ff.) disagreed.

COMPARATIVE NUMERATION

TERPANDER

Loeb	Page	Bergk	Diehl
1	6 *S.L.G.*	—	—
2	697 *P.M.G.*	2	2, 3
3	698 *P.M.G.*	1	1
4	adesp. 941 *P.M.G.*	3	pop. 49
5	adesp. 1027c *P.M.G.*	4	adesp. 23
6	*P.M.G.* p. 363	5	[4]
7	*P.M.G.* p. 363	6	[4]
8	*P.M.G.* p. 363	7	—
9	*P.M.G.* p. 363	8	—

ALCMAN

The numeration used in the present volume is that of Page, *P.M.G.* Fragments published in *Oxyrhynchus Papyri* since the appearance of *P.M.G.* have been numbered as follows (S1–5 are the numbers in Page, *S.L.G.*):

P.Oxy.	Loeb
2737 (=S1, S2)	12A, 12B
2801 (=S3)	4B
2812 (=S4)	12C
2802 (=S5)	test. 29
3209	4C
3210	9A
3213 (+2443)	4A

Fr. 120A does not appear in *P.M.G.*

Loeb/ P.M.G.	Bergk	Diehl	Garzya	Calame
1	23	1	1	3
2	9 + 74A	2 + 89	2 + 70	2
3	—	—	—	26–56
4	—	—	—	57–78
5	—	—	—	79–81 + 83 + 277–281
6	—	—	—	259–260
7	—	—	—	19
8	—	—	—	20–21
9	—	—	—	22
10	—	—	—	82 + 295 + test.5
11	—	—	—	24
12	—	—	—	25
13	—	—	—	8 + test.6 + 32 + 40

ALCMAN

Loeb/ P.M.G.	Bergk	Diehl	Garzya	Calame
14	1+4+6	7	6	4–6
15	10–11	11	9	7
16	24	13	10	8
17	33	49	42	9
18	—	—	—	10
19	74B	55	46	11
20	76	56	47	12
21	13	—	127	210
22	13adn.	—	127	273
23	14	—	140	211
24	—	—	—	test.29
25	—	—	138	212
26	26	94	74	90
27	45	67	55	84
28	59	40	34	85
29	2	9	7	89
30	7	10	8	86
31	95	42	35	88
32	152	—	122	208
33	146A	—	117	200
34	125	—	103	183
35	98	19	16	141
36	65	18	15	139
37	77–78	17+21	14+18	151+138
38	66	20	17	137
39	25	92	72	91
40	67	93	73	140
41	35	100	78	143
42	100	3	3	133
43	51	25	21	111
44	104	—	128	220
45	86	32	26	113
46	85A	34	28	114
47	61	31	25	117
48	17	33	27	118
49	73	29	23	115
50	83–84	30+39	24+33	116+124
51	102	—	124	219

COMPARATIVE NUMERATION

Loeb/ *P.M.G.*	Bergk	Diehl	Garzya	Calame
52	103	—	132	213
53	18	62	51	119
54	101A	64	53	120
55	21	35	29	121 + 221
56	34	37	31	125
57	48	43	36	93
58	38	36	30	147
59	36–37	101–102	79–80	148 + 149
60	16	24	20	126
61	111	—	126	218
62	105	—	153	223
63	—	—	135	94
64	62	44	37	105
65	69	45	38	107
66	108	—	123	108
67	119	—	134	81
68	68	77	61	95
69	56B	76	60	96
70	52–54	113 + 74 + 47	40 + 59 + 91	169 + 98 + 286
71	113	—	130	216
72	107	—	131	222
73	88	—	125	99
74	72	84	64	101
75	109	—	136	214
76	110	—	137	215
77	40	73	58	97
78	149	—	139	202
79	87	72	57	100
80	41	80	63	102
81	29	16	13	150
82	28	15	12	157
83	31	106	84	156
84	32	82	66	174
85	3 + 30	4 + 46	4 + 39	123 + 127
86	148	—	120	205
87	adesp. 34–37	12 + 22 + 27 + 85 + 79	54 + 160– 162 + 177	122 + 142 + 112 + 103 + 172

ALCMAN

Loeb/ _P.M.G._	Bergk	Diehl	Garzya	Calame
88	56A	88	69	104
89	60	58	49	159
90	58	59	50	162
91	39	105	82	136
92	117	53	150	134
93	43	54	175	160
94	20	63	52	132
95	70–71	52 + 51	44–45	131 + 92
96	75	50	43	130
97	144	—	115	198
98	22	71	56	129
99	143	—	97	226
100	90	114	92	135
101	91	99	77	144
102	81	110	88	108
103	99	115	93	170
104	42	81	65	168
105	89	78	62	171
106	47	48	41	87
107	27	95	83	152
108	116	—	99	110
109	112	—	156	206
110	80	107	85	155
111	26adn.	112	90	173
112	92	83	67	158
113	101B	—	98	145
114	93	87	68	164
115	94	23	19	153
116	55	103	81	128
117	97	14	11	154
118	64	111	89	175
119	49	116	94	176
120	44	28	22	177
120A	(3rd ed., 78)	—	—	—
121	79	57	48	161
122	96	90	71	165
123	50	108	86	109
124	46	38	32	163

COMPARATIVE NUMERATION

Loeb/ *P.M.G.*	Bergk	Diehl	Garzya	Calame
125	63	109	87	293
126	82	97	75	146
127	120	—	100	179
128	123	—	102	180
129	121	—	104	166
130	132	—	106	187
131	133	—	107	188
132	135	—	108	190
133	145	—	109	191
134	136B	—	110	193
135	137	—	111	181
136	139	—	112	194
137	—	—	96	178
138	140	—	95	167
139	141	—	113	195
140	142	—	114	196
141	85B	98	76	197
142	—	—	116	199
143	146B	—	118	201
144	147A	—	119	203
145	114	—	155	225
146	151	—	129	106
147	153	—	121	209
148	118	—	151–152	207 + 229
149	124	—	141	182
150	127	—	142	184
151	128A	—	143	227
152	128B	—	144	185
153	129	—	145	228
154	131	—	146	186
155	134	—	154	189
156	136A	—	147	192
157	147B	—	149	204
158	—	—	—	test.4 + 36
159	—	—	—	test.9
160	—	—	—	test.27
161	—	(74B)	—	test.35 + test. metr.

Loeb/ P.M.G.	Bergk	Diehl	Garzya	Calame
162	—	—	—	239, 240, 242–251
163	—	—	—	236
164	115	—	157	237
165	—	—	—	235
166	126	—	180	233
167	130	—	105	234
168	adesp.43A	5	158	267
169	adesp.42	26	163	265
170	adesp.46B	65	167	263
171	57	96	178	268
172	adesp.43B	91	173	299
173	19	61	166	264
174	adesp.45	104	174	269
175	p.78	—	—	274
176	p.78	—	—	275
177	—	—	—	306 + 307

COMPARATIVE NUMERATION

ALCMAN: REVERSE INDEX

(Read: 3 Bergk = 85 *P.M.G.*, 7 Garzya = 29 *P.M.G.*, etc.)

Loeb/ *P.M.G.*	Bergk	Diehl	Garzya	Calame
1	14	1	1	12A (S1)
2	29	2	2	2 + 12
3	85	42	42	1
4	14	85	85	14a
5	—	168	adesp.1012	14b
6	14	—	14	14c
7	30	14	29	15
8	adesp.1012	adesp.983	30	16 + 13(a)
9	2	29	15	17
10	15	30	16	18
11	15	15	117	19
12	—	87	82	20
13	21 + 22adn.	16	81	—
14	23	117	37	—
15	—	82	36	—
16	60	81	35	—
17	48	37	38	—
18	53	36	37	—
19	173	35	115	7
20	94	38	60	8.1–6
21	55	37	43	8.7–11
22	98	87	120	9
23	1	115	49	—
24	16	60	50	11
25	39	43	47	12
26	26	169	45	3.1, 3
27	107	87	48	3.4
28	82	120	46	3.5
29	81	49	55	3.6
30	85	50	58	3.7
31	83	47	56	3.8

ALCMAN

Loeb/ *P.M.G.*	Bergk	Diehl	Garzya	Calame
32	84	45	124	3.9
33	17	48	50	3.10
34	56	46	28	3.11
35	41	55	31	3.12
36	59	58	57	3.13
37	59	56	64	3.14
38	58	124	65	3.15
39	91	50	85	3.16
40	77	28	70	3.17
41	80	adesp.954B	106	3.18
42	104	31	17	3.19
43	93	57	96	3.20
44	120	64	95	3.21
45	27	65	95	3.22
46	124	85	19	3.23
47	106	70	20	3.24
48	57	106	121	3.25
49	119	17	89	3.26
50	123	96	90	3.27
51	43	95	53	3.28
52	70	95	94	3.29
53	70	92	54	3.30
54	70	93	87	3.31
55	116	19	27	3.32
56	(A)88, (B)69	20	98	3.33
57	171	121	79	4.1
58	90	89	77	4.2
59	28	90	70	4.3
60	89	adesp.955	69	4.4
61	47	173	68	4.5
62	64	53	105	4.6
63	125	94	80	4.7
64	118	54	74	4.8
65	36	170	104	4.9
66	38	pop.872	84	4.10
67	40	27	112	4.11

COMPARATIVE NUMERATION

Loeb/ P.M.G.	Bergk	Diehl	Garzya	Calame
68	68	adesp.1016	114	4.12
69	65	adesp.942	88	4.13
70	95	adesp.954A	2	4.14
71	95	98	122	4.15
72	74	79	39	4.16
73	49	77	40	4.17
74	(A)2, (B)19 + 161	70	26	4.18
75	96	adesp. 1011A	126	4.19
76	20	69	141	4.20
77	37	68	101	4.21
78	37	105	41	4.22
79	121	87	59	5.1
80	110	80	59	5.2 (i.1–22)
81	102	104	116	5.2 (ii. 22ff., iii) + 67
82	126	84	91	10(b)
83	50	112	107	5.49
84	50	74	83	27
85	(A)46, (B)141	87	110	28
86	45	adesp.972	123	30
87	79	114	125	106
88	73	88	102	31
89	105	2	118	29
90	100	122	111	26
91	101	172	70	39
92	112	39	100	95(b)
93	114	40	103	57
94	115	26	119	63
95	31	107	138	68
96	122	171	137	69
97	117	126	99	77
98	35	141	113	70(b)
99	103	101	108	73
100	42	41	127	79
101	(A)54, (B)113	59	—	74

ALCMAN

Loeb/ *P.M.G.*	Bergk	Diehl	Garzya	Calame
102	51	59	128	80
103	52	116	34	87(d)
104	44	174	129	88
105	62	91	167	64
106	—	83	130	146
107	72	110	131	65
108	66	123	132	102
109	75	125	133	123
110	76	102	134	108
111	61	118	135	43
112	109	111	136	87(c)
113	71	70	139	45
114	145	100	140	46
115	164	103	97	49
116	108	119	142	50(a)
117	92	adesp.974	33	47
118	—	148	143	48
119	67	—	144	53
120	127	—	86	54
121	129	—	147	55
122	—	—	32	87(a)
123	128	—	66	85(a)
124	149	—	51	50(b)
125	34	—	73	56
126	166	—	61	60
127	150	—	21 + 22	85(b)
128	(A)151, (B)152	—	44	116
129	153	—	146	98
130	167	—	71	96
131	154	—	72	95(a)
132	130	—	52	94
133	131	—	163	42
134	155	—	67	92
135	132	—	63	100
136	(A)156, (B)134	—	75	91
137	135	—	76	38

517

COMPARATIVE NUMERATION

Loeb/ P.M.G.	Bergk	Diehl	Garzya	Calame
138	—	—	25	37(b)
139	136	—	78	36
140	138	—	23	40
141	139	—	149	35
142	140	—	150	87(b)
143	99	—	151	41
144	97	—	152	101
145	133	—	153	113
146	(A)33, (B)143	—	154	126
147	(A)144, (B)157	—	156	58
148	86	—	—	59(a)
149	78	—	157	59(b)
150	—	—	92	81
151	146	—	148	37(a)
152	32	—	148	107
153	147	—	62	115
154	—	—	155	117
155	—	—	145	110
156	—	—	109	83
157	—	—	164	82
158	—	—	168	112
159	—	—	adesp.983	89
160	—	—	87	93
161	—	—	87	121
162	—	—	87	90
163	—	—	169	124
164	—	—	adesp.954B	114
165	—	—	adesp.955	122
166	—	—	173	129
167	—	—	170	138
168	—	—	pop.872	104
169	—	—	adesp.1016	70(a)
170	—	—	adesp.942	103
171	—	—	adesp. 1011A	105

ALCMAN

Loeb/ P.M.G.	Bergk	Diehl	Garzya	Calame
172	—	—	adesp.972	87(e)
173	—	—	172	111
174	—	—	174	84
175	—	—	93	198
176	—	—	adesp.954A	119
177	—	—	87	120
178	—	—	171	137
179	—	—	adesp.974	127
180	—	—	166	128

Loeb/ P.M.G.	Calame		Loeb/ P.M.G.	Calame
181	135		205	86
182	149		206	109
183	34		207	148
184	150		208	32
185	152		209	147
186	154		210	21
187	130		211	23
188	131		212	25
189	155		213	52
190	132		214	75
191	133		215	76
192	156		216	71
193	134		217	66
194	136		218	61
195	139		219	51
196	140		220	44
197	141		221	(55)
198	97		222	72
199	142		223	62
200	33		224	—
201	143		225	145
202	78		226	99
203	144		227	151
204	157		228	153

COMPARATIVE NUMERATION

Loeb/ *P.M.G.*	Calame	Loeb/ *P.M.G.*	Calame
229	148	266	ad.1039
230	ad.1012	267	168
231	S2	268	171
232	—	269	174
233	166	270	ad.954(a)
234	167	271	ad.954(b)
235	165	272	ad.974
236	163	273	22
237	164	274	175
238	S3	275	176
239	162.1	276	—
240	162.2	277	cf. 5.49
241	—	278	cf. 5.49
242	162.3	279	cf. 5.49
243	162.4	280	cf. 5.49
244	162.5	281	cf. 5.49
245	162.6	282	ad.1016
246	162.9	283	ad.942
247	162.10	284	ad.955
248	162.11	285	pop.872
249	162.12	286	70(c)
250	162.13	287	ad.983
251	162.14	288	ad.972
252	—	289	ad.1014
253	—	290	ad.1011(a)
254	—	291	ad.1011(b)
255	—	292	ad.965
256	—	293	125
257	—	294	(49 Edm.)
258	—	295	10(a)
259	6.4	296	ad.1045
260	6.21	297	ad.857
261	—	298	ad.952
262	54	299	172
263	170	300	—
264	173	301	ad.1042
265	169	302	ad.945

ALCMAN

Loeb/ _P.M.G._	Calame
303	ad.980
304	—
305	—
306	177
307	177
308	—
309	—

INDEX OF AUTHORS AND SOURCES

523

INDEX OF AUTHORS AND SOURCES

INDEX OF AUTHORS AND SOURCES

525

INDEX OF AUTHORS AND SOURCES

INDEX OF AUTHORS AND SOURCES

INDEX OF AUTHORS AND SOURCES

INDEX OF AUTHORS AND SOURCES

INDEX OF AUTHORS AND SOURCES

GENERAL INDEX

535

GENERAL INDEX

Aphidnus, eponymous king of Aphidna: 413

Aphrodite, goddess of love and beauty: 41, 43, 45, 55, 133, 147, 167, 201, 209, 223, 229, 231, 233, 245, 363, 389, 431, 433, 435; *see also* Cypris, Cythere, Paphian.

Apodeixeis, Arcadian festival: 325

Apollo, god of music, prophecy etc.: 7, 71, 143, 147, 157, 187, 262, 275, 279, 291, 295, 315, 317, 319, 343, 399, 403, 405, 426, 427, 429, 431, 433; *see also* Phoebus.

Araxae or Araxi, people of Illyria: 493

Arcadia, mountainous region of central Peloponnese: 264, 415, 505

Archias of Corinth, founder of Syracuse *c.* 734 B.C.: 287

Archidamus, Spartan king, *c.* 665–*c.* 645 B.C.: 399

Ardys, king of Lydia, *c.* 652–*c.* 619 B.C.: 268, 337

Areïphilus, father of Melanthus: 157

Areitus, *see* Areius

Areius, son of Hippocoon: 361, 371

Ares, god of war: 79, 151, 185, 199, 281, 353, 363, 399, 427

Areta, mentioned by Alcman as choir-member: 367, 373

Arete, wife of Alcinous: 453

Arganthonius, king of Tartessus: 79

Argiphontes, Hermes as Slayer of Argus (Io's guardian): 433

Argos, city of E. Peloponnese: 264, 445

Ariadne, daughter of Minos, wife of Dionysus: 145

Aristoclides, mourned by Anacreon: 97

Aristocritus, father of Anacreon?: 23

Arne, name of towns in Thessaly and Boeotia: 295

Artemis, goddess of wild places and animals: 47, 121, 147, 369, 427, 431, 433, 461, 503, 505

Artemon, mocked by Anacreon: 65, 75, 77

Arybba, place in Epirus (?): 493

Ascalaphus, son of Ares, Greek warrior killed at Troy: 399

Asia: 383

Assus, city in Troad: 495

Astaphis, mentioned by Alcman: 367, 373

Asteropaeus, Paeonian warrior, Trojan ally: 141

Astymeloisa, choir-leader mentioned by Alcman: 379, 381

Atarneus, city on W. coast of Asia Minor: 343, 375, 495

Athamantis (daughter of Athamas), name for Teos: 121

Athamas, husband of (1) Nephele, (2) Ino; driven mad by Hera: 429

Athamas, son of Aeolus and founder of Teos: 121

Athena, virgin warrior goddess: 45, 157, 183, 233, 281, 383, 427, 453, 477; *see also* Pallas.

Athens: 3, 4, 10, 27, 31, 71, 179, 263, 413, 415

Atreus, brother of Thyestes, the flesh of whose children he served to him: 455

GENERAL INDEX

Atridae (sons of Atreus), Agamemnon and Menelaus: 193

Attica, region round Athens: 91, 155

Attis, young devotee of Cybele, castrated himself: 175

Bacchant, worshipper of Dionysus: 55, 159, 165, 167, 217, 397, 433, 439

Bacchiadae, rulers of Corinth, c. 750–650 B.C.: 265, 289

Bacchus, title of Dionysus: 7, 33, 169, 211, 213, 215, 223, 225, 241

Bactria, district in Asia, corresponding roughly to Afghanistan: 179

Balearic Islands (Maiorca, Minorca etc.): 268, 497

Bassarid, female worshipper of Dionysus: 91

Bathyllus, Samian boy loved by Anacreon: 4, 6, 27, 33, 85, 125, 143, 167, 175, 181, 185, 187, 189

Bear (Arctos), see Wain.

Beauty (Kallos): 189

Berecyntians, Phrygian tribe: 481

Black Sea (Pontus): 375

Boeotia, district of central Greece: 295, 445

Boeus, father of Terpander?: 295

Briareus, one of the Hundred-handed: 395

Bromius, cult title of Dionysus: 139, 189, 221

Cadiz (Gadeira), city on S. coast of Spain: 179

Cadmus, mythical founder of Thebes: 193, 397

Calaesus, mentioned by Alcman: 389

Callicrite, mentioned by Anacreon: 115

Calliope, senior Muse: 417

Calliteles, dedicator of herm: 153

Cambyses, Persian king 529–522 B.C.: 22, 23

Candaules, king of Lydia, early 7th c. B.C.: 339

Canobus (Canopus), town in Egypt: 179

Caria, district of S.W. Asia Minor: 85, 101, 179

Carnea, Dorian festival: 265, 295, 297, 303, 431

Carneus, Trojan; Carnea said to have been named after him: 431

Carystus, place in Laconia: 457, 458

Castor, one of Dioscuri, sons of Zeus and Leda: 317, 361, 363, 377, 389, 397, 399, 401, 413, 415

Cayster, river of W. Asia Minor: 243

Cepheus, king of Tegea: 445

Cerbesian, Phrygian place and tune: 481

Chalcidice, Macedonian peninsula: 403

Chalcis, name of cities in Euboea, Ionia, Thessaly and Aetolia: 403

Chios, large island off Asia Minor: 145, 481

Cicones, Thracian tribe: 33

Cimmerians, people of S. Russia; invaded W. Asia Minor mid-7th c. B.C.: 149

Cinyras, legendary king of Cyprus: 381

537

GENERAL INDEX

Circe, goddess with magic powers: 449

Claros, oracle of Apollo in W. Asia Minor: 177

Cleënorides, lost at sea: 173

Cleësippus, mentioned by Alcman (?): 505

Cleësithera, mentioned by Alcman as choir-member: 367, 373

Cleobulus, boy loved by Anacreon: 4, 57, 59, 85, 125

Clesimbrota, mentioned by Alcman: 383

Cleta, one of the Graces: 439

Cnacalus, mountain in Arcadia: 505

Cnidos, city of S.W. Asia Minor: 433

Colaxaeans, Scythian people (?): 365, 375

Colophon, city of W. Asia Minor: 267, 335

Corcyra, island of Ionian Sea: 473

Corinth: 11, 153, 179, 262–265, 287, 289, 293

Crates, unknown musician: 275

Crete, most southerly island of Aegean: 11, 179, 327, 463, 501

Critias, loved by Anacreon; grandfather of the 5th c. politician and poet: 3, 91, 137

Crius, a Titan, father of Perses: 395

Croesus, king of Lydia 560–547 B.C.: 223

Cronus, father of Zeus: 145, 153

Curetes, Cretan protectors of baby Zeus: 327

Cyane, mother of Callicrite: 115

Cybele, Cybebe, great mother-goddess of Anatolia: 175, 243, 275, 281

Cyce, mother of Artemon: 77

Cydonia, city of N.W. Crete: 463

Cyllarus, horse of Polydeuces: 415

Cyme, city of N.W. Asia Minor: 295

Cypris, 'the Cyprian', title of Aphrodite, who emerged from the sea at Paphos in Cyprus: 7, 41, 133, 169, 199, 215, 225, 235, 237, 363, 395, 435

Cyprus, most easterly island of Mediterranean: 381, 431, 433, 473

Cypselus, Chest of, dedicated to Hera at Olympia, c. 600 B.C.: 293

Cyrus, founder of Persian empire, king 559–529 B.C.: 3, 22, 23, 101

Cythere, Cythereia, title of Aphrodite, born on Cythera: 7, 167, 181, 183, 185, 189, 199, 207, 211, 219, 233, 243

Cyzicus, city on Propontis: 31

Damareta, mentioned by Alcman: 367, 373, 377

Damas, father of Alcman?: 337, 339, 341

Damotimus, father of Hagesidamus: 401

Danaus, brother of Aegyptus; his daughters killed their husbands, the sons of Aegyptus: 455

Daphne, girl pursued by Apollo; turned into a bay-tree: 7, 243

538

540

GENERAL INDEX

Moon, *see* Selene.

Musaeus, mythical singer: 359

Muses, goddesses of poetry, music and dance, daughters of Zeus: 33, 43, 71, 73, 77(?), 147, 161, 165, 189, 207, 225, 231, 239, 243, 291, 299, 307, 317, 319, 339, 341, 379, 391, 399, 401, 407, 417, 419, 427, 437, 441; *see also* Calliope.

Myron, sculptor, worked *c.* 480–445 B.C.: 159, 161

Mysia, district of N.W. Asia Minor: 69, 273, 277, 495

Mytilene, chief city of Lesbos: 495

Naiads, nymphs of rivers and springs: 439

Nanno: mentioned by Alcman as choir-member: 367, 373

Nature (Physis): 195

Naucrates, dedicator: 157

Naucratis, Greek emporium on Nile delta: 51, 107, 137

Nausicaa, Phaeacian princess of *Od.* 5–6: 385, 449, 451

Neptune, *see* Poseidon.

Nereids, daughters of Nereus: 385

Nereus, sea-god: 361

Nile, river of Egypt: 195

Niobe, daughter of Tantalus; boasted of the number of her children, whom Apollo and Artemis killed; turned into a stone: 193, 447

Nymphs, nature-spirits of mountains, water, etc.: 55, 115, 233, 439

Nyrsylas, unknown place: 505

Nyssa (Nysa), nurse of Diony-

sus; city in India, his birth-place: 319

Odysseus, Homeric hero: 385, 449, 451, 453

Oenopion, son of Dionysus and Ariadne: 145

Oenus, place near Sparta: 459

Olympia, sanctuary of Zeus, site of Games: 297, 373

Olympus, mountain, home of gods: 69, 233, 379, 397

Onogli, place near Sparta: 459

Onomacritus, oracle-monger, late 5th c. B.C.: 325

Orestes, son of Agamemnon: 173

Orion, constellation: 167

Orpheus, legendary musician of Thrace: 264, 275, 307, 311, 327, 441

Orth(e)ia, Spartan goddess identified with Artemis: 373, 399

Orthria, goddess of morning twilight (?): 367, 369

Pain (Lupē): 211

Pallas, title of Athena: 45, 71

Pan, Arcadian god, player of *syrinx* (Pan-pines): 61, 264, 273

Pandion, king of Athens, father of Procne and Philomela: 193

Paphian, title of Aphrodite, who emerged from the sea near Paphos: 7, 187, 191, 237

Paphos, city of Cyprus: 431

Paris, *see* Alexander.

Parthenius, father of Anacreon?: 23

Parthia, Asiatic country S.E. of Caspian Sea: 11, 197

GENERAL INDEX

Promētheia, *see* Foresight.

Psyra, island N.W. of Chios: 481

Pyrrhicus of Crete, said to have invented pyrrhic dance: 327

Pythagoras of Samos, philosopher, *fl.* 532/1 B.C.: 25, 441

Pythian Games, at Delphi: 299, 324, 333

Pythomander, mentioned by Anacreon: 83

Python, serpent killed at Delphi by Apollo: 279, 283

Python, soldier: 157

Rhipae, mountain of N. Europe (?): 457

Rhodes, island of S.E. Aegean: 49, 179, 183

Rome: 10

Sambas, piper: 471

Samos, island off W. Asia Minor: 3, 4, 6, 23, 27, 53, 63, 115, 125, 131, 135, 143, 187

Sardis, capital of Lydia: 171, 268, 337, 339, 401, 405, 409

Satyrs, attendants of Dionysus, half-animal: 167

Sciapods, *see* Shadow-foots.

Scythia, country N. of Black Sea: 55, 365, 375, 483, 497

Scythinus, father of Anacreon?: 23

Seasons (Hōrae), goddesses of the seasons: 167

Sebrus, son of Hippocoon: 349, 361

Selēnē (Moon), 435

Semele, mother of Dionysus: 157

Shadow-foots (Sciapods): 491

Sibyl of Erythrae, prophetess: 287

Sicily: 95, 501

Sidon, Phoenician city: 231

Silenus, old attendant of Dionysus: 221

Simalus, mentioned by Anacreon: 75

Sintians, early inhabitants of Lemnos: 149

Sirens, mythical singers: 369, 419, 489

Sirius, the dogstar: 367, 375

Smerdies (Smerdis), Thracian youth loved by Anacreon: 4, 33, 45, 63, 85, 93, 99, 125, 143

Socrates, Athenian philosopher, 469–399 B.C.: 39, 115, 137, 143

Sparta: 263–269, 291, 299–303, 307, 313, 319, 323, 325, 329, 337, 339, 341, 343, 345, 349, 353, 355, 361, 363, 379, 385, 387, 415, 419, 425, 439, 457, 459, 461, 463, 477

Stathmi, place near Sparta: 459

Steganopods, *see* Umbrella-foots.

Stoics: 11, 441

Strattis, metioned by Anacreon: 75

Strife (Eris): 489

Stroebus, father of Leocrates: 161

Strymo, mother of Priam?: 445

Sulla, Roman general and politician, *c.* 138–78 B.C.: 349

Sun (Hēlios): 117

Syloson, brother of Polycrates: 143

Syria: 11, 179, 433

Tantalus, legendary king of

GENERAL INDEX

GENERAL INDEX